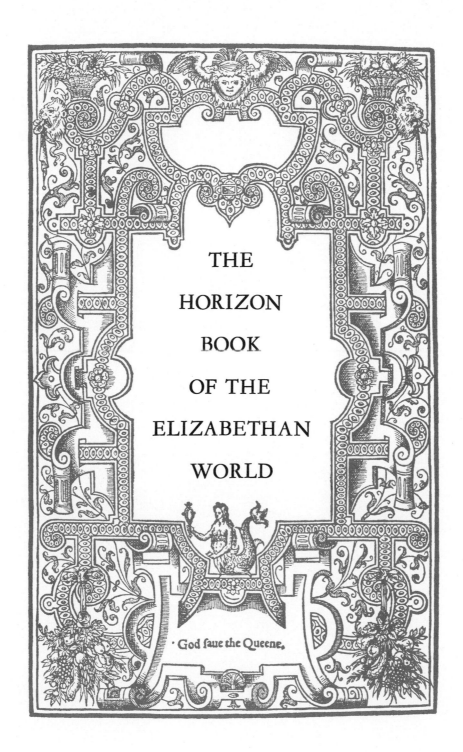

THE

HORIZON

BOOK

OF THE

ELIZABETHAN

WORLD

· God saue the Queene.

BY THE EDITORS OF HORIZON MAGAZINE

EDITOR IN CHARGE NORMAN KOTKER

AUTHOR LACEY BALDWIN SMITH

PUBLISHED BY AMERICAN HERITAGE PUBLISHING CO., INC., New York

BOOK TRADE DISTRIBUTION BY HOUGHTON MIFFLIN COMPANY, Boston

PUBLISHED SIMULTANEOUSLY IN CANADA BY McCLELLAND AND STEWART LTD., Toronto

THE HORIZON BOOK OF THE
ELIZABETHAN WORLD

AMERICAN HERITAGE
BOOK DIVISION

EDITORIAL DIRECTOR
Richard M. Ketchum

GENERAL EDITOR
Alvin M. Josephy, Jr.

Staff for this Book

EDITOR
Norman Kotker

ART DIRECTOR
Emma Landau

ASSOCIATE EDITORS
Jay Jacobs

Jane Hoover Polley

PICTURE EDITORS
Ellen Bates

Martha Fine, *Assistant*

COPY EDITORS
Kaari I. Ward

Jill Felsen, *Assistant*

EDITORIAL ASSISTANT
Julia Bozzelli

EUROPEAN BUREAU
Gertrudis Feliu, *Chief*

Mary Jenkins

AMERICAN HERITAGE
PUBLISHING CO., INC.

PRESIDENT
James Parton

EDITORIAL COMMITTEE
Joseph J. Thorndike, *Chairman*

Oliver Jensen

Richard M. Ketchum

SENIOR ART DIRECTOR
Irwin Glusker

PUBLISHER, HORIZON MAGAZINE
Paul Gottlieb

Horizon Magazine is published quarterly by American Heritage Publishing Co., Inc., 551 Fifth Avenue, N.Y., N.Y. 10017. Printed in the United States of America. Library of Congress Catalog Card Number: 67–22393

Ivory knife handles, from a set depicting English rulers, show (left to right) Henry VII, Henry VIII, Edward VI, and Elizabeth.
VICTORIA AND ALBERT MUSEUM; CROWN COPYRIGHT

HALF-TITLE PAGE: *The design is adapted from the title page of the* Chronicles, *published in 1577 by the most noted Elizabethan historian, Raphael Holinshed.*
HOLINSHED, *Chronicles,* 1577

TITLE PAGE: *In a detail of a painting done near the close of her reign, Queen Elizabeth is shown riding to Tilbury in 1588 to review the troops assembled there to guard against the Spanish Armada.*
ST. FAITH'S CHURCH, KING'S LYNN, NORFOLK

SHETLAND IS.

NORWAY

HEBRIDES

SWEDEN

SCOTLAND

Edinburgh

North Sea

DENMARK

Copenhagen

Baltic Sea

IRELAND

Dublin

Lübeck
Hamburg

York

ENGLAND

Norwich

Warsaw

Plymouth
London
Dover
Amsterdam
Brielle
Antwerp
Calais
Brussels

NETHERLANDS

HOLY

ROMAN

EMPIRE

Prague

Cracow

English Channel

A t l a n t i c   O c e a n

Route of the Spanish Armada

Paris

FRANCE

Dijon

Augsburg

Vienna

AUSTRIA

Lyons
Geneva

Milan
Venice

El Ferrol
Corunna

Bay of Biscay

La Rochelle

Genoa

Florence

Santander

PORTUGAL

El Escorial
Madrid

Barcelona

CORSICA

ITALY
Rome

SPAIN

Lisbon

BALEARIC IS.

SARDINIA

Naples

Seville

M e d i t e r r a n e a n

Cadiz

SICILY

Tunis

BARBARY STATES

S e a

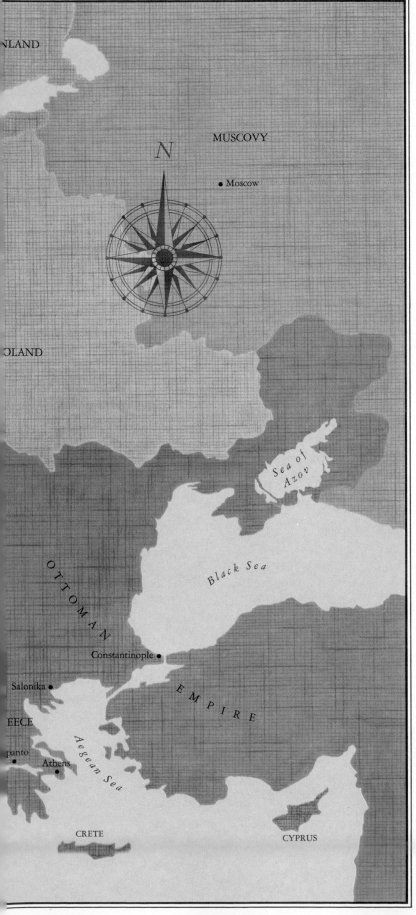

THE KINGDOMS OF EUROPE, 1560

The world seemed a far larger place to men of the Elizabethan age than it had to earlier generations. New kingdoms had been discovered in America, and the distant Orient had become more accessible. Yet Europe remained the center of the Elizabethan world —and politically, if not geographically, the center of Europe was Spain. The land of Philip II was the Continent's greatest power, with wide possessions in Italy and the Netherlands. Spain's formidable navy dominated both the Mediterranean and the Atlantic. But eventually its dominance was challenged, first by the Dutch, who rebelled against their Spanish masters in 1566, and then by the English, whose privateers attacked Spanish ports and captured Philip's treasure ships. The defeat of the Spanish Armada, in 1588, and its utter ruin on the long voyage home, through dangerous waters north and west of the British Isles, signaled the end of Spanish sea power. Nevertheless the lions and castles of Spain's coat of arms (shown bordering the map along with devices of other European powers) continued to command respect. France, potentially Spain's greatest rival, was rendered ineffective by internal dissension, and the chaotic Holy Roman Empire was impressive only on the map.

Except for the Ottoman empire and England, the peripheral states of Europe hardly mattered. The Scandinavian kingdoms and Scotland were rarely involved in European politics. To most Elizabethans, Muscovy was a barbaric wilderness, as was, to a lesser extent, its neighbor Poland. The Ottoman empire was important, however. It had grown enormously over the previous centuries—overrunning the Balkans and reaching into Central Europe. And England was slowly becoming important too. Under the forceful rulers of the new Tudor dynasty, the small and relatively isolated island kingdom was emerging as a force to be reckoned with in European affairs.

ENGLAND AND SCOTLAND

HENRY VII — Elizabeth *of York*

Catherine *of Aragon* — HENRY VIII — Jane Seymour

EDWARD VI

Philip II *of Spain* — MARY

Anne Boleyn

ELIZABETH

JAMES IV *of Scotland* — Margaret — Archibald Douglas, *Earl of Angus*

Mary *of Guise* — JAMES V

Margaret — Matthew Stewart, *Earl of Lennox*

Francis II *of France* — MARY *Queen of Scots* — Henry Stuart, *Lord Darnley*

JAMES VI *of Scotland and I of England*

FRANCE

HENRY II — Catherine de Médicis

Mary *Queen of Scots* — FRANCIS II

Philip II *of Spain* — Elizabeth

CHARLES IX — Elizabeth *of Austria*

HENRY III

Francis, *Duke of Alençon*

Margaret — Henry *of Navarre* (HENRY IV)

SPAIN AND THE HOLY ROMAN EMPIRE

FERDINAND — ISABELLA

Joanna the Mad — Philip the Handsome

Isabella *of Portugal* — CHARLES V, *Emperor*

FERDINAND I, *Emperor* — Anne *of Hungary*

Maria — MAXIMILIAN II, *Emperor*

Maria *of Portugal* — PHILIP II — Elizabeth *of France*

Carlos

Catherine

Isabella — Albert

RUDOLF II, *Emperor*

Elizabeth — Charles IX *of France*

Mary Tudor *of England*

PHILIP III — Anne

TUDORS AND STUARTS

The Stuart line goes back to a twelfth-century clan of hereditary stewards (Stuarts) of Scotland; the ancient Welsh family of Tudor became prominent when Owen Tudor, Henry VII's grandfather, wed Catherine of Valois, the widow of England's King Henry V. James IV's marriage to a Tudor gave the Stuarts a claim to England's throne.

VALOIS

The Valois dynasty began in 1328 when Philip VI acceded to the French throne. Upon the death of Charles VIII in 1498, the direct Valois line was superseded by family alliances: Valois-Orléans under Louis XII, and at his death in 1515, the Valois-Angoulême line, which began with Francis I, father-in-law of Catherine de Médicis.

HAPSBURGS

The Hapsburgs (whose name comes from a Swiss castle) ruled Austria from 1282 on. The marriage of Maximilian I to Mary of Burgundy brought most of the Low Countries under Hapsburg rule, and their son Philip's marriage to Joanna, the mad daughter of Ferdinand and Isabella, resulted in Hapsburg rule of Spain as well.

THE GREAT DYNASTIES

During the sixteenth century, marriages, not armies, were usually the decisive factor in struggles for political power and territorial expansion. An armed conflict might drag on inconclusively for decades, but the wedding of two royal houses could instantly transform the boundaries of an empire or the fortunes of a nation. Princesses brought dowries of land—sometimes whole kingdoms—to the altar; and since many of them died in childbirth, kings could often make successive additions to their domains through a series of advantageous marriages. Spain's unification was begun when Ferdinand and Isabella, the heirs of Castile and Aragon, wed. Subsequent marriages were far more significant than military conquest in building the Spanish empire in Europe. In France, Catherine de Médicis ceaselessly plotted marriages that would bring crowns to her children. Marriage did not result in territorial expansion in England until after Elizabeth's death, when James VI of Scotland—the great-great-grandson of Henry VII—inherited the throne. Almost a century earlier, Henry VII himself had ended the War of the Roses by marrying Elizabeth of York. Their son, Henry VIII, did not marry to effect political changes; he had no hesitation about changing his politics in order to divorce and remarry as fancy dictated. A genealogical chart at left shows the family trees and symbols of the major dynasties, and the various marriages that linked them all.

From top to bottom, reading left to right: NATIONAL PORTRAIT GALLERY, LONDON   NATIONAL PORTRAIT GALLERY, LONDON   COURTESY OF THE MARQUESS OF SALISBURY   MUSEE CONDE, CHANTILLY; GIRAUDON   BIBLIOTHEQUE NATIONALE; GIRAUDON   PHOTO BULLOZ   NATIONAL MUSEUM OF FINE ARTS, MADRID   NATIONAL MUSEUM OF FINE ARTS, MADRID   THE PRADO, MADRID   THE PRADO, MADRID

Anna
Berkin

Marx
herwart

Comrat
im hoff

Regina
artztin

lauv
langenmantel

vlerich
Waltzrin

Achilus Bund

lucas Nielern

1

THE
OLD ORDER
PASSES

"I appeal," said Charles VII of France, "to the sharp end of my sword." As the medieval world slowly dissolved in the fifteenth century, Europe fell prey to barbarism, sacrilege, and selfishness, in which man's inhumanity to man knew no limits and all men made appeal to the sharp ends of their swords. On every side the alchemy of change and the shock of catastrophe generated despair and foreboding, inducing men to forsake and pervert the old standards. In poetry and art, in sermons and chronicles, in actions and even in aspirations, a tone of despondency prevailed. As early as the fourteenth century, the French poet Eustache Deschamps set the tone for most of late medieval Europe when he sadly asked:

Why is our life so cruel and dark
That men no longer speak to friend?
Why does evil so clearly mark
The monstrous government of men?
Compare what is with what is past
And see how fraud and sorrow stand,
While law and justice fade so fast
That I know no longer where I am.

Compared with the preceding centuries, the fifteenth century presented a tableau of royal murders, clerical corruption, international anarchy, and spiritual neurosis. Traditionally the medieval ideal had been one of universalism, which in practice had been balanced by diversity. Christendom was seen as a seamless cloak, a single corps in which the universal Catholic Church and the Holy Roman Empire shared the two swords of Christ—the spiritual and temporal.

Religious unity had at one time been a reality, but political union had never been more than a myth, the phantom of Roman imperium living on in the moribund body of the Holy Roman Empire. By 1400 medieval Christianity was falling apart. The Holy Roman Empire was a specter in which real power rested not with the emperor but with a myriad of principalities scattered throughout Germany, the Lowlands, and northern Italy. Each prince, prelate, and imperial town possessed sovereignty within the empire, and the emperor was little more than a cipher burdened with endless duties but exercising only nominal rights. The empire itself was a soulless, artificial relic of the past, held together by hollow pomp and gaudy circumstance.

Spiritually the Christian world was also in chaos. Religious unity had disintegrated; now Europe witnessed the degrading spectacle of rival popes, one at Avignon, the other in Rome, each claiming for himself the keys to the kingdom of heaven and each thundering dire anathemas and maledictions at any Christian who dared challenge his authority. The Great Schism lasted thirty-nine years, from 1378 to 1417. Significantly Europe divided along national lines: England and Germany sided with Urban VI in Rome, and France and Scotland followed Clement VII at Avignon—a sure sign that the medieval ideal of universality was giving way to international anarchy, in which God was French or German, English or Scottish.

On all sides medieval institutions survived, but the spirit that had once sustained them withered and died. Kings continued to rule, but subjects complained that "the law serveth for naught else but to do wrong"; the chivalric creed persisted, but the feudal knight, encased in iron, became a military

During the Renaissance the bourgeoisie gained wealth and power; opposite, an assembly of prosperous German citizens.

Throughout the Hundred Years War troops ravaged the French countryside. Even in times of truce, companies of discharged soldiers and their women (like those above) lived off the land.

anachronism; the cleric retained his privileged position in society, but his flock learned to use such expressions as "fat as a canon," "lazy as a monk," and "lewd as a Carmelite." In crown, baronage, and Church, the fifteenth century experienced a failure of leadership.

From Germany to England, from the Lowlands to Spain, the dynasties of Europe were afflicted with incompetency and insanity and stricken by sudden death. The medieval concept of kingship had incorporated three ideals: piety, justice, and courage. The king was supposed to be the fountain of justice and the model of faith and bravery. He lived on his own, using his private wealth to sustain his regal office. He ruled by law, defending and recognizing the rights of his subjects, and he dedicated his energies to the defense of the Holy Church, championing the true faith against the infidel. Such a king had been Louis IX of France in the thirteenth century, and both Church and state agreed that he deserved the name of saint.

Kingly reality in the fifteenth century was far different from the ideal exemplified by Saint Louis. In France the realm fell prey to internal discord, foreign invasion, and governmental paralysis. When Charles V died in 1380, the crown passed to a twelve-year-old minor, Charles VI, who moved from adolescence into insanity. From the moment Charles took control of the government, he proved to be a monarch of inordinate passion: immoderate in work, in generosity, in war, and in pleasure. The expenses of

the court rose from the 94,000 livres that had been spent by his predecessor each year to 450,000 livres, and during the periods of his madness, officially termed the king's absences, the land was torn by the bitter rivalry between the princely houses of Burgundy and Orleans. For fifty years France bled; neither "the fear of God, nor love of our neighbors, nor anything else," as a contemporary witness said, was sufficient to restrain Frenchmen from "doing violence to one another."

The lunatic king and the quarreling nobility offered England the chance to regain its lost province of Normandy and to initiate a second bout of the Hundred Years War. The war was a horror story punctuated with appalling atrocities, guerrilla tactics, and broken promises, both sides fighting to the point of total exhaustion. The little village of Neville-sur-Saône was sacked six times in three years by the mercenary troops hired by each side. By the end of the war the population of the diocese of Rouen had fallen from fifteen to six thousand.

France finally cast out the Goddamns, as the English were called, but its success had less to do with royal leadership than with the mounting weakness of its enemy, for England was handicapped in 1422 by the succession of Henry VI, a nine-month-old sovereign who ruled off and on for the next fifty years with varying degrees of pious incompetence. The fifteenth century in England was little better than in France. Ever since 1399, when Richard II, the last of the direct Plantagenet kings, had been deposed by his cousin, Henry, duke of Lancaster, the kingdom had suffered disputed succession. Feuding among the great magnates was momentarily set aside when the new king, Henry v, led his barons to victory at Agincourt in 1415; but once the conqueror died in 1422, leaving an infant son to the tender mercies of avaricious relatives, and once the tide of victory in France had ebbed, England fell prey to party discord and civil war.

Defeat in France was the signal for strife to begin at home, for, as one French commentator put it: "Upon their return into England not one of the English lords thought of lessening his estate; and the whole revenue of the kingdom was not sufficient to satisfy them all." The Wars of the Roses between the house of Lancaster, with its red rose, and the house of York, with its white, lasted by one computation until 1471 when Edward, duke of York, finally made good his claim to the throne and ruled as Edward iv. By another reckoning, the wars endured until 1485 when Yorkist Richard iii fell at Bosworth field and Henry Tudor, the grandfather of Queen Elizabeth, seized the crown—quite literally according to one legend, which maintains that he snatched it from a thornbush on which Richard had hung it.

The paralysis of regal leadership throughout Europe was no more vividly revealed than when the Holy Roman Emperor Wenceslas and Charles vi of France met in an effort to heal the religious schism of Christendom. The meeting, in 1398, had to be conducted by underlings since the emperor was too drunk and Charles was too mad to confer. The conference did nothing but magnify Europe's woes; instead of ending schism, it called for the election of a third pope to settle the controversy. In 1400 Wenceslas was deposed; he had shocked even his hardened age by roasting his cook on a spit when that unfortunate servant spoiled his dinner. But he refused to abdicate, and for ten years thereafter the German empire was torn by disputed elections until eventually there were three warring emperors, roughly corresponding to the three rival popes.

Elsewhere in Europe royal dynasties were cursed by a similar madness and violence. The epithets given to the kings of Castile are evidence of the brutality, injustice, poverty, and weakness that plagued the Iberian peninsula. There was Peter the Cruel, Henry the Invalid, and Henry the Impotent, more aptly called the Degenerate. Castile, like England and the empire, suffered the prolonged rule of a well-meaning but ineffectual monarch, John ii, who announced at the close of a reign of forty-eight years that he would have been happier had he been born the son of a poor artisan. The humanist Lucio

Conflicting royal claims and the succession of children to many thrones added to Europe's chaos. Above, Henry VI, England's child-king, is crowned king of France as well.

As knights lost their importance in warfare, their love of display increased. Above, knightly contenders holding colorful banners confront each other at the beginning of a tournament.

Marineo Siculo painted a picture of almost total anarchy in Spain: the kingdom, he said, was worn out by a multitude of murderers, adulterers, and thieves who scorned the law, "both human and divine," shamelessly violated wives, virgins, and nuns," and "cruelly assaulted and robbed tradesmen, travelers, and people on their way to fairs."

Only in the Lowlands was the scene somewhat different. There the dukes of Burgundy had constructed a vast and formless realm through conquest and the accident of feudal inheritance. In contrast to France or England, the dukes' rambling possessions, particularly the wealthy city of Bruges, that "Florence of Flanders," were accounted an earthly paradise. The dukes of Burgundy—Philip Without Fear, Philip the Good, Charles the Rash—were the first nobles of Europe, calling themselves dukes by the grace of God and aspiring to the title of king. Their chivalric order of the Golden Fleece was the most coveted knightly association in Europe, and the nobility of the entire Continent eagerly sought to enter the order, which was limited to twenty-four *gentils hommes de nom et d'armes et sans reproche."*

But even in the rigid magnificence of their feudal court at Dijon, the house of Burgundy did not escape the taint of madness. Its last duke, Charles the Rash, was well named. Introverted, fanatic, and stubborn, he symbolized the worst and most unyielding aspect of the feudal spirit, insatiable pride. In the end his reckless ambitions and boundless greed, and his unreasoning hatred for the king of France, to whom he owed feudal fealty, destroyed him. His death in 1477 and the collapse of his feudal army, impaled upon the pikes of modern Swiss mercenaries hired by France, demonstrated that medieval knighthood was as moribund as feudal monarchy.

Never was the contrast between theory and reality so marked as in the gulf that existed between the ideals and actions of the feudal nobility. The knight remained the social paradigm of the fifteenth century, but the reasons for his existence had vanished in the face of royal law and government bureaucracy, Swiss pikemen, English longbows, and that costly but "final argument of kings," the cannon. At one time the mounted feudal knight had been the effective, if unruly, instrument by which princes had been able to maintain a reasonable degree of security. Above all else, the knight had been a warrior, and the ethics and structure of feudalism had been geared to his military activities. The virtues of his caste were those of the hero; he was expected to "protect the Church, to fight against treachery, to reverence the priesthood, to fend off injustice from the poor, to make peace in his own province, to shed his blood for his brethren, and if need be, to lay down his life" for his overlord.

By the end of the Middle Ages reality was quite otherwise. "Only the name of nobility remains," wrote one fifteenth-century critic of the knightly order, branding it as "a nutshell, without a kernel, which was full of worms." The medieval knight may have been well adapted for private brawls or religious crusades, but now he was obsolete; the advent of gunpowder had made killing so easy that it was no longer the work of experts. Although war remained in the estimation of knighthood "a glorious thing," more and more the knight had to leave war to mercenaries, who were not made immobile by cumbersome suits of armor and who fought for money not for diversion or glory.

As knightly existence lost military significance and political purpose, it gained in ceremony and formality. The chivalric code went to seed and became mere politeness, ostentation, and extravagance. Knights wore shoes with beaks so long that they impeded walking; their ladies adorned themselves with peaked caps two feet high; cloaks were pieced together from three thousand sable skins, and the duke of Orleans used seven hundred pearls to embroider a song upon his sleeve. Extravagance of attire became the mark not only of a bottomless exchequer but also of nobility itself. The knightly order was more than once dismissed as "mere disorder," and throughout Europe the picture of the overmighty noble, proud, predatory, and unruly, claiming a privileged place in society as his ancestral birthright, became the symbol for violence, mismanagement, and anarchy. Their irresponsibility became proverbial: "The nobles make promises," it was said, "and the peasants keep them."

But the century's "greatest scourge" and "the source and germ of all disorders" was the Church, where men who were ignorant and impious had raised themselves to high pastoral office. In a world surrounded by perpetual pain and accustomed to death, which struck at infants in their cradles and at wives in childbirth, God's Church stood as a sentinel against evil and offered to man the hope of salvation. It enveloped every human act from birth to death with meaning and richness, and always it held out to mankind the picture of paradise. Hope, faith, and charity were the pillars of its doctrine, and it assured all men, irrespective of rank or profession, that God's mercy was available to them. The es-

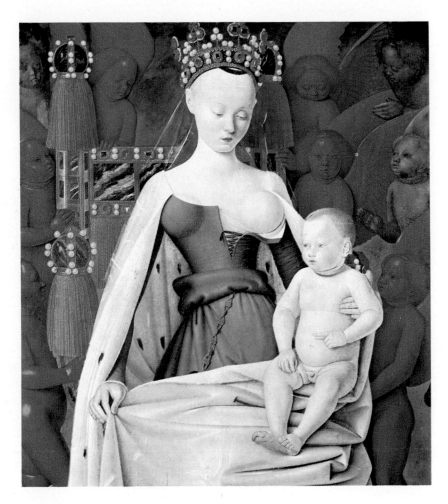

Jean Fouquet's Madonna is typical of fifteenth-century religious art in which sensuality was as evident as spirituality.

sence of medieval Christianity was the doctrine of hope and moderation—hope of salvation and moderation in life. "Man," said Saint Thomas Aquinas, "is called by nature to live in society that he may not only live but live the good life." The good life was, in effect, the exercise of moderation and charity in the affairs of this world and the constant hope that God's mercy would bring man safely into the next world. For the man who lived by these standards, the gates of heaven were forever open.

In the attainment of this ideal the role of the Church was vital. Not only did the Church maintain a tight hold upon the keys to the kingdom of heaven but it also kept a sharp eye on man's actions on earth. Men woke, slept, and worked to the knelling of bells. They were baptized, confirmed, married, confessed, and shriven within the fold of the universal Church. Their wills were probated, their charity administered, their children taught, their minds shaped, and their transgressions judged by clerics. Great and small, prince and pauper were expected to render account to God's vicar on earth, and every act, from the bureaucrat's financial peculations to the peasant's petty adulteries, was judged in terms of man's ultimate purpose on earth—his

A detail from The Triumph of Death *by Peter Brueghel the Elder shows the forces of death overcoming the living. Death appears at upper left on horseback and armed with a scythe.*

salvation or damnation. A careful regulation of the economic impulses of society was considered as essential to man's spiritual welfare as it was to his material well-being. There was a righteous price in commerce, based on considerations of morality, as well as an economic price, reflecting the laws of supply and demand. Gluttony and lack of moderation—be they found in capitalistic ventures, usurious rates of interest, baronial pretensions, or monarchical sharp practices—were condemned as being cancerous to society and dangerous to the soul's salvation. Nothing burned more fiercely in a medieval Christian hell than pride, the mother of egotism, greed, and treason, and "the whole puddle and sink of all sins against God and man."

By the fifteenth century the Church's way of life had long since ceased to correspond to its ideals. In becoming rich, autonomous, privileged, and complacent, it began to forsake the virtues that had originally been the source of its strength. The medieval world learned to despise the unpreaching prelate "loitering in his lordships," the tricky ecclesiastical lawyer extracting the last penny in legal fees, and the papal tax collector bent on fleecing God's flock. It was not so much that churchmen were more

corrupt than royal servants or aristocratic brigands; it was merely that the ecclesiastical body was judged by a higher standard. The ignorant peasant was a source of humor, the slothful priest was scandalous; the profiteer in commerce was secretly admired, the greedy cleric was shocking; the Machiavellian bureaucrat was honored, the conniving clergyman was condemned. Ideally priests and prelates were the curators of souls and the representatives of a higher way of life, in fact they were lawyers, tax collectors, and financiers. Whether the Vatican by 1499 had in fact become the sewer of the world, as it was later claimed, is debatable, but certainly religion and morality were parting company, the former degenerating into a business and the latter all but disappearing from the Church. When Cardinal Borgia, later Pope Alexander VI, was criticized for selling pardons for criminal offenses, he is supposed to have replied: "God desires not the death of sinners but that they should pay and live."

Ideally the Church was unified and universal, the keeper of Europe's conscience and the curator of Christian souls. In reality, it presented to the world the picture of religious schism in which popes and even saints squabbled over the keys of paradise, and

Christians wondered whether Urban at Rome was the rightful heir to Saint Peter's throne and Clement at Avignon was the anti-Christ, as Saint Catherine of Siena stated, or whether the situation was reversed, as Saint Vincent claimed. In the face of such spiritual strife, there seemed to be no certainty in life, and men whispered abroad that nobody could be saved while the Great Schism endured.

On all sides there was growing evidence that a spiritual cancer was crippling the Church, profaning its ideals, and making a mockery of its aspirations. The image of the Madonna and Child, symbolizing the infinite compassion of the Virgin and the innocence of the Christ Child, was a cherished Christian theme; by the fifteenth century that ideal had degenerated into an artistic convention, meaningless and profane, in which ladies of high fashion posed for their portraits holding naked children in their laps. In the hands of Jean Fouquet the Virgin became a fashionable whore surrounded by cherubs who looked like red imps. Legend says that the model was Agnes Sorel, mistress to Charles VII of France. Even Hans Memling, one of the greatest of the Rhenish religious painters, did an altarpiece in which he portrayed the duchess of Burgundy as Saint Barbara. She was dressed in the height of fashion, her eyebrows carefully plucked, her temples shaven, and her head adorned with a brightly jeweled turban. One of Memling's disciples went further, profaning the Assumption of the Virgin by representing the Mother of God as a nude Venus. Moralists complained, with some cause, that "nowadays, there is not an altar but a harlot stands thereon. . . . What sort of piety does this breed in a young cleric when he prays his *confiteor* and sees these pretty statues in front of him?"

The calamities of late medieval society seemed to be without end, and men warned that disease, death, suffering, and war were manifestations of God's wrath directed against a depraved and corrupt Church and against those individuals who had allowed the devil to enter into their lives. It seemed that the voice of Cassandra spoke nothing but the truth, for in 1348 death struck in proportions that annihilated hope and came close to destroying society itself. Possibly one fourth to one half of Europe died in a bubonic plague epidemic, during which there remained neither priest nor grave digger to attend the dead and dying. With terrifying perversity the Black Death struck down the healthiest and most vigorous elements within society. Between forty to sixty per cent of the clergy were liquidated; entire villages were wiped out; and one educated guess presents the total mortality at twenty million persons. Economically the plague came close to destroying Europe. Trade stagnated and incomes for every section of society began to wither. As the death tolls increased, the nobility faced ruin with rents from their land slowly diminishing and their peasants demanding higher and higher wages and greater and greater freedom. Merchants and artisans were caught up in a vast depression cycle of contracting markets and increasing violence, for barons and peasants, artisans and bankers alike were willing to risk political gangsterism and economic sharp practices to save what little remained.

On the heels of internal crisis came the shock of invasion from the east. For centuries Europe had been secure; Christianity had been the aggressor not the defender, and the boundaries of Christendom had been pushed forward at the expense of the followers of Allah. In 1396 Sultan Bayazid, called the Flash of Lightning, destroyed the last of Europe's crusading armies and took a great oath that he would not rest till he could hitch his horse to the altar of St. Peter's Church. A century later, the sultan's descendants seemed on the verge of fulfilling that oath when on May 29, 1453 the imperial city of Constantinople fell to the Ottoman Turks, and a militant Moslem faith turned Santa Sophia into a mosque. The fall of Constantinople meant the loss of the largest city in Christendom and the end of the eastern Roman empire. More important, it opened eastern and southern Europe to the expansion of the Moslem faith. Athens fell in 1458; Italy was invaded, and the city of Otranto was taken and put to the sword in August, 1480.

Popes and bishops regularly preached the desperate need for a new crusade against the infidel, but the response was apathetic. The Christian world was too torn by internal strife to react against the Moslem aggressor, and the medieval crusading spirit had long since died. Kings, princes, and merchants talked much of a crusade, but their words were meaningless. Their crusading zeal was limited to one of the most extraordinary extravaganzas in the history of chivalry: the magnificent Feast of the Pheasant, which was held at the city of Lille in 1454 by Philip, duke of Burgundy. The knights of the Golden Fleece, dressed in vermilion velvet and gold cloth, were entertained at lavishly decorated tables: on one stood a church complete with ringing bells and singing choir, and on another was a pie in which twenty-eight musicians played. The climax of the banquet occurred when a fair damsel entered the great hall riding on an elephant led by a giant dressed in Turkish costume. The symbolic meaning was clear: the Holy Church was in chains to the infidel, and the lady herself appealed to the knights of the Golden Fleece to liberate the ecclesia and free

Constantinople. Philip and his knights were presented with a pheasant bedecked with gold and precious jewels, whereupon the duke and his company rose and in the name of the pheasant and the Virgin Mary vowed to take up the sword in defense of the true faith. Not a member of this chivalric company had any real intention of going on a crusade. In the end what saved Europe from Turkish conquest was the death of Mohammed II in 1481 and the voluntary withdrawal of Turkish troops from Italy.

As the medieval world stood on the threshold of a new century, all that contemporaries could see was the misery of life, the cold of the night, and the heat of the day. From the curses directed against the lice and fleas that made life hideous for all, to the cries of the victims of the Black Death, "thick fogs of lamentation" lay heavy upon Christendom. Confronted by the disgusting death reserved for those tortured by the plague and for those unfortunate enough to fall into the hands of bandits, Christians asked themselves what kind of God could bring such suffering to his flock and what terrible sins had humanity committed to warrant such punishment.

Europe was in panic, in a state of shock, the repercussions of which lasted long into the Elizabethan age. Surrounded by inordinate death, senseless destruction, and awful suffering, moderation seemed to be impossible, and men looked to a life of extremes as the only way out of their fear and disillusionment. Some men turned their backs on the old way of life and took refuge in worldly excesses and material success. "If," said Cosimo de Medici, "Saint Peter is to keep the keys . . . to the tree of knowledge as well as those of the gates of heaven and hell . . . nine tenths of us would prefer to go to Beelzebub at the beginning, instead of having to do so at the end." In the Lowlands, where, despite economic decline, the profits of commerce and sin could still be enjoyed to the full, fat burghers who had "no God but their belly and their moneybags" were almost as successful as Cosimo in his Florentine palace. They were content to concentrate on their account books and drown their consciences in beer and schnapps.

Others, generally the less successful, condemned the life of the commercial cities as vicious and depraved, and turned instead to religious fanaticism. The idea of hell, "where there is no voice but of weeping, no face but of the tormentors," drove men of tender conscience to all sorts of emotional extremes—masochistic religious practices, witchcraft, diabolism, superstition, and mysticism. Satan covered the world with his black wings, and men sought in a variety of fantastic ways either to escape his clutches or to join his ranks. Flagellant monks,

garbed in white, bearing red crosses, and ceaselessly chanting their prayers, wandered the highways and byways of Europe. They denounced the evils of humanity and renounced the Church's path to salvation through the sacraments, claiming that self-flagellation was the true communion, for only when the blood of man was joined to that of Christ could the sinner find redemption. Religious sensationalism of every variety was on the increase. In 1429 Friar Richard of Paris thundered dire warnings for ten consecutive days, beginning at sunrise and continuing without stop for five or six hours. He urged his listeners, who numbered between five and six thousand, to burn their lewd books, cast away their rich apparel, and renounce the evil in their lives.

Though churchmen struck out against the religious extremists whose depiction of hell "milked an old woman to tears" or made "her blood run cold," spiritual emotionalism and the appeal to the imagination became the dominant motif of late medieval religious expression. At the monastic hospital of Isenheim, which specialized in the care of syphilitics, Mathias Grunewald was commissioned to paint his greatest altarpiece. The Christ that he portrayed was even more diseased than the inmates of the hospital. Twisted, bleeding, and decayed, the Saviour's body hung in agony. To those afflicted with incurable venereal disease, which inevitably ended in madness and death, the sight of the dying Christ and the imaginative and sensual witnessing of his suffering were the only reliefs available.

In the general breakdown of morality and moderation there were some who argued that if there was no escape from damnation then they might as well invoke the devil and enjoy his company. Alchemy and astrology were old and recognized professions; in the fifteenth century, however, a new urgency entered the efforts of men of letters and of wealth who sought furiously for the philosopher's stone of knowledge, the well of eternal youth, and the magic of transmuting base metals into gold. The most notorious of these was Gilles de Rais, colleague of Joan of Arc, marshal of France, humanist, and sorcerer, who practiced the black arts, worshiped the devil, and butchered more than one hundred forty children in ritualistic murders. After eight years of satanic orgies he was finally detected and in 1440 was hanged in flames.

Nothing more clearly revealed the degree to which the old standards had lost their hold over society during this time than the decline of orthodox religion itself. More and more, religion was viewed as a means of propitiating an ill-natured deity. Most men firmly believed that "a candle offered to Saint Lowye" would protect their cattle from disaster and that a gift made to the Virgin would stave off evil. For the late medieval world, religion was a variety of magic: the scrupulous and absolute fulfillment of the teachings of the Church bestowed magic power upon the performer. As the peasant burned a candle for Saint Lowye, so King Louis XI of France endowed chapels and monasteries. When the Lord faltered in his bargain, as He so often did, and failed to reward the faithful with material success, both king and peasant were justifiably enraged.

The desire to warrant salvation in the midst of sin and to propitiate the anger of a vengeful god by any means possible led men not only into superstition but also into the elaboration and repetition of Church ritual. A form of galloping mechanization seized religion. If the collecting of relics, the saying of prayers, and the burning of candles were desirable, then it seemed to follow that the more candles offered and the more relics collected, the greater a man's chance of salvation. At Wittenberg Frederick the Wise of Saxony was seized by exactly such a quantitative approach to faith and became an avid collector of relics. By 1509 he had gathered a museum of holy treasures that included four hairs from the Virgin's head, three pieces from her cloak, four from her girdle, and seven from her veil, a wisp of straw from the manger, a piece of gold presented by the Wise Men, a strand of Jesus' beard, a thorn from his crown, a morsel of bread left over from the Last Supper, and a nail certified to have pierced the Saviour's hand. In all, there were 19,013 sacred bones stored in the castle church. No wonder the Florentine reformer Savonarola thundered that "all fervor and inward worship are dead, and ceremonies wax more numerous, but have lost their efficacy."

Exaggeration, elaboration, and proliferation came to predominate in architecture, in dress, in vows, and speech just as it did in religion. Sermons became marathons; vows grew longer and more elaborate, but they always had some tricky qualifications that prevented their fulfillment; clothing became flamboyant and erotic as grotesque codpieces for men and low-cut gowns for women emphasized the sensuality of the age. Architectural design tended to become all form and no soul as ornamental details and ostentatious magnificence began to replace the simplicity of the early Gothic perpendicular outline. Cathedrals became houses of light, not of God, monuments to man's architectural inspiration, where humanity worshiped its own ingenuity and not God's presence.

As inward worship withered, fascination with mortality increased. Later, Elizabethans would find that the ever-present threat of death kindled not a

One of the most forceful fire and brimstone preachers was Saint Bernardino, seen here speaking in his native Siena.
OPERA DEL DUOMO, SIENA; SCALA

morbid terror of death but a passionate preoccupation with living; but in the fifteenth century and the early years of the sixteenth it engendered necrophilia, a fascination with death and bodily decay. The ugly process that turns all to "earth, ashes, dust, and worm's meat" and devours "thy beautiful face, thy fair nose, thy clear eyes, thy white hands, thy goodly body" was feared and yet revered. The equality and the unexpectedness of death caught and held the medieval mind. Places of execution—Tyburn, outside of London, where the Marble Arch now stands, or the giant gibbet of Montfaucon in Paris—became centers of entertainment and sources of perverse fascination. Montfaucon with its colonnade of gibbets and its iron-grated grave pit, into

Prints from Holbein's Dance of Death *show death seizing an abbess, merchant, and knight.*

HOLBEIN, *The Dance of Death*

which the blackened bodies were thrown, was a picknicking place for young gallants, who took their girls to the execution grounds for an evening of good cheer.

The most famous and revered sight in Paris was the ancient Cemetery of the Innocents, where almost a million people, mostly paupers and plague victims, had been buried in nameless graves. By the end of the twelfth century the Innocents had been walled-in and a cloistered arcade constructed, where Parisians promenaded of an evening. The walls were lined with shops and vendors' stalls, and within the cloister, resting on open shelves, were great piles of human bones and skulls, which had been exhumed to make room for new arrivals as the cemetary filled up. There the bones slowly decomposed into dust and were eventually swept on to the pavement where the living walked and joked and speculated upon the grim dance in which not even the dead found rest. In 1424 the danse macabre was painted on the cloister wall. There, in stately elegance, was depicted the endless dance of death in which a skeleton dragged pope, peasant, and priest into the grave. Death held the hand of an abbess fresh from hearing Mass; he seized the scholar in the midst of his books; he awaited the emperor rejoicing upon his throne; he welcomed the usurer clinging to his gold; and he led the blind man to his destruction. Standing in the middle of the cemetery was a figure of Death himself, in cold stone, with raised arm and tightly clenched fist—the ultimate conqueror. Day after day immense crowds were drawn to this place where the odor of corruption prevailed. Lumps of earth from the cemetery were thrown into the graves of those who could not be buried in its hallowed grounds and visitors from every corner of Europe came to view and pay their respects to Death.

Among those who came to behold the charnel house and the thirty scenes of the danse macabre was the English poet John Lydgate, and in 1460 he commissioned a reproduction of the sequence in the cloister of Pardon Church, next to St. Paul's Cathedral in London. All of Europe imitated and embellished this theme of mortality and despair. The greatest of the dances of death was completed by Hans Holbein the Younger in 1526. His prints were published in 1538, and such was their popularity that they went through eleven editions before 1562; by 1573 no less than five plagiarized versions appeared on the market. Numerous imitations of the Holbein *Dance*—possibly a hundred—were published during the sixteenth century, for Elizabeth and her world were still somewhat touched with necrophilia. The graveyard scene remained a stock dramatic ploy; poor Yorick found as little rest as the Innocents of Paris, and John Knox took pleasure in warning Mary Queen of Scots that "foul worms will be busy with this flesh, be it never so fair and tender." Yet by the middle of the sixteenth century the tone had begun to change. The Cemetery of the Innocents slowly lost its hold and was all but forgotten, its stores were closed, and its crowds dispersed. Eventually it was destroyed in the name of progress.

Even in the fifteenth century, amidst an aura of decay, there still lingered the breath of hope; the generation that erected the monument to Death in the Cemetery of the Innocents also produced the statue of René of Chalons. René commissioned his wife to have an effigy done of him as he would look three years after death. The form is that of the familiar and grotesque cadaver, yet there is an exalted quality about the pose, for the old warrior is shown holding up a representation of his soul—the one element of his humanity that is still untouched by corruption and death. When Elizabeth's grandfather, Henry VII, the founder of the Tudor dynasty, came to the throne in 1485 life expectancy was no greater than it had been a hundred years before; but the reaction to death was slowly changing, for new impulses and new ideas were beginning to lift Europe out of the despair and depression of a dying civilization. The scent of optimism was growing stronger as the fifteenth century gave way to the sixteenth.

For the picture of despair, the sense that all men go wandering about without any goal and without knowing what is happening to them, is only one side of the fifteenth-century profile. The Cimmerian darkness contained the hint of a new dawn; in the midst of chaos lay hope of new order. Imperceptibly throughout the century the archaic feudal image of depraved clerics, indolent monarchs, unruly barons, clubfisted usurers, and ranting fanatics receded, and a new outline began to emerge. Old bottles were filled with new wine, ancient dynasties were fortified with new blood, and unprofitable economic pursuits were replaced by new and vigorous enterprises. In state, Church, and business, men of novel views and aggressive practices began to take over from those who lacked confidence in the future.

The harbingers of change were feared and hated because they advocated exactly those practices and doctrines most deplored by the defenders of the medieval way of life. On all sides the antithesis of the Christian doctrine of moderation seemed to be triumphant: excessive concern with money among capitalistic venturers, inordinate and unscrupulous power exercised by the New Monarchs, immoderate religious sensibilities in the persons of Martin Luther and his disciples, and above all, a satanic view of life

in which man became not only the measure of all things but the equal of God Himself. In Italy Leon Battista Alberti announced that "men can do all things if they will," and Michelangelo was called divine. Man's ultimate conceit, and to the medieval mind his unforgivable blasphemy, was reserved for the German painter Albrecht Dürer, who in 1500 portrayed himself as Christ. The medieval doctrines of balance and moderation, which had died in the communal graves of the plague victims and in the anarchy of war and economic recession, were never resurrected. Instead, immoderation in government, in business, and in personal conduct triumphed and slowly came to be accepted as the norm.

Merely to describe the new spirit as secular is to misrepresent its flavor, the essence of which was individualism. In Church, state, art, and economic organization, men were breaking with the corporate society of the medieval past. In religion Martin Luther set private judgment "against the faith held by all Christians for a thousand years." In economics Cosimo de Medici knew that the Church's laws against usury and unethical commercial practices did not apply to him, for he had the Church itself, God the Father, God the Son, God the Holy Ghost "in his books as debtors." In government kings demanded a monopoly of power in which the rights and privileges of chartered towns, the ancient nobility, and the universal Church were sacrificed on the altar of the divine-right monarch, who claimed reasons of state as the highest justification for action.

The growing rigidity of the old guild system accelerated the process whereby a more rational, efficient, and competitive system of business enterprise was developed. The medieval guild, with its corporate and monopolistic economic structure, protected the artisan from predatory competitors and the buying public from shoddy merchandise, but it had deteriorated into a self-perpetuating and niggardly organization, incapable of change and so encumbered with petty regulations as to make efficient production almost impossible. More and more, individual merchants and artisans—cloth makers, mining operators, tanners, importers of silks and spices —broke away from the older restrictions and went into business for themselves in defiance of the guild codes, the Church laws against usury, and the traditional system of ethics. They moved to the new centers of trade and prospered, because they lived by the standard that "conscience is a pretty thing to carry to Church," but he who "pursueth it in fair market or shop may die a beggar." Business shifted to Antwerp and Augsburg, where freer trade regulations and sharper mercantile practices helped trans-

The love of money became respectable as the Middle Ages drew to a close. This painting by the Antwerp artist Marinus van Reymerswael portrays a rich money-changer with his wife.

form the hard-working craftsman into a prince of commerce and finance. The acquisitive spirit in northern Europe may have hesitated at linking God and economic success in quite the same fashion as did the Italian trader Francisco di Marco Datini, who inscribed each of his account books with the words "in the name of God and of profit"; yet the German merchant Jacob Fugger of Augsburg considered it perfectly appropriate to write one of the most arrogant epitaphs ever conceived: "To God, All Powerful and Good! Jacob Fugger of Augsburg, ornament to his class and and to his country, Imperial Councilor under Maximilian I and Charles V, second to none in the acquisition of extraordinary wealth, in liberality, in purity of life, and in greatness of soul, as he was comparable to none in life, so after death is not to be numbered among the mortal." A revolution had taken place, for what had once been branded as a vile and sordid love of money was now entertained as wisdom. Christopher Columbus could greedily avow before those Most Catholic Monarchs of Spain that "gold is most excellent—with gold is treasure made; he who has it can do whatever he wants."

In England, and to a lesser extent in the Lowlands and France, the spirit of commerce filtered down to the gentry, who began to discard their feudal outlook and judge nobility in terms of "the abundance of worldly goods." Younger sons of landed stock went into trade, and merchants sought to transform the profits of commerce into landed wealth. In doing so they brought to the control of land a business spirit that viewed the management of estates as a mercantile venture. Early in the fifteenth century Englishmen had acquired the reputation of being a race "vainglorious of money." The swan song of medieval religious standards was sung, and the full measure of commercial respectability in town and shire was attained when in 1510 Dean John Colet chose to place the management of St. Paul's School in the hands of solid London "citizens of established reputation," because he had lost confidence in the good faith of priests and noblemen. There was, he said, "nothing certain in human affairs, he yet found the least corruption" in men of business.

Similar changes were taking place in the palaces of kings who were as anxious to modernize their kingdoms as financiers were to calculate the risks and profits in usury. It has been said of King Louis XI of France that he represented the worst side of the fifteenth century. Cold, deceitful, and suspicious, he viewed both God and man as purchasable and was so cautious that when he imported a particularly holy hermit from Italy, he insisted on testing the saintliness of his acquisition by placing before him the temptations of the flesh. Yet the very qualities that earned Louis the sinister description of "the universal spider" were what made his reign successful and won him a place among the New Monarchs of Europe, rulers who were taking the first hesitant steps toward converting their medieval kingdoms into sovereign national states. Upon the thrones of England, France, and Spain sat monarchs who made up in success what they may have lacked in legitimacy or the traditional virtues of medieval kingship. The insanity and turpitude that had dogged royal leadership, and the forces that had been tearing the feudal monarchies asunder began to diminish during the final decades of the fifteenth century. Louis XI of France, Henry VII of England, Ferdinand and Isabella of Spain were strong-minded sovereigns determined to be masters in their own realms, and they brought to their offices the two essentials of success that had already been applied to the counting house —hard work and calculation.

Debate continues as to whether the New Monarchs were in fact as new as historians once considered them to be or whether they were simply modeling themselves upon older medieval sovereigns who also had worked to establish financial solvency and endeavored to liberate royal government from ecclesiastical interference and the meddling of overmighty magnates. Yet something new had been added. There existed in government a degree of efficiency that had been unknown to the feudal world. Under the New Monarchs law enforcement loomed higher than strict legality; the reality of power was more highly regarded than political theory; and the duties of subjects were of greater concern than the rights of peers, priests, and principalities. The old institutional forms remained, but a new spirit had entered them. Success was in the air, and the New Monarchs were as concerned with it as any calculating commercialist or enterprising landlord might be. In England, for the first time, a king was praised not for his heroism or his piety but for those achievements attained by "acts of peace alone without sword or bloodshed." Henry VII was "full of notes," and with infinite care he initialed each page of the exchequer accounts and amassed a comfortable surplus in the treasury. Attention to the details of government and an astute understanding of the importance of finance were characteristic of Louis XI as

well. Both monarchs knew the truth of the contemporary saying that in peace as well as in war "three things must be made ready: money, money, and once again money," and both were willing to pay the price of success: the scorn of the old nobility who despised their bourgeois tastes, the hatred of all who envied their authority, and the endless hours of work that stood behind their achievement.

But it was their insistence on power, and not their hard work, that underlay the success of the New Monarchs. In England, France, and Spain the only conditions under which government could function were draconian, and monarchs demanded and achieved a measure of obedience that no feudal sovereign had ever enjoyed. In France the tradition of immensely powerful and independent ducal families, who coined their own money and disregarded the king's law, was finally ended when Charles of Burgundy was destroyed. By 1483, the year of Louis XI's death, not only had the duchy of Burgundy been reunited to the French crown but so had Anjou, Maine, and Provence. Feudal nobles, chartered towns, and rebellious provinces had to learn that "obedience is best in each degree." No matter how unjust, brutal, and costly it was, the prince's will had to be accepted as law. Louis XI enacted more legislation than any sovereign since the days of Charlemagne. Under his rule the burden of taxation steadily rose as the king successfully increased his nonfeudal revenues from one and a half million livres to nearly five million. Yet the price appeared small to Frenchmen who admired, even if they did not love, a monarch who argued that "the notable cities of Christianity have become great . . . not by exploits of arms but by good government."

In England the same steps were taken when Henry VII and his son, Henry VIII, insisted that the only peace that might prevail was the king's peace, the only justice to be allowed was royal justice, and the only loyalty that mattered was devotion to the crown. The divine right of aristocracy slowly receded before the divinity that "doth hedge a king," and the old nobility reluctantly learned that the meanest servant of the crown had "sufficient warrant to arrest the greatest peer of this realm." Private armies, private justice, and private war had to give way if Englishmen were to live under a single law. Henry VII's income rose astonishingly from 52,000 pounds to 142,000 pounds. His subjects who lived lavishly were persuaded to part with their gold for their high living was evidence of their ability to contribute generously to the king's exchequer; conversely, those who lived in poverty were also relieved of their money on the grounds that their frugality was proof of great savings, a part of which should be offered to defray the kingdom's operating expenses.

Events in Spain followed a somewhat different path. No tradition of Iberian unity had ever existed. Disunited as England and France may have been, the theory of feudal unity remained. In fifteenth-century England royal justice may have been perverted by the great barons, but it remained royal. In France the dukes of Burgundy may have regarded themselves as divine-right rulers, but they did fealty to the kings of France. Spain, in contrast, was not reunified, it was liberated. The common memory of the peninsula was not political union but a Christian crusade against the infidel. In 1469 the accident of dynastic marriage joined two of the peninsula's three major kingdoms together when Isabella, queen of Castile, and Ferdinand of Aragon were married. Though Ferdinand was as ruthless and calculating as any monarch of Europe, and Isabella as hard working, the forces that underlay Spanish union were spiritual, not political. More important than the need for internal security and good government was the demand that Spain, the citadel of the faith, be strengthened and prepared for its final victory over the Moors. The laws were codified and enforced, a hundred fifty mints throughout the country were reduced to five, the currency was standardized, and the historic tariff barriers within the realm were abolished. The aristocracy were forbidden their cherished symbols of independence— the right to include a crown in their coats of arms, the license to be preceded by a macebearer, and the right to build castles. Above all else, the nobility were persuaded to part with the lavish grants and sinecures that they had been able to extort from countless feudal kings, and the Catholic monarchs found themselves thirty million maravedis richer each year than their predecessors had been. The argument that induced the aristocracy to disgorge such sums and to accept correction was, significantly enough, the plea that money and discipline were necessary to expel the Moors from Spain.

By 1500 a new phenomenon had materialized in Europe: the sovereign national state. Feudal government had been a composite of rights, liberties, and privileges, and feudal subjects had been united by frail ties of allegiance only to the king. Man's first loyalty had rested with his village, his profession, his overlord, and his Church. On occasion feudal monarchs had been inspired leaders of men, but rarely, except possibly in England, did they view themselves as the regal symbol of state. Now, however, change was everywhere apparent. The medieval world had looked on government as a necessary evil at best; sixteenth-century man was beginning to suggest the strange notion that it might be a posi-

tive good. Slowly an image of society was evolving in which the state was viewed as a living organism with a will and rationale of its own. The ambassador no longer spoke for his province or for his profession but for the common good. The business of the ambassador, said one Venetian civil servant, was to "do, say, advise, and think only whatever may best serve the preservation and aggrandizement of his own state."

The truth was no longer to be sought only in God's laws or in Christian morality; it could be created to suit the needs of the state. "The opinion of the world," said Henry VIII, "is often stronger than the truth"; and public opinion was a commodity that the sixteenth century quickly learned could be molded to conform to the purposes of national policy. For reasons of state Francis I of France could ally himself with the infidel Turk in defiance of Christian opinion, even though Suleiman the Magnificent was about to attack Vienna. In the name of state diplomacy a Scottish arch-

A sixteenth-century woodcut entitled An Allegory of Trade *depicts the house of a Nuremberg merchant, who sits at the center overseeing his workers as they pack goods and count gold.*

bishop was assassinated by order of a Christian king of England. In the name of the welfare of the state an English bishop so far forgot higher laws as to argue that "in matters of state individuals were not to be so much regarded as the whole body of the citizens."

The more the state was heralded as the altar on which private and feudal rights had to be sacrificed, the more men and women sang the praises of their own land and noted their neighbor's defects. National consciousness, a sense of Englishness, Spanishness, or Frenchness, was relatively new to the sixteenth century, but dislike of strangers had been a common characteristic of the medieval world. The traveler from southern France who ventured as far north as Paris found Parisian French almost incomprehensible; Englishmen spoke a babble of dialects; neighboring villages eyed one another with suspicion; and Frenchmen were convinced that Englishmen were born with tails. The birth of the state converted man's inherent prejudice for his family, his

village, and his faith into a larger loyalty, so that by 1500 one traveler could complain that Englishmen think "there are no other men than themselves, and no other world but England; and whenever they see a handsome foreigner, they say that 'he looks like an Englishman'." England had been transformed into "this other Eden, demiparadise," while Spain, with its religious preoccupation, was becoming a land in which all men should seek to live and die "because of the faith there, which is so Catholic, so firm, and so true."

The indispensable conditions of statehood—linguistic unity and nationalistic pride—were rapidly developing in Spain, England, and France during the fifteenth century. London English, Parisian French, and Castilian Spanish came to predominate over rival dialects, and each became the medium through which the state sang the praises of its own uniqueness and virtues. The first grammar of any modern language was presented to Queen Isabella in 1492, and Spaniards were so convinced of the su-

Louis XI, *a portrait attributed to Fouquet* *Henry* VII, *by an unknown artist*

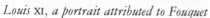

periority of their tongue that they boasted that "one can more rightly fear its descent than hope for its elevation." Englishmen were even more extreme in their defense of their native language, and one devotee asserted that his Anglo-Saxon tongue may not be "as sacred as the Hebrew or as learned as the Greek," but it was "as fluent as the Latin, as courteous as the Spanish, as courtlike as the French, and as amorous as the Italian."

When the New Monarchs associated themselves with national prejudice, and Bluff King Hal and Gloriana became the symbols for all that was best and English, or Francis I became for all Frenchmen *mon Roi, mon Seigneur, mon César,* then sovereigns became not kings to be obeyed but idols to be worshiped. This demanded the destruction of one of the most sacred and essential elements of the medieval formula—the balanced obligation offered to both God and Caesar. Lord, commoner, and clergyman learned that he owed his first duty to the crown. The full measure of Tudor authority was voiced when it was said of Bishop Fox that to "serve the king's turn [he] would agree to his own father's death." The great humanist scholar Erasmus spoke little more than the simple truth when he said that before the threat of princes "the people tremble, the senate yields, the nobility cringe, the judges concur, the divines are dumb, the lawyers assent, the law and constitution give way, neither right nor religion, neither justice nor humanity avails."

New nations, New Monarchs, new financiers were symptomatic of a new spirit. Optimism was in the air, in government, in commerce, and even in religion, and Erasmus could confidently predict a future in which true Christian piety, sound scholarship, and public peace would prevail. An increas-

ing and articulate coterie of scholars, artists, magistrates, and popes was beginning to look away from the danse macabre and turn instead to the dance of life. In Venice, where a golden shower of ducats had produced a society in which artists, scholars, courtesans, and merchants were judged by the single standard, talent, the visiting painter Albrecht Dürer suddenly discovered he was a gentleman, although at home in Germany he was still "a parasite." In the early years of the sixteenth century the rich vitality of Renaissance Italy moved northward, bringing with it a view of the world in which the individual was held up as the highest expression of divine wisdom. In man, as Pico della Mirandola said, was to be "found all and every ratio and proportion by which God reveals the innermost secrets of nature." In England and France, the second generation of the New Monarchs seemed to herald a new age in which "the heavens laugh, the earth exults, and all things are full of milk, of honey, and of nectar!"

The spirit that transformed the youthful courts of Henry VIII and Francis I into pavilions of Renaissance brilliance was heavily classical in flavor, deeply humanistic in its insistence upon the worth of man, childishly naïve in its expectations, and blatantly defiant in denying the medieval view of man's role in the divine order of things. The sin that the medieval world had most warned against— the exaltation of the individual—was the very virtue that the humanists most loudly extolled. Where the past had preached against pride, the Renaissance praised the virtuosity and creative genius of human talent in every field. Where the medieval Church had thundered against preoccupation with the affairs of this world, the early sixteenth century applauded the universal man who tasted deeply of every facet of life. Where man's humility in the face of the mysteries of life and death had once been acclaimed, now it was condemned. The individual was urged on to dare all, to test all, to inquire into the secrets of heaven and hell.

In Italy and in parts of northern Europe men agreed that a golden age had undoubtedly arrived, restoring the light of the liberal arts that had almost been destroyed. In France the humanist Louis Budé sang paeans to "sacred truth" which, he claimed, was beginning "to shine forth from the filth of the sophist school." In the Lowlands Erasmus of Rotterdam begged to be rejuvenated for a few years so as to enjoy the approaching golden age of learning. In Germany Ulrich von Hutten wrote: "Oh world, oh letters, it is a delight to live."

Yet in the midst of this enthusiasm the need for spiritual authority remained. Humanism, with its pedantic overtones and naïve individualism, proved to be distasteful to those of non-intellectual appetite. It was all very well for Erasmus to purge the Church with laughter, to wash away abuse with mirth, and expose the foibles of society to friendly ridicule. But the weight of clerical corruption was too heavy to be lifted by mere laughter. Scholarly reform within the Church lacked the strength to do more than reveal the sickness of Christendom, it could not cure it. It was Erasmus himself, the prince of all humanists, who confessed the underlying weakness of the reforming scholar when he sadly acknowledged that not everyone had "the courage to be a martyr. I am afraid if I were put to the trial, I should be like Peter."

The medieval ecclesia faced little danger from humanism; the enemy lay closer to home, within the Church itself. The path of religious revolution was not cut with the sharp axe of humanism but with the heavy sword of Martin Luther's spiritual despair. Luther was no child of the Renaissance. He was born of peasant stock in 1483 in Saxony, where men of piety still said their paternosters and attended Mass. He was a young man of deep religious sensibilities, who united a persistent conviction of his own impending damnation with a pressing sense of God's dreadful omnipotence and ruthless justice. Like a good son of the medieval Church, he turned in 1505 to a monastery—to the Augustinian community at Erfurt—to seek religious solace. By a life of fasting, prayer, and self-discipline and by the meticulous observation of every detail of the monastic rule, he sought to find salvation. "True it is," he confessed, "I was a good monk and . . . if ever a monk got to heaven by his monkery, it was I." Monkery seemed to fail in its purpose, however, for his sense of guilt remained until one day when he happened to ponder anew the words of Saint Paul: "The just shall live by faith." Thereupon he knew himself to have been reborn and the endless night of doubt and anguish receded; Luther had "gone through open doors into paradise." The path to heaven was through the doctrine of justification by "faith alone." The old medieval balance between good works and faith was demolished. It was not necessary to light candles, renounce life, retreat into a monastery, or endow chapels, for the excellent reason that heaven could not be bought with pious works. Man was saved by God's infinite mercy, and humanity could in no way warrant, merit, or purchase salvation; all it could do was to have faith in divine charity.

The implications of the new doctrine were revolutionary. To the claims of the medieval Church, to an absolute control of the channels by which God's grace was dispensed to man, Luther proclaimed that individuals were saved by their own faith without

Under Francis I, the French court was a center of Renaissance learning. Here the king listens to a scholar reading.

benefit of sacrament or cleric. To the Church's assertion of a monopoly of the roads to salvation, Luther set up the priesthood of all the faithful in which there was no distinction between a priest and a layman. To the Church's insistence that God spoke only through the ecclesiastical hierarchy of popes, bishops, and priests, Luther maintained the right of the individual, inspired by his faith, to comprehend God's word as revealed in Scripture.

Luther did not learn his theology all at once. From the monastery he was called to the new University of Wittenberg, where he lectured on the Bible and slowly formulated his religious views. It was only in 1516 that the sequence of events commenced that ultimately led him to challenge the entire edifice of medieval Catholicism and to destroy forever the spiritual unity of Christendom. The episode involved one of the most flagrant abuses of good works and one of the most startling examples

27

In this Cranach painting of Reformation leaders, Luther is seen at the left of his protector, John Frederick of Saxony. Luther's followers, Zwingli and Melancthon, are shown at the right.

of the sterile mechanization and soulless ceremonialism into which the medieval Church had slipped. The papacy of Leo X was in need of silver to pay for the construction of that magnificent monument to Renaissance grandeur, the new basilica of St. Peter at Rome. In order to raise the money, the pope turned to the international banking house of the Fuggers to supervise the collection. Johann Tetzel, a Dominican monk, acted as chief collector and canvassed Germany, selling indulgences, which were guaranteed to deliver souls from purgatory. He assured his listeners that:

> As soon as the coin in the coffer rings
> The soul from purgatory springs.

When Tetzel approached Wittenberg, Luther struck out against the belief that remission of sin could be bought, and on October 31, 1517, he posted on the castle church door his ninety-five theses, calling into question the purpose of the indulgences, their spiritual value, and the pope's authority to issue them to individual Christians.

Unexpectedly a personal and somewhat academic vendetta became the signal for spiritual revolution. Luther was acclaimed a hero by those who resented the draining away of German money to Rome in order to build the "insatiable basilica" of St. Peter and by those who wished to rid the Church of its commercialism, ritualism, and sterility. Every effort to discipline the wayward monk produced stronger words of defiance, until Luther stood in open rebellion against the entire Catholic Church. At the Imperial Diet at Worms in April, 1521, he voiced the final logic of his heresy: "Unless I am convicted by Scripture and plain reason—I do not accept the authority of popes and councils, for they have contradicted each other—my conscience is captive to the Word of God. I cannot and will not recant anything, for to go against conscience is neither right nor safe. God help me. Amen. Here I stand, I cannot do otherwise." To the Emperor Charles V, who sat listening to Luther's presumptuous challenge, it seemed intolerable that "a single monk, led astray by private judgment," should have impudently concluded "that all Christians up till now have erred." But pope and emperor, medieval Church and empire reckoned without "the marvelous comfort and quietness" that Luther's message held for all who felt close upon them the fires of damnation or who could find no relief in the bosom of the Catholic ecclesia. The reformer's books sold everywhere and six hundred copies of his theses were sent to France, Spain, and England, where men of similar heart were eager to receive them. Plagued by the same sense of despair, they followed in his footsteps or sought their own brand of spiritual solace in defiance of established authority and ancient formulas.

In religion, in politics, in commerce, and in the governments of men, change surged and swelled, and by 1533, the year of Elizabeth's birth, the main outlines of modern Europe were clearly discernible. Although Elizabeth and her generation stood on the threshold of modernity, the ghost of medievalism lingered on, fettering the minds of men and holding captive their imaginations. Scratch an Elizabethan deeply and a medieval man lies revealed. The humanist scholar Sir Thomas More has been called the first man to apply human reason to the study of a sane and realistic society, yet More sacrificed his life for the medieval concept of a unified Christendom. The Frenchman Jean Bodin was capable of perceiving that the curse of inflation that afflicted Europe in the sixteenth century was the result of a glut on the money market caused by gold and silver from the New World. Yet Bodin wrote in defense of witchcraft and carried the title of Satan's Attorney General. The attraction of the Cemetery of the Innocents was passing, but the human body in various stages of decomposition remained a popular theme of tombstone art.

Everywhere the medieval heritage died hard, and the new impulses in society faced constant challenge from the past. Feudal castles still stood, ties of fealty and blood remained strong, and most men's image of society continued to be medieval. Throughout Europe the social order was still supposed to be static, closed, hierarchical, and religiously inspired. The Elizabethan state was no human contrivance constructed to advance the material well-being of man. It remained a divinely ordained structure into which individuals were born with prescribed duties and fixed status. The favorite political metaphor of the age was the beehive in which all members knew their place and over which the queen and her aristocracy ruled. From Madrid to London, from Paris to Rome, the sixteenth century insisted upon "a head to rule, priests to pray, counselors to counsel, judges to judge, noblemen to give orders, soldiers to defend, farmers to till, tradesmen to do business, and artisans to take care of mechanical matters."

The much proclaimed sovereign national state was as yet no leviathan, and though it demanded the loyalty of all its subjects, it still lacked the machinery to make its claims completely effective. During much of the sixteenth century Parisians were "so ready to uproars and insurrections that foreign nations wondered at the patience of the kings of France." Royal patience, however, was unavoidable, for 12,000 royal officials endeavored, rather ineffectually, to govern fifteen million Frenchmen, a figure that represents a ratio of one official for every 1,250 inhabitants. By today's standards and proportions, which work out to one official for every seventy Frenchmen, France was scarcely burdened with an overabundance of government. The era of private armies and feudal revolts was far from ended. Overmighty subjects still retained vast military and economic resources and did not hesitate to appeal to clan, custom, and feudal privilege. During the winter of 1569–70 the feudal north in England made a last bid to return to "the good old days," and in France the tottering realm was engulfed by a series of bitter dynastic, regional, and religious wars that lasted for over a generation.

National states were increasing in strength, yet the myth of European political unity still excited the imagination; the fatuous dignities of the Holy Roman Emperor were still held in awe; and the European family of states was still considered to be subject to divine governance. Medieval theory and contemporary reality stood at total variance with one another, but most men—even rebels like Luther—still desired a return to the days when there had been but one truth, one faith, and one Church. The existence of two absolute truths—one Catholic, the other Protestant—meant not toleration but religious controversy, in which the faithful were urged to sacrifice all other concerns for the defense and aggrandizement of their particular brand of orthodoxy. The clash of loyalties to God, to fellowman, to state, to family, and to feudal overlord imposed strains on society as great as those that had existed in the fifteenth century and produced equally violent extremes of despondency and delight. In France, the Lowlands, and parts of Germany, society dissolved into civil war and religious bloodshed; in Spain, the state became the hallowed instrument of Catholic truth; and in Geneva, an equally belligerent Protestant orthodoxy prevailed. It was in England alone that a more moderate political and religious pattern of behavior came to triumph thanks to the magic of a virgin queen.

A
WORLD
REBORN

By the end of the fifteenth century Europe was emerging from an age of uncertainty. A new world had been discovered and an old one revitalized. Life and thought were being transformed as men abandoned the ideals of medieval times and looked back to classical antiquity for inspiration. In technology, the sciences, and in the arts, startling advances were made. The Atlantic ports were being enriched by the plunder of the Indies, and the economy of western Europe was coming to life again after centuries of stagnation. Men and women were filled with a new exuberance, a new desire to exploit all their potentialities—a new confidence that led them to dare anything.

A new spirit of nationalism was in the air, too, and nowhere was it more apparent than in Spain, where not even the concept of unity had existed previously. Spanish consolidation had begun with the marriage of Ferdinand of Aragon to Isabella of Castile; by 1492, with the royal couple's triumphant entry (right) into Granada, the last Moslem stronghold in Spain, the divided land had been transformed into a sovereign Catholic state. In that year of conquest and discovery, the foundations were laid for an empire that was to dominate the Elizabethan world, an empire far greater than even the Romans had envisioned.

THE NEW TECHNOLOGY

The invention of movable type in Germany around 1440 and the spread of printing throughout Europe revolutionized society. Almost at once, the exchange of information and ideas accelerated enormously. Even impecunious scholars were able to buy books, and people in remote districts were brought into contact with the cities by itinerant peddlers who sold printed broadsides devoted to politics, religion, and the latest scandals. More than anything else, it was printing that enabled the ideas of the Renaissance and the Reformation to spread as rapidly as they did. At the same time, the art of war was undergoing a revolution too; books about new developments in tactics and weaponry were in demand everywhere. Theories of fortification became increasingly sophisticated as cannon and firearms improved. By 1500 the feudal knight, like the medieval scribe, had become an anachronism. Warfare was no longer a glorified blood sport played by the rules of chivalry.

The widespread employment of compositors, pressmen, and proofreaders like those in the Paris printer's shop opposite helped revitalize the European economy. Machiavelli's Art of War, *shown above in an English translation of 1560, was a best-seller everywhere.*

OVERLEAF: *The battle of Pavia in Italy in 1525, at which the forces of Francis I of France were defeated by the Holy Roman Emperor Charles V, clearly demonstrated the advances that had lately taken place in the use of artillery and in the employment of infantry.*

A sixteenth-century woodcut shows various aspects of man's nature, with intelligence at the top.

THE NEW MAN

The Renaissance was based upon a new belief in the dignity of man. Man was no longer considered to be limited by his birth as he was during the Middle Ages; now he was envisioned as a being capable of transformation through acts of his own will, a demigod to whom all things were possible. Michelangelo's sonnets were hardly less magnificent than his paintings, sculpture, and architecture; and Leonardo da Vinci, having mastered all earthly pursuits, tried to lift himself, literally, into the heavens. Baldassare Castiglione's book *The Courtier* fired the imagination of the age; men were taught to cultivate learning, connoisseurship, and the social graces, not as ends in themselves, but in order to enable them to act—and, above all, fight—more effectively. Thus Cellini was as admired for his swordplay as for his art, and in England poets like Wyatt, Raleigh, and Sidney were far less concerned about their literary reputations than they were about their standing as courtiers and soldiers. Castiglione's book and the ideas it introduced became extremely popular, especially in England, where the enduring tradition of the gentleman—an accomplished amateur, literate, dashing, and always cool under fire—was derived directly from it.

Few paintings summarize the interests and attitudes of Renaissance man as succinctly as does Titian's Portrait of Jacopo Strada *(opposite). The love of antiquity is indicated by a classical sculpture, books are shown as emblems of learning, and the coins and a sword symbolize trade and action.*

THE NEW WOMAN

The rise of individualism and the desire for new experiences were not confined to Renaissance men. Women too found their lot less confining. The daughters of prosperous families were often given fine educations, learning classical and modern languages, music, dancing, and sonnetizing. Husbands were usually older men preoccupied with worldly affairs, and wives were free to devote themselves to personal adornment, elaborate flirtations, and the cultivation of the arts. Italian women were the first to benefit from the changes, but by the time Elizabeth Tudor was born, the Renaissance had reached England and the future queen was taught much as a prince might be—to ride well and to dance skillfully, to read Latin, Greek, French, and Italian, and write English prose and verse with a graceful style.

English women such as those shown in the sketch above by a Flemish traveler managed considerable variety of costume despite ordinances regulating dress. In the painting at left, a young woman pursues the literary life.

CITIES OF THE WEST

The discovery of the New World brought with it the decline of the Mediterranean port cities and the emergence of those on the Atlantic. As the sixteenth century advanced, western Europe grew increasingly prosperous, and many small towns found themselves transformed into great cities. The population of Seville, which monopolized Spanish trade with the New World, nearly quadrupled between 1517 and 1594; Bristol, Amsterdam, Cadiz, and Lisbon replaced Venice, Lübeck, Visby, and Genoa as shipping terminals; and Antwerp—partly because the river Zwyn, the only sea access of its rival city Bruges, silted up—became the chief commercial center of the north. Wool from Bilbao, spices from the Indies, gold and silver from Mexico and South America, naval stores, flax, timber, and furs from the Baltic nations, and salt fish and herring from the North Sea—all were traded through Antwerp. The city became the site of the first exchange and a center of international finance. It was to the wealthy merchants of Antwerp that German princes and the kings of France and England applied for the blatantly usurious loans that were necessary in order to finance costly wars.

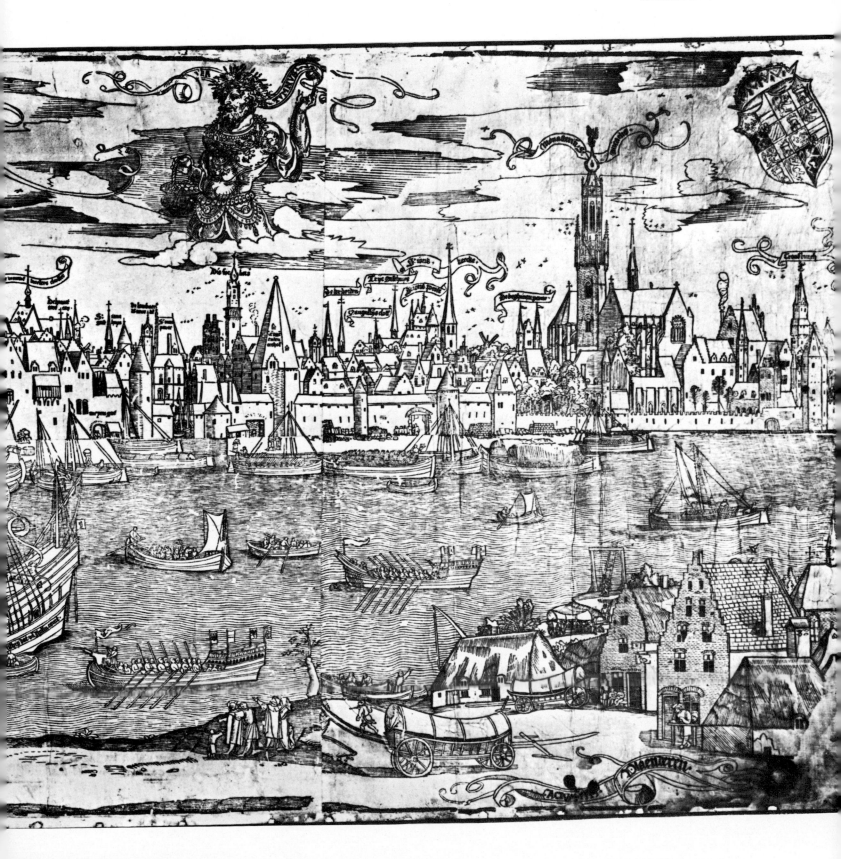

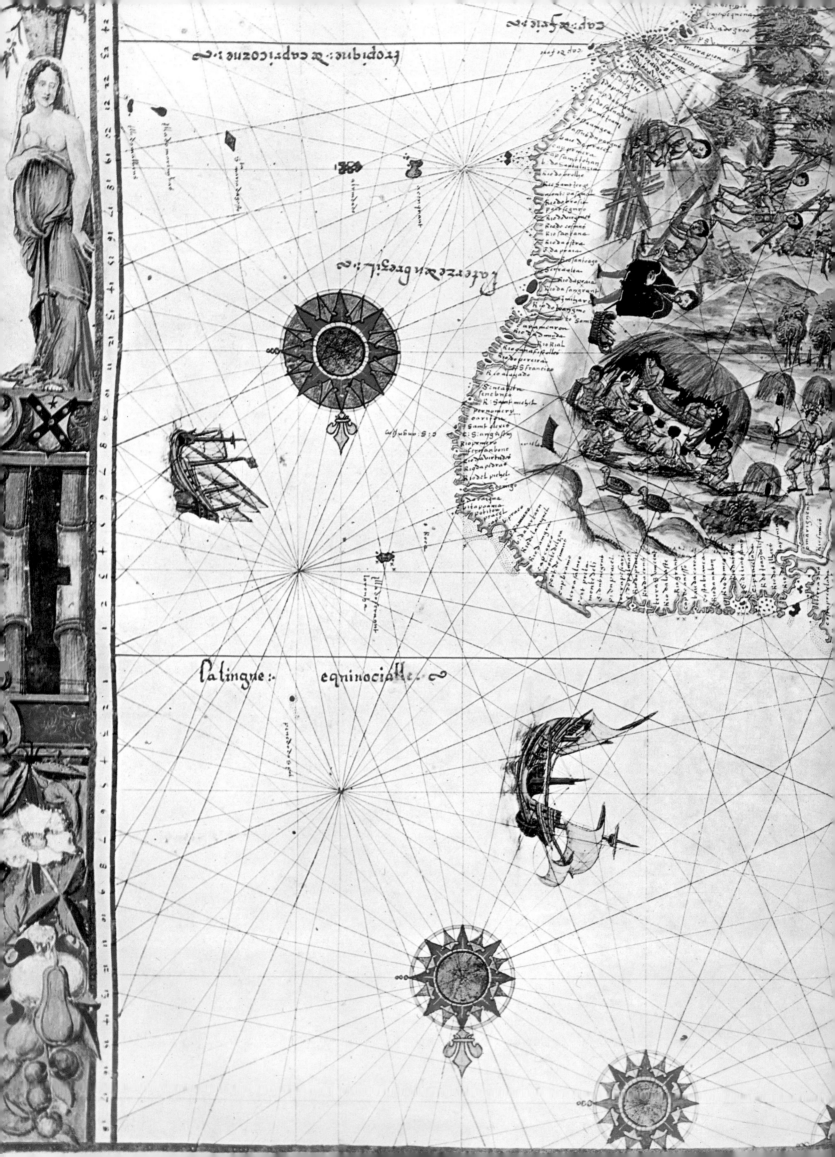

A papal bull directed against Luther

THE REFORMATION

When Martin Luther began the Reformation by posting ninety-five theses debating Church practices, printed broadsides quickly spread the news throughout Europe. Luther himself was motivated by medieval piety, yet it was Renaissance ideas that promoted the spread of the Reformation. The new bourgeoisie hated Church restraints on usury and trade; humanistic scholars like Zwingli, Hutten, and Melanchthon questioned Church prerogatives; nationalism prompted many countries to sever old ties. Nevertheless most Europeans remained vehemently Catholic, and inevitably wars broke out between adherents of the rival religions. Europe would not know peace until a century later in a world transformed by the converging currents of Reformation and Renaissance.

Lutheran tracts showed the pope as an ass.

One section of an altar, which was painted by Lucas Cranach, the greatest artist of the Reformation, shows Martin Luther pointing to a passage in his Bible as he preaches a sermon about the dying Christ to an enraptured Protestant congregation.

ANNO · ÆTATIS · · SVÆ · XLI

2

SIN AND SCHISM

Elizabeth may not have been born in sin as the Catholic Church claimed, but she was certainly the child of schism, and her sex was a source of bitter disappointment to a parent who had risked his crown and kingdom in the hope of fathering a legitimate male heir. From the moment of her conception, the princess' sex and legitimacy were crucial factors in the course of European history. Elizabeth was born into a world that viewed her birth and continued good health as the cardinal stumbling block to the spiritual reunification of Christendom and the extinction of the Protestant heresy. Most of Europe, and possibly even a majority in England, regarded her as the product of adultery, a royal bastard who could not legally succeed to the throne. Only a few militant Protestants greeted her arrival with fervent prayers of thankfulness, and even they were dismayed that the future of their faith should be tied to the frail life of a girl child. As for her father, that giant of a sovereign who conjoined in his royal person the savage pride of a Lucifer and the irresistible charm of a Falstaff, he was outraged that God and fortune had made him ridiculous by presenting him with still another heiress to his kingdom.

The story of Elizabeth's birth goes back to sometime before the year 1527 when Henry VIII was forced to contend with three interrelated emotions: mounting concern over his queen—Catherine of Aragon's—advancing years and her failure to bear a living son; the sting of conscience for having married his deceased brother's wife; and a violent sexual attraction for a young lady of the court, who obstinately insisted that sharing her sovereign's crown

was going to be a prerequisite to sharing his bed.

As a young man Henry had fulfilled his father's deathbed request that he marry Catherine, daughter of Isabella and Ferdinand of Spain and widow of Henry's brother, Prince Arthur. Special papal dispensation had been arranged so that the king might not violate the law in the Book of Leviticus that clearly stated: "If a man shall take his brother's wife, it is an unclean thing . . . they shall be childless." Marriage with Catherine had not actually been barren and the queen had done her best. Five children had been born, but only a daughter survived. This the most learned and politic men of the land regarded as a sure invitation to disputed succession and civil war. By 1527 Catherine was an aging and rotund lady of forty-two, and her husband, who was six years her junior, began to ponder, despite papal assurances to the contrary, whether he was not in fact an incestuous king and the unhappy object of Heaven's righteous anger.

Whether the sequence of events that culminated in history's most celebrated divorce suit stemmed from Henry's tender conscience or his far from tender infatuation with the ebony-eyed beauty Anne Boleyn is more a matter of personal judgment than of verifiable historic fact. What is clear is that the case was presented to the world as a question of political necessity; no matter what the price, England had to have a legitimate male heir to secure the succession and save the kingdom from a bitter civil war between the advocates of the king's legitimate daughter, Mary, and his only son, the illegitimate duke of Richmond.

Henry VIII, *one of several portraits painted by Hans Holbein*

Every consideration seemed to call for divorce, a step that was hardly unique in the annals of dynastic history. Wives of royalty promised to be "bonair and buxom in bed and at board," and when they went so far as to forget their wedding vows, it was accepted procedure to put them aside in favor of someone who was capable of providing sons and heirs—those most precious assets in an age of high infant mortality. In a world that made exceptions for kings and princes and looked kindly upon the matrimonial requirements of sovereigns, Henry anticipated no problem in obtaining a divorce. The pope had obliged him by making it possible to marry Catherine in the first place, so now, eighteen years later, it was expected that His Holiness would grant his faithful son and Defender of the Faith the privilege of breaking the rules again and allow him to divorce the lady. In this pleasant and easy solution to domestic matters, Bluff King Hal reckoned without his wife's Spanish pride, her European relatives, and the conscience of Christendom.

The fact that the king's "great matter," as Henry's divorce was referred to in the chanceries of Europe, took six interminable years to run its course is evidence not so much that Henry had the patience of Job but that the pace of diplomacy in the sixteenth century was leisurely in the extreme. The world of the Renaissance still thought in terms of distances that took weeks and months to cover, and foreign policies were implemented by ambassadors who spent a large portion of their waking hours jogging along painfully on sluggish mules. Diplomatically London and Paris were at best two-days journey

apart, and during the winter months official dispatches might take over four weeks to get through. Madrid and Rome were more than a fortnight distant, and in 1603 couriers took three days, riding at breakneck speed, to carry dispatches bearing the news of Elizabeth's death to Edinburgh, where her expectant heir, James, was awaiting them.

The fastest, but at times the most dangerous, mode of transportation was by sea, and Mediterranean galleys, stroked by countless slaves and helped along by a favorable breeze, might achieve one hundred twenty-five miles a day. The great galleons, propelled only by sail but capable of surviving in the gray waters of the Atlantic, were considerably slower, but they could still outdistance equestrian travelers who attained at most eighty-five miles a day. The great disadvantage of ocean travel lay in contrary winds, high waves, and unpredictable currents. At the Strait of Gibraltar, for instance, where the Atlantic rushes into the Mediterranean at a rate of five to six knots an hour, ships sometimes had to wait for weeks for a wind strong enough to carry them into the Atlantic. Whether it was for Henry waiting for information from his ambassadors in Rome, Elizabeth expecting word of the Armada, or Philip II of Spain scheming his moves in the game of international cold war, news traveled at a pace unimaginably slow.

Early sixteenth-century Europe was composed of six major powers, all of which claimed the special attention of the deity but none of which ever allowed spiritual concerns to interfere seriously with questions of state. There was Henry of England, who proudly bore the title of Defender of the Faith; Francis I, the Most Christian King of France; His Holiness, the pope, possessed of the keys to the kingdom of heaven; Suleiman, the sultan of the Ottoman empire, caliph of all true believers; and finally Charles V, who was both emperor of the Holy Roman Empire and His Most Catholic Majesty of Spain. Of all the sovereigns of Europe, the Emperor Charles and the Sultan Suleiman were the most powerful. The Great Suleiman had indeed penetrated "the bulwark of Christendom," overrun Hungary, razed the Christian churches of Buda, replacing them with mosques, and slain in battle the emperor's brother-in-law, the twenty-year-old king of Hungary. Six times Suleiman had led his armies to the very gates of Vienna. Yet the sultan's successes were in large measure based not on his own strength but on his opponent's weakness. For Charles' ramshackle empire imposed on him so many obligations that he could never marshal his full military potential against the forces of the infidel.

Charles' vast domain was the result of dynastic

An eagle emblematic of the Holy Roman Empire displays coats of arms of fifty-six member states on its wings.

HANS BURGKMAIR

accident and was historic proof of the effectiveness of the maxim by which his ancient dynasty, the Hapsburgs, lived: "Others make war but you, happy Austria, make marriages." From his paternal grandfather, the Emperor Maximilian, Charles inherited the Hapsburg possessions in Austria and the Low Countries. Through his mother, mad Joanna, daughter of Ferdinand and Isabella, he was heir to the kingdom of Spain and the riches of the New World. The imperial dignity to which he was elected in 1519, the military might of the Spanish infantry, the wealth of the silver mines of Peru, and the economic prosperity of the Netherlands were united under a single hand, and Charles was told in all seriousness that God had placed him "on the road to universal monarchy," raising him above all other kings and princes. The imperial shepherd discovered, however, that for every sheep he gathered into the fold there lurked a wolf outside. Each new title burdened Charles with added obligations and brought him new opponents.

The emperor was never able to isolate his enemies, to crush the Lutheran heretics in Germany, to curb the independence of the great princes of his empire, to surround and destroy Valois France, and to expel the forces of Allah from Europe. Charles spent a lifetime preserving the status quo, fighting delaying actions, and hurrying from Milan to Antwerp and back to Madrid in an effort to save what he had inherited. In one area alone was he successful: the kings of France, who had been attempting to extend their domain into Italy, were thrown out of the country, and the whole peninsula fell under imperial domination. This turned out to be of supreme importance to the success of Henry's "great matter," for only the Roman pontiff could grant the divorce, and Clement VII had become, in effect, the emperor's chaplain.

Unfortunately for Henry, the wife he wanted to divorce was the aunt of the man who controlled the wealth of the Indies, the markets of the Netherlands, the armies of Spain, and the conscience of the pope. Worse still, middle-aged Catherine proved to be something more than a dowdy spouse with spreading hips and domestic tastes, content to count her sovereign's laundry and preside over his household. Beneath a placid surface lay hidden the furious pride and unbending obstinacy of her Iberian blood. The queen was, as she reminded her royal husband, "no English woman but a Spaniard born," and she set her heart and soul against any idea of a divorce. Henry might have as many concubines as he desired, but no common lady in waiting would ever replace her as rightful queen, and no child of sin would displace her daughter as legal heir to the Tudor

In a painting that was completed before his rift with the Church, Henry is portrayed with Pope Leo X and Charles V.

throne. Humility and loyalty were the words of her motto; but Henry quickly learned that her humility was for God, her loyalty to her blood. In her determination to thwart her husband's matrimonial plans, she called upon the formidable influence of her family and the dynastic pride of her powerful nephew, the Emperor Charles.

For six years Henry applied persuasion and coercion to his wife and used all the weapons of diplomacy on Charles and Clement VII, but by 1532 time and patience were running out. In September Anne Boleyn's resistance gave way, having been substantially weakened by her elevation to the peerage as marchioness of Pembroke, with an annual income of one thousand pounds. By December she was pregnant, and on January 25, 1533, Anne and Henry were secretly married. If the child was to be legitimate and the father saved from bigamy, only seven months remained in which to secure the divorce from Catherine.

49

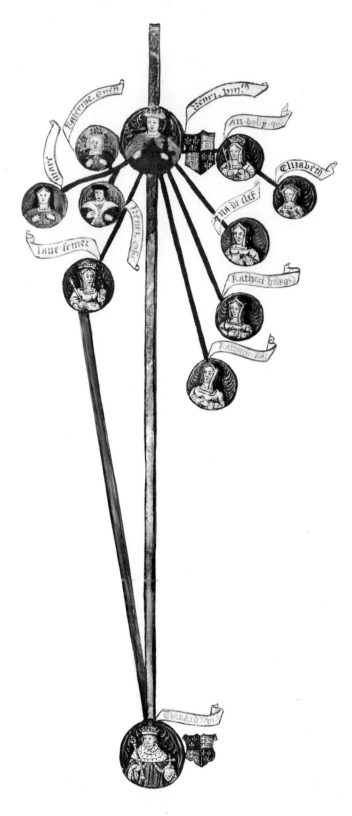

This genealogical table, apparently painted during the reign of King Edward VI (at bottom), shows Henry surrounded by his disposable wives and the issue of his six marriages. Elizabeth, still a young princess, is at right.

From January on, the pace of events quickened, culminating in a religious revolution. The archbishop of Canterbury had recently died and in his place was appointed Thomas Cranmer, a Cambridge don who had been one of the king's strongest supporters in his efforts to obtain a divorce from Catherine. With Cranmer's elevation to the see of Canterbury, the shape of revolutionary things to come was clearly revealed, but a frightened pope, still anxious to placate Henry though unwilling to grant him a divorce, blessed the appointment; and the new archbishop was legally installed in March, 1533. Cranmer was ready and willing to grant the king a divorce himself, but any decision rendered in the archbishop's court would be subject to review and possible reversal in Rome. In April, therefore, the irrevocable step was finally taken; by the Act in Restraint of Appeals the legal fabric binding England to Rome was cut and the court of the archdiocese of Canterbury decreed to be the highest spiritual forum for Englishmen. In May Henry was requested to appear before a tribunal of his own kingdom, presided over by Cranmer, a prelate of his own creation. The decision, in the king's favor, surprised no one; Henry was now free to announce publicly his marriage to Anne and to crown her queen on June 1, 1533. The stage had been prepared with studied care, new statutes had been passed and old laws violated, a Spanish queen had been sacrificed and an English one created, all in anticipation of the birth of a legitimate male heir. It was almost too much to endure when on September 7, 1533, the prince born to Anne Boleyn turned out to be Elizabeth Tudor.

The Catholic world guffawed and perceived evidence of divine judgment; Anne was despondent and Henry indignant at this trick of fate. Comfort, however, could be taken from the fact that the child was healthy and the new queen fertile, and the forty-two-year-old monarch had no doubts about his own fecundity. More children would certainly follow. The immediate problem was to complete the break with Rome and create a Church of England that would be independent of the pope but not of the king. The new ecclesia had to be free of foreign interference, and more important, all its authority and fiscal perquisites had to be transferred to the crown. By the second Act of Annates, in 1534, the financial links with Rome were severed, and Church revenues were redirected into the royal coffers. New legislation gave Henry the right to make all ecclesiastical appointments, and in November, 1534, the constitutional revolution reached its climax in the Act of Supremacy, whereby the king assumed the title of Supreme Head on Earth of the Church of England. Henry became, in his own memorable words, "pope, king, and emperor" in England.

Transfer, not reform, was the theme of the English Reformation. The vicar of Christ at Rome had been displaced by God's lieutenant on earth in London. The revenues, powers, and privileges of His Holiness had been conferred upon His Majesty, the sovereign king of England. The Church of England remained Catholic and orthodox, for the man who assumed the mantle of spiritual authority was no heretic. All of "his devout subjects" were "as obedient, devout, Catholic, and humble children of God and the Holy Church as any people be within any realm of Christendom." Henry had abolished the pope but not popery, and those who desired to see the reform of the Church after the transfer of papal authority from the Vatican to Westminster were disappointed. They suspected, and with some justification, that, as one Protestant said, "the rich treasures, the rich income of the Church, these are the gospel according to Harry." In doctrine and in many of its forms, Henry's Church was still thoroughly Catholic. Canon law remained valid, spiritual violators were put to public penance, the Church's power to excommunicate was still held in awe, ecclesiastical

courts continued to hear divorce cases and handle the probation of wills, and the archbishop of Canterbury retained authority to grant special dispensations for those who infringed upon the laws of God. The only change was that the source of all of this authority was now the king and not the pope.

Henry had achieved the means to his end, but the end itself—a legitimate male heir—continued to elude him. His situation at home was eased in January, 1536, when Catherine died, probably of heart disease, although it is possible she was murdered. Henry's reaction was to thank God and to make much of the infant princess Elizabeth. He celebrated his wife's death by holding a court ball, which he attended "clad all in yellow from top to toe." Though much was made of the royal babe, time was running out, for Anne Boleyn was proving to be as unproductive of male heirs as her predecessor had been. Again the king was touched in his conscience for fear that his second marriage was displeasing to God. Proof of divine wrath seemed manifest when on January 29 Anne miscarried of a baby boy, supposedly after she found her husband in the embraces of one of her maids in waiting, the demure and af-

An allegory of Tudor succession shows Bloody Mary at left with Philip and the god Mars, Henry
VIII, *Edward* VI, *and Elizabeth, last of the line, who ushers in Peace and Plenty at right.*

The reformed Church issued its first Bible in 1539. In this detail from its title-page illustration Henry presents copies to Cromwell and Archbishop Cranmer for public distribution.

fable Jane Seymour. By May the queen had been accused of high treason and adultery; on the nineteenth of the month she was executed, and eleven days later Henry married Jane Seymour. On October 12, 1537, the king was granted his wish, for the new queen fulfilled her nuptial vows and gave birth to Prince Edward. The heir, however, was born at a price; in twelve days Queen Jane was dead.

The old king was to marry thrice more, once for reasons of diplomacy, once for love, and once to find a companion in his advancing years and a nurse to his diseased and dying body; but with Edward the number of his children was complete—Catholic and Spanish Mary, Protestant and English Elizabeth, sickly and legitimate Edward. In the end Henry willed his throne as if no breath of scandal had touched his dynasty: first to Edward, then to Mary, and finally to Elizabeth, and if the children of his own body should die without issue, the crown was bequeathed to the offspring of his younger sister Mary, duchess of Suffolk.

Throughout Henry's reign, the tide of religious passion in England and Europe had been steadily rising, engulfing Christendom in the strife and bloodshed of sectarian discord. With almost apocalyptic speed Lutheran ideas spread, breeding social and spiritual revolution. By 1547 Prussia, Denmark, Sweden, and Brandenburg had gone over to the new heresy, while England was schismatic and the Netherlands and northern France were hearkening

to the stern word of God as revealed by John Calvin. The fact that reform spoke not with a single voice but in a babble of warring tongues, each claiming a monopoly of the truth, was of little comfort to men of the old school who bewailed the existence of so much error in the world. Every new Protestant faction seemed more quarrelsome and sententious than the one before. Luther at Wittenberg, Bucer at Strasbourg, Zwingli at Zurich, Calvin at Geneva, and the Anabaptists at Münster thundered militant threats at Rome and at each other. In every country the leadership of the Protestant movement seemed to be falling into the hands of fervent and aggressive reformers, who sought not to countenance society but to remodel it into a community of saints.

In England Henry faced a growing and exultant minority of saints, righteous in their spiritual strength and adamant in their stand against evil, who saw the break with Rome as a prelude to the establishment of the kingdom of heaven on earth. To such men the pope was the devil's disciple and the Roman Church was the "painted whore of Babylon." In their stern eyes the popery that remained in the Church of England was as pernicious as the pope, and the cry went up to "get rid of the poison with the author." As long as Henry lived the call went unheeded, but at his death England was caught in a religious maelstrom.

Princess Elizabeth was thirteen when her father died in the early morning of January 8, 1547, and the control of the state passed to her brother, a precocious child of nine, and to his naïve but well-meaning uncle, Edward Seymour, duke of Somerset. The princess' formal education as a woman of the Renaissance was the work of tutors appointed by her father, but her training in statecraft commenced the day the old king died. Under Edward and Mary, Elizabeth learned exactly what it meant to be a Tudor heir and how true was the saying: "Slippery is the place next to kings." Elizabeth's miraculous achievements in later years in restraining religious passions and preserving the unity of her realm were an outgrowth of her experiences during the tragic reigns of her brother and older sister. A decade of indecent Protestant fanaticism under Edward and Catholic bigotry under Mary demonstrated to her what unrestrained religious hatred and social violence could do to the kingdom.

The man most responsible for the failure of Edward VI's reign was Edward Seymour, who, as the sovereign's uncle, was appointed Lord Protector of the realm and governor of the king's person. The new *alter rex* endeavored to substitute sweet reason and tolerance for the old king's draconian measures, and as a result the country came close to being torn to pieces. The moment the government indicated its willingness to discard Henry's *via media* of Catholicism without the pope, the clamor for religious revolution rose to deafening heights. The alehouse and the tavern, the royal household and the bishop's palace became the arenas of religious strife, where the holy Mass was referred to as a jack-in-the-box and the time-honored words spoken at the consecration of the host—*Hoc est corpus*—were translated as "hocus-pocus."

Edward Seymour tried to solve the problem by demanding a massive and comprehensive religious conformity aimed at bringing into a single fold a Catholic faction, made more desperate by the growing force of heresy, and a determined Protestant minority, made more radical by the arrival of reformers from the Continent. The Book of Common Prayer of 1549 tried to satisfy all parties and ended by alienating them, for it obscured the central issue of dispute: whether the Mass was a ceremony in which the body and blood of Christ were actually present and resacrificed for the benefit of mankind or whether it was a commemorative service recalling Christ's sacrifice and redemption. Written by Archbishop Cranmer and reflecting the richness of his language and the softness of his compromise, the prayer book was a literary masterpiece but a religious debacle. It irritated reformers, who insisted that in religion it was "more proper to call a spade a spade than to throw ambiguous expressions before posterity," and it drove the conservative shires of southern England into open revolt, with the peasants calling for a return to the good old days that they had enjoyed under Henry VIII.

The Lord Protector was no more successful at satisfying the ambitions of his family than in uniting his sovereign's kingdom. Edward Seymour had a younger brother, Thomas, "fierce in courage, courtly in fashion, in personage stately, in voice magnificent, but somewhat empty in matter." While the elder brother was aloof and tactless, the younger was ruthless and charming; while the Lord Protector had greatness, title, and wealth thrust upon him, Thomas Seymour had been left with the crumbs of high office—Lord High Admiral of England. Thomas was critical of his brother's policies, covetous of his authority, and infuriated by the lordly bearing of a man who was his own flesh and blood. The Lord Admiral's ambitions were built upon his personal magnetism, his charm with the ladies, and his way with small boys, especially young Edward VI. He offered himself as a suitable husband for either Elizabeth or Mary, and when the king's Council dismissed the suggestion he secretly married the dowager queen, Catherine Parr.

His wife did not long survive her nuptials, dying in childbirth a year and a half later. Thomas next cast his net at Elizabeth and Edward IV. The way to the king's heart was through his pocket money; Thomas tried to turn him against his other uncle by telling Edward that the Lord Protector had kept him "a very beggarly king" and had treated him like a small boy. To Elizabeth he made advances even while Catherine lived, entering her bedchamber in nightgown and bare legs to romp with his wife's royal stepdaughter. After Catherine's death the romping took on more serious overtones, and Thomas again began to hint at marriage.

What Thomas' ultimate plans were—kidnapping the king, replacing his brother, leading an insurrection, or marrying Elizabeth—remain a mystery. The results, however, were clear: the Lord Admiral was destroyed, and eventually his brother was too, and Elizabeth's life was placed in jeopardy. To avoid being suspected of involvement in his brother's indiscretions, the Lord Protector was forced to act; and on January 17, 1549, he ordered Thomas' arrest. A full-scale investigation was conducted into the relationship between the Lord Admiral and Elizabeth, and the princess was grimly reminded that "she was but a subject." If nothing else, the future queen learned discretion, and when Thomas Seymour was executed in March, she remarked: "This day died a man of much wit and very little judgment."

The death of the Lord Admiral was a prelude to the fury of factional discord and backstairs politics that swept the Lord Protector from his office in 1549 and then, two years later, to the execution block. In 1550 a palace revolution took place, and Seymour's rival, John Dudley, earl of Warwick and later duke of Northumberland, seized control of the Council and the king's person. Historians have rarely had a good word to say about Northumberland. Although he was a Catholic by conviction, he was a ruthless Protestant by politics. Under the duke, full-scale plunder of the ecclesia began, and extreme Calvinistic Protestantism was officially fostered. Religious reformers and tough court politicians had one idea in common: clerical wealth and property were harmful to the spiritual vigor and purity of God's Church. Pious sentiment and economic self-interest made it highly desirable to relieve the bishops of as many lordships as possible. Northumberland, therefore, found it profitable to support the extreme Protestant position: the Mass was purely a commemorative service, priests were teachers of morality and the Bible, altars should be replaced by tables, and the Church should be returned to its pristine ceremonial purity. By the new ordinal of 1550 the divinely ordained priest became a parson appointed by the government, and in 1552 the wind of religious change reached gale force with the issuance of a revised version of the 1549 prayer book, which ended any pretense at compromise with Catholicism.

How long a worried realm, still attached to the ancient ritual and outward trappings of Catholicism, would have tolerated doctrinaire radicalism in religion and the brazen plundering of the Church is difficult to surmise, for in 1553 the rock on which Northumberland's power rested turned to sand. He was suddenly informed by the royal doctors that Edward VI was dying of consumption and had less than six months to live. The duke had tied his star to a priggish, humorless, and desperately ill monarch who had never had a chance to live a normal childhood, and to an advanced variety of Protestantism popular in London and almost nowhere else. Northumberland was feared but not loved, not even by reformers who saw him as "an intrepid soldier of Christ." In the face of Catholic Mary, who was the next in line of succession, he embarked upon the desperate gamble of kingmaking. The Tudor throne was too strong to usurp, but Northumberland hoped that the succession could be altered and Henry's will set aside. He convinced the dying Edward to strike a blow for God, and incidentally for Northumberland, by declaring Princess Mary to be illegitimate and by willing his imperial crown to Lady Jane Grey, the granddaughter of Henry VIII's sis-

ter Mary and the duke's own daughter-in-law.

The night of Edward's death was dark and stormy, and men whispered that Henry's grave at Windsor had cracked open and that the old king had risen up in ghostly wrath against those who dared upset his will. Northumberland's desperate calculations reckoned without the loyalty that the Tudor dynasty had gathered to itself. When Edward, "tormented by constant sleeplessness" and spewing forth sputum, "livid, black, fetid, and full of carbon," finally died, England rallied to Catholic Mary, who claimed her throne by rightful inheritance. Forsaken by the Council in London and by his own army, the duke of Northumberland surrendered and even went so far as to apologize for the arrogant presumption that had led him to defy the divinity of kings and the will of Henry VIII.

Mary was a Catholic but she was also a Tudor, and except in the austere and jaundiced eyes of a Protestant minority, she was of unimpeachable descent, claiming her throne by parliamentary statute and divine succession. She was her father's daughter, which was sufficient for most men, and though John Knox, safe in the Calvinist citadel in Geneva, thundered against the "monstrous regiment of women," Englishmen were willing to risk a woman, even a Catholic one, on the throne in order to avoid undergoing again the nightmare of factionalism, strife, and the "dolorous experience of the inconstant government" that they had suffered for five years during the reign of King Edward.

With the forces of factionalism utterly destroyed and the duke of Northumberland safely in the Tower, Mary insisted, as her father had before her, that all her subjects subscribe to the same faith, to be followed "for life and death." The new monarch was no daughter of the Renaissance. The soft glow of Catholic humanism had long since blistered and died in the face of Mary's Spanish pride and granite conviction. Mary joined the dogged determination of Catherine of Aragon with Henry Tudor's ruthlessness and intelligence, yet she lacked her mother's compassion and her father's tact and magnetism. The combination was disastrous, for the new queen came to the throne with a single mission: to return her errant realm to the Roman fold. Of all the Tudors, it was Mary who listened most to the small voice of conscience.

The arrival upon the throne of a neurotic thirty-seven-year-old maiden was dangerous enough; what made matters more serious was that the Church that Mary so desperately desired to restore was, in 1553, no longer the same institution that her father had defied and discarded two decades earlier. The fires of Protestant heresy had purged the comfortable but corrupt papacy of Clement VII. Revenge, recantation, and purgation were the order of the day, and conservative churchmen who had been imprisoned under Edward VI came out of the Tower upon Mary's accession determined that reformers would soon discover that "their sweet shall not be without sour sauce."

It proved relatively easy for the government to achieve the first steps in undoing the Reformation, and the clock was quickly turned back to the days of Henry VIII. In October, 1553, the Edwardian spiritual reformation was destroyed as it had been created, by act of Parliament. An anxious and willing House of Commons reversed the divorce of Catherine of Aragon, absolved the new queen of bastardy, repealed the Edwardian acts of uniformity and the statutes that had reformed church furnishings, ceremonies, and the nature of the Mass. England returned to the Henrician *via media* of Catholicism without the pope.

Mary could go no further than this, however, for Parliament refused to go along with her. Two barriers yet remained to block the return to Rome—the Act of Supremacy, in which Parliament had acknowledged the prince as the Supreme Head on Earth of the Church of England, and the fate of the mo-

nastic lands that had been nationalized under Henry VIII. To Mary her spiritual title was a burning crown upon her head, the work of Satan; yet Parliament politely but firmly declined to discharge the queen from her duties as supreme head or make it legally possible to recognize the authority of Rome until the ultimate fate of the monastic lands had been decided. Reflecting the interests of the landed classes, Commons refused any religious settlement that involved a return of the monastic lands to the Church. The soul's salvation would have to wait upon political considerations. Only after the Church lands had been secured for their new owners by statutory decree was Parliament willing, in 1554, to repeal the antipapal legislation of Henry's reign and to petition for reunion with Rome and spiritual absolution for the kingdom.

In foreign policy as well as in religion Mary was determined to cast out time and return to the conditions that had made possible the marriage of her Spanish mother and Tudor father. She set her royal heart upon marrying her cousin, the son and heir to the Hapsburg possessions, young Philip of Spain. Times, however, had changed, and English and Spanish imperial interests were rapidly parting company. Spain, not France, was emerging as the colos-

In a satirical painting done shortly after his death, Henry is shown confounding the pope and preventing the restoration of Catholicism by naming Edward VI as successor to his throne.

55

The port of Calais, with its heavily fortified heights, had been an English possession since 1347; it fell to the French during the bitter final days of Bloody Mary's reign.

sus of the world, the arbiter of Europe, and England's commercial competitor in the Mediterranean and Caribbean. Against the bitter opposition of the public, Parliament, and the Privy Council, Mary insisted on the marriage, and in July, 1554, Prince Philip became coruler of England.

The queen had her way, but even before the marriage she learned that a large and vocal segment of the population refused to follow her lead. Kent rose up against the prospects of a Roman faith and an alien king. Led by Sir Thomas Wyatt, some three thousand men from Kent came as close as any rebels ever did to upsetting the Tudor throne. The revolt proved conclusively that London was the heart of England and the bastion of Tudor rule. Mary followed the advice of the Spanish ambassador, who warned her that "if you value your crown stay in London, for once you leave Elizabeth will be queen, and the true religion thrown out." Wyatt knocked at the gates of the city, but when most of the populace, including even the Protestants, remained loyal to the daughter of Henry Tudor, his forces evaporated. He ended his career where other critics of the Tudor throne had—upon Tower Hill on the execution block.

Two other victims were beheaded along with the leaders of this ill-starred venture. Lady Jane Grey, Northumberland's nine-day puppet-queen, and her husband paid the price of Wyatt's treason. The depth of the queen's mercy had been sounded, and Mistress Grey could not be forgiven a second time for her heretical faith and proximity to the throne. Elizabeth's fate hung by the slenderest thread of sisterly affection, and for a moment it looked as if the logic of realpolitik would prevail. The princess as heir presumptive was too dangerous to live, and the Spanish ambassador put his finger on the insecurity that surrounded Elizabeth's life when he noted that she was "greatly to be feared; she has a spirit full of incantation." Every effort was made to connect her with Wyatt's rebellion, and she was ordered to the Tower for safekeeping while her future was being decided. As she was being conducted through Traitor's Gate and up the stairs from the river into the fortress, Elizabeth suddenly sat down and refused to go farther. The lord lieutenant of the Tower appealed to her sense of dignity and said: "You had best come in, Madam, for here you sit unwholesomely." The princess answered with a simple truth: "Better sit here than in a worse place." In the end she sat in a worse place for three months, and such was her hopelessness that she resigned herself to death and requested only that the sword be sharp and the executioner be French, for French executioners were considered most proficient. What saved Elizabeth was the queen's compassion and

Philip's realization that should his wife die childless, he would have a better chance of maintaining his diplomatic hold over England as Elizabeth's brother-in-law and prospective husband than as a bystander impotently watching the struggle for succession that would inevitably follow her death. The Spanish king was never one to forget the advice: "Wary is the man who assures his own retreat."

The year 1555 was the turning point of Mary's reign. During her first three years the queen had hoped that spiritual absolution and the return to Rome would bring peace of mind to her people, and that marriage to Philip would perpetuate the Tudor dynasty in the Catholic faith. The last twenty-four months of her reign brought nothing but disillusionment, despair, and defeat, and earned for Mary the infamous epithet of "Bloody." To her sorrow the queen realized that godliness and loving kindness were not sufficient to lead her flock back into the bosom of the Church. Laws would have to be written in blood; heresy would have to be put to the torch; and early in 1555 the Smithfield fires were lighted. The first victims were few—Cranmer, Ridley, Hooper, Latimer, and two others—in the expectation that the terrible fate of the leaders of Protestantism would silence the voice of heresy. Mary's government, however, badly miscalculated the faith that sustained the Protestant martyrs. It failed to realize the strength of mind and body that led Hugh Latimer to turn to Nicholas Ridley as they stood chained to the stake and say: "Be of good comfort, Master Ridley, and play the man. We shall this day light such a candle, by God's grace, in England, as I trust shall never be put out." The death of the Protestant leaders showed not so much the horrors of incineration as the path to glory and gave others the strength to play the man.

Responsibility for burning three hundred Protestant martyrs must ultimately rest upon the conscience of humanity, for the explanation, if not the justification, resides in the spirit of an age that believed that "there can not be a greater work of cruelty against the commonwealth than to nourish or favor [heretics] . . . who, as it were, undermining the chief foundation of all commonwealths, which is religion, make an entry to all kinds of vice in the most heinous manner." Protestants and Catholics alike viewed heresy as an insidious social disease that could not only destroy the soul but also lead men into rebellion and perdition. Purgation by fire was the deplorable but accepted method of dealing with the problem.

No matter how hard she labored, Mary had not won "the favor of God, nor the hearts of her subjects, nor yet the love of her husband." Her mar-

This 1556 manuscript illumination wishes long life to Philip and his spouse Queen Mary, who died two years later.

riage was a travesty, barren of love as well as of children. The queen was wedded to a husband who regarded his matrimonial vows as a matter of diplomatic convenience and demanded that his wife prove her affection by leading England into war with France on the side of Spain. Dutifully Mary dragooned her subjects into a war for which they were militarily unequipped and emotionally unprepared. The consequences were almost as disastrous as her religious policy. The memory of Agincourt and Crécy was blackened by defeat when the city of Calais, the last English possession in France, was lost in January, 1558. It is alleged that Mary said on her deathbed that if her heart were opened up her doctors would find the word *Calais* written across it. The unrelieved tragedy of her reign, however, was not the loss of Calais, whose importance was mostly symbolic, nor the loss of her husband's love, which she had never really possessed, nor even the sterility of her loins; it was her dreadful and gradual realization that righteous intent does not necessarily prevail over evil. As Mary lay dying on November 16, 1558—Hope Wednesday, her subjects called the day—she must have known that although she had shown the way, England had obstinately failed to follow. It now remained to be seen whether the realm would follow the last of Henry's children—Queen Elizabeth.

THE KING'S PLEASURE

The youthful attractiveness and good-natured demeanor of Henry VIII, who mounted the throne in 1509, immediately won him the love of his subjects. The new king seemed to be concerned with little besides pleasure, as the splendid festivities at the Field of the Cloth of Gold demonstrated. (At right Henry is shown approaching the field to meet the king of France.) At that time there was hardly a hint of the complex, forceful, and intelligent nature that he would reveal in later years. There was no indication that eventually he would develop into a calculating tyrant, or that some day it would be the king's pleasure to revolutionize the country by changing his subjects' religion.

Henry was too impulsive to keep England out of war, yet he became skillful in his handling of international politics. He was incapable of concentrating on the details of government, yet he managed his realm brilliantly. He chose sycophantic councilors who were notorious for filling their own pockets, yet from them he got advice that could rarely be faulted. He gradually deteriorated in character, yet even as he did he grew as a king. His strength and personal magnetism were such that he influenced England more profoundly than any other monarch who ruled the kingdom. Despite his wars and murders and numerous marriages, despite high taxation and religious strife, he made England more powerful than it had ever been before.

PASTIME AND GOOD COMPANY

Later portraits and reports that depict Henry as corpulent and crass, intolerant and cruel contrast sharply with accounts of the charming and graceful youth who succeeded to the throne at seventeen. Henry was a handsome giant of a man, a fine athlete, and an avid outdoorsman who enjoyed hawking and hunting. He could ride tirelessly for hours, and he easily defeated any man matched against him in the colorful tournaments that he loved to stage. Indeed he was so accustomed to winning that once when Francis I of France threw him in a wrestling contest only the tactful intervention of councilors prevented an international incident. But it was not only physical prowess that interested the king. Henry read widely and prided himself on his ability to quote appropriate scriptural verses for any occasion. He encouraged learning and invited important European scholars to visit his court. He was both a patron of music and a considerable musician and composer himself. "Pastime with good company/I love, and shall until I die," one of his songs begins, for the king delighted in feasting and drinking, dancing and attending masquerades.

Above, a miniature shows Henry at a tournament jousting before the admiring gaze of Catherine of Aragon (under the canopy) and her ladies in waiting. A piece of the young king's shattered lance can be seen flying through the air as a result of the direct hit that Henry has scored against his opponent. The queen's initial, the letter K, appears surrounded by hearts in the elaborate device embroidered on Henry's saddle cloth.

His Psalter shows Henry playing the harp in imitation of King David.

Henry is seen in his chamber engaged in one of his favorite pastimes, reading.

William Warham Arch
bishop of Canterbury

Edward Stafford
Duke of Buckingham

POWER
AND
PARLIAMENT

Henry could sense the mood of his subjects better than any of his advisers, and he had the boldness and intelligence to act when others wavered. His revolt against Rome was risky but it was successful; his subjects accepted it, just as he had guessed they would. The consequences of the revolt were felt far beyond the realm of religion. England was pushed out of the Middle Ages to become the first modern state, where the citizen owed allegiance primarily to his king and nation rather than to a feudal or celestial lord. In the process Henry became a despot, yet he set in motion the machinery that would destroy absolutism in England. To assure popular support, he was forced to call on Parliament to ratify his actions, and from that time it sat frequently to "approve" other moves. Under Elizabeth Parliament was to prove less easy to manipulate, and a century after Henry died, it would depose an English king.

Henry by the Grace of God Kinge of England &c.

A solemn Henry is shown above holding his scepter as he marches in stately procession, with the spiritual and temporal lords of the realm, to the opening of Parliament at Westminster. The painting was done on a vellum roll very early in Henry's reign, and it shows the king with the features of his father, Henry VII, whose face was more familiar to the painter.

Anne Boleyn

Catherine of Aragon

Jane Seymour

Anne of Cleves

Catherine Parr

Catherine Howard

HENRY'S WIVES

It was Henry's ardent desire for a legitimate male heir that was responsible in large part for his many marriages and for the ruthlessness with which several of them were ended. Anne Boleyn had fascinated the king while he was still wed to Catherine of Aragon, but after their marriage her shrewishness disenchanted him. The disenchantment was made complete when she failed to produce a son. When Anne was accused of adultery, Henry was ready to believe the charge, and she was beheaded. One of Anne's ladies in waiting, Jane Seymour, had caught Henry's attention, and soon after Anne's death they were married. Henry doted on her and was genuinely grieved when she died in childbirth. He took his fourth bride, Anne of Cleves, at the behest of his adviser Thomas Cromwell. The marriage was planned to cement an alliance with Germany, but the alliance failed. Even worse, Cromwell had represented Anne as being attractive, and Henry found her to be unaccountably ugly. The marriage was annulled and Cromwell was punished by being beheaded. Next the king wed Catherine Howard, whose beauty and manner delighted him. When she was accused of premarital dalliance, he was distraught and wanted to overlook her youthful indiscretions; but he ordered her execution when he learned that she had been unfaithful to him. His last wife, Catherine Parr, survived the king. Once when she disagreed with him in a theological discussion he ordered her arrest, but she mollified him by pleading that her remarks had been designed only to elicit a profound lecture on theology from him. Before she had the chance to offend him again, Henry died.

THE KING'S ADVISERS

For almost twenty years Thomas Wolsey virtually ruled England as Henry's chief councilor while the king himself concentrated on enjoying life. Wolsey was envied and hated by the aristocrats and commoners alike for his arrogance and ruthlessness, but he maintained his immensely powerful position for as long as he was useful to the king. When he mishandled Henry's divorce from Catherine of Aragon, he was charged with treason, but he died before he could be brought to trial. Because he had consolidated the power and income that had previously been scattered among nobles and officeholders, Wolsey had enormously strengthened the crown. Henry, beneficiary of Wolsey's legacy, decided to rule in his own stead, and he chose advisers who would implement his will without question. Thomas More was made chancellor, but he proved to be too scrupulous; his outspoken disapproval of the new Church cost him his head. Because he helped Henry settle the divorce problem, Cromwell earned the king's favor, but only temporarily; he too ended on the execution block. Of all the king's major advisers only Thomas Cranmer outlived Henry, because he adapted so well to his master's demands.

Four of Henry's most famous advisers are shown here. Above is Cardinal Wolsey, the king's deputy for twenty years. Wolsey's protégé, Thomas Cranmer, who enriched himself in the royal service, is shown at left. At lower right is a painting by Hans Holbein of Thomas Cromwell, who also filled his pockets while acting as Henry's agent. A drawing by Holbein at top right depicts Sir Thomas More and his family. More is best known as author of Utopia, *written before he became Lord Chancellor.*

THE ROYAL FORCES

During Henry's reign England often found itself embroiled in wars on the Continent, although they were rarely waged on a large scale. As a young king, Henry fancied himself a warrior, and he chafed until he got to the battlefield, where he enjoyed himself immensely, dashing vaingloriously about. When he got older he contented himself with supervising military affairs from afar. Despite his involvement with the army, it scarcely improved during his reign, and England usually lost the wars that it engaged in. This was in part because the country could not afford a standing militia, and in part because Henry and his advisers failed to appreciate the potential importance of firearms. The navy was a different matter. Henry built up a fleet manned by professionals and foresaw the value of maneuverable and heavily armed ships. As a result of his efforts Elizabeth was to inherit the nucleus of the powerful navy that would make England mistress of the seas.

The illustration of the Peter *(above), one of the ships in Henry's fleet, appears in an inventory of the English navy that was completed in the year 1546; according to the report the royal fleet was well equipped. At right is a unit of Henry's army in about 1540. The troops are armed with pikes and bows, weapons that were obsolescent on the Continent, but they also have a few up-to-date cannons pulled along by horses.*

ne Henry the eights Army.

OVERLEAF: *A detail from a painted wall panel shows Henry promising royal protection to the bishop of Chichester Cathedral. The picture was probably commissioned by the bishop to symbolize his acceptance of the new Church that was formed when Henry broke with the pope.*

Pro amore
tui χpi
qu prtuo
coretero

quttumr
Rait Crolrbella

OPERIB

…R͘ · sup̄ · ōneꝭ · Reges ᛁ

CREDITE

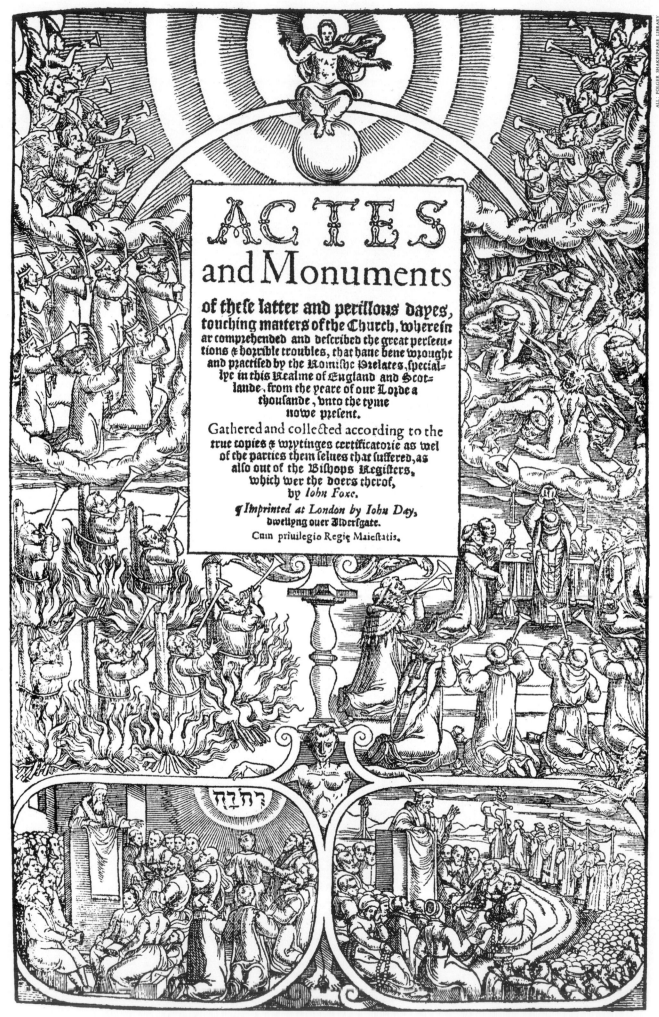

ACTES and Monuments of these latter and perillous dayes, touching matters of the Church, wherein ar comprehended and described the great persecutions & horrible troubles, that haue bene wrought and practised by the Romishe Prelates, speciallye in this Realme of England and Scotlande, from the yeare of our Lorde a thousande, vnto the tyme nowe present.

Gathered and collected according to the true copies & wrytinges certificatorie as wel of the parties them selues that suffered, as also out of the Bishops Registers, which wer the doers therof, by Iohn Foxe.

Imprinted at London by Iohn Day, dwellyng ouer Aldersgate.

Cum priuilegio Regiæ Maiestatis.

One result of Henry's revolution was the martyrdom of Protestants under Mary. Tales of the victims and depictions of their deaths appear in John Foxe's Acts and Monuments, often called the Book of Martyrs

The archbishop of Canterbury, Thomas Cranmer, was executed by Mary; he is seen with Henry Cole, Catholic dean of St. Paul's.

Burning at the stake was the usual way of dispatching heretics, but a few men like the ones on the gibbet suffered easier deaths.

John Rogers, the first victim, "broke the ice valiantly," Foxe reports, "washing . . . in the flame as though it had been cold water."

Protestants, roped together, are being led to London for trial. In five years under Mary three hundred people were burned.

The most famous execution of Mary's reign was that of bishops Latimer and Ridley, who were burned in the autumn of 1555.

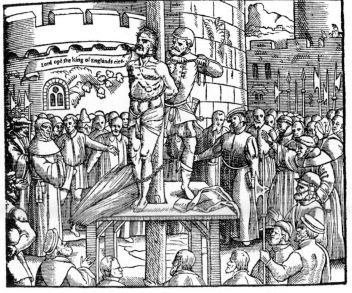

William Tyndale, translator of the Bible, fled to the Netherlands, where he was seized and strangled; his body was then burned.

3

THE
CALM AND QUIET
SEASON

The bells that sounded and the fires that blazed on that dark evening of November 17, 1558, bespoke England's relief that Catholic Mary, worn out by sickness and embittered by failure, was mercifully dead. Yet "the darksome clouds of discomfort" appeared as black as ever, and Englishmen "went about their matters as men amazed that wist not where to begin or end." The kingdom had floundered leaderless for more than a decade, and in 1558 no one could see an end to discord, bigotry, and uncertainty. Once again the "wolves" were "coming out of Geneva and other places of Germany," where the Protestant exiles of Mary's reign had failed to learn either humility or compassion and had absorbed the acrid theological air of Calvin's Switzerland. The religious pattern of things to come remained unclear, but on one matter the soldiers of the Lord were adamant: "even the slightest vestiges of popery" had to be driven from the land and out of men's minds. Under Northumberland, desperate and ambitious men had led the kingdom to the brink of civil war, and five years of Catholic Mary had neither softened Protestant hearts nor taught them tolerance. Now, in the cold days of November, another woman, another member of that "monstrous regiment," wore the crown. Elizabeth inherited a kingdom that was humiliated in war, paralyzed by ineptitude, and sinking into spiritual and financial bankruptcy. Men predicted nothing but further agony in which Protestant zealots would replace Catholic ones, and Puritan martyrs would

make way for papists. Throughout the realm it was agreed that "our remedy must be prayer," for no other help seemed to be in sight.

That the ranks were re-formed, that new life and vitality were infused into the moribund body of the state, and that police and moderate men undertook the leadership of government were marvels that Elizabeth's own age attributed to the special intercession of God and the divine genius of their new sovereign. God and destiny loomed large in the affairs of states when France could be catapulted into two generations of religious war by the sudden death of Henry II in 1559, and England, against all prognostications, could be saved from religious fire and political dismemberment by the magic of Elizabeth's personality and the accident that she survived disease and escaped assassination for seventy years.

Elizabeth was her father's daughter: athletic, red-haired, autocratic, inordinately vain, and "of stately and majestic deportment." Time and again her subjects saw the reflection of that iron-willed giant in the slender person of their monarch; indeed, when Londoners first beheld their queen they exclaimed, "Remember old King Henry VIII!" The Spanish ambassador immediately sensed the similarity and reported to his master that Elizabeth seems to be "incomparably more feared than her sister and gives her orders and has her way as absolutely as her father did." Later in the reign her godson Sir John Harington noted the same quality and concluded that "she left no doubtings whose daughter she

One of the few portraits probably painted from life shows Elizabeth around 1575.

Robert Dudley, earl of Leicester

Elizabeth is shown receiving a manuscript from the laurel-crowned poet George Gascoigne. This miniature, drawn by the poet himself, appeared in Gascoigne's Hermit's Tale, *along with a plea for royal patronage.*

was." Elizabeth spent a lifetime making capital of her sex, indulging her vanity, and excusing her womanly frailty, but on one subject she never wavered: she had "the heart and stomach of a king" and she would be master in her own house. To Robert Dudley, the first of the youthful heroes of her reign who aspired to win her hand, she fulminated: "God's death! My Lord . . . I will have here but one mistress and no master." After the execution of Robert Devereux, earl of Essex, who sought not her hand but her throne, she coldly commented: "I warned him that he should not touch my scepter."

There were many reasons why Elizabeth never married—political reasons, sexual reasons, historic reasons—but an adroit Scottish ambassador may have come closest to the truth when he boldly told the queen: "Ye think that if ye were married, ye would be but queen of England, and now ye are king and queen both. Ye may not suffer a commander." The decision to remain single was not easy; both public sentiment and political necessity rebelled at the idea of a queen who was childless and alone. John Knox had been unbending in his views on women; they were "weak, frail, impatient, feeble, and foolish," and the whole world knew them to be "inconstant, variable, cruel, and void of the spirit of council." The sixteenth century also agreed wholeheartedly with Martin Luther when he said of the weaker sex: "Let them bear children till they die of it; that is what they are for." Though Tudor society was emphatic in its demand that the queen should marry, it was not nearly so united on the subject of a proper husband. No man in the Elizabethan age would have settled for a position secondary to that of his wife, and when the wife was queen, a husband had to be king. This was the insurmountable obstacle to marriage, and Elizabeth quickly learned from her affair with Robert Dudley that only in lonely virginity could she ever hope to rule her jealous subjects.

Lord Robert Dudley was, as the saying went, descended from "a tribe of traitors." His grandfather had been a ruthless and despised minion of the first Tudor king; his father, the duke of Northumberland, had tried his hand at kingmaking; his brother, Guildford Dudley, had married Lady Jane Grey; and each had ended his life on the execution block. Elizabeth could not have given her heart to anyone better calculated to arouse the hatred and fear of every faction at court. Young, handsome, and lusty, Lord Robert had been a friend of the princess during those perilous days under Mary, and he had been created Master of the Horse almost the moment the new reign began. Later, when the queen created him baron of Denbigh and earl of Leicester, it was noted with alarm that she tickled her young gallant's neck, and it was rumored that "Her Majesty visits him in his chamber day and night." A more sinister piece of gossip was soon spread abroad by the Spanish ambassador: Elizabeth, he said, was only waiting for Dudley's wife to die in order to marry him, and the handsome husband was scheming to hasten that moment with poison. Suddenly, on September 8, 1560, idle and malicious tongues had even more startling news to discuss: the lady in question had conveniently fallen down a flight of stairs and broken her neck! The coroner's inquest decided it was an accident, Dudley's household suspected suicide, and the world whispered murder. The scandal rattled at the foundations of Elizabeth's shaky throne. In Paris the English ambassador could not find an answer when Parisians asked: "What religion is this, that a subject shall kill his wife, and the prince not only bear withal but marry with him?" Mary Stuart was delighted by her cousin's embarrassment and told everyone: "The queen of England is going to marry her horsekeeper who has killed his wife to make room for her." In England statesmen feared that Elizabeth would prove that John Knox's dreary evaluation of womankind was indeed correct.

During the winter of 1560 Elizabeth stormed and stamped, threatening marriage one moment and disdaining it the next; but she quickly began to perceive that although her position as a maiden and barren queen might be dangerous, it was still safer than marriage to a man who would stir every court clique to violence and insist upon all his husbandly prerogatives. To Gloriana's "stately stomach" marriage was incompatible with sovereignty, and though Dudley always remained her "Robin," he had to make do with the title of earl of Leicester.

The miracle of Gloriana's reign, as one seventeenth-century observer wrote, was the queen's ability "to gain obedience thus without constraint." In more modern phraseology, it was the extraordinary fashion in which Elizabeth got her own way without a standing army, without a clear and absolute title to her throne, and without even being the right sex. She was coarse, vulgar, bawdy, and extroverted. She spat and picked her teeth and swore great "mouth-filling oaths." She boxed her ministers' ears and threw slippers at them in her rage, and her councilors so despaired of her ever making up her mind that they turned to prayer and the hope of miracles as England's only recourse. She could be exasperating, officious, and meddlesome; she corrected her councilors' reports, criticized their Latin, and drove

the long-suffering Sir Francis Walsingham, her principal secretary, into complaining: "I would to God Her Majesty could be content to refer these things to them that can best judge of them, as other princes do." She believed in astrology, clairvoyance, and black magic; her temper was uncertain, her wit cruel, and her tongue razor-edged; and as she aged, her nose, "somewhat rising in the midst," grew hooked as a harridan's, her sharp eyes turned dim and near-sighted, her red hair faded and gave way to a wig, and her teeth decayed and blackened.

Elizabeth took every advantage of her sex and sovereignty to indulge her wit and sarcasm, and not even the wife of the archbishop of Canterbury was immune from her barbed and royal tongue. The queen disliked clerical marriages on principle, and after a visit to Lambeth Palace she thanked Archbishop Parker's wife with the words: "Madam I may not call you; mistress I am ashamed to call you, so I know not what to call you; but yet I thank you." When she discovered herself to be the subject of a sermon on the sins of vanity and costly dress, she turned to her maids in waiting and said of the presumptuous ecclesiastic that if he "held more discourse on such matters," she would "fit him for heaven—but he would walk thither without a staff and leave his mantle behind him." Of the two men who probably knew her best during the autumn of her life, one, the devious Robert Cecil, concluded that the queen was "more than a man, and (in truth) sometimes less than a woman," and the other, the earl of Essex, raged that she was "cankered, and her mind as crooked as her carcass."

Yet behind the façade of gaudy vulgarity, shallow egotism, and feminine caprice, there lay toughness of mind, innate caution, deep humility, and unmatched magnetism, for "when she smiled, it was a pure sunshine." Few monarchs ever worked at royalty as hard as did Elizabeth. The ceaseless ceremony, the endless interviews, and the exhausting spectacles, in which the queen was always the central figure, were integral parts of her role as sovereign. Her ministers complained of overwork, yet William Cecil, Lord Burghley, her chief councilor, admitted that it was Gloriana herself who "knew all estates and dispositions of all princes and parties." Courtiers were dismayed by the boundless energy that not only kept their queen dancing to tabor and pipe at the age of sixty-six but also allowed her to endure the rigors of a royal progress through the realm. When some of her entourage complained, she bade "the old stay behind, and the young and able" go along with her.

The queen knew the business of kingship. She

had a marvelous memory, kept meticulous notes, and was never frightened or bored by details, especially when they concerned shillings and pence. She knew that "the greatest clerks are not the wisest men," and though she could never abide a fool, Elizabeth sensed that even the wisest man is not without his folly. With unerring eye she recognized the worth of a good servant. Her judgment of those who served her was rarely in error, even though a winning smile and a well-turned calf could gain her indulgence. On occasion Elizabeth "would set the reason of a mean man before the authority of the greatest councilor she had," and she never forgot the basis on which she first selected William Cecil as her principal secretary. "This judgment I have of you," she had said to him, "that you will not be corrupted with any manner of gift, and that you will be faithful to the state, and that without respect of my private will, you will give me that counsel that you think best." In lonely pre-eminence the queen learned the trade of royalty and in anguish wrote:

I grieve; and dare not show my discontent!
I love; and yet am forced to seem to hate!
I do; yet dare not say, I ever meant!

Elizabeth was nothing if not a realist, rarely allowing passion to overshadow wisdom and always looking "into things as they are." She could couple mildness with majesty and she never hesitated to stoop to conquer. Instinctively she realized that in government the line between good and evil, honesty and corruption, was not always clear. She knew herself for what she was, a child "of corrupt seed" and "a most frail substance" living in a "world of wickedness, where delights be snares." The queen was the first to admit she was no angel, for her sins were manifold, and in the quiet of her chapel she even confessed the possibility that she was "unworthy of eternal life, if not of the royal dignity."

Elizabeth could be ridiculous, deceitful, and vindictive, but her humor, humility, and self-criticism saved her from becoming vicious and monstrous. She gave God credit for pulling her "from the prison to the palace," and she confessed her "ignorance in this my calling" and her "need of good advice and counsel." To God she was thankful and to men she was merciful, for the queen knew from youthful experience that all men are fortune's playthings and that in the bloody game of politics, "my lot today, tomorrow may be thine." Throughout her life Elizabeth had a sense of mission, for she believed that God and time were on her side. At her coronation she looked about her at the splendor of the occasion and whispered, "Time has brought me hither." Delay, procrastination, reconsideration were her great-

est assets, for the queen was a past master of the art of biding her time. Early in her reign her ambassador to France, Sir Nicholas Throckmorton, warned her to walk warily and allow no party or faction to understand fully what she had in mind. Elizabeth needed no such advice, for she intuitively sensed that watchfulness, finesse, secrecy, and prudence were her surest political weapons. Presiding over a court filled with quarrelsome, hotheaded children who posed as heroic adults and were always more willing to pay back "wrongs than good turns," and living in an age of international hypertension, Elizabeth saw that in politics problems are rarely solved, they are only replaced by other, more pressing ones. Given time, men and nations could be led into forgetfulness. The dramatic moments of her reign—the beheading of Mary Queen of Scots, the defeat of the Armada, and the execution of Essex—were events thrust upon her by circumstances.

Left to herself, Elizabeth almost always elected half measures and delays in preference to rash solutions and impetuous actions. She was a thoroughly conservative female who shied away from newfangledness in religion, in politics, and in science. Legend reports that Gloriana did not even take kindly to that most dangerous of mechanical devices, the flush toilet, and though she thanked its inventor, she preferred more tried-and-true methods of sanitation. Without royal support the contraption died out in England and had to be reinvented one hundred seventy-five years later.

Elizabeth gloried in her nationality; she was, as she boasted, "mere English" and was confident that her subjects were all on her side, which the Spanish ambassador admitted was indeed true. "She was queen of the small as well as the great," and if there was a secret to her success, it lay, as her courtier Sir Christopher Hatton said, in the fact that "the queen did fish for men's souls, and had so sweet a bait that no one could escape her network." Robert Dudley was not only her "Sweet Robin" but also her "Eyes," William Cecil her "Spirit," Hatton her "Mutton" and "Bellwether," Francis Walsingham her "Moor," and Robert Cecil her "Pygmy." She caught each "poor fish," Hatton continued, "who little knew what snare was laid" for him.

Gloriana wooed and won her people because she was in tune with the spirit of her generation. If Mary belonged to a dying past, Elizabeth was at home in a dynamic present. If one sister was consumed by the bright flame of conscience, the other held to the glorious and brilliant standards of the Renaissance in which calculation displaced conviction, virtuosity was praised more highly than beatitude, and beardless boys carved out their kingdoms in the sky and proclaimed to the world what "bliss was it in that dawn to be alive." No finer tribute to her achievement was ever written than the verse that was inscribed on dishes and was scribbled by schoolboys in the margins of their textbooks:

> The rose is red, the leaves are green.
> God save Elizabeth, our noble queen.

Personality may ultimately explain the Elizabethan age, but good luck and some highly astute politics were also evident behind the steps that Elizabeth took to restore peace and order to the realm. Elizabeth had one advantage: though a woman, only other women could make claim to her throne. Catherine and Mary, sisters of Lady Jane Grey, were hardly serious contenders, and Mary Stuart, queen of Scots and Henry VIII's grandniece, was the wife of the young dauphin of France and consequently tied by marriage and sympathy to England's traditional enemy. Though good Catholics loudly denounced Elizabeth as a usurper and a bastard, most of her subjects accepted her as Henry's lawful daughter and heir; and her brother-in-law, Philip of Spain, defended her rights at Rome against the voice of France that urged the pope to declare her a heretic with no legal title to her crown. Spain preferred an English queen of somewhat doubtful religious conviction to a devout Catholic monarch controlled by the Valois interests of France. That Elizabeth in part owed the peaceful succession of her throne to Philip II would become within a decade the grand irony of both their lives.

Once acknowledged queen, Elizabeth turned to men of moderation, regardless of their faith, as the prop and stay of her reign. Her Council was reduced from forty-four men to fewer than twenty and purged of its episcopal members, for Elizabeth preferred laymen as her associates in government. In part the secular spirit of her administration was a matter of taste, in part it was the result of circumstances. As the child of Anne Boleyn, Elizabeth could be nothing except Protestant, but her faith was not the militant and burning Protestantism of the Marian exiles returning from Geneva. Instead, it was that strange spiritual mixture her father had brutally enforced on his kingdom, a muddled and headless Catholicism that insisted on outward conformity but allowed sufficient doctrinal breadth so that both Protestant and Catholic could find it acceptable. The new queen desired to open no windows into men's souls and to light no fires to consume their bodies. For Elizabeth the essence of religion remained mystical and personal. There was, she said, "only one Christ Jesus and one faith; the rest is a dispute about trifles." Politically speaking

Her subjects' admiration for their queen is evident in the doggerel that embellishes this commemorative majolica dish. The building shown is the Tower of London, where Elizabeth had been briefly confined as a young princess.
LONDON MUSEUM

those trifles were highly combustible and dangerous to the state, and Elizabeth decided that the wisest course to follow was to persuade the moderates of her father's reign to undertake a second break with Rome, reintroducing Henrician Catholicism, which she regarded as the safest religious solution. In this she signally failed.

In their salad days such men as Cuthbert Tunstall, bishop of Durham, and Nicholas Heath, archbishop of York, had accompanied Henry VIII into schism, but under Edward VI they had drawn the line at heresy and had resigned rather than accept the Edwardian prayer books and the Protestant doctrines they proclaimed. They had welcomed the return to Rome under Catholic Mary, and now, in 1559, they refused to oblige their new queen by sanctioning what Elizabeth demanded: independence for the Church of England, Catholicism without the pope. The episcopal conservatives had learned through bitter experience the truth of the words: "Whatever is contrary to the Catholic faith is heresy; whatever is contrary to unity is schism. . . . It is the same thing, so far as schism is concerned, to do a little or to do all."

Thwarted by the Catholic party, Elizabeth perforce turned for religious support to those of a more Protestant and obliging nature, but she avoided the radical ideas of extremists fresh from Calvinistic Geneva, relying instead on men who had stayed in England and had bent with the wind. Her new archbishop of Canterbury personified the comfortable compromise of Elizabeth's religious settlement. Matthew Parker was no martyr. He was a loyal, obedient, and efficient servant of the crown, more interested in peaceful government than in religious purity. Parker was a scholar and an antiquarian who cultivated academic obscurity. He had, however, known the queen's mother and had been a chaplain in her house, and for these reasons he felt honor bound to serve the daughter. Like his royal mistress he detested the religious extravagance that was found in Geneva and Scotland, and he prayed long and loud that God might preserve the kingdom "from such a visitation as John Knox has attempted in Scotland; the people to be orderers of things."

In temporal matters as well as spiritual, the queen chose cautious men, dexterous in the ways of politics. William Cecil was to the state what Matthew Parker was to the Church. The new principal secre-

tary had been a Protestant under Edward, a reluctant but conforming Catholic under Mary, and he was a politique under his new sovereign. The rise of the Cecils is a perfect sixteenth-century success story. They started out as yeomen, who through good management, good marriages, and good political judgment rose to become country gentlemen and minor officials at the court. The most famous of them, William Cecil, was born in 1520 with a passion for hard work and an instinct for survival in the slippery warfare of Tudor politics. He received his political education under the dukes of Somerset and Northumberland, but he nimbly escaped the fate of his noble patrons. Under Mary, Cecil quietly retired to the country; but on Elizabeth's succession he became first principal secretary, then Master of the Wards, and finally, in 1572, Lord Treasurer. His reward was one of the few noble titles conferred by Elizabeth. William Cecil of yeoman stock became Baron Burghley of Stamford Burghley. "Of all men of genius," said the contemporary chronicler William Camden, "he was the most a drudge and of all men of business, the most a genius." He suited the needs of his sovereign perfectly, and he became the artful stage manager for Elizabeth's equally artful performance in the role of Gloriana. Cecil and Parker were typical of the men who succeeded in rebuilding England, working on the hypothesis that Catholics were better losers than Protestants and were more easily controlled since their devotion to the crown was greater than their sense of duty to their religion.

Throughout the long, bitter struggle to achieve religious unity and a workable doctrinal compromise, Elizabeth and her ministers never forgot Thomas Howard's warning that England would not bear yet another radical change in religion, for the kingdom had "been bowed so oft that if it should be bent again it would break." The utter confusion of four changes in religion in as many decades was revealed at Oxford. Under Edward VI the Italian Protestant theologian Peter Martyr had been appointed canon of Christ's Church. To his new post Martyr brought not only his learning but his wife, who died in 1552 and was buried in the cathedral. On Mary's succession, Mrs. Martyr's remains were cast out upon a dunghill in the back garden. When the queen died, the canons were eager to restore the lady to her tomb, but were filled with indecision when they discovered on the dunghill the bones of Saint Frideswide, the patron saint of Oxford, which had been discarded earlier during the reign of Edward VI. In their uncertainty the canons wrote to Elizabeth, asking which set of bones should be honored. There is a legend that she answered with the

William Cecil, Lord Burghley, Elizabeth's chief adviser

laconic phrase: "Mix them." Whatever her exact words, an elaborate funeral was arranged and the Catholic saint and the Protestant Mrs. Martyr were duly buried together. In honor of the occasion, one of the canons, with a fine sense of irony, caught the spirit of Elizabeth's solution to the religious troubles of her age when he wrote:

> Papists and Protestants should now
> In peace abide,
> As here religion true and false
> Lie side by side.

During the spring of 1559 the Elizabethan settlement was legislated; it mixed elements of both religions in the hope that papists and Protestants would "in peace abide." It restored the royal supremacy, but softened it by styling the queen Supreme Governor, not Head of the Church of England. The Book of Common Prayer of 1552 was reintroduced, but in a slightly modified form, with ambiguous language added to avoid defining the exact nature of the Mass. A new Act of Uniformity was passed, prescribing punishment for clergymen who refused to use the prayer book and for laymen who refused to conform to the new Church; and four years later, in 1563, the final pronouncement on what an Englishman should believe was set forth by convocation in the Thirty-Nine Articles. The old Church came to heel without a fight; the Marian bishops quietly resigned their sees, and their places on the episcopal bench were filled with men of Protestant mettle and pragmatic flexibility. Even the militant Protestants, who persisted in regarding Elizabeth's Church as the sanctuary of "dumb dogs, unskillful, sacrificing priests, destroying drones, or rather caterpillars of the Word," were silenced for the time by a queen who was quite evidently determined to be mistress in her own house.

The Elizabethan religious settlement and the ceaseless labors on the part of the queen and her servants were aimed at a single purpose: a commonwealth composed of balanced and harmonious elements in which all men would know their place and no man would hanker after what was not rightly his. Every century and every generation has its own preconceptions and habits of thought. The twentieth century talks noisily of the equality of man, but half a century ago reference to the equality of races was rarely heard, and four centuries before that, in Tudor England, the equality of man, except as a spiritual entity in the eyes of God, would have been regarded as a dangerous and preposterous supposition. The medieval concept of a great chain of being, commencing with God and working down through the hierarchy from angels and saints to men, beasts, and

An antipapal satire shows Elizabeth as the goddess Diana sitting in judgment on Pope Gregory XIII, who hatches eggs symbolizing the Inquisition, the St. Bartholomew's Day Massacre, and the assassination of William of Orange.

vegetables, was still the normal mental picture of the universe. The system was authoritarian, hierarchical, and organic; every element played a prescribed role and contributed to the totality of the divine structure. Man's society was both a part and a mirror of this grand design. Poet and queen, statesman and courtier, all held the view of society that was recorded by Shakespeare when he wrote: "Take but degree away, untune that string, and hark! What discord follows."

Nothing stirred the sixteenth century so deeply as the thought of chaos and mutability, if only because the sight of disorder was everywhere present and the means of suppressing treason were so pathetically inadequate. The benefits of order, degree, and balance were trumpeted from every pulpit, written into every statute, and dramatized by every playwright. Dramatists and preachers never wearied of reminding their audiences of "the sweetness of unity, the fatness and substance of religion, the wine of obedience," and the assurance that those who rebel "against the prince get unto themselves damnation." Humility was considered the chief virtue of all ranks, and subjects were expected to hearken to the advice: "We should not look at what we cannot reach, nor long for what we should not have. Things above us are not for us."

The Tudor state was constantly compared with

A Flemish traveler in England painted a series of pictures showing Elizabethans in characteristic costumes. Above, two peers of the realm, wearing their traditional robes of office, are accompanied by a uniformed halberdier.

the human body. The prince was the head that guarded the body politic from anarchy; the ministers of God were "the eyes to watch and not to wink or sleep"; the judges were the ears to hear complaints; the nobility were "the shoulders and arms to bear the burden of the commonwealth, to hold up the head, and defend the body with might and force"; and men of the lower orders were "set as inferior parts painfully to travail" for the support of those worthier than themselves. The sixteenth-century gentleman, whether he lived in Madrid, Paris, or London, had a low opinion of the many-headed mob, and one and all agreed that, except for the natural leaders of society, man was "wild, without judgment, and not of sufficient experience to govern himself." This Elizabethan concept of an ordained and paternalistic commonwealth was enshrined in the Statute of Apprentices of 1563, which required all men to remain in their birthplace and practice the same occupation as their fathers. The act was predicated on the theory that all men had a social and moral obligation to labor. It assumed the existence of a universal order, and it arrayed the major occupations of the kingdom on a scale of utility, with agriculture ranked at the top and foreign trade at the bottom. The statute tacitly presumed that town and country, court and shire were separate but interdependent parts of the commonwealth. The structure of society was fixed and static, permitting neither a fluid labor force nor any form of social mobility; and the claims of blood, education, and land were considered ample justification for both social and political inequality.

The states of Europe were everywhere as authoritarian and totalitarian as the instruments of coercion could make them. In England fines were levied for truancy from church on Sunday; prices, wages, and working conditions were regulated; beggars were shipped home to their parishes; and Elizabeth commanded her subjects to wear hats in order to help the felt business and to eat fish at least two days each week in order to support the fishing industry. Spaniards were forbidden the use of all precious metal ornaments upon their clothes, and when such sumptuary legislation was ignored by the ladies of the court, Philip II tried to shame them into compliance by giving the whores of the streets the sole right to bedeck themselves in silver and silks. In Spain ruffs were limited to two pleats, not more than three inches in width, and could be cut from white linen only. The fine for disobedience was twenty thousand maravedis for the first offense; it rose to eighty thousand and a year's banishment for the third. The sixteenth-century traveler was as harassed by the officiousness of bureaucrats and the actions of government officials as is any twentieth-century tourist. No one was allowed to leave England without license; passports were issued to all persons entering or leaving the kingdom; and strict currency regulations were enforced. Travelers "upon pain of confiscation" could take no more than twenty pounds out of the country, and one visitor reported that each member of his party "was obliged to give his name, the reason for his visit to England, and the place to which he was going." Moreover, their valises and trunks were opened and "most diligently examined for the sake of discovering English money."

The aim of most social legislation of the century was not the welfare state, since few Elizabethans thought in terms of human well-being. What induced Elizabeth as "the godly prince," and the aristocracy as the natural leaders of society to maintain an authoritarian state in which society endeavored to protect the individual from his predatory neighbors was the fear of social revolution. According to Sir Walter Raleigh the gentry were "the garrisons of good order throughout the realm," and good order rested on full bellies, cheap food, steady employment, and a society that was carefully watched over by a vigilant gentry born and educated to rule.

At the apex of society stood the queen, "the life, the head, and the authority of all things that be done in the realm of England." Elizabeth was "the wellspring of all that was good and evil," the fountain of justice, the symbol of national unity, and the ultimate source of the lavish rewards that came to men in political life. Gloriana was God's anointed lieutenant on earth, and though the queen rarely bothered to mention the fact, no one, least of all Elizabeth, doubted that she was a god on earth. Elizabeth was addressed on bended knee; like her father she was referred to by the weighty title of Your Majesty and not by the older medieval term of Your Grace; and wherever Gloriana was in residence there was the vital center of government and the source of all political authority. To the queen's court came not only the representatives of foreign states and the suitors for her hand but also all who sought wealth, power, and renown. Like pale satellites to Gloriana's sun, statesmen and favorites, scamps and saints, heroes and bounders, financiers and vendors, patron-seekers and parasites, entertainers and educators were all pulled into the royal orbit, where they reflected the glittering light of the queen's favor.

To be banished from court was to be exiled into outer darkness, for a word spoken by the queen was worth the riches of the Indies and a favor bestowed by Her Majesty was a greater honor than the most ancient noble title in the land. The favorite or minister, who by flattery, masculinity, hard work, or

ability controlled the approach to the throne, in effect controlled the kingdom. Elizabethan politics remained personal and intimate and consisted primarily in getting oneself and one's protégés as close to the queen as possible. The prolonged duel between the Essex and Cecil factions during the last years of Elizabeth's reign was fought over the placement of friends and followers in positions at court where they could exert influence on the queen. The essential axiom of Tudor politics was not merely "out of sight out of mind," but "out of sight, in evil mind." In the end Essex was destroyed when he was maneuvered into accepting a position away from the court, and he wrote bitterly to the Council in London that he could defend himself "on the breast, but not on the back" from the dagger thrusts of malicious gossip.

Elizabeth's household may have been an academy of Renaissance learning, a rich and ceremonial setting for royalty, and the political heart of the kingdom; yet falsehood and greed, callousness and spitefulness were everywhere in evidence. Political morality under the queen remained almost as predatory and just as susceptible to corruption as in the past. Lord Burghley is reported to have planted a spy on Drake's ship in order to sabotage his venture; Secretary Walsingham had the queen's correspondence with her Lord Treasurer intercepted by hirelings; and all men expected tips to insure prompt service. Moralists and political failures agreed with

The wool trade brought prosperity to Gloucestershire shepherds like those shown above in a woodcut from Michael Drayton's Poly-Olbion, *a rhymed description of England.*

83

The ordinary of the Company of Bakers of the city of York contained regulations governing the production of bread. Maxims in the woodcuts shown above urged good measure and the use of wholesome ingredients.

the playwright Anthony Munday, who found that:

... falsehoods sat in fairest looks
And friend to friend was coy;
Court favor fill'd but empty books
And there I found no joy.

The court was perambulating, elaborate, and un-hygienic. It included everybody from the children of the squillery and the grooms of the stool to the Lord Chamberlain and the great dignitaries of the household, possibly a thousand persons in all. The most coveted positions, and consequently the most inaccessible, were those that permitted entree to the queen's chamber. Like any private household the court was divided along traditional lines—above stairs and below stairs. In the case of the queen's establishment, however, the divisions were not so fixed, for the royal household was a public institution as well as a private home. At one time Elizabeth's ancestors had kept their treasure in chests under their beds, like any private individuals who regarded the bedchamber as the safest room in the house, and they had used their servants to aid them in their public duties. Consequently the domestics of the household—the chamberlain, the steward, the butler, the marshal, the treasurer—evolved into state dignitaries, holding such titles as Lord Chamberlain, Lord Steward, and Lord Treasurer.

Below stairs was the preserve of the Lord Steward, who presided over a host of court servants ranging in social and governmental importance from the Lord Treasurer, the Keeper of the Queen's Jewels, and the Clerks of the Green Cloth, to the master and apprentice cooks and the grooms of the stable. Above stairs was the domain of the Lord Chamberlain. His was a far smaller organization than the domestic staff of the Lord Steward; it was the world of the politically elite, numbering no more than one hundred seventy-five privileged men and a dozen women. The Lord Chamberlain attended upon the queen's person; he was responsible for the operation of her privy chamber and the organization of the ceremony that surrounded her every waking moment and lent dignity and glamour to her life; and he controlled the appointment of those influential and greatly envied officials about the queen—the well-born grooms and yeomen of her chamber and her ladies in waiting. Of all the functionaries at court the Lord Chamberlain was politically the most important, for his were the juiciest plums of patronage.

Outside the court and the immediate entourage of the queen, but linked closely to the royal household by overlapping personnel, was the slender structure of government through which the sovereign ruled. The Tudor bureaucracy was intimate, hardworking, and underpaid, and by modern standards incredibly small and understaffed. The mainspring of government in England as well as in France, Spain, and elsewhere in Europe was the Council surrounding the monarch, which, wrote James I, "does watch for me when I sleep and in my absence are so careful to snip and trim the house against my return." Under Elizabeth the Privy Council was composed of a dozen or more ministers, who managed the realm "as if it had been the household and estate of a nobleman under a strict and prying steward." The Council handled foreign affairs, drafted official communiqués, issued proclamations that had the authority of law, and scrutinized and regulated every facet of Tudor life. County officials such as justices of the peace, chief constables, sheriffs, and lord lieutenants were appointed and supervised by the Council in the queen's name. The price of wheat, the level of wages, the drainage of rivers, the apprehension of criminals, the supervision of the shire militia, the construction of bridges, the petitions of soldiers and sailors grown old and infirm in the queen's service—all these and more were the daily concern of a group of ministers who were Elizabeth's men of all work.

Beneath the Council were the major divisions of state: the secretariat, which numbered no more than fifteen; the judicial machinery, with a staff of fifty persons at the most; the regional administrations such as the duchy of Lancaster, with its own petty treasury and some forty officials, the earldom of Chester, the Council of the North, and the government of Wales—all four run by no more than one hundred forty-five officials; and the largest office, the treasury, with its cadre of two hundred custom officials and some sixty-five clerks of the exchequer at Westminster. Although Elizabeth ruled her kingdom with a bureaucracy of scarcely five hundred salaried persons, she also had at her command an unsung and unpaid regiment of amateur officials who brought the paternalism of Tudor government directly to the countryside. These were the fifteen hundred justices of the peace. Never, said Sir Thomas Smith, one of the queen's secretaries, was there "in any commonwealth devised a more wise, a more dulce and gentle, a more certain way to rule the people." Chosen from among the men of birth and substance who lived in each county, the justices of the peace united the two essentials of good government—knowledge of the law and understanding of local conditions. Justices were often members of Parliament, and all of them had friends and relations among the luminaries of the court and the great nobles of the realm. They were the eyes, ears, and hands of the Privy Council, informing the govern-

Much of life in Elizabethan England remained crude for people of both high and low estate. Punishment for even minor transgressions was quick and direct, as malefactors locked into stocks (above) discovered to their discomfort. Even at formal meals like the one below, food was plain —and often rank—and meat was eaten with the hands.

ment of local crises, fixing wages, watching over the parish poor, supervising weights and measures, maintaining the peace, collecting parliamentary taxes, and inspecting the county levies. There was nothing like them anywhere else in Europe, where kings were forced to rule through paid servants who were placed in charge of local administration.

Just as the queen, the heart and head of the state, was considered to rule by divine right, the "better part" of society—the nobility and the gentry—were believed to have divine sanction for their positions too, having been ordained by God to help her. In solitary and wealthy grandeur near the apex of society stood the sixty or so peers of the realm, who were worth anywhere from 20,000 to 100,000 pounds and rivaled even the queen in the lavishness of their hospitality and the magnificence of their semifeudal households. Although the Tudor aristocrat vigorously maintained his privileged and almost divine position in society, he differed from his colleague in France in one essential quality—he had become domesticated. The cherished tradition of baronial feuding and independence lingered on in the northern shires, but the Tudor crown never tolerated such princely houses as the Guises and Bourbons, whose wealth and political influence allowed them to act as laws unto themselves. Below the great peers, but closely related by blood and interest, were the country gentlemen and their mercantile and professional cousins in trade, in law, and in the Church. They numbered no more than three to four thousand, and most of them possessed upward of fifty pounds a year in an age that accounted two pounds, ten shillings a marginal but adequate income. These were the real governors of the kingdom, a select and intimate group from whom the queen appointed her paid and unpaid servants and to whom she offered the richest prizes of office. Elizabeth may have given unity and leadership to the kingdom, but the crown existed only in federation with the local, regional, and class interests of these natural leaders of society.

The highest authority of the realm was not the solitary voice of a willful and capricious sovereign but the authority of the organ that spoke for all interests within the commonwealth—king in Parliament. When Elizabeth sat in the midst of her Lords and Commons and when legislation was enacted by the whole Parliament, then the kingdom spoke *ex cathedra*. The voice of the realm might in fact be that of the monarch, but constitutionally it was assumed that it was the sound of all elements singing but a single song. Parliament was ideally considered to be the "highest and most absolute power of the realm" because "every Englishman is intended to be there present . . . from the prince . . . to the lowest

person in England." No one knew better than Elizabeth how to play upon the heartstrings of her loyal Commons or how to produce a perfect political accord. Within the mystical union of Lords, Commons, and crown, the strong voice of the queen and her Council established the pitch and set the tempo of government. The proper role of Parliament, especially that of the lower house, was to beseech and petition, not to command or initiate. It was true that members belonged to the "better part" of society and were expected to give leadership to the vulgar multitude in town and shire, but policy belonged to the head, the prince, and the Privy Council. Justices of the peace, overseers of the poor, sheriffs, and even lord lieutenants of the county were merely vessels through which authority was translated into local administration. When Elizabeth firmly informed a rebellious House of Commons, which was demanding the death sentence for Mary Queen of Scots, that "if I should say unto you that I mean to grant your petition, I should then tell you more than is fit for you to know," she was stating her regal conviction that the members of the Commons were no more than humble petitioners.

The queen was acutely aware that her political control of Parliament would continue so long as she was financially solvent. During the first years of the reign Elizabeth was parsimonious to an extreme, hoarding her regular non-parliamentary income of 200,000 pounds a year, cutting her expenses by half, liquidating her sister's debt, building up a slight surplus, and establishing on the Continent such a solid credit that she was able to borrow at eight per cent interest, whereas Philip of Spain was charged as much as eighteen per cent. In Elizabeth's estimation it was important that the crown should never have to come to Commons to beg for money. Unfortunately war made the queen insolvent, and potential bankruptcy made her dependent upon Parliament. She did everything she could to avoid frequent sessions and requests for money, and she mortgaged the Stuart future by consuming her capital in order to avoid excessive taxation. In a single year she divested the crown of 120,000 pounds worth of land in order to finance her costly Irish war. In the end the weight of financial reality proved overpowering; Henry VII had been able to manage with an average yearly parliamentary grant of 11,500 pounds to supplement his ordinary revenues; his son's dependence rose to 30,000 pounds, and Elizabeth's reached 50,000 pounds a year. When Elizabeth's Secretary of State, Sir Thomas Smith, wrote that what a commonwealth desired most was "peace, liberty, quietness, little taking of their money, few parliaments," he unconsciously linked two crucial elements—taxation and representation. There could be neither few nor obedient parliaments so long as there was much taking of money.

Toward the close of her long reign, a new voice was being heard in parliamentary committees, in Commons' chamber, and in country mansions. Slowly, hesitantly, and inarticulately, the landed classes, speaking through the House of Commons and using the weapons of finance to add weight to their demand, were urging a partnership in which crown and Parliament would sing duet. So long as the queen and her loyal Commons shared the concept of a divinely inspired and carefully regulated society and agreed on what was best for the common sort, harmony prevailed. When crown and Parliament parted company in their views, the harsh sounds of constitutional discord were heard with increasing frequency until they reached a crescendo in the civil war of 1642.

The structure and pattern of Elizabethan govern-ment were deceptively simple. The ordered ranks, that tidy hierarchy of queen, Privy Council, regional governments, law courts, Parliament, and local administration, provided a framework for the most vital aspect of Tudor government: sensitivity to the shifting nuances of public sentiment. The greatness of Elizabeth's accomplishment lay in the sixth sense that led her to demand of her subjects only what they wished to give, in the talent of bestowing upon the socially prominent elements of society the fruits of office while depriving them of the power of government, and in the artistry by which she enveloped functions of state in a magic veil of pomp and circumstance. As a result of that magic, "mere English" Elizabeth Tudor was elevated to a goddess-queen and her beardless boys at court became Olympian heroes in worshipful attendance.

All Elizabethans knew that "in pompous circumstances a secret of government doth much consist." Government was always on display, and the imagina-

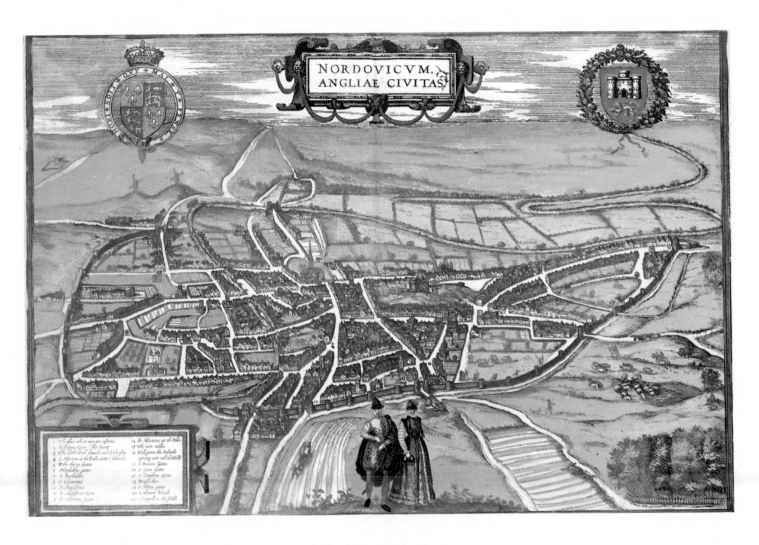

Norwich, shown here around 1577, was the second city of Elizabethan England. A center of the cloth trade to which many workers emigrated from the Netherlands, the city had some 20,000 inhabitants in the sixteenth century—more than one fifth of them foreign-born.

87

*As head of state Elizabeth presided over a rapidly pro-
liferating army of bureaucrats. This portrait, showing
the queen surrounded by Tudor symbols, appeared in the
account book of the duchy of Lancaster's receiver general.*

tion of the multitude was captivated by gorgeous
dress, robes of state, gold brocade, and majestic
processions. The symbols of state and authority
were human, but authority was dull and unimpres-
sive without the sound of cannon, the glitter of
gold, and the clatter of horses' hoofs. The goddess-
queen had to be decked in silver bodice, satin gown,
and silken farthingale, she had to live in gorgeous
establishments and be surrounded by the trappings
of endless wealth, for without ceremony she was but
another woman. Richmond Palace was "a splendid
and magnificent house"; Hampton Court was "a
noble and uniform pile" and all its walls shone with
gold and silver; Whitehall, that most ancient of all
royal establishments, contained more than two
thousand rooms; and Nonsuch, so called because
there was none other like it, was so adorned with
gold that Elizabeth thought it afire when she saw
it sparkling in the light of the setting sun.

If the fairyland quality surrounding kings was
intended to captivate the eye, royal generosity was
designed in order to win men's hearts and loyalty.
Robert Cecil spoke from a lifetime of experience
when he said that "bounty is an essential virtue of
the king." The key to Tudor politics rested upon
the control of this generosity, for no Elizabethan
official ever received a salary that was commensurate
with his position: the Lord Keeper of the Great Seal
earned a stipend of 919 pounds a year; the Lord Admiral 200 pounds, and the principal secretary 100
pounds, but in 1601 all three posts were actually
valued at approximately 3,000 pounds a year. Gra-
tuities and fees for promoting a friend, urging a
favor, giving information, and above all, for tapping
and directing the bounty of the queen made up the
difference between official salary and actual income.
They were considered as the legitimate perquisites
of office in an age that regarded governmental posts
as both public trusts and private sinecures.

At the sovereign's disposal were pensions, annu-
ities, leases, monopolies, titles, and honors, including about twelve hundred positions, which ranged
in importance and profit from the principal offices
of the realm down to the gunners of the Tower
and the stewards and bailiffs of the crown lands. Between the sovereign and a swarm of suitors anxious
to partake of royal bounty, there existed an inner
core of councilors and favorites, who attracted to
themselves the admiration and the wealth of lesser
men desirous of protection or advancement in society. When old Lord Burghley died, a forsaken patron seeker wrote to his son, Robert Cecil, expressing
a desire "to be protected . . . under the shadow of
your wings," which he rightly judged to be as extensive as his father's. As the medieval baron had held

A detail from a drawing done by a Dutch traveler shows Greenwich Palace, overlooking the river Thames. Elizabeth had been born in the palace and stayed there occasionally.

men loyal to him by ties of lordship, so the sixteenth-century aristocrat based his political power upon the exercise of influence and built up personal followings held together by ties of patronage. "My good Lord," wrote one Elizabethan wise to the realities of political life, "advancement in all worlds be obtained by mediation and remembrance of noble friends." Remembrance was always made easier by the presentation of a well-timed gift. The amount was expected to be commensurate with the favor demanded; when the countess of Warwick was offered one hundred pounds to influence the queen in a law case in chancery, she considered the sum to be too small. The essence of Elizabethan politics was clearly perceived by Lord Burghley in the simple formula for success that he offered his son. "Be sure," he said, "to keep some great man thy friend but trouble him not for trifles."

That a political system based on patronage, graft, influence, factionalism, ceremony, and queen worship did not deteriorate into simple jobbery, fawning corruption, and senseless ritualism was one of the marvels of the Elizabethan age. Elsewhere in Europe, and particularly in France, personal hatreds, party factions, and human avarice palsied the hand of royal government, but in England Gloriana succeeded in ruling by factions and parties, which she herself "made, upheld, and weakened, as her own great judgment advised." On the Continent, men placed loyalty to God, to overlord, and to estate higher than their duty to the sovereign, but during the "calm and quiet season" of Elizabeth's reign,

subjects agreed with Lord Burghley when he said that he had "no affection to be of a party, but for the queen's majesty." The ruling classes of England were tied to Elizabeth by links of air that were as strong and enduring as iron, for the queen knew how to appeal to their self-interest and their love, and when she accounted it "the glory of my crown that I have reigned with your loves," she spoke no more than the truth.

Elizabethan England was exposed to all the disrupting forces of the century, feudal privileges, Renaissance pride, religious zeal, and commercial cupidity, but instead of destroying the kingdom they gave new vitality and dynamism to the medieval ideal of balance, order, and degree. In Spain respect for class descended to pride in caste, the harmonious commonwealth stiffened into a rigid bureaucracy ruled by a pettifogging and pedantic monarch, and tranquility and concord deteriorated into an orthodoxy of thought so rigid that Spaniards preferred to be illiterate rather than risk the charge of heresy. In France another woman of the age, Catherine de Médicis, endeavored to do for her adopted land what Elizabeth had done for England, to preserve "the reverence wherewith a king is girt about from God" and to cast the mantle of her feminism over all factions. But in France the queen regent's magic was no more than clever legerdemain, her aspirations mere family and dynastic aggrandizement, her policy subtle intrigue; and though her methods were no more devious than Elizabeth's, the results were discord, bloodshed, and monstrous civil war.

89

GLORIANA

Elizabeth the Great, Gloriana, a woman who imprinted
her name on an age, seemed to most of her subjects more
mythical than human. Yet they saw much of her since she
went into public often, as on the occasion depicted at right
in a painting by Marcus Gheeraerts, which shows courtiers
carrying the queen in a palanquin to attend a wedding.
Her appearance never failed to thrill the populace, for she
tempered her naturally majestic mien with a smile here and
a gracious word there. To her intimates, however, Elizabeth was as much a woman as a queen. She often seemed
womanishly indecisive, but her delaying tactics usually
gave her the time that was needed to raise money, an army,
or public support. She had an uncanny instinct for choos-
ing councilors, and when she did choose unwisely—as
with Essex—it was because of the promptings of her heart.
Despite her exalted position she was able to maintain
friendships with many women who were generally loyal,
intelligent, and kind; with them she enjoyed lusty gossip
as well as intellectual discussion. The queen had a violent
temper and had little reluctance about expressing it; but
she never held a grudge, and her temper was balanced by
a sense of humor, which helped her laugh her way out of
many tight diplomatic situations. Whatever the queen did
she did well and with gusto: she was a brilliant liar, a
pinchpenny of great talent, an egoist of royal magnitude

One side of Elizabeth's official seal shows the queen with symbols of her authority.

THE CORONATION

Elizabeth's coronation in Westminster Abbey, where English monarchs had been crowned since the time of William the Conqueror, was calculated to summon up an image of the new queen as the embodiment of majesty; contemporaries report that it was entirely successful. The coronation procession, which took place the day before the ceremony, began at the Tower and wound through the streets of London and Westminster. The queen's ceremonial guards were garbed in crimson, and each of the thousand mounted courtiers who accompanied the gold-draped royal litter vied to outdo his fellows in sartorial splendor. Londoners jammed streets, which were hung with banners, tapestries, silks, and paintings; they stood for hours in the icy air waiting for a glimpse of their new monarch. Music and cheers greeted Elizabeth all along her route, and as she passed by certain sites, tableaux symbolizing the greatness of England and its queen were presented for her delectation,

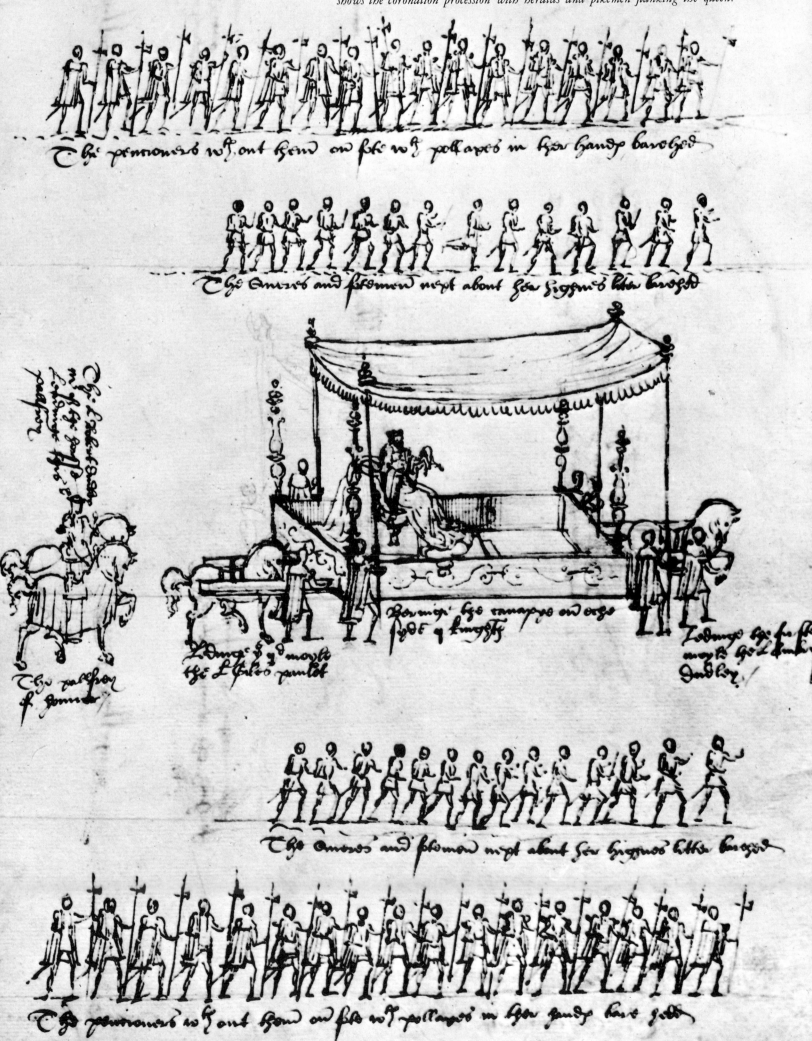

QUEEN AND RULER

From the moment Elizabeth was proclaimed queen an apprehensive nation waited to see how she would cope with the religious problem. She did not delay; being far more interested in national unity than in the niceties of religious differences, she proposed a return to the Church of Henry VIII, which would allow her subjects inner freedom though demanding public conformity. "I will do as my father did,' she announced, and then proceeded along her own course with great political skill. In signing her first document she refused to add "Supreme Head of the Church" to her other titles; in its place she diplomatically wrote "&c"—a brilliant move that antagonized neither Catholic nor Protestant. Since she was anxious not to incur the pope's condemnation until she was certain of her subjects' loyalty, she kept Mary's ambassador in Rome—but she also pleased the Protestants by allowing the publication of English Bibles again. By the time Elizabeth's coronation took place most Englishmen were no longer worried about religious strife, for now they had found a ruler as well as a queen.

A portrait (opposite) painted at the time of the coronation shows the twenty-five-year-old queen dressed in robes of state. In the miniature above, Elizabeth (front center) is shown with her bishops at the traditional maundy ceremony, during which the queen washed the feet of her subjects in imitation of Christ.

95

Falconry was one of Elizabeth's favorite sports.

Tharlton, a comic actor, entertained the queen.

At a hunt the queen is about to bleed a slain deer.

96

Elizabeth *(upper left) picnics with her courtiers.*

A huntsman announces the sighting of a deer.

PLEASURES OF THE COURT

Most of Elizabeth's courtiers and maids of honor spent part of each year in residence with the queen, where they found themselves caught up in a round of almost continuous revelry; in fact a good part of the highly complex organization of the court was oriented toward providing entertainment. Although she disliked spending money, Elizabeth encouraged the Office of the Revels to prepare elaborate masques and dramas. The officer of the queen's barge arranged parties on the Thames, and the master of the bears and two keepers of mastiffs set up bear-baiting contests, which were as popular at court as they were with the commonalty. Other functionaries supervised the resident singing group and musicians and organized banquets and the balls at which Elizabeth loved to dance. The queen staged tournaments and athletic contests and undoubtedly bet on them, for she liked to gamble when she played cards and backgammon. An accomplished rider and hunter, Elizabeth delighted in combining a picnic with a hunt. And her courtiers, informed by their monarch's spirit, found as much enjoyment in them as she.

In the drawing above, Elizabeth is seen riding in the chariot of Fame.

THE ROYAL EGO

Only a queen could indulge an ego the size of Elizabeth's. She thrived on—and demanded—constant compliments, professions of adoration, and gifts from those around her. She encouraged her subjects' veneration, accepting the grossest and most obvious flattery with relish, and took it amiss when her ladies in waiting seemed more interested in an attractive courtier than in herself; the courtier reciprocating their attention often lost favor. The queen was inordinately vain; even when her beauty had gone and her hair had faded, her passion for sumptuous clothes and costly jewelry to "set off" her figure and face did not abate. She wore a different dress almost every day; when she died she left some two thousand dresses and a treasure of jewels. Her vanity as well as her virtues promoted the "Cult of Gloriana"—and poets and painters produced numerous allegorical works that placed Elizabeth in the role of goddess or muse. The results include some of the greatest English poetry ever produced and some of the worst English painting.

In Queen Elizabeth and the Goddesses *Elizabeth decides whether Juno, Minerva, or Venus is most beautiful; the implication is that Elizabeth, loveliest of all, is in the best position to judge.*

ELIZABETH   REGINA

4

RAGE IN HEAVEN

The years preceding the birth of Elizabeth were heavy with foreboding. In 1531 the heavens broke out into astronomic display, and an ominous comet, bright with fire and with a giant yellow tail, lit up the western sky. The same year two flying standards had been seen moving across the sky, and in Germany it was reported that the air was filled with soldiers, headed God knew where but certainly sent to do the Lord's bidding. Everywhere there were signs of frantic battle, mysterious claps of thunder, fireballs, strange and terrifying lights, and flaming crosses in the sky. Rage in heaven had commenced, and all the omens pointed to great and terrible events on earth. God and Satan were once again in mortal conflict, and as never before, men's souls stood in jeopardy. On both sides the ranks were closing, and men were called upon to stand up and be counted, to declare themselves, and to give their lives in defense of the truth.

Two events of those years passed without notice amidst all the divine and atmospheric commotion. In 1531 three students attending the University of Paris—Pierre Lefèvre, Francis Xavier, and Ignatius Loyola—tacked a picture of Jesus on the door of the room they shared, and in contempt other students dubbed the inmates the *Societas Jesu*. Such was the quiet beginning of those militant shock troops of the Church, the Jesuits. Two years later another scholar at the University made history also; John Calvin suddenly became overwhelmed with the knowledge that he had been made the chosen vessel

of the Lord. A great light broke upon him as he realized "in what a quagmire of errors" he had wallowed and with "what filth and shame" he had covered himself.

Two students—Calvin and Loyola—both men of iron will and inflexible conviction, began the reordering of the religious ranks, the recasting of Christendom into two armed and militant Churches, and the reforging of the metal of which martyrs and heroes are made. The religious energy marshaled by the two leaders represented a far greater break with the past than had the new learning of Erasmus or the new religion of Martin Luther, for in both the Protestant and Catholic camps the medieval atmosphere had continued to predominate until well into the 1530's. Luther was a medieval man, closer to Wycliffe and Huss than to Calvin or to Knox.

His words brought fear to his enemies, his voice struck down the walls of Satan, and his faith moved mountains, but his appeal was to the heart, not the mind. Luther had begun as an academic reformer of abuses; and even when driven into open revolution, he was unhappy about throwing out the baby with the bath water, casting out ancient ceremonies simply because they had been misused by evil men. Always, if in vain, the hope of religious reconciliation remained, the expectation that Christian men of good faith could somehow settle their differences and live together in brotherhood and peace.

Even in open defiance, Luther continued to be a cherubic-faced monk with more of the publican than

This portrait of Ignatius Loyola was painted in 1585, after his death.

A sixteenth-century painting shows John Calvin in his study, perusing a copy of his Institutes of the Christian Religion.

of the fanatic about him. He hurled ink pots at the devil in an understandable fashion, and for all his reasoned logic about *The Bondage of the Will*, he wondered whether it was "not against reason that all mankind should be subject to toil, sickness, and death just because one man took a bite out of an apple."

Luther's spiritual despair and shocked conscience at the sight of clerical corruption had driven him into revolt, yet the medieval background from which he emerged—his monastic experiences and his scholastic education—prevented him from crossing the threshold into the modern world. It remained for the second generation, for John Calvin, to provide the Reformation with a modern outlook and outfit Lutheranism in the armor of military discipline and doctrinal orthodoxy.

The first generation of the Catholic Counter-Reformation experienced a similar change. The humanistic Christianity of Erasmus at Basle and the mysticism of Lefèvre d'Etaples in France represented a unique mixture of learning, laughter, and piety. Early sixteenth-century Catholic reform within the Church was tolerant, humane, and individualistic. The ranks of reformers were filled with men who in their innocence expected that good will, good scholarship, and good fellowship would free the Church of corruption, heal the wound of schism, and do away with error. In the end, however, the old Church died in the fury of the Protestant heresy. In defeat and humiliation the Catholic Church was forced to find new strength and new spiritual resources with which to roll back the armies of the devil; but the means were those of a new generation, the tempered and flexible will of Ignatius Loyola and his Society of Jesus, and not the soft compromise and idle words of humanistic scholars and mystics.

Calvin began his career as a French scholar and lawyer of petty bourgeois extraction who eventually overcame pathological shyness and grinding ill health to do the Lord's bidding. Loyola was an untutored Spanish soldier and court reprobate of impoverished noble descent who willed himself to sainthood. The Frenchman was a theologian with the strength to live by the terrifying conclusions of his own logic; the Spaniard was a sixteenth-century psychiatrist and catcher of men's souls, who by the sheer strength of his will turned imagination into reality. Both men fought to conquer the world of the spirit and to fashion a disciplined and ordered army dedicated to God's service. Calvin and Loyola—like the faiths they represented—were adversaries in an irreconcilable conflict, yet never were there two men so different in their background and their approach and so similar in their achievement. The French lawyer-theologian would not permit a marker for his grave (it might be venerated by the superstitious); and the Spanish soldier-saint would not sit for his portrait (there was never time.) Each became the model that his devoted followers aspired to emulate, and each branded his movement with the force of his personality. By 1558, when Elizabeth succeeded to the throne, Protestantism was no longer Lutheran and German but Calvinistic and international; Catholicism was no longer humanistic and Roman but militant and Jesuitic.

John Calvin was born on July 10, 1509, the son of Gerard Cauvin, the registrar of the town of Noyon in France. For two generations the community had been divided into furiously hostile camps over the bones of Saint Eloi. Who possessed the authentic remains and who the fake? The canons of the cathedral or the monks of the abbey? Later in life Calvin commented on the confusion and profusion of relics throughout France, and he calculated that the wood guaranteed to come from the true cross amounted to "a good shipload," the nails of the cross numbered fourteen, and the worshipers of sacred relics ran "the risk of reverencing the bones of some thief or robber, or of an ass, a dog, or a horse."

Calvin was brought up to be a cleric. He was made a chaplain of the cathedral of Noyon at the age of eleven; at fourteen he was sent to the University of Paris, where he studied the great schoolmen of the medieval past—Aquinas, Bonaventure, Scotus, and Gerson. Shy, introspective, and hypersensitive, the young scholar was intellectually precocious, morally priggish, and so unyielding in his opposition to vice and weakness that legend records that he was referred to as the accusative case for his didactic and argumentative spirit. At Paris Calvin was swept up by the warm breath of Renaissance humanism. His first published work was a gloss on Seneca's *De clementia*. It was written in impeccable Latin, bristled with classical learning, and exuded high ethical principles. In 1528, at his father's sudden demand, Calvin added training in the law to classical learning and medieval scholarship, and by 1533 his education was complete and the vessel was ready to receive the spirit of God. He had made himself into a jurist, theologian, and Latinist. Yet for all his intellectual feats he remained deeply dissatisfied and found, as he later wrote, that "the more closely I examined myself the more was my conscience tormented by sharp stings so that there was no solace or comfort left to me save that of deluding myself by oblivion."

Oblivion was not John Calvin's fate, for in 1533 he heard the Lord speak and became "inflamed with so intense a desire to progress" that he resolved to re-

nounce his ecclesiastical offices and raise his voice against the evils of the Roman Church. He fled to Basle and in 1535 commenced that true, perfect, and final pronouncement on God's Word—*The Institutes of the Christian Religion*. First published in 1536, *The Institutes* was brief by theological standards, little more than five hundred pages long, yet it did for Protestant knowledge what the *Summa theologica* of Thomas Aquinas had done for the medieval Church and what the Council of Trent would shortly do for sixteenth-century Catholicism. In it Calvin summarized and systematized the creed, and disciplined and ordered the ranks of the believers, so that the truth could be defended against any heresy that might arise within Protestantism as well as against the papal Antichrist and the Romish court of darkness. *The Institutes* was the quintessence of the Protestant thought, which had been formulated by Luther, Zwingli, Erasmus, and Melanchthon. It was a faultlessly rational and convincing statement of the ultimate logic of the Protestant Reformation, a work that Jonathan Edwards was to call "a delightful doctrine, exceeding bright, pleasant, and sweet." Within nine months of its publication every copy had been sold to men who were desperate to be told the truth.

The book's central tenet, around which all others revolved, was the existence of an inscrutable God

Giuseppe Arcimboldo caricatured Calvin as neither fish nor fowl, but an unappetizing combination of the two.
GRIPSHOLM, SWEDEN

The Catholic Church struggled to preserve its traditions despite widespread persecution in the north. These sixteenth-century woodcuts show a monk (top), cardinal (center), and priest.

who was bound neither by compassion nor by the laws of science but was "the Arbiter and Governor of all things," a sovereign, omniscient, and capricious force, who "by His own power executes what He has decreed." The inescapable corollaries to such a thesis were the doctrines of predestination and election. For Calvin it was impossible for a leaf to fall or a decision to be formed without the express command of the deity, and the gates of the kingdom of heaven were open to those few who were the elect of God. Man, according to the Calvinist creed, was sinful and still bore the stain of Adam's disobedience; in justice God, who was omnipotent, would find it inconsistent to save any man. Nevertheless He selected for salvation certain men, irrespective of their deserts, in order to reveal to the world the complete freedom and total power of His authority. Calvin's God would not even be bound by his own sense of justice. That Adam disobeyed God and brought upon posterity the wrath of heaven by divine command and that the hand that grasped the apple was moved by God's will were historic facts that might seem unjust to man's faulty reason; but in the divine scheme of things they were in no way illogical, for God was "above logic; indeed, God made logic just as he made the apple."

The Institutes was a call to arms, to labor, to do battle, and above all to witness God's glory and spread His Word abroad. To Calvin the whole world was "the theatre of God's glory." God's doctrine, however, could never be victorious without commotion and suffering, for only Satan's creed was ever accepted by all without contention. And so Calvinists expected opposition. By definition they were poor security risks, for no earthly authority could claim their obedience. They were the soldiers of the Lord, and true believers, said Knox, could never be expected to "frame their religion according to the appetite of their princes." In Calvinism, Protestant minorities found the strength to resist and the justification to disobey established authority. Puritans in England, Presbyterians in Scotland, and Huguenots in France considered themselves the chosen instruments of sublime grace. In abandoning themselves to the majesty of God's will, they felt themselves to be the equals of any earthly king. The structured and hallowed hierarchy of social and political authority, so dear to the hearts of the custodians of the well-ordered commonwealth, was meaningless to men who hearkened to the voice of inner conscience. The Word of God was heard in their hearts and it was of greater import than the most weighty pronouncements of pope, magistrate, or king. Calvin never argued the right of revolution, but the spirit of disobedience was implicit in his statement that "where the glory of God is not made the end of the government, it is not a legitimate sovereignty, but a usurpation." Peter Wentworth summed up the Puritan position in England and elsewhere in Europe when, during a debate in Parliament, he presumptuously but positively told Archbishop Parker and the other bishops: "We will pass nothing before we understand what it is; for that were but to make you popes."

His vision of heaven on earth led John Calvin to make one of the grand experiments of all times—the founding of that "most perfect school of Christ that ever was on earth since the days of the apostles," the theocratic community of Geneva in Switzerland. In July, 1536, Calvin had chanced to visit Geneva, where an impetuous, if irritating, member of the elect, William Farel, was waging a furious battle against the forces of popery. Farel was as fiery as his brilliant red hair. On one occasion, earlier in his tempestuous career, he had risen while Mass was being celebrated, walked up to the surprised priest, knocked the consecrated bread from his hand, and calmly announced to the astonished audience that God was above in heaven and not in a piece of ritualistic trickery on earth. A short time before Calvin's arrival in Geneva, Farel had succeeded in getting the city council to proclaim political independence from the House of Savoy and spiritual liberation from Rome, and to vote "to live henceforth according to the Law of the Gospel and the Word of God, and to abolish all papal abuses." Such an ardent reformer could spearhead a revolu-

tion, but he could not discipline the revolutionists; the iron will and organizational talents of Calvin were needed to complete the transformation of the city of Geneva into the kingdom of God.

To the ordinary ordeal of living Farel and Calvin added the ordeal of saintliness. Both men were possessed by a beatific vision in which all of God's people were arrayed within the fold in tidy and disciplined ranks. For those who refused to "submit themselves wholeheartedly to the Word of God in complete obedience," excommunication was prescribed. In Geneva there were many obstinate folk who preferred sinfulness to saintliness and sloth to salvation. Calvin was ready to meet their challenge by instituting a government of God's elect, who had a stake in paradise as well as in mundane society.

In January, 1537, the "perfect school of Christ" was outlined in a series of articles establishing a system of Church-state government that from the start smacked more of the schoolhouse than the house of God. Geneva was transformed into a theocracy where the two swords of Christ—the civil and the ecclesiastical—acted together in perfect harmony, with the Council of Two Hundred ruling the city and the Venerable Company of clergymen overseeing morality and governing the Church. The Council retained the power to legislate and punish, but the Venerable Company was expected to scrutinize the life of every citizen and report any moral lapses and to inspire the secular government to acts of devotion and godly legislation. Discipline and her handmaid, inspection, were the symbols of the

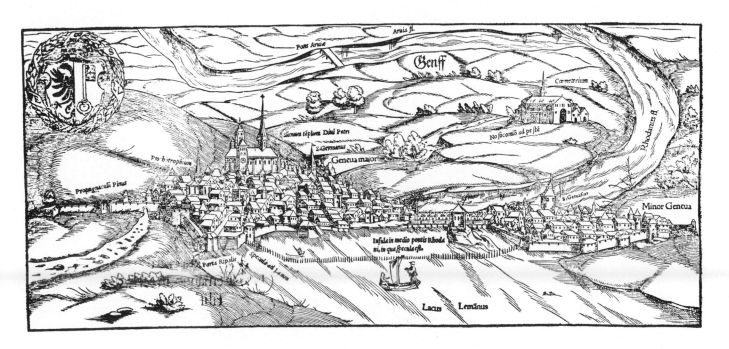

The earliest known view of Geneva shows the citadel of militant Calvinism as it appeared in 1548. St. Peter's Cathedral, where Calvin preached for thirty years, dominates the city.

113

new Geneva, for if the Church consisted of all the believers and not merely the clergy, then it was essential that every member be wholesome of heart and pure of mind. "To accomplish this," Calvin wrote, "we have decided . . . to appoint and choose certain persons of upright life and good reputation among all the faithful" who shall have "an eye to the life and conduct of each one." For the good citizens of Geneva there were not only to be windows into their souls but also great doors into their domestic, business, and social affairs. The grand experiment in applied theology had begun, and thenceforth the life of every man was to measure up to the scriptural standards of purity.

Attendance at church and at morning prayers was strictly enforced. Popery was exterminated root and branch, and even the celebration of Christmas was prohibited under pain of imprisonment as a devil's Mass and bacchanalian brawl. The theatre was denounced, especially the new and degenerate Italian custom of allowing women to perform on the stage instead of employing boys to play female roles. The women who appeared in theatrical productions, according to Calvinistic argument, had no purpose in mind other than "to expose their bodies, clothes, and ornaments to excite the impure desires of the spectators," all of which was utterly "contrary to the modesty of women, who ought to be shamefaced and shy." The initials *IHS* were placed on all public buildings, coins, and city flags; the number of bowling greens was reduced sharply, and in every respect Geneva became a Protestant Sparta.

It is far too easy to caricature Calvin's Geneva as a dreadful combination of a reformatory and a Christian revival meeting and school for saints, a veritable "dictatorship of the praying classes," in which neither common sense nor common happiness prevailed. Calvinism, however, was never "the haunting fear that someone somewhere may be happy," as H. L. Mencken has described it, for Calvinistic Genevans, Puritan English, and Huguenot French were not devoid of laughter and joy. Puritans danced, wined, and made merry in the privacy of their homes. Good fellowship, which was the fruit of godliness, was to be welcomed. It was gaiety for man's sake that was to be avoided. The trouble with God's elect in the eyes of more politic men was their determination to thunder against the evils of this world and their conviction that it was the minister's duty to God to speak as "a dying man to dying men." Calvinist preachers were rarely known for their tact or moderation, for Calvin never regarded the clerical office as being so limited in its scope that "when the sermon is delivered we may rest as if our task were done."

The preacher had to take care to see that souls were not lost as a result of his own lack of vigilance. The need to bring the Lord's way to all men made the Calvinist a busybody, and nothing was too obscure, nothing too inconsequential to be considered by the Church elders. The consistory, a body of the clergy sitting in company with twelve lay elders who were elected by the city council, decided cases involving fortunetelling, the singing of obscene songs, overindulgence, blasphemy, adultery, as well as more serious problems such as witchcraft and heresy. Matters of apparel, women's hair styles, and two cases of adultery involving Calvin's own sister-in-law and his stepdaughter were brought to the consistory's attention. The names given children at baptism were carefully culled, and if any was found to be objectionable, it was prohibited. Such Catholic names as Claude and Martin were barred as indicating a secret and idolatrous reverence for saints, whereas such questionable designations as Sepulcher, Sunday, and Jesus were outlawed as being in poor taste. Calvin, however, did not have to struggle with the English Puritan habit of bestowing such godly and imaginative names as Renewed, Fear-not, Accepted (an English archbishop carried that name), Be-thankful, Faint-not, Love-God, Live-well, and the mouth-filling Fight-the-good-fight-of-faith.

In 1546 the inns of Geneva were reorganized as "abbeys" and placed under strict government supervision; and a precise code of behavior for guests and hosts was laid down. Among other items it included the following:

If any one blasphemes the name of God or says, "By the body, 'sblood, zounds" or anything like, or who gives himself to the devil or uses similar execrable imprecations, he shall be punished. . . .

Item: The host shall not allow any person of whatever quality he be to drink or eat anything in his house without first having asked a blessing and afterward said grace.

Item: The host shall be obliged to keep in a public place a French Bible, in which anyone who wishes may read. . . .

Item: The host shall not allow any dissoluteness like dancing, dice, or cards, nor shall he receive anyone suspected of being a debauchee or ruffian.

Item: He shall only allow people to play honest games without swearing or blasphemy, and without wasting more time than that allowed for a meal. . . .

Item: Nobody shall be allowed to sit up after nine o'clock at night except spies.

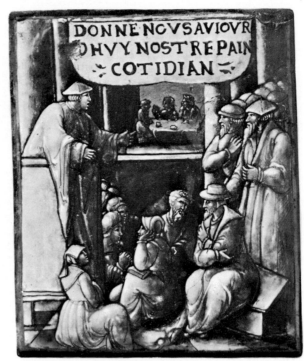

Two Protestant enamels show a Calvinist at prayer despite carnal temptation and a sermon being preached by the reformer Pierre Viret. Calvin himself can be seen at extreme right.

Calvin demanded that the city of Geneva become the armed citadel of God, and that absolute discipline of behavior and orthodoxy of thought be maintained as an example to all Europe. The self-appointed pope of the Protestant world was more than a pastor, he was a general and his followers were soldiers in the Lord's service. It was essential to success that God's army be built upon obedience to the divine Word as revealed in Scripture and interpreted by Calvin.

One of the first to clash with Geneva's warden of morality was a man named Pierre Ameaux, whose ancestral livelihood, the manufacture of playing cards, had been destroyed by the new discipline. In 1546, at a supper party given in his own house, Ameaux indulged in the ill-advised luxury of calling Calvin a preacher of false doctrines and prophesied that the government would soon be in the hands of fanatical French religious exiles who were flocking by the hundreds to the city. Ameaux's confidences were reported to the consistory by one of his own guests. His attack was not viewed merely as a personal affront to one of God's ministers, but as an insult to "the honor of Christ" whose servant Calvin knew himself to be. The Council of Two Hundred ordered Ameaux to present himself and on bended knee seek humble pardon of Calvin. But that outraged defender of the Lord would have no such mildness shown to a man who had insulted the "name of God," and he prevailed upon the Council to reconsider its verdict and change the

punishment to a more suitable one: Ameaux, clad only in a shirt, was ordered to walk through the streets of the city and kneel down in public to beg the mercy of God and the city magistrates for his ill-advised words.

Ameaux's opposition to Calvin was largely the result of economic grievance; the case of Michael Servetus was far more dangerous. Servetus was a Spanish physician whom history has treated as a hero, but whom contemporaries, both Protestant and Catholic, viewed as the most dangerous of criminals, for he denied the Trinity and the doctrine of original sin. He was thought of as a murderer of the soul, and his death by slow fire, in 1553, was greeted with applause by the entire Christian world. Calvin had known of Servetus in their university days in Paris, and he had been horrified even then by the Spaniard's pseudo-unitarian arguments. Servetus represented a pernicious threat from within the Protestant ranks, for he symbolized the tendency of the Protestant faith to disintegrate into a flock of warring sects ranging in alphabetical lunacy from Adventists, Biddelians, Boehmenists, and Christadelphians, to Salmonists, Traskites, and Tyronists.

Servetus lived in France for a decade, but finally fled to Vienna and in 1553 published the *Restitution of Christianity*, a work that immediately brought him to the attention of the Catholic authorities. He escaped from their prison and for reasons bordering on insanity sought safety in the city of the man who had denounced him in his university days, who had

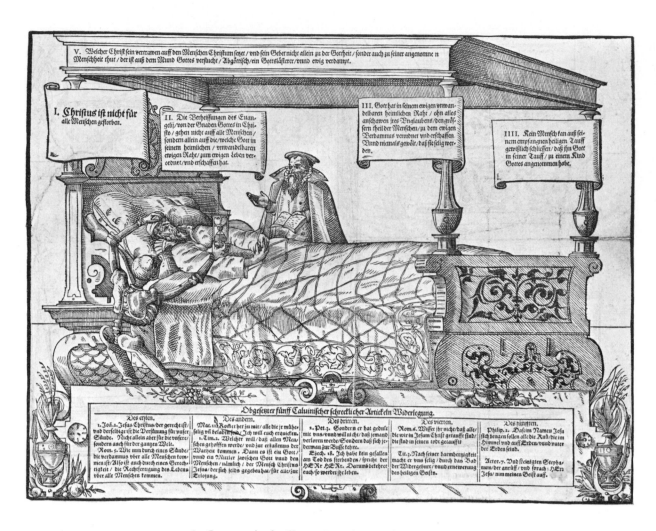

A German book illustration shows John Calvin on his deathbed. Numbered texts above the reformer are articles of faith to which Calvinists were required to subscribe.

BIBLIOTHEQUE DE L'ECOLE DES BEAUX ARTS, PARIS

been writing vicious attacks upon his views, and who may in fact have betrayed his identity to the Catholic inquisition in Vienna. The moment Servetus set foot in Geneva, he was recognized, arrested, tried, found guilty of heresy, and sentenced to death by slow burning. Still possessed of Satan, he died on October 27, 1553, at the hands of men who accounted the agony of the stake as slight compared to hell's fire. To Calvin the ranks of the faithful had to be preserved and heresy stamped out, for his Geneva was more than a Protestant stronghold and *The Institutes* more than a statement of righteousness. His city was the tabernacle of the Lord and a model for all believers, and his book was the tablet of God's Word.

For all the portraits of the man that survive and the intimate details that were recorded by his flock, John Calvin remains strangely inhuman. With his emaciated body and his uncompromising face dominated by a beaked nose, an unsmiling mouth, and eyes that looked with sorrow on a world filled with ignorance and evil, Calvin the man was re-

placed by Calvin the elect of God. His anger was monumental, his will uncompromising, his logic irrefutable, and his task Herculean. He was never beset by doubt, only by ill health and exhaustion, both of which he willed away. Fastidious to the point of madness, he could not endure even a speck of dust to mar the blackness of his gown. No detail was too trifling for him, no task done in the Lord's name too inconsequential. John Calvin must be numbered among the saints, if only because of the intensity of his emotions and the strength of his convictions. Like the saints he is of interest to humanity, but he lies outside its power of compassion or comprehension, for, as he said himself, his strength was not his own but belonged to the Lord. Calvin's reputation rests not simply on his record as master of that "perfect school of Christ" but even more on his achievement in building his rival to Catholicism, a tightly organized, self-sufficient, and international Church dedicated to bringing the standards of heaven to earth.

Roman Catholics considered Calvin's Geneva as

116

the center of an international and diabolical conspiracy to overthrow all established order and to subvert the true faith; but to Protestants the city was a source of inspired preachers and organizers who went forth in God's name to every country of Europe. Calvin himself was tireless in his efforts to organize the faithful on an international scale. His correspondence was voluminous, his advice endless, and his encouragement to stand firm in the knowledge of the Lord a source of strength throughout Europe. He was in touch with Queen Elizabeth and the king of Lithuania. He advised Thomas Cranmer in England, John Knox in Scotland, Jan Laski in Poland, and Admiral Coligny in France, and in each case his militant message was the same: "If He pleases to make use of you even to death in His battle, He will uphold you by His mighty hand to fight firmly, and will not suffer a single drop of your blood to remain useless." In May, 1559, Calvin founded his Academy, the spawning ground for religious revolutionists, and in its first year thirty-two ministers were dispatched to strengthen the army of the Lord in its struggle against Catholicism. Geneva began to attract the faithful from all over Europe. Each year the flood of exiles pouring into the city mounted: eighty-one in 1549, one hundred and forty-five in 1550, five hundred and eighty-seven in 1557, and over sixteen hundred in 1559. The great majority of them came from France, but several hundred flocked in from Italy, fifty or so from England, a scattering from Spain, and even a small colony from Greece and Tunis, which was under Spanish control at the time.

Geneva under the firm leadership of Calvin had become the haven and oracle for militant Protestantism. After his death, at the age of fifty-four, on May 27, 1564, it was the source of endless propaganda, which poured from the city's new printing presses and from the sharp pens of reformers eager to instruct the elect of other lands on how to build their Churches in the face of persecution and bitter official opposition. In France an entire state within a state was organized illegally with the establishment of dozens of interconnected religious cells or consistories, each modeled on the Church of Geneva and staffed with a pastor, elders, and deacons. The first of these was organized in Paris in 1555; four years later, Calvinist Presbyterian congregations had sprung up in seventy-two other French towns. The spirit that directed the new Church and the ministers who guided God's flock came from Geneva. In 1559 thirty-two preachers went forth to labor among the Lord's followers in France; in 1560 twelve more followed; and the next year the number rose to ninety. By the outbreak of the French civil war in

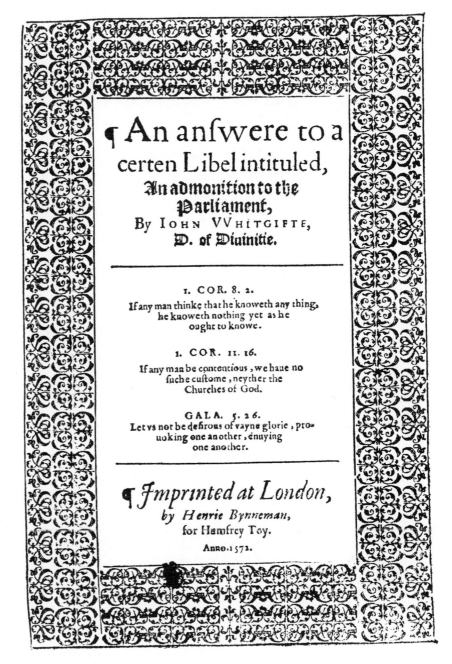

John Whitgift wrote his tract An Answer to a Certain Libel *in 1572 in response to a Puritan treatise that advocated the reform of the Church of England. During the second half of Elizabeth's reign Calvinists increased their agitation against the English Church.*

A detail of a painting by De Valdés Leal shows Loyola receiving permission of Pope Paul III to found the Jesuit order.

1562, a religious organization had been fashioned that rigidly disciplined and controlled the faith and personal lives of possibly a million and a half Frenchmen out of a population of sixteen million.

The consistory, which exercised inquisitorial powers over the beliefs and the activities of each French congregation, was the basic ecclesiastical unit. Above the consistory rose a tightly disciplined hierarchy, extending from the regional and provincial colloquies to the national synod, a governing body of ministers and elders who trained Calvinist preachers and passed final judgment on doctrine and oversaw the actions of the faithful. The structure was as authoritarian and paternalistic as anything that could be found in Geneva itself. Pastors were chastised for being too dull or too flippant; husbands were ordered to keep their household staffs disciplined or warned about beating their wives; and entire congregations were admonished to attend church more regularly.

The French Calvinists were called Huguenots or Night Specters for the quiet and stealthy way in which they slipped to church meetings in the dark of the night. Militant, disciplined, and elite, they felt themselves to be separate from the corrupt society of God's saints on earth. Throughout the 1560's cells were founded to spread the Word of God, to defend His faith, and transform the realm into a kingdom of heaven. Under their impact the religious spectrum in France was polarized: pacifistic Lutheranism, with its doctrine of quiet submission to authority, slowly gave way to Calvinism and a granite determination to resist. To men of the new persuasion who viewed life as a spiritual drama, the claims of religion dwarfed any sense of loyalty to either dynasty or state. The Huguenot felt closer to his Dutch, Scottish, and English brethren than he did to his countrymen—the overwhelming majority of whom remained Catholic. France in 1560 stood on the brink of ideological and civil war. "At one time," a contemporary observed, "friends and enemies were distinguished by the frontiers of provinces and kingdoms and were called Italians, Germans, French, Spaniards, English, and the like; now we must say Catholics and heretics, and a Catholic prince must consider all Catholics of all countries as his friends, just as the heretics consider all heretics as friends and subjects whether they are their own vassals or not."

Whether civil war would actually have erupted in France without the agitation of a numerically small but persistent community of "precise folk," who would "offer their goods and bodies to prison rather than they should relent," is a matter of guesswork. In sixteenth-century France forces were operating that had little to do with religion, but that happened to coincide fatally with the gathering spiritual storm. A degenerate monarchy, mounting feudal and provincial resistance to the incompetent royal bureaucracy, and the growing irresponsibility of an aristocracy confronted with economic ruin, contributed heavily to the disaster of civil war that broke out in 1562, two years before Calvin died in Geneva. The language of sedition remained religious, however; discontented Frenchmen, whether bourgeois or aristocratic, sought support from the one really organized and disciplined body within the state, the Calvinist Presbyterian Church.

In England the story was similar but the conclusion different. Calvinists hot out of Geneva had been frustrated in their original efforts to influence the Elizabethan religious settlement of 1559 strongly in their favor, but within a decade they launched a new campaign to seize the Church from within and to legislate the New Jerusalem into existence by means of parliamentary statute. Everywhere during the 1570's Puritan cells, similar to those in France and the Netherlands, were organized. In the universities, in the mansions of the aristocracy, in the houses of great financiers, and above all in Parliament, the "unspotted lambs of the Lord" forged a party, dedicated to the work of God's will, in which the voice of the divinity spoke more clearly than the dictates of political belly wisdom. In the eyes of fervent reformers the Church of England remained in desperate need of purification and redemption. It lacked a pope and a Mass, but otherwise it retained the lavish trappings of the Whore of Rome. Worse yet, the Church was the child of worldly necessity and not of God. In the words of one Puritan agitator, John Field, it had been "framed out of man's own brain and fantasy" and was even worse than popery.

The campaign against the Church commenced in 1570, when both press and pulpit were utilized to re-educate the queen and her people. Led by a defrocked Cambridge don named Thomas Cartwright, the Puritans spoke out against the ignorance and inefficiency of the Established Church; they branded cathedrals as "dens of lazy, loitering lubbards," and the prayer book a thing "picked out of that popish dunghill, the Mass-book, full of abominations."

The crisis, however, did not come until 1587, when the Puritan party tried to reform the Anglican Church by act of Parliament. In doing so, they blatantly defied the queen's prerogative, incurred her wrath, and attempted to usurp a constitutional function that Elizabeth firmly believed belonged to the crown. Cope's Bill and Book, as the two Puritan statutes were called, demanded the abolition of the Anglican episcopate and prayer book and their re-

placement by a prayer book and Church modeled on those of Geneva. The Bill and Book received short shrift from the queen, who ordered both withdrawn from Commons.

English Puritanism from the start was faced with a dilemma almost as old as man himself—the problem of double loyalties. In a clash between man's law and God's decree, the faithful had no choice but to follow the higher authority. Yet there was no doubt that the Puritans were loyal to Elizabeth as well as to their religion; and when one good evangelist had his hand struck off for writing against the queen's proposed marriage to a French and Catholic prince, he raised his hat with his remaining hand and shouted: "God save the queen." Yet Elizabeth was adamant in her opposition to Puritanism in whatever form it happened to appear, for she sensed from the start a fundamental truth about the sect—Puritan creed and organization were totally incompatible with the Tudor theory of paternalism and the doctrine of the organic state. More specifically, it was evident to her that a community of saints claiming spiritual authority derived directly from God was contrary not only to the theory of episcopacy but also to the very existence of a monarchy that exercised historic and extensive religious prerogatives and claimed divinity from God. As early as 1573 the Established Church had acknowledged the threat, and the dean of York pointed out the dialectic of Puritanism when he wrote: "At the beginning it was but a cap, a surplice, and a tippet over which these preachers complained; now, it is grown to bishops, archbishops, and cathedral churches, to the overthrow of the established order, and to the queen's authority in causes ecclesiastical." If the divinity of bishops was denied, could the divinity of monarchs be far behind? Elizabeth's reaction was to growl that these Puritans "did not wish to recognize either God or the king," but she dared not destroy her loyal Puritans, their provoking ardor and arrogant defiance notwithstanding, for at the other end of the religious scale an even more dangerous phenomenon was beginning to be seen —the Jesuit.

Ignatius Loyola made his first recorded appearance in history as a "bold and defiant" court delinquent, "armed with sword and pistol," who had come to the attention of the authorities for brawling in the streets and molesting women during the carnival season of 1515. In the words of his indictment he was "perfidious, brutal, vindictive." Loyola himself described the depravity of his youth in somewhat less harsh but nevertheless sufficiently damning terms. "Up to my twenty-sixth year, I was entirely given up to the vanities of the world and felt a keen

A contemporary drawing shows a crowd of Swiss peasants, newly converted to Protestantism, torturing a monk.

and empty craving to excel.'' Loyola was born in 1491, the product of a Spanish aristocratic and chivalric tradition that had already degenerated into pride of caste, license to brawl, and an excuse for idleness. The unique quality that this empty-headed young man possessed was insatiable ambition, a driving desire to excel as a bravo, a warrior, and a leader of men. He had been placed through family influence as a page at the royal palace at Arevalo, where tournaments were the routine amusements of life. Gorgeously arrayed youths thrust and hacked at one another with blunted swords and lances while gaily attired damsels cheered their gallants on. When his patron at court fell from royal favor, Loyola suddenly found himself the victim of a palace upheaval. His career as a court parasite in jeopardy, he turned to soldiering and was stationed on the barren, mountainous frontier between Spain and France.

As a palace page Loyola had perceived a basic truth about worldly power: success in society depended on influence and on the ability to control men and women in high office. In the frontier province of Navarre he learned another lesson: grinding discipline and unthinking obedience were essential to any military organization. Realization of the facts of sixteenth-century life did not, however, diminish his ambition; the courtier-soldier still yearned to achieve chivalric renown and splash the name of Loyola across the length and breadth of Europe. His chance came in May, 1521, when war broke out between the Emperor Charles V and Francis I of France. What followed was a nightmare: instead of glory and honor came defeat and horror. The young knight was crippled by the engines of modern war, his leg smashed by a cannon ball. Knightly heroism proved itself to be no match for modern science, and Loyola found himself a prisoner of the sickroom, his military career shattered along with his injured leg. A limping knight was out of the question, for chivalric heroes could not be allowed to hobble. Loyola endured a living hell to overcome the results of his injury; his leg was rebroken and reset, part of the bone was sawed off, and he suffered for weeks lying on an orthopedic rack in order to stretch the shrunken limb back to its proper size. No matter what the cost, he felt he had to avoid deformity, and he set his mind and soul to willing himself whole again.

From the torture of the rack and the surgeon's saw, he moved into the deadly tedium of convalescence. He daydreamed for hours, trying to capture in imagination the sight of flashing armor, the scent of perfumed ladies, and the sound of clashing swords. He became so bored that he was even reduced to reading, and he called for the *Amadis de Gaula*, the book of courtly love, to help his imagination. Unfortunately the castle of Loyola possessed but two books—Ludolphus of Saxony's *Life of Christ* and a collection of legends about the lives of the saints. With intense distaste he read about saintly suffering and degrading humility while longing for tales of heroism and romance. In his desperation he tried to think of saints as knights of God, and suddenly a new world opened: the deeds of saints became equal to the grandest feats of knightly arms, and he pictured himself as a valiant knight in the service of Christ. As he lay in bed dreaming about the exploits of Saint Francis and Saint Dominic, Loyola yearned to cast aside sword and armor and don cowl and girdle to do battle for Christ. The enemy was no longer a French invader or a rival knight but Satan himself and his host of demons, and the court maidens seemed insignificant in contrast to the queen of heaven for whom Loyola longed to do heroic deeds.

He had become in his imagination a crusader in

the old medieval tradition. If he was too deformed and crippled to fight for fair princesses and feudal lords, he could at least slay satanic dragons in honor of God. He determined to make the name of Loyola ring through the halls of time as the champion of the heavenly kingdom. The moment he could walk, he donned beggar's garb and went to Manresa, a tiny village in Catalonia, where he lived in a cave, practicing the art of sainthood as it was vividly depicted in early Christian literature. He knelt in prayer for seven hours a day and whipped and mortified his body. He wore a belt made of wire and a shirt woven with iron barbs, and he slept on the floor of the cave at night and fasted during the day. When he came down from his cave to beg in the village, even the beggars in the street called him Father Sack, so thin and filthy had he become.

In the midst of his suffering Loyola made a terrifying discovery: the strength that sustained him and the will that endured months of self-inflicted torture came not from God but from his own satanic pride. He knew that he sought martyrdom on earth to be great in heaven and desired to excel at saintliness in order to achieve recognition from God and man. The miracle of his conversion, the final consequence of those endless nights of torture in which he came to see the truth within himself, was the purgation of his pride and dedication of his will power to the service of God. He became the drill sergeant of his own soul. His will, once it had been purged of pride, became master of his reason, of his emotions, and above all, of his imagination. Loyola discovered that imagination, disciplined by an iron resolution, could move mountains and change darkness into light.

When he emerged from his ordeal he was as much an instrument of the Lord as was John Calvin, but there was a vital difference between them. Loyola was not, like Calvin, an empty vessel filled with God's grace; he was a mortal man who by the sheer magnitude of his will had set out to be a saint and meet God halfway. He had drilled his imagination, analyzed his conscience, scrutinized and inspected his soul, and regimented his body. The novice was now ready to join the ranks and do battle for the kingdom of heaven. Only the problem of finding, training, and organizing his spiritual recruits remained; to this end he set about writing the greatest of all do-it-yourself books, his *Spiritual Exercises*, in which the initiate was told, step by step, how to exercise his will. The book is one of the most powerful and perceptive ventures into psychoanalysis ever written, describing in detail how the recruit might harness and discipline all his senses in order to sharpen his imagination to the point where fantasy

A Catholic satirical engraving depicts a three-way spiritual dispute involving Calvin, the pope, and Luther.

and reality would become one. The *Exercises* were divided into four steps, or weeks, during which the recruit moved from a general examination of his conscience to an intense meditation on sin and its punishment in hell, and on the miracle of Christ's life.

The method was emotional and physical rather than intellectual. By an act of will the novice imagined himself to hang in agony upon the cross, to taste the bread and the fish that Jesus delivered to the people, to sit with the disciples at the Last Supper, and to visualize Christ as the king of heaven enthroned in His majesty and directing His armies against Satan. Throughout the *Exercises* Loyola insisted that every sense be controlled by the imagination. "It will be necessary," he explained, "to see in imagination the length, breadth, and depth of hell. . . . to beg for a deep sense of the pain which the lost suffer. . . . to see the vast fires and the souls enclosed, as it were, in bodies of fire; to hear the wailing, the howling, cries and blasphemies against Christ our Lord. . . . with the sense of smell to perceive the smoke, the sulphur, the filth, and

corruption; to taste the bitterness of tears, sadness, and remorse of conscience; with the sense of touch to feel the flames which envelop and burn the souls."

The *Exercises* was not written to be read as literature, but rather to be studied as a manual of instruction in preparation for action on the battlefield, and from the start Loyola's methods met with violent opposition from the very Church he sought to serve. Ecclesiastical authorities were alarmed by the hint of hysteria evident in his system of spiritual analysis. His converts suffered convulsions and fainting spells; they endured moments of suicidal depression and raptures bordering on madness. More serious, Loyola's doctrine of absolute free will rested as uncomfortably upon the shoulders of Catholic theology as did Luther's thesis of the bondage of the human will and the sovereign power of divine grace. The Church remained darkly suspicious of Loyola's assertion that he could discover God whenever he wished and that, "as the body can be exercised by going, walking, and running, so the will of man can be trained by exercises to find the will of God."

At the age of thirty-three Loyola was forced to conclude that if he was to lead anything other than a rabble of repentant prostitutes and idle and disappointed wives of the rich, he would have to return to school in order to meet and catch the men who had the strength to wield the sword of Christ. He started at the beginning, joining children to memorize lists of Latin words and learn basic grammar. Each step in his education led him to recognize the need for further learning, and in 1527, in his thirty-seventh year, he left his native Spain to study at the University of Paris.

Loyola shared a room with two other university students—the gentle and scholarly Pierre Lefèvre and the handsome and athletic Francis Xavier. Both

men were his junior by at least a dozen years, and both were ideally suited as recruits and lieutenants in the army of Christ if only Loyola could stimulate their interest and inveigle them into reading the *Exercises*. With Lefèvre the conquest was easy. By careful and quiet scrutiny Loyola discerned that behind the mind of this young Aristotelian philosopher there lingered the spirit of a superstitious Savoyard cowherd. Lefèvre started out teaching his elderly and untutored roommate the secrets of scholastic logic and ended by becoming a convert to the *Spiritual Exercises.*

With Francis Xavier the problem was more difficult, for the quarry was more wary. Moreover, the dicethrowing swordplayer Xavier had nothing but distaste for his Bible-reading, limping roommate. Loyola, however, won the younger man's respect by his learning and gained his love by his generosity, and in the end Xavier was induced to partake of the

A follower of Titian painted the Catholic bishops assembled at Trent. The Council, convened in 1545, continued intermittently for eighteen years in three sessions, which introduced needed reforms into the Catholic Church.
LOUVRE

Spiritual Exercises. By 1531 the leader had two converts and together they posted upon the door of their bedroom a picture of Jesus. By 1534 six disciples had been trapped by a saint who possessed the cunning of a soldier and the tact of a courtier. One he caught the morning after a night of debauchery, another he captured by the force of his words, and still another he led into a friendly game of dice, the loser pledging to take the *Exercises*. From the start Loyola adopted two controversial doctrines, which were to characterize the Society: the end justifies the means; and be all things to all men.

Armies of seven are rarely more than bands of

The persecution of English Catholics is shown in a print from a 1592 book published in France and considered so inflammatory that the English ambassador demanded its suppression.

fanatics or idealists. Yet in the case of Loyola and his followers, quality somehow made up for quantity, for these seven were men of steel. They left Paris and dedicated themselves to the service of the pope and the Catholic Church. Somewhat hesitantly Pope Paul III accepted these naïve but magnificently trained and enthusiastic champions, and on September 27, 1540, he blessed the foundation of the order of the Society of Jesus and named Loyola as its first general. The aim of the new organization was clear—to restore the medieval Church to the position of uncontested spiritual and political power that it had enjoyed in the thirteenth century. If the aim was medieval, the means were modern. The Jesuits were no medieval monastic order serving God by renouncing this world and retreating into a monastery. They were a military company in which every facet of life and every intellectual premise was subordinated to efficiency. The Jesuit ideal was the creation of a military corps in perfect fighting trim, a force in which every man would be ready to believe, if necessary, that "what seems black is white if the hierarchical Church so teaches." Every recruit was "like a corpse, which can be turned this way or that

. . . or a ball of wax that might be moulded in any form." Jesuits wore no special habit but dressed to suit the needs of the occasion. They did not spend their days in contemplation and prayer, but trained their minds and steeled their hearts to meet and defeat all men on their own terms. Jesuits were expected to talk finance to the Fuggers, scholarship to the intellectual, politics to the minister of state, and military tactics to the general. They were ordered not to shun the world of riches and power politics, but to join battle with Satan by becoming the confessors of the great and mighty. Loyola knew from early experience that power over the souls of the influential few was more useful than the support of the masses in the war against evil. Deliberately and with calculated results Jesuits set out to control the confessional of kings, the education of princes, and the minds of the men and women who counted.

At the same time that Loyola sought to place his disciples in the councils of the monarchs of Europe, he turned his attention to the organization of social welfare on a scale unheard of in the past. He sought to stamp out pauperism, prostitution, unemployment, and famine. In every major city of Europe,

Loyola established an office to co-ordinate begging, find jobs for the unemployed, and urge the local community to build homes for the old and infirm. For the first time the problem of human suffering was being attacked on a rational and organized scale.

The institution that slowly evolved during the 1540's and 1550's was carefully designed to fight social evil, to counter the monster of heresy, to reconquer Europe for the Roman fold, and to win new converts throughout the globe. The growth of the order was spectacular; in four years Italy, Spain, Portugal, France, Germany, and the Netherlands had Jesuit cells, and by the time Loyola died in 1556, the Society had grown from seven members to an elite and highly trained following of one thousand five hundred men, who were organized in twelve provinces and sixty-five residences in most of the major cities of Europe. In every case recruits were selected for their effectiveness as soldiers of God. Loyola once told his secretary that "in those who offered themselves" he looked "less to purely natural goodness than to firmness of character and ability for business," for he was of the opinion that "those who were not fit for public business were not adapted for filling offices in the Society."

By 1556 the order had become a world power: Jesuits heard confession in the most august courts of Europe, sat amidst the privy councils of kings, and maintained their representatives at the Imperial Diet in Germany. They held distinguished positions in the universities of the Continent, where they exercised control over the shaping of young minds. They whispered advice to Philip of Spain and Catherine de Médicis of France, and they were feared and detested by Protestants, who viewed them as Satan's most pernicious instrument. By the time Elizabeth came to the throne in 1558, the tide of Protestant victory had begun to ebb. Before long, central Europe was made safe for Catholicism, and the Protestant heresy was contained and limited to a northern arc of Europe extending from Prussia and Sweden through the Netherlands to England. By 1585 the religious struggle had been carried into the enemy camp; Antwerp had returned to the Catholic fold, Holland was under attack, and England itself was exposed to Catholic invasion and conversion. In each case Jesuit leadership stood behind Catholic resurgence.

Outside Europe Jesuit missionaries were on the move, carrying Christianity to the Far East, America, and Africa. Only two years after the Society was founded, Loyola sent his most trusted lieutenant, Francis Xavier, to India. In May, 1542, Xavier arrived in Goa, the rich trading center of the Portuguese East Indian empire. He was made vicar of all the lands washed by the Indian Ocean, with a potential flock of millions upon millions of souls who might yet be saved. Arabs, Hindus, Gujarats, and Persians, speaking a host of different languages, following false prophets or worshiping graven images, all awaited the coming of God's Word, if only it could be made comprehensible to their heathen ears and minds. Xavier began the task of learning the babble of Eastern tongues, of explaining the message of Christ, of meeting every kind and manner of man, and of urging them to come to him with their troubles and accept him as their confessor. From Goa, with its Kafir slaves and Portuguese hidalgos, he moved to the pearl fisheries of Kerala, where simple folk who worshiped fire demons and serpents were struck by his black gown and monk's cowl and listened to his clanging bell and the few words of Tamil that he had mastered. The entire East lay before him, and Xavier was not one to tarry when the hordes of China and Japan had yet to hear his message. Thousands of Japanese received his blessings, but he never reached China, for as he prepared to sail to Canton he was struck down with fever and died, a single soldier who had given his life to the greater glory of God—*ad majorem dei gloriam.*

To the greater glory of God was the secret of Jesuit power. It was the grossest kind of blasphemy to the Calvinist, for the doctrine presumed that man's efforts could add to or detract from God's glory; nevertheless it was the source of the vitality

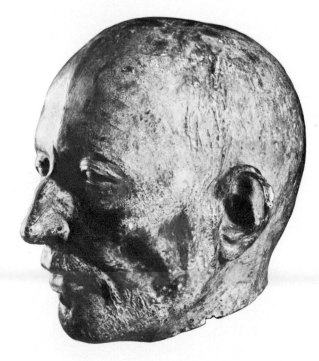

Loyola died in 1556 and was canonized six years later. The portrait of him above was cast from his death mask.

125

S·P·FRĀCISCUSXAVERIVSSOCIEᴀᵀISV

A sixteenth-century Japanese, working in a western style, portrayed the Jesuit missionary Francis Xavier.

that led Xavier ever eastward and enabled Loyola to shoulder enormous administrative labors. Loyola's headquarters consisted of three cells in a Roman slum. He worked twenty hours a day at a wooden trestle table and slept on a cot. He subsisted on chestnuts, bread, and water, never finding the leisure to sit down and eat a meal. All day he read reports, answered letters, and issued precise military communiqués, for each of his lieutenants reported to him in writing upon every particular of his life and the lives of those who served under him, and subordinates were expected to comment upon the success and quality of their superiors. Loyola became an administrative machine in absolute control of himself and of his army of spiritual soldiers. There was no time for contemplation, for friendship,

or for humanity, for he had willed himself to become a saint and in doing so he ceased to be human. The ranks of the sanctified had been joined by a "saint of will."

Loyola was born Spanish and he stamped his creation with his Iberian personality. In turn the Society of Jesus branded the entire Catholic Counter-Reformation with its proselytizing zeal, its efficiency, its insistence on quick action, and its creed that, in the name of God, the end justifies the means. The energy of the Jesuits was symptomatic of the new vigor that was becoming manifest throughout Catholicism. A steeling of the soul, a formulation of fundamental doctrine, and a sharpening of the weapons to destroy diversity of thought and faith were evident in every phase of the Catholic revival. The medieval inquisition, that sharp-eyed shepherd against the wolf of heresy, was re-established in Spain in 1478, in the Netherlands in 1523, and in Italy in 1542. The quality of the new leadership and the spirit of the inquisition were summed up in the words of an inquisitor who coldly stated: "It is no great matter whether they that die on account of religion be guilty or innocent, provided we terrify the people by such examples."

In 1545 Catholicism met in religious council to reform the Church and clarify the creed. The labors of the Council of Trent lasted on and off for eighteen years. Controlled by papal interests and later guided by Jesuit and Spanish leadership, its final pronouncement was a clear and unified statement of what the believer must profess in order to be numbered among the Catholic fold. Good works and faith and the seven sacraments were proclaimed to be the sole road to man's salvation. The Council further announced that only the Catholic Church held the keys to the kingdom of heaven and that the priesthood possessed supernatural powers transmitted directly from Christ. Latin was named the language of prayer and worship; the Church was made the interpreter and arbiter of the Bible; celibacy of the clergy was insisted upon; monasticism was pronounced to be the high road to salvation and the noblest attainment of mankind; and the existence of a celestial hierarchy of saints and angels was restated. As a final measure of defense an Index of prohibited books was established in order to protect the minds of future generations against the poison of heresy and unorthodoxy.

On both sides extremism was triumphant, the faith was prescribed and the faint of heart proscribed. In England Catholics were now told that religion stood higher than duty to the queen; one Catholic voiced the spirit of the rejuvenated Church when he said: "If I heard that the entire destruction of England was for the greater glory of God and the welfare of Christianity, I should be glad of it being done." In 1568 William Allen established an English college in Flanders in order to train missionaries for the dangerous work of re-catholicizing England and bringing hope and renewed strength to those believers who still clung to their ancient faith. Six years later the first three missionaries arrived in the country; by 1578 their number had risen to fifty and by 1580 there were over a hundred. The Catholic revival in England received still further impetus with the arrival of the Jesuits led by Edmund Campion and Robert Parsons. Their charge was "to preach the gospel, to minister the sacraments, to instruct the simple, to reform sinners, [and] to confute errors."

Whether the Jesuits, who were smuggled into the realm, were in fact traitors—fifth columnists sent to destroy the Protestant Jezebel and to incite regicide —is difficult to judge. Officially the order preached obedience even to heretical sovereigns, but as revolution was implicit in the militant creed of John Calvin, so sedition was inherent in the Jesuit judgment that matters of faith stood higher than the concerns of daily life and that the spiritual end justified the material means. When Campion was caught and then dismembered in the name of state security and political orthodoxy, he died blessing Elizabeth—"your queen and mine"; but Robert Parsons was a professional revolutionist, and his fine touch discernible in almost every plot to overthrow Elizabeth.

Throughout Europe Calvinist and Jesuit were setting the pace. Each represented a supra-national creed enforced by a militant, international organization. Both were politically and socially dangerous movements, for neither recognized the limitations of common sense or common decency, and each was a haven for men, some deeply pious, others viciously evil, who enjoyed extreme action, whether it be raping nuns in the name of religion or torturing men with rack and fire for the sake of their souls. The Puritan and the Jesuit were strangely alike. Father Gerard, a Jesuit missionary in England, was an outlawed and hunted man. Once, in search of a hiding place, he came to the country house of an English Catholic only a few hours ahead of the law. At great risk to himself, his host offered Gerard sanctuary; as he led him up the stairs to a place of concealment, the hunted priest saw on the landing a stained-glass window in which was depicted a naked Venus. In outraged righteousness Gerard put his fist through the window and shouted that the sight of such nudity was blasphemous to God. The normal dictates of courtesy were not sufficient to restrain the man possessed of Truth.

Ignatious Jurdain was a Puritan member of the Elizabethan House of Commons and a merchant from Exeter. He was returning to his city in company with another member of Parliament, who invited him to lodge the night at his manor house. Jurdain's host was a country gentleman addicted to profanity, and the godly Puritan accepted the invitation only on condition that the squire, his wife, and servants refrain from using bad language in his presence, and that there be a godly sermon both at the parish church in the morning and at the manor house in the afternoon. Again the limits of hospitality were being strained by a man eaten up by the zeal of his faith. The similarity between the two extremes did not go unnoticed in the sixteenth century, and it was that "wisest fool in Christendom" and coiner of bons mots, James of Scotland, who noted that "one Puritan presbyter equals one papist priest." Both Elizabeth of England and Catherine de Médicis of France would have agreed fervently, though Philip of Spain undoubtedly would have missed the point.

128

PORTRAIT OF AN AGE

The Elizabethans were nothing if not communicative. The age's abundance of drama, poetry, and fiction attests to that. Along with this, they left behind millions of letters, pamphlets, broadsides, diaries, account books, journals, and contemporary histories, which tell us far more about the people of the time and their concerns than the age's nobler literature does.

The sixteenth-century English loved to write letters; Elizabeth sometimes wrote a dozen a day apparently without disrupting her busy schedule, and she liked receiving them so much, she specifically requested personal communiqués from absent courtiers. Aristocrats knew any letter might be intercepted —but they had to correspond, and so they used code numbers to designate important members of the court. Diarists abounded, and their journals have left a fascinating record of the day-to-day life of Elizabethan England. The affluence of the growing middle class gave them time to worry about "improving themselves," and they began to buy books and pamphlets that instructed them in every aspect of life from manners to morality. During the century their tastes widened, and their hunger for reading matter deepened, and hard-pressed printers managed to fill the bookstalls at St. Paul's with romances, jest books, histories, plays, prayer collections, and encyclopedias, all of which were eagerly purchased. Histories, whether legendary accounts of England's past or memoirs of the current reign, were very popular, and a number of notable historians appeared, who have greatly enriched our knowledge of the era. The widest possible spectrum of religious and political views was reflected in pamphlets and broadsides, which were the prototypes of newspapers. Usually written in ballad form, they recounted sensational crimes and grotesque events.

On the pages that follow, excerpts from the various literary forms of the age are presented in an anthology that depicts Elizabethan life in all its variety.

The happy couple opposite illustrated a popular Elizabethan ballad.

GLORIANA'S COURT

The backbiting and intrigues as well as the gaiety and grandeur of Elizabeth's court are revealed in the voluminous correspondence of courtiers and in other eye-witness accounts that have survived.

Queen and huntress

Tuesday, pleasant passing of the time with music and dancing: saving that toward night it liked Her Majesty to walk afoot into the chase over the bridge: where it pleased her to stand, while upon the pool out of a barge fine appointed for the purpose, to hear sundry kinds of a very delectable music; thus recreated, and after some walk, Her Highness returned. *Wednesday*, Her Majesty rode into the chase, ahunting again of the *hart of fors*. The deer, after his property, for refuge took the soil: but so mastered by hot pursuit on all parts, that he was taken quick in the pool. The watermen held him up hard by the head, while at Her Highness' commandment, he lost his ears for a ransom, and so had pardon of life.

from A letter: Wherein, part of the entertainment untoo the Queen Majesty . . . in this Soomerz Progress, 1575, is signified *by Robert Laneham*

The royal presence

We were admitted into the Presence Chamber, hung with rich tapestry, and the floor, after the English fashion, strewed with hay, through which the queen commonly passes in her way to chapel. At the door stood a gentleman dressed in velvet, with a gold chain, whose office was to introduce to the queen any person of distinction that came to wait on her. It was Sunday, when there is usually the greatest attendance of nobility. In the same hall were the archbishop of Canterbury, the bishop of London, a great number of councilors of state, officers of the crown, and gentlemen, who waited the queen's coming out; which she did from her own apartment when it was time to go to prayers, attended in the following manner:

First went gentlemen, barons, earls, knights of the Garter, all richly dressed and bareheaded; next came the Lord High Chancellor of England, bearing the seals in a red silk purse, between two, one of whom carried the royal scepter, the other the sword of state in a red scabbard studded with golden fleurs-de-lis, the point upwards. Next came the queen, in the sixty-fifth year of her age, as we were told, very majestic; her face oblong, fair, but wrinkled; her eyes small, yet black and pleasant; her nose a little hooked; her lips narrow, and her teeth black (a defect the English seem subject to, from their too great use of sugar). She had in her ears two pearls, with very rich drops. Her hair was of an auburn color, but false; upon her head she had a small crown. Her bosom was uncovered, as all the English ladies have it till they marry, and she had on a necklace of exceeding fine jewels. Her hands were slender, her fingers rather long, and her stature neither tall nor low. Her air was stately, her manner of speaking mild and obliging. That day she was dressed in white silk, bordered with pearls of the size of beans, and over it a mantle of black silk shot with silver threads; her train was very long, the end of it borne by a marchioness; instead of a chain, she had an oblong collar of gold and jewels.

The ladies of the court followed next to her, very hand-some and well shaped, and for the most part dressed in white. She was guarded on each side by the gentlemen pensioners, fifty in number, with gilt halberds. In the antechapel next the hall where we were, petitions were presented to her, and she received them most graciously, which occasioned the acclamation of "God save the Queen Elizabeth!" She answered it with, "I thank you, mine good people."

from an account of a visit to England in 1598 by a German traveler

The carter's indiscretion

The remove from this place [the royal residence of Hampton Court] is quite dashed, conformable to the speech of the carter, that three times had been at Windsor with his cart to carry away upon summons of a remove some part of the stuff of Her Majesty's wardrobe; and when he had repaired thither once, twice, and the third time, and that they of the wardrobe had told him the third time that the remove held not, clapping his hand on his thigh, said these words: "Now I see," quoth the carter, "that the queen is a woman as well as my wife." Which words being overheard by Her Majesty, who then stood at the window, she said: "What a villain is this?" and so sent him three angels to stop his mouth. Bryan Annesley, Francis Harvey, James Crofts, and John Parker, all four gentlemen-pensioners, three days agone were robbed, and in their absences at six of the clock at night their chamber door, which is in one of the five towers of the tiltyard, was broke open, and all their trunks likewise, out of all which the thieves took and carried away of jewels and ready money from these four to the value of 400 pounds and no news heard of them since. And surely I do not marvel at this, weighing the number of poor suitors, soldiers, and others . . . [without] a bit of bread to put in their mouths.

from Memoirs of the Reign of Queen Elizabeth, *edited by Thomas Birch*

Elizabeth's suitors

By and by after, comes Rambouillet from the French king, and a month after, Semier, from the duke of Anjou, a refined courtier, who was exquisite in the delights of love, and skillful in the ways of courtship . . . whom Queen Elizabeth received forthwith very lovingly at Richmond. Then began Leicester to grow discontented, seeing himself fallen from the hope which he had so long conceived to marry her . . .

from Annales: The true and royall history of the famous empress Elizabeth *by William Camden*

The troublesome Essex

Things have fallen out very strangely against me since last being with you. Yesternight the queen came to Worth Hall . . . She came to speak of Raleigh, and it seemed she could not well endure any thing to be spoken against him; and taking hold of one word, "disdain," she said there was no such cause why I should disdain him.

This speech troubled me so much that as near as I could I described unto her what he had been and what he was, and then I did let her see whether I had cause to disdain his competition of love, or whether I could have comfort to give myself over to the service of a mistress that was in awe of such a man.

I spake, what of grief and choler, as much against him as I could, and I think he standing at the door might very well hear the worse that I spoke of himself.

In the end I saw she was resolved to defend him, and to cross me . . . I told her . . . I had no joy to be in any place but loathe to be near about her when I knew my affection so much thrown down, and such a wretch as Raleigh highly esteemed of her.

To this she made no answer, but turned away to my lady of Warwick.

This strange alteration is by Raleigh's means, and the queen that hath tried all other ways now will see whether she can by these hard courses drive me to be friends with Raleigh, which rather shall drive me to many other extremities.

from the earl of Essex to Edward Dyer, July 21, 1587

A letter from Lady Leicester to her son, the earl of Essex

You gave us an alarm, sweet Robin, to make us believe we should see you. But I hope your stay is to your better contentment: otherwise you had made the company of Drayton proud with your presence. I shall exceedingly long to hear of your good satisfaction, which I wish might somewhat fit with your deserts and heart's desire, as my trust is it will for all the cross-working of your subtle enemies. My friend [her husband, Sir Christopher Blount] is now to come up very shortly to the term about some business; and were it not for the unseasonable time and foul traveling, I should accompany him to see you; especially if matters stood so well as you might hope to obtain some favor for us, then I would come also presently up: otherwise a country life is fittest for disgraced persons. But if you found reason to wish my coming, then must you presently send some coach horses to fetch me, for my own will never be able to draw me out of the mire. I pray you ask my sister of Warwick's counsel, and my sister Layton's in this case; and let me hear accordingly from you by this bearer. So wishing you as to my own heart, my dear son, I ever rest

Your mother
infinitely loving you,
L. Leicester

Sir Francis Bacon finally offers help to his jailed friend Essex, after not having communicated with him for nine months.

My Lord,

No man can better expound my doings than your lordship, which maketh me say the less. Only I humbly pray you to believe that I aspire to the conscience and commendation of first *bonus civis*, which with us is a good and true servant to the queen, and next of *bonus vir*, that is an honest man. I desire your lordship also to think that, though I confess I love some things much better than I love your lordship, as the queen's service, her quiet and contentment, her honor, her favor, the good of my country and the like, yet I love few persons better than yourself, both for gratitude's sake and for your own virtues, which cannot hurt but by accident or abuse. Of which my good affection I was ever and am ready to yield testimony by any good offices, but with such

reservations as yourself cannot but allow. For as I was ever sorry that your lordship should fly with waxen wings, doubting Icarus' fortune, so for the growing up of your own feathers—especially ostrich's or any other save of a bird of prey—no man shall be more glad. And this is the axle-tree whereupon I have turned and shall turn. Which to signify to you, though I think you are of yourself persuaded as much, is the cause of my writing. And so I commend your lordship to God's goodness. From Gray's Inn, this 20th day of July, 1600.

Your lordship's most humbly,
Fr. Bacon

Essex doubts Bacon's friendship, but accepts his offer of help.

Mr. Bacon,

I can neither expound nor censure your late actions, being ignorant of them all save one [Bacon had attacked Essex before the royal councilors], and having directed my sight inward only to examine myself. . . . Your profession of affection and your offer of good offices are welcome to me. For answer to them I will say but this: that you have believed I have been kind to you, and you may believe that I cannot be other, either upon humor or mine own election. I am a stranger to all poetical conceits, or else I should say somewhat of your poetical example. But this I must say, that I never flew with other wings than desire to merit, and confidence in my sovereign's favor, and when one of these wings failed me, I would light nowhere but at my sovereign's feet, though she suffered me to be bruised with my fall. And till Her Majesty—that knows I was never bird of prey—finds it to agree with her will and her service that my wings should be imped [repaired] again, I have committed myself to the mue [cage]. No power but my God's and my sovereign's can alter this resolution of

Your retired friend,
Essex

Mr. Davison writes his father that he understands his disappointment about the preferment of Robert Cecil to the post of secretary to the queen.

Miserable estate of times, and more miserable estate of men that live in them, where great virtue is a man's ruin; either none or else ill merits the highway to advancement, and a man's noblest and most glorious actions nothing but weighs to thrust down himself and his friends, and bring up his enemies in the balance of his prince's favor! But my noble lord [of Essex], I doubt not, being rooted in Her Majesty's favor and countenance by so great an enterprise as this his journey hath fallen out to be, will be able himself to ride out both this and any other storm, as well as he hath done those heretofore. But whether he shall be able to bring in any of his friends to strengthen him (of which all the world thinks he hath need) or keep out his greatest enemies who will seek by all possible means to overthrow him, I now neither see nor hope for. I write perhaps more liberally than the dangers letters are subject to would permit. But where good words will prevail, nothing, nor ill can reduce a man into worse estate than he is in, there is both want of judgment and liberty not to disburden his own passions.

from Memoirs of the Reign of Queen Elizabeth,
edited by Thomas Birch

A COURTIER IN EXILE

The courtier Sir Robert Sydney was often out of favor with the queen, and on occasion was barred from England. His friend Rowland Whyte kept Sydney well informed and pressed his suits at court. A sampling of Whyte's many letters to Sydney is presented here.

To Mr. Secretary I first delivered your letter, which, when he had read, he used these words unto me: "If you mistrust me with the delivering of the letter to the Lords, you may deliver it yourself." But, observing in his words and countenance some dislike, I answered him thus: "I am very sorry your honor should have any such opinion of me, seeing by my lord governor's directions I am expressly commanded to deliver it to your honor's hands, unless it were your pleasure I might deliver it at the Council board." He then took the letter of me and said that I should have a test for the receipt of it.

My lord of Essex comes out of his chamber in his gown and night cap. I presented your humble service unto him, and acquainted him with your letter to the Lords, and delivered to Mr. Secretary. He said that he made no doubt but you would give good reason for the thing the queen much blamed you for here . . .

There is a Flushing skipper here that hath had often conference with his lordship, who is lodged and dieted upon his charges in a victualing house by Charing Cross, where, I hear, he domineers and means to drink my lord out of debt. He is said to come from you.

Full fourteen days his lordship [Essex] kept in; Her Majesty, as I heard, resolved to break him of his will and to pull down his great heart, who found it a thing impossible, and says he holds it from the mother's side; but all is well again, and no doubt he will grow a mighty man in our state.

My lord of Cumberland makes some doubt of his going to sea because my Lord Thomas Howard and Sir Walter Raleigh were to be joined with him in equal authority. The queen told him of it, and he to herself, refuses to go, which he was well chidden for.

Mr. Smith told me that the queen, in words to him, did blame you about the shipping passed for Spain; but he tells me that you were not by any letter you had from the Lords, warranted to stay them by force . . .

January, 1597

My Lord Treasurer told me this evening that the queen will not grant your leave in these doubtful times of war and peace, which he is sorry for; that the queen is made acquainted with your letter about the merchants coming to Flushing, but she likes it not; that he will write unto you himself more of it. You see one day brings forth hope, the other despair. It should seem there is a constant revolution to keep you away. Here is a speech that Sir Edward Stafford shall be sworn a councilor to attend Her Majesty's service in Mr. Secretary's absence; but I will believe it when it is done.

A chief servant of 200 [Sir Robert Cecil] bid me assure myself that if you have leave to come over, you shall assuredly be pushed over to Ireland, but I see no probability of it.

My Lord Herbert is dead, my lord of Worcester's son. My Lord Mountjoy is not half well. My lord of Sussex in parting two of his men that quarreled, run one of them through with his rapier, but it is hoped he will live. My Lord Rutland, as I hear, is waxen more cold in the matter of marriage with your niece.

The quarrel of my Lord Southampton to Ambrose Willoughby grew upon this. That he, with Sir Walter Raleigh, and Mr. Parker, being at primero [a game of cards] in the Presence Chamber, the queen was gone to bed; and he being there, as Squire for the Body, desired them to give over. Soon after he spoke to them again, that if they would not leave, he would call in the guard to pull down the board, which Sir Walter Raleigh seeing, put up his money and went his ways. But my Lord Southampton took exceptions at him and told him he would remember it; and so finding him between the tennis court wall and the garden, struck him, and Willoughby pulled off some of his locks.

The queen gave Willoughby thanks for what he did in the Presence and told him he had done better, if he had sent him to the porter's lodge to see who durst have fetched him out.

Summer, 1599

Nine thousand [Lord Herbert] is highly favored by 1500 [the queen] for at his departure he had access unto her and was private an hour; but he greatly wants advice and extremely longs for you here. This day he is gone to see 2000 [the earl of Pembroke's father], but will be here again before Christmas. He bids me assure you privately that he will undertake to bring 2000 to resign over unto you presently, the place desired by you [i.e. to be appointed Lord President of Wales], if you found yourself strong in friends at 160 [the court] to compass it. He desires it above all things, and the matter is of greatest moment; and his offer and care to be exceedingly respected. But in my opinion it is not to be stirred in, but when you are present. And you have this to grace you that you have done Her Majesty great service in her wars and employments with foreign princes; that you never received denied, I shall think you will never obtain any suit. Nine any reward; that this being a voluntary resignation, if it be thousand is very well beloved here of all, especially by 200 [Sir Robert Cecil], and 40 [Sir Walter Raleigh], who protests in all places they love him. I have some cause to believe that 600 [the earl of Nottingham] would desire to have him match in his house. I only answer that a fitter instrument than yourself cannot be found out, if you may be brought to deal in it, which peradventure you might do, if you were here.

My lady was this morning brought safely to bed of a goodly girl; and God be thanked her pains were but short.

My Lord,

Here is Sir William Russell come, but for anything I see, the great places being disposed of, he is to be either a lieutenant general to the General of Horse, or Foot; but he stands to have a better place or to accept of none. All the noblemen of England are sent for to be here by the twentieth of this month to attend Her Majesty's person with horse and foot. . . . Dispatches are made and sent every way, and all the clerks of Council, Signet, and Privy Seal even wearied and tired with writing. Mr. Beale and Mr. Mainard and Mr. Secretary himself doth take exceeding pains and is not able to endure it long.

My lord of Worcester helping the queen from her horse, it trod on his foot, and this morning she went to see him but it is no great matter. Here is just come news from my lord of Essex that he hath given some overthrow to the rebel at Ophale, and that part of Connaught is revolted from the rebel and come to Her Majesty's obedience. I do verily believe that if the Spaniards land here you will be sent for. Nonsuch, this Sunday noon, August 5, 1599.

GUIDES TO CONDUCT

Everyone gave counsel, and if no one followed it, many at least seemed willing to listen. Noblemen penned instructions to their sons, while middle-class lads were forced to resort to books for advice; these were available on almost every subject. The most popular topics were how to choose a wife and how to run a family. Some of the differences and similarities between upper- and middle-class attitudes are apparent in the selections that are presented here.

Fatherly admonitions
Son Robert . . .

I think it fit and agreeable to the affection I bear to help thee with such advertisements and rules for the squaring of thy life as are gained rather by much experience than long reading, to the end that thou, entering into this exorbitant age, mayest be the better prepared to shun those cautelous courses whereinto this world and thy lack of experience may easily draw thee. And because I will not confound thy memory, I have reduced them into ten precepts, and next unto Moses' tables, if thou do imprint them in thy mind, then shalt [thou] reap the benefit and I the contentment. And these are they.

1. When it shall please God to bring thee to man's estate, use great providence and circumspection in the choice of thy wife, for from thence may spring all thy future good or ill; and it is an action like a stratagem in war where man can err but once. If thy estate be good, match near home and at leisure; if weak, then far off and quickly. Inquire diligently of her disposition and how her parents have been inclined in their youth. Let her not be poor how generous soever, for a man can buy nothing in the market with gentility. Neither choose a base and uncomely creature altogether for wealth, for it will cause contempt in others and loathing in thee. Make not choice of a dwarf or a fool, for from the one thou mayest beget a race of pygmies, the other may be thy daily disgrace; for it will irk thee to have her talk, for then thou shalt find to thy great grief that there is nothing more fulsome than a she-fool. Touching the government of thy house, let thy hospitality be moderate and according to the measure of thine own estate, rather plentiful than sparing— but not too costly—for I never knew any grow poor by keeping an orderly table. But some consume themselves through secret vices and their hospitality must bear the blame. Banish swinish drunkards out of thy house, which is a vice that impairs health, consumes much, and makes no show, for I never knew any praise ascribed to a drunkard but the well-bearing of drink, which is a better commendation for a brewer's horse or a drayman than for either gentleman or servingman. Beware that thou spend not above three of the four parts of thy revenue, nor above one-third part of that in thine house, for the other two parts will do no more than defray thy extraordinaries, which will always surmount thy ordinaries by much. For otherwise shalt thou live like a rich beggar in continual want, and the needy man can never live happily nor contented, for then every least disaster makes him ready either to mortgage or to sell, and that gentleman which then sells an acre of land loses an ounce of credit, for gentility is nothing but ancient riches. So that if the foundations sink, the building must needs consequently fail.

2. Bring thy children up in learning and obedience yet without austerity; praise them openly; reprehend them secretly; give them good countenance and convenient maintenance according to thy ability; for otherwise thy life will seem their bondage, and then what portion thou shalt leave them at thy death they may thank death for it and not thee. And I am verily persuaded that the foolish cockering of some parents and the overstern carriage of others causeth more men and women to take evil courses than naturally their own vicious inclinations. Marry thy daughters in time, lest they marry themselves. Suffer not thy sons to pass the Alps, for they shall learn nothing but pride, blasphemy, and atheism. And if by travel they attain to some few broken languages, they will profit them no more than to have one meat served in diverse dishes. Neither by my advice shalt thou train them up to wars, for he that sets up his rest only to live by that profession can hardly be an honest man or good Christian, for war is of itself unjust unless the good cause may make it just. Besides it is a science no longer in request than use, for "soldiers in peace are like chimneys in summer." . . .

4. Let thy kindred and allies be welcome to thy table, grace them with thy countenance, and ever further them in all honest actions, for by that means thou shalt so double the bond of nature as thou shalt find them so many advocates to plead an apology for thee behind thy back. But shake off these glowworms—I mean parasites and sycophants—who will feed and fawn upon thee in the summer of prosperity, but in any adverse storm they will shelter thee no more than an arbor in winter.

5. Beware of suretyship for thy best friend, for he which payeth another man's debts seeks his own decay; but if thou canst not otherwise choose, then rather lend that money from thyself upon good bond though thou borrow it, so mayest thou pleasure thy friend and happily also secure thyself. Neither borrow money of a neighbor or friend but rather from a mere stranger, where paying for it thou mayest hear

no more of it, for otherwise thou shalt eclipse thy credit, lose thy freedom, and yet pay to him as dear as to the other. In borrowing of money be ever precious of thy word, for he that cares to keep day of payment is lord commander many times in another man's goods. . . .

7. Be sure ever to keep some great man thy friend, but trouble him not for trifles, compliment him often, present [him] with many yet small gifts and of little charge, and if thou have cause to bestow any great gratuity let it then be some such thing as may be daily in sight, for otherwise in this ambitious age thou mayest remain like a hop without a pole, live in obscurity, and be made a football for every insulting companion to spurn at.

8. Toward thy superiors be humble yet generous; with thy equals familiar yet respective; towards inferiors show much humility and some familiarity, as to bow thy body, stretch forth thy hand, and to uncover thy head, and suchlike popular compliments. The first prepares a way to advancement; the second makes thee known for a man well-bred; the third gains a good report which once gotten may be safely kept, for high humilities take such root in the minds of the multitude as they are more easilier won by unprofitable courtesies than churlish benefits. Yet do I advise thee not to affect nor neglect popularity too much. Seek not to be E. [Essex] and shun to be R. [Raleigh]. . . .

10. Be not scurrilous in conversation nor stoical in thy jests; the one may make thee unwelcome to all companies, the other pull on quarrels and yet the hatred of thy best friends. Jests when they savor too much of truth leave a bitterness in the mind of those that are touched. And although I have already pointed all this inclusive, yet I think it necessary to leave it thee as a caution, because I have seen many so prone to quip and gird as they would rather lose their friend than their jests, and if by chance their boiling brain yield a quaint scoff they will travail to be delivered of it as a woman with child. Those nimble apprehensions are but the froth of wit.

Lord Burghley's letter of advice to his son

Choosing a wife

. . . although I persuade thee to associate thyself with thy betters, or at least with thy peers, yet remember always that thou venture not thy estate with any of those great ones that shall attempt unlawful things, for such men labor for themselves and not for thee. Thou shalt be sure to part with them in the danger but not in the honor, and to venture a sure estate in present in hope of a better in future is mere madness. And great men forget such as have done them service when they have obtained what they would, and will rather hate thee for saying thou hast been a mean of their advancement than acknowledge it. I could give thee a thousand examples, and I myself know it and have tasted it in all the course of my life. When thou shalt read and observe the stories of all nations, thou shalt find innumerable examples of the like. Let thy love, therefore, be to the best so long as they do well, but take heed that thou love God, thy country, thy prince, and thine own estate before all others, for the fancies of men change and he that loves today hateth tomorrow. But let reason be thy schoolmistress, which shall ever guide thee aright.

The next and greatest care ought to be in choice of a wife,

and the only danger therein is beauty, by which all men in all ages, wise and foolish, have been betrayed. And although I know it vain to use reasons or arguments to dissuade thee from being captivated therewith, there being few or none that ever resisted that witchery, yet I cannot omit to warn thee as of other things which may be thy ruin and destruction. For the present time it is true that every man prefers his fantasy in that appetite before all other worldly desires, leaving the care of honor, credit, and safety in respect thereof. But remember that though these affections do not last, yet the bond of marriage dureth to the end of thy life; and therefore better to be borne withal in a mistress than in a wife, for when thy humor shall change thou art yet free to choose again (if thou give thyself that vain liberty). Remember, secondly, that if thou marry for beauty thou bindest thyself for all thy life for that which perchance will neither last nor please thee one year; and when thou hast it, it will be unto thee of no price at all, for the desire dieth when it is attained and the affection perisheth when it is satisfied. . . .

Yet I wish thee above all the rest, have care thou dost not marry an uncomely woman for any respect, for comeliness in children is riches if nothing else be left them. And if thou have care for thy races of horses and other beasts, value the shape and comeliness of thy children before alliances or riches. Have care, therefore, of both together, for if thou have a fair wife and a poor one, if thine own estate be not great, assure thyself that love abideth not with want, for she is the companion of plenty and honor, for I never yet knew a poor woman exceeding fair that was not made dishonest by one or other in the end. . . .

Have, therefore, evermore care that thou be beloved of thy wife rather than thyself besotted on her, and thou shalt judge of her love by these two observations: first, if thou perceive she have care of thy estate and exercise herself therein; the other, if she study to please thee and be sweet unto thee in conversation without thy instruction, for love needs no teaching nor precept. On the other side, be not sour nor stern to thy wife, for cruelty engendereth no other thing than hatred. Let her have equal part of thy estate whilst thou livest if thou find her sparing and honest; but what thou givest after thy death, remember that thou givest it to a stranger and most times to an enemy, for he that shall marry thy wife will despise thee, thy memory, and thine, and shall possess the quiet of thy labors, the fruit which thou hast planted, enjoy thy love, and spend with joy and ease what thou hast spared and gotten with care and travail. Yet always remember that thou leave not thy wife to be a shame unto thee after thou art dead, but that she may live according to thy estate, especially if thou hast few children and them provided for. But howsoever it be or whatsoever thou find, leave thy wife no more than of necessity thou must, but only during her widowhood; for if she love again, let her not enjoy her second love in the same bed wherein she loved thee nor fly to future pleasures with those feathers which death hath pulled from thy wings; but leave thy estate to thy house and children in which thou livest upon earth whilst it lasteth. To conclude, wives were ordained to continue the generations of men . . . therefore thy house and estate, which liveth in thy son and not in thy wife, is to be preferred.

from Instructions to His Son and to Posterity *by Raleigh*

The drunkard's lot

Take especial care that thou delight not in wine, for there never was any man that came to honor or preferment that loved it; for it transformeth a man into a beast, decayeth health, poisoneth the breath, destroyeth natural heat, brings a man's stomach to an artificial heat, deformeth the face, rotteth the teeth, and, to conclude, maketh a man contemptible, soon old and despised of all wise and worthy men, hated in thy servants, in thyself, and companions, for it is a bewitching and infectious vice.

from Instructions to His Son and
to Posterity *by Raleigh*

The deportment of women

Instead of song and music let them [housewives] learn cookery and laundry. And instead of reading Sir Philip Sidney's *Arcadia* let them read the grounds of good housewifery. I like not a female poetess at any hand. Let greater personages glory their skill in music, the posture of their bodies, their knowledge in languages, the greatness and freedom of their spirits, and their arts in arraigning of men's affections at their flattering faces: this is not the way to breed a private gentleman's daughter.

from Tom of all trades, or the plaine path-way
to preferment *by Thomas Powell*

Husbandly duties

The duties of a husband toward his wife are . . . (1) The first that he give honor to his wife as the weaker vessel, for she is partaker of the grace of life. (2) The second, he must patiently brook the hastiness of his wife, for there is nothing in the world more spiteful than a woman if she be hardly dealt withal, or egged to indignation. (3) The third duty, the husband in any case must not have carnal copulation with any other but his own wife. A woman is jealous and naturally suspicious, and, sith her husband breaketh with her, she will not stick to break with him and privily borrow a night's lodging with her neighbor. (4) The fourth duty, the husband must not injury his wife by word or deed, for a woman is a feeble creature and not endued with such a noble courage as the man; she is sooner pricked to the heart, or moved to passions, than man; and again, he that injurieth his wife, doth as if he should spit into the air and the same spittle return back upon his own self. (5) The fifth, the husband, in disputations with his wife, must sometimes confess himself vanquished by her. . . .

from The golden-grove *by William Vaughan*

Wives must not speak too familiarly to their spouses.

Remember the fearful issue that had like to have fallen out by reason of such compellations given by Sarah and Rebekah to their husbands. Not unlike to those are such as these, *Sweet, Sweeting, Heart, Sweetheart, Love, Joy, Dear,* etc., and such as these, *Duck, Chick, Pigsney,* etc., husbands' Christian names, as *John, Thomas, William, Henry,* etc., which if they be contracted (as many use to contract them thus, *Jack, Tom, Will, Hal*) they are much more unseemly: servants are usually so called. But what may we say of those titles given to a husband by his wife, not seldom in passion, but usually in ordinary speech, which are not fit to be given to the basest men that be, as *Grub, Rogue,* and the like, which I am even ashamed to name . . .

from Of domesticall duties *by Reverend William Gouge*

Intermarriage between social classes is bad.

For men will sooner match their daughters with my young master, a rich cobbler's son, though they be their heirs, than with a gentleman of a good house, being a younger brother, hereby comes the decay of ancient gentility, and this the making of upstart houses . . . But full of covetousness, that is the root of all mischief; for men that have enough to make their daughters gentlewomen, by matching them with houses of no small antiquity, will, with the desire they have thereunto, woo men of great living with large offers, to match their sons and heirs with them . . .

from an anonymously written pamphlet,
The passionate Morrice

An unhappy marriage can be avoided.

The first cause . . . is a constrained love, when as parents do by compulsion couple two bodies, neither respecting the joining of their hearts, nor having any care of the continuance of their welfare, but more regarding the linking of wealth and money together, then of love with honesty: will force affection without liking, and cause love with jealousy. For either they marry their children in their infancy, when they are not able to know what love is, or else match them with inequality, joining burning summer with sea-cold winter, their daughters of twenty years old or under, to rich cormorants of threescore or upwards.

from an anonymously written pamphlet,
Tell-trothes new yeares gift

On very rare occasions wife-beating may be in order.

But if she will rail upon him with most reproachful terms, if she will affront him with bold and impudent resistances, if she will tell him to his teeth that she cares not for him, and that she will do as she lusts for all him; if she will fly in his face with violence, and begin to strike him, or break into such unwomanly words or behavior; then let him bear a while, and admonish and exhort, and pray; but if still she persist against reproofs and persuasion, if her father be living, let him be entreated to fight; if she have none, or he cannot, or will not, I think the husband shall not offend, in using a fool according to her folly, a child in understanding; like a child in years, and a woman of base and servile condition in base and servile manner.

from A bride-bush: or, a direction for married persons
by William Whately

135

LIFE IN ENGLAND

The infinite variety of Elizabethan thought and activity was captured by contemporary diarists and registrars as well as historians.

Physical perfection

Such as are bred in this island are men for the most part of a good complexion, tall of stature, strong in body, white of color, and thereto of great boldness and courage in the wars. As for their general comeliness of person, the testimony of Gregory the Great, at such time as he saw English captives sold at Rome, shall easily confirm what it is, which yet doth differ in sundry shires and soils, as also their proportion of members. . . . Such hath been the estimation of our soldiers from time to time, since our isle hath been known unto the Romans, that wheresoever they have served in foreign countries, the chief brunts of service have been reserved unto them. Of their conquests and bloody battles won in France, Germany, and Scotland, our victories are full: and where they have been overcome, the victors themselves confessed their victories to have been so dearly bought that they would not gladly covet to overcome often after such difficult manner. In martial prowess there is little or no difference between Englishmen and Scots: for albeit that the Scots have been often and very grievously overcome by the force of our nation, it hath not been for want of manhood on their parts but through the mercy of God showed on us, and his justice upon them, since they always have begun the quarrels and offered us mere injury with great despite and cruelty.

England as a fountain of youth

The comeliness of our living bodies do continue from middle age (for the most) even to the last gasp, specially in mankind. And albeit that our women through bearing of children do after forty begin to wrinkle apace, yet are they not commonly so wretched and hard favored to look upon in their age, as the French women, and diverse of other countries with whom their men also do much participate; and thereto be so often wayward and peevish that nothing in manner may content them.

I might here add somewhat also of the mean stature generally of our women, whose beauty commonly exceedeth the fairest of those of the main, their comeliness of person and good proposition of limbs, most of theirs that come over unto us from beyond the seas.

both from The Description of England *by William Harrison*

Ladies of leisure

Although the women there are entirely in the power of their husbands except for their lives, yet they are not kept so strictly as they are in Spain or elsewhere. Nor are they shut up, but they have the free management of the house or housekeeping, after the fashion of those of the Netherlands and others their neighbors. They go to market to buy what they like best to eat. They are well dressed, fond of taking it easy, and commonly leave the care of household matters and drudgery to their servants. They sit before their doors, decked out in fine clothes, in order to see and be seen by the passers-by. In all banquets and feasts they are shown the greatest honor; they are placed at the upper end of the table, where they are the first served; at the lower end they help the men. All the rest of their time they employ in walking and riding, in playing at cards or otherwise, in visiting their friends and keeping company, conversing with their equals (whom they term "gossips") and their neighbors, and making merry with them at childbirths, christenings, churchings, and funerals; and all this with the permission and knowledge of their husbands, as such is the custom. Although the husbands often recommend to them the pains, industry, and care of the German or Dutch women, who do what men ought to do both in the house and in the shops, for which services in England men are employed, nevertheless the women usually persist in retaining their customs. This is why England is called "The Paradise of Married Women."

from an account of a visit to England by Emanuel van Meteren

Subjects of the realm

The multitude (or whole body) of this populous city is two ways to be considered, generally and specially: generally they be natural subjects, a part of the commons of this realm, and are by birth for the most part a mixture of all countries of the same, by blood gentlemen, yeomen, and of the basest sort, without distinction: and by profession busy bees, and travelers for their living in the hive of this commonwealth; but specially considered, they consist of these three parts, merchants, handicraftsmen, and laborers. Merchandise is also divided into these three sorts, navigation—by the which merchandises are brought and carried in and out over the seas—invection—by the which commodities are gathered into the city and dispersed from thence into the country by land—and negotiation, which I may call the keeping of a retailing or standing shop. In common speech they of the first sort be called merchants, and both the other retailers. Handicraftsmen by those which do exercise such arts as require both labor and cunning as goldsmiths, tailors, and haberdashers, skinners, etc. Laborers and hirelings I call those *quorum opere non artes emuntur*, as Tullie sayeth, of which sort be porters, carmen, watermen, etc. Again these three sorts may be considered either in respect of their wealth, or number: in wealth, merchants and some of the chief retailers have the first place; the most part of retailers have the first place; the most part of retailers and all artificers, the second or mean place; and hirelings the lowest room: but in number they of the middle place be first and do far exceed both the rest: hirelings be next, and merchants be the last.

from A Survay of London *by John Stow*

A comparison of London with Paris

. . . instead of a beastly town and dirty streets, you have in London those that be fair, beautiful, and cleanly kept; instead of foggy mists and clouds, ill air, flat situation, miry springs, and a kind of staining clay, you have in London a sun-shining and serene element for the most part, a wholesome dwelling, stately ascension, and delicate prospect; instead of a shallow, narrow, and sometimes dangerous river, bringing only barges and boats with wood, coal, turf, and such country provision, you have at London a river flowing twenty foot, and full of stately ships that fly to us with merchandise from all the ports of the world, the sight yielding astonishment, and the use perpetual comfort.

from The Glory of England *by Thomas Gainsford*

English weather
This year [1590] in the month of May fell many great showers of rain, but in the months of June and July much more, for it commonly rained every day or night . . . in the month of August, there followed a fair harvest, but in the month of September fell great rains, which raised high waters, such as stayed the carriages and bare down bridges at Cambridge, Ware, and elsewhere.

from Annales of England *by John Stow*

London traffic
The number of cars, drays, carts, and coaches more than hath been accustomed, the streets and lanes being straitened, must needs be dangerous, as daily experience proveth. The coachman rides behind the horse tails, lasheth them and looketh not behind him; the drayman sitteth and sleepeth on his dray and letteth his horse lead him home. I know that by the good laws and customs of this city, shod carts are forbidden to enter the same except upon reasonable causes, as service of the prince or suchlike, they be tolerated; also that the forehorse of every carriage should be led by hand —but these good orders are not observed. Now of late years the use of coaches brought out of Germany is taken up and made so common as there is neither distinction of time nor difference of persons observed; for the world runs on wheels with many whose parents were glad to go on foot.

from A Survay of London *by John Stow*

Sweet charity
In London, and other such places, it would move a stony heart to hear one crying up and down the streets, "Bread and meat for the poor prisoners of Newgate, for Christ Jesus' sake!", and the prisoners crying out of their grates and holes, "One penny or half-penny, for Christ His sake, to buy some bread, to buy some bread!"

from The rowsing of the sluggard *by William Burton*

The playgoers
In our assemblies at plays in London you shall see such heaving and shoving, such itching and shouldering, to sit by women—such care for their garments, that they be not trod on—such eyes to their laps that no chips light in them —such pillows to their backs that they take no hurt—such masking in their ears I know not what—such giving them pippins to pass the time—such playing at foot-saunt without cards—such ticking, such toying, such smiling, such winking, and such manning them home when the sports are ended.

from The schoole of abuse *by Stephen Gosson*

The wicked theatre
Sundry great disorders and inconveniencies have been found to ensue to this city by the inordinate haunting of great multitudes of people, especially youth, to plays, interludes, and shows—namely, occasion of frays and quarrels; evil practices of incontinency in great inns having chambers and secret places adjoining to their open stages and galleries; inveigling and alluring of maids, specially orphans and good citizens' children under age, to privy and unmeet contracts; the publishing of unchaste, uncomely, and unshamefast speeches and doings; withdrawing of the queen's majesty's subjects from divine service on Sundays and holidays, at which times such plays were chiefly used; unthrifty waste of the money of the poor and fond persons; sundry robberies by picking and cutting of purses; uttering of popular, busy, and seditious matters; and many other corruptions of youth and other enormities—besides that also sundry slaughters and mayhemings of the queen's subjects have happened by ruins of scaffolds, frames, and stages, and by engines, weapons, and powder used in plays.

from an act of the Common Council, December 6, 1574

A new play   *February 2, 1601*
At our feast [at the Inns of Court] we had a play called *Twelfth Night, or What You Will*, much like the *Comedy of Errors*, or *Menaechmi* in Plautus, but most like and near to that in Italian called *Inganni*. A good practice in it to make the steward believe his lady widow was in love with him by counterfeiting a letter as from his lady in general terms, telling him what she liked best in him, and prescribing his gesture in smiling, his apparel, etc., and then when he came to practice making him believe they took him to be mad.

A goodly sport
Turner and Dun, two famous fencers, played their prizes this day at the Bankside, but Turner at last ran Dun so far in the brain at the eye that he fell down presently stone dead; a goodly sport in a Christian state, to see one man kill another!

both from the diary of John Manningham, a law student

Water for Londoners
This year Bevis Bulmar, a most ingenious gentleman, set up an engine at Brokenwharf, thereby, from thence to convey Thames water up into the city, sufficient to serve the whole west part thereof, being conveyed into men's houses by pipes of lead.

from Annales of England *by John Stow*

EVIL TIMES

Nations are never perfect, and Elizabethan England was no exception. Disease, dearth, social ills, and moral laxity were common, and the plague, as described here, was an ever-present threat.

The purple whip of vengeance, the plague, having beaten many thousands of men, women, and children to death, and still marking the people of this city every week by hundreds for the grave, is the only cause that all her inhabitants walk up and down like mourners at some great solemn funeral, the City herself being the chief mourners. The poison of this lingering infection strikes so deep into all men's hearts that their cheeks, like cowardly soldiers, have lost their colors; their eyes, as if they were in debt and durst not look abroad, do scarce peep out of their heads; and their tongues, like physicians ill-paid, give but cold comfort. By the power of their pestilent charms all merry meetings are cut off, all frolic assemblies dissolved, and in their circles are raised up the black, sullen, and dogged spirits of sadness, of melancholy, and so, consequently, of mischief. Mirth is departed and lies dead and buried in men's bosoms; laughter dares not look a man in the face; jests are, like music to the deaf, not regarded; pleasure itself finds now no pleasure but in sighing and bewailing the miseries of the time. For, alack! what string is there now to be played upon whose touch can make us merry? Playhouses stand like taverns that have cast out their masters, the doors locked up, the flags, like their bushes, taken down—or rather like houses lately infected, from whence the affrighted dwellers are fled, in hope to live better in the country.

from Worke for armorours *by Thomas Dekker*

What an unmatchable torment were it for a man to be barred up every night in a vast silent charnel house—hung (to make it more hideous) with lamps dimly and slowly burning in hollow and glimmering corners; where all the pavement should, instead of green rushes, be strewed with blasted rosemary, withered hyacinths, fatal cypress, and yew, thickly mingled with heaps of dead men's bones; the bare ribs of a father that begat him lying there, here the chapless hollow skull of a mother that bore him; round about him a thousand corses [bodies], some standing bolt upright in their knotted winding sheets, others half-mouldered in rotten coffins that should suddenly yawn wide open, filling his nostrils with noisome stench and his eyes with the sight of nothing but crawling worms; and to keep such a poor wretch waking, he should hear no noise but of toads croaking, screech owls howling, mandrakes shrieking! Were not this an infernal prison? Would not the strongest-hearted man (beset with such a ghastly horror) look wild, and run mad, and die?

And even such a formidable shape did the diseased city appear in. For he that durst (in the dead hour of gloomy midnight) have been so valiant as to have walked through the still and melancholy streets, what think you should have been his music? Surely the loud groans of raving sick men, the struggling pangs of souls departing—in every house grief striking up an alarm, servants crying out for masters, wives for husbands, parents for children, children for their mothers. Here he should have met some franticly running to knock up sextons; there, others fearfully sweating with coffins, to steal forth dead bodies lest the fatal handwriting of death should seal up their doors. And to make this dismal consort more full, round about him bells heavily tolling in one place and ringing out in another. The dreadfulness of such an hour is unutterable.

from The wonderfull yeare *by Thomas Dekker*

The land-grabbers

There is no life more pleasant than a yeoman's life, but nowadays yeomanry is decayed, hospitality gone to wrack, and husbandry almost quite fallen. The reason is because landlords, not contented with such revenues as their predecessors received, nor yet satisfied that they live like swinish epicures quietly at their ease, doing no good to the commonwealth, do leave no ground for tillage, but do enclose for pasture many thousand acres of ground within one hedge, the husbandmen are thrust out of their own, or else by deceit constrained to sell all that they have.

from The golden-grove *by William Vaughan*

Religious decline

And for my parishioners, they are a kind of people that love a pot of ale better than a pulpit, and a corn rick better than a church door, who, coming to divine service more for fashion than devotion, are contented after a little capping and kneeling, coughing and spitting, to help me to sing out a psalm, and sleep at the second lesson, or awake to stand up at the gospel, and say "Amen" at the peace of God, and stay till the banns of matrimony be asked, or till the clerk have cried a pied stray bullock, a black sheep or a gray mare, and then, for that some dwell far off, be glad to be gotten home to dinner. *from* A merrie dialogue betwixt the taker and mistaker *by Nicholas Breton*

Vanity and venery

Dr. Dene made a sermon against the excessive pride and vanity of women in apparel, etc., which vice he said was in their husbands' power to correct. This man the last time he was in this place taught that a man could not be divorced from his wife, though she should commit adultery.

He reprehended Mr. Egerton, and such another popular preacher, that their auditory, being most of women, abounded in that superfluous vanity of apparel.

from the diary of John Manningham, a law student

A warning to profiteers

Because of the great dearth of corn this year proclamation is made against those ingrossers, forestallers, and ingraters of corn that increase the price of corn by spreading a false report that much quantity of corn is being carried out of the realm by sea and thereby occasion given of want. Likewise it is straitly forbidden to carry any corn by sea out of the realm. Moreover sundry persons of ability that had intended to save their charges by living privately in London or towns corporate, thereby leaving their hospitality and the relief of their poor neighbors, are charged not to break up their households; and all others that have of late time broken up their households to return to their houses again without delay.

Royal proclamation, 1596

KNAVES AND NE'ER-DO-WELLS

A large, active criminal class fascinated both writers and readers.

A Ruffler goeth with a weapon to seek service, saying he hath been a servitor in the wars, and beggeth for his relief. But his chiefest trade is to rob poor wayfaring men and market women.

A Prigman goeth with a stick in his hand like an idle person. His property is to steal clothes off the hedge, which they call "storing of the rogueman."

A Whipjack is one that, by color of a counterfeit license (which they call a "gibe," and the seals they call "jarks"), doth use to beg like a mariner; but his chiefest trade is to rob booths in a fair, or to pilfer ware from stalls, which they call "heaving of the booth."

A Frater goeth with a like license to beg for some spittal-house or hospital. Their prey is commonly upon poor women as they go and come to the markets.

A Quire Bird is one that came lately out of prison, and goeth to seek service. He is commonly a stealer of horses, which they term a "prigger of palfreys."

An Upright Man is one that goeth with the truncheon of a staff, which staff thay call a "filchman." This man is of so much authority that, meeting with any of his profession, he may call them to account and command a share or "snap" unto himself of all that they have gained by their trade in one month. And if he do them wrong, they have no remedy against him—no, though he beat them, as he useth commonly to do. He may also command any of their women, which they call "doxies," to serve his turn. He hath the chief place at any market walk and other assemblies, and is not of any to be controlled.

from The fraternitye of vacabondes *by John Awdeley*

The folly of fair-going

Let my pen gallop over a few lines, and it shall bring you, without spurring, swiftlier into Gloucestershire than if you rode upon Pacolet. There if you please to alight near Tewkesbury, at a place called Durrest Fair (being kept there upon the two Holy Rood days), you shall see more rogues than ever were whipped at a cart's arse through London, and more beggars than ever came dropping out of Ireland. If you look upon them, you would think you lived in Henry VI's time, and that Jack Cade and his rebellious ragamuffins were there mustering. And these swarms of locusts come to this lousy fair from all parts of the land within a hundred miles' compass. To describe the booths is lost labor, for, let the hangman show but his wardrobe, and there is not a rag difference between them. None stands here crying, "What do you lack?" for you can ask for nothing that is good but here it is lacking. The buyers and sellers are both alike, tawny, sunburned rascals, and they flock in such troops that it shows as if Hell were broke loose. The shopkeepers are thieves and the chapmen rogues, beggars, and whores; so that to bring a purse-full of money hither were madness . . .

from O per se O *by Thomas Dekker* (?)

A talented purse snatcher

Faith, I have had a foolish odd mischance that angers me. Coming over Shooter's Hill there came a fellow to me like a sailor and asked me money; and whilst I stayed my horse to draw my purse, he takes th' advantage of a little bank and leaps behind me, whips my purse away, and, with a sudden jerk I know not how, threw me at least three yards out of my saddle. I never was so robbed in all my life.

from Endimion and Phoebe *by Michael Drayton*

The hazards of travel

Certes I believe not that chapman or traveler in England is robbed by the way without the knowledge of some [innkeepers] . . . for when he cometh into the inn and alighteth from his horse, the hostler forthwith is very busy to take down his budget or capcase in the yard from his saddlebow, which he peiseth [weighs] slyly in his hand to feel the weight thereof: or if he miss of this pitch, when the guest hath taken up his chamber, the chamberlain that looketh to the making of the beds will be sure to remove it from the place where the owner hath set it, as if it were to set it more conveniently somewhere else, whereby he getteth an inkling whether it be money or other short wares, and thereof giveth warning to such odd guests as haunt the house and are of his confederacy, to the utter undoing of many an honest yeoman as he journeyeth by the way. The tapster in like sort for his part doth mark his behavior, and what plenty of money he draweth when he payeth the shot, to the like end: so that it shall be a hard matter to escape all their subtle practices. Some think it a gay matter to commit their budgets at their coming to the goodman of the house: but thereby they oft betray themselves. For albeit their money be safe for the time that it is in his hands (for you shall not hear that a man is robbed in his inn), yet after their departure the host can make no warranty of the same, so his protection extendeth no further than the gate of his own house: and there cannot be a surer token unto such as pry and watch for those booties than to see any guest deliver his capcase in such manner. In all our inns we have plenty of ale, beer, and sundry kinds of wine, and such is the capacity of some of them that they are able to lodge two hundred or three hundred persons and their horses at ease, and thereto with a very short warning make such provision for their diet as to him that is unacquainted withall may seem to be incredible. Howbeit of all in England there are no worse inns than in London, and yet many are there far better than the best that I have heard of in any foreign country, if all circumstances be duly considered.

from The Description of England *by William Harrison*

How curious, how nice also, are a number of men and women, and how hardly can the tailor please them in making it fit for their bodies! How many times must it be sent back again to him that made it! What chafing, what fretting, what reproachful language doth the poor workman bear away! And many times when he doth nothing to it at all, yet when it is brought home again it is very fit and handsome; then must we put it on, then must the long seams of our hose be set by a plumb line; then we puff, then we blow, and finally sweat till we drop, that our clothes may stand well upon us. I will say nothing of our heads, which sometimes are polled, sometimes curled, or suffered to grow at length like woman's locks, many times cut off above or under the ears, round as by a wooden dish. Neither will I meddle with our variety of beards, of which some are shaven from the chin like those of Turks, not a few cut short like to the beard of Marquess Otto, some made round like a rubbing brush, others with a *pique devant* (O fine fashion!) or now and then suffered to grow long, the barbers being grown to be so cunning in this behalf as the tailors. And therefore if a man have a lean and straight face, a Marquess Otto's cut will make it broad and large; if it be platterlike, a long slender beard will make it seem the narrower; if he be weaselbecked, then much hair left on the cheeks will make the owner look big like a bowdled hen and so grim as a goose. Sume lusty courtiers also and gentlemen of courage do wear either rings of gold, stones, or pearl in their ears, whereby they imagine the workmanship of God not to be a little amended. But herein they rather disgrace than adorn their persons, as by their niceness in apparel, for which I say most nations do not unjustly deride us, as also for that we do seem to imitate all nations round about us, wherein we be like to the polypus or chameleon, and thereunto bestow most cost upon our arses, and much more than upon all the rest of our bodies, as women do likewise upon their heads and shoulders.

from The Description of England *by William Harrison*

Dicing

They egged me to have made one at dice and told me it was a shame for a gentleman not to keep gentlemen company for his twenty or forty crowns: nevertheless, because I alleged ignorance, the gentlewoman said I should not sit idle, all the rest being occupied, and so we two fell to saunt, five games a crown . . . I passed not for the loss of twenty or forty shillings for acquaintance, and so much I think it cost me, and then I left off. Marry the dice-players stuck well by it and made very fresh play, saving one or two, that were clean shriven, and had no more money to lose. In the end, when I should take my leave to depart, I could not by any means be suffered so to break company, unless I would deliver the gentlewoman a ring for a gage of my return to supper, and so I did; and, to tell you all in few words, I have haunted none other since I got that acquaintance: my meat, and drink, and lodging is every way so delicate that I make no haste to change it.

from A Manifest detection of Dice-play *by Gilbert Walker*

Dancing was a favorite pastime in Elizabethan England, and all classes, from the queen to the lowliest peasant, enjoyed it.

Yet is there one, the most delightful kind,
    A lofty jumping, or a leaping round,
When arm in arm two dancers are entwined
    And whirl themselves, with strict embracements bound,
    And still their feet an anapaest do sound—
An anapaest is all their music's song,
Whose first two feet are short, and third is long.

Anonymous

Ills of the flesh

After private prayer I dined, and soon after, I went to Walsingham's house, where I saw my Lady Rich, my Lady Rutland, and my Lady Walsingham: after I came home I was pained in the toothache which continued with me four days after, in which time I exercised, praying and reading as I was able, and took physic of Dr. Lister, who, coming to see me the fourth day after my pain . . . told me of my lady of Bedford's death the night before, which was the Lord's day, who was well at the sermon in the afternoon, and dead that night.

from the diary of Lady Hoby

Christmas was much loved by Elizabethans of all ages, although the rising tide of Puritanism was soon to cast a pall over Yuletide celebrations. Here, the amenities of the season are described.

It is now Christmas, and not a cup of drink must pass without a carol; the beasts, fowl, and fish come to a general execution; and the corn is ground to dust for the bakehouse, and the pastry. Cards and dice purge many a purse, and the youth show their agility in shoeing of the wild mare. Now "Good cheer" and "Welcome," and "God be with you," and "I thank you," and "Against the new year," provide for the presents. The Lord of Misrule is no mean man for his time, and the guests of the high table must lack no wine. The lusty bloods must look about them like men, and piping and dancing puts away much melancholy. Stolen venison is sweet, and a fat coney is worth money. Pit-falls are now set for small birds, and a woodcock hangs himself in a gin. A good fire heats all the house, and a full alms-basket makes the beggars prayers. The masquers and mummers make the merry sport; but if they lose their money, their drum goes dead. Swearers and swaggerers are sent away to the ale-house, and unruly wenches go in danger of judgment. Musicians now make their instruments speak out, and a good song is worth the hearing. In sum, it is a holy time, a duty in Christians for the remembrance of Christ, and custom among friends for the maintenance of good fellowship. In brief, I thus conclude of it: I hold it a memory of the Heaven's love and the world's peace, the mirth of the honest, and the meeting of the friendly.

from Fantastickes *by Nicholas Breton*

The woodcut opposite graphically itemizes the prizes offered in a state lottery of 1567.

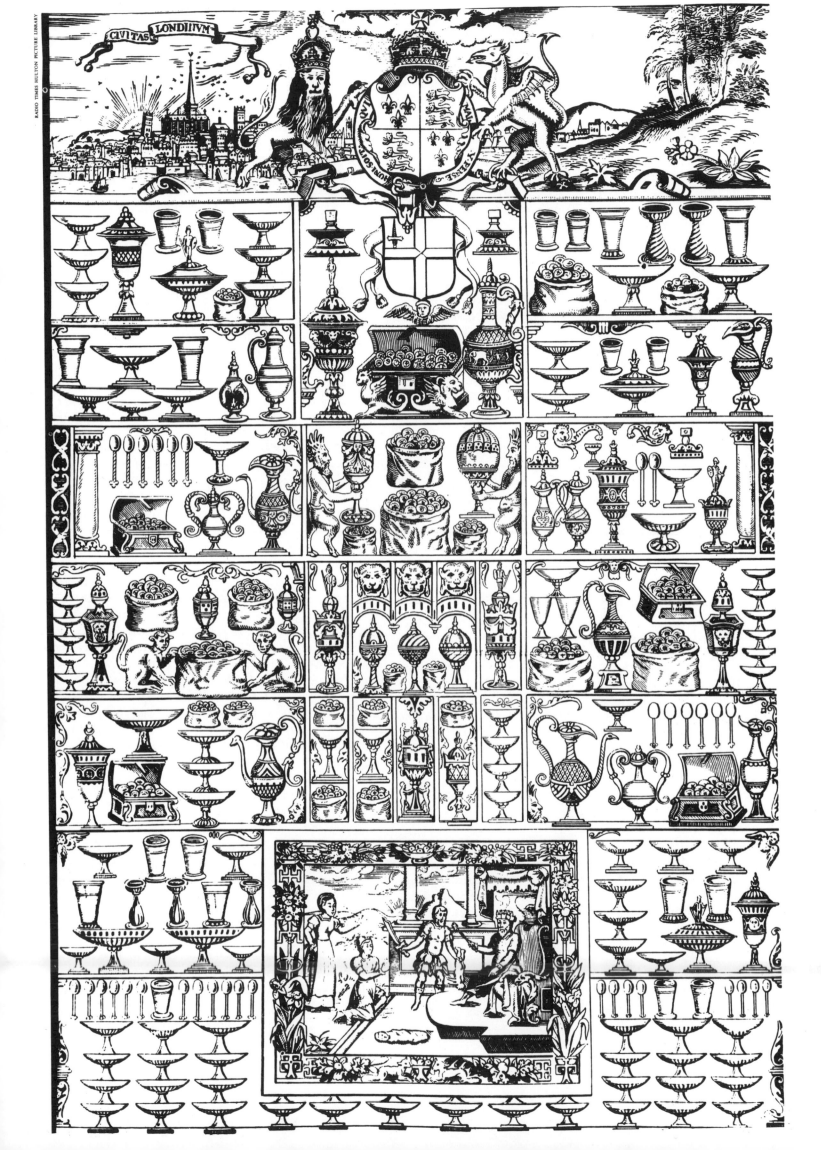

ENGLISH HOMES

Lavish banquets were a common upper-class pastime in Tudor England. The Elizabethans collected recipe books and wrote about the pleasures of the table, which included—along with good food —elegant settings and the latest innovations in table implements.

To make a tart that is a courage to a man or woman

Take two quinces and two or three burr roots and a potato, and pare your potato, and scrape your roots, and put them into a quart of wine, and let them boil till they be tender, and put in an ounce of dates, and when they be boiled tender, draw them through a strainer, wine and all; and then put in the yolks of eight eggs and the brains of three or four cock-sparrows, and strain them into the other, and a little rose-water, and seethe them all with sugar, cinammon and gin-ger, and cloves and mace, and put in a little sweet butter, and set it upon a chafing dish of coals between two platters, and so let it boil till it be something big.

from The good huswifes jewell *by Thomas Dawson*

A diet for sanguine men

Sanguine men be hot and moist of complexion, wherefore they must be circumspect in eating of their meat, consider-ing that the purer the complexion is, the sooner it may be corrupted and the blood may be the sooner infected. Where-fore they must abstain to eat inordinately fruits and herbs, and roots as garlic, onions, and leeks. They must refrain from eating of old flesh, and eschew the usage of eating of the brains of beasts and from eating the udders of kine.

A diet for choleric men

Choler is hot and dry, wherefore choleric men must abstain from eating hot spices, and to refrain from drinking of wine and eating of choleric meat—howbeit choleric men may eat more grosser meat than any other of the complexions. The things following doth purge choler—fumitory, centory, wormwood, wild hops, violets, mercury, manna, rhubarb, eupatory, tamarindes, and the whey of butter.

both from A compendium regimen
or dietarie health *by Andrew Borde*

Vulgar and genteel tippling

Clowns and vulgar men only use large drinking of beer or ale. Gentlemen carouse only in wine, with which many mix sugar—which I never observed in any other place or king-dom to be used for that purpose. And because the taste of the English is thus delighted with sweetness, the wines in taverns (for I speak not of merchants' or gentlemen's cellars) are commonly mixed at the filling thereof, to make them pleasant.

A novel implement

I observed a custom in all those Italian cities and towns through the which I passed that is not used in any other country that I saw in my travels, neither do I think that any other nation of Christendom doth use it, but only Italy. The Italians, and also most strangers that are commorant in Italy,

do always at their meals use a little fork when they cut their meat. For while with their knife, which they hold in one hand, they cut the meat out of the dish, they fasten their fork, which they hold in their other hand, upon the same dish, so that whatsoever he be that, sitting in the company of any others at meal, should unadvisedly touch the dish of meat with his fingers, from which all at the table do cut, he will give occasion of offense unto the company, as having trans-gressed the laws of good manners, in so much that for his error he shall be at the least brow-beaten if not reprehended in words. This form of feeding I understand is generally used in all places of Italy, their forks being for the most part made of iron or steel, and some of silver, but those are used only by gentlemen. The reason of this their curiosity is, because the Italian cannot by any means endure to have his dish touched with fingers, seeing all mens' fingers are not alike clean. Hereupon I myself thought good to imitate the Italian fashion by this forked cutting of meat, not only while I was in Italy, but also in Germany, and oftentimes in England since I came home: being once quipped for that frequent using of my fork by a certain learned gentleman, a familiar friend of mine, one M. Laurence Whitaker, who in his merry humor doubted not to call me at table *furcifer*, only for using a fork at feeding, but for no other cause.

from Coryats crudities *by Thomas Coryat*

Household luxury

The furniture of our houses also exceedeth and is grown in manner even to passing delicacy: and herein I do not speak of the nobility and gentry only, but likewise of the lowest sort in most places of our south country that have anything at all to take to. Certes in noblemen's houses it is not rare to see abundance of arras, rich hangings of tapestry, silver vessel and so much other plate as may furnish sundry cupboards to the sum oftentimes of a thousand or two thousand pounds at the least, whereby the value of this and the rest of their stuff doth grow to be almost inestimable. Likewise in the houses of knights, gentlemen, merchantmen and some other wealthy citizens it is not geson [rare] to behold generally their great provision of tapestry, Turkey work, pewter, brass, fine linen, and thereto costly cupboards of plate . . .

from The Description of England *by William Harrison*

The popularity of glass

It is a world to see in these our days, wherein gold and silver most aboundeth, how that our gentility, as loathing those metals because of the plenty, do now generally choose rather the Venice glasses, both for our wine and beer, than any of those metals or stone wherein beforetime we have been ac-customed to drink. And as this is seen in the gentility, so in the wealthy communalty the like desire of glass is not neg-lected. The poorest also will have glass if they may, but, sith the Venetian is somewhat too dear for them, they content themselves with such as are made at home of fern and burned stone.

from The Description of England *by William Harrison*

Various stipends

MR. TREASURER. He hath for his entertainment 130 pounds

16 shillings 8 pence a year, and 10 dishes of meat to his first mess, and 6 dishes to his second, every meal. He and Mr. Comptroller (there being no Lord Steward) have the government of the whole household, and placing of all Her Majesty's servants. They are likewise to be counseled and assisted by the officers of the board; but they two together are absolute of themselves.

GROOMS. These have 4 marks a year apiece, and meat as aforesaid; they have for fee a penny out of the yeomen's fee, and they have also the drippings of all the meats roasted throughout the year for their fee.

CHILDREN. These have 40 shillings yearly apiece, and 6 pence a day boardwages.

from The Booke of Household of Queene Elizabeth, as it was ordained in the 43ᵈ yeare of her Reigne

Bringing up children
Sweetheart,

By Captain Brown, Davy, and Patrick, I have received four letters from you. I am glad to hear that you and all my children are well; and for your coming over, I desire it as much as you, and would not have let you have been so long from me, but in respect of your own unfitness to come over, and the hope I had to have gotten ere this into England. But herein I well perceive the practice of those, which like not my company at the court; and I trust, if all things fall out well, that they shall have done me no hurt in it. Touching your coming over, toward the middle of May, I will send Captain Goring, and Captain Brown, and a couple of men-of-war from hence, if you do not desire rather to come over in one of the queen's ships; and therein your own credit is sufficient with my Lord Admiral; and for the bringing over of your children, I am still of my first opinion, that I think it very unfit to bring the three bigger ones; I know your delight in them makes you not care what is best for them; and rather than you will part with them, you will not hear of any place where to leave them behind you. Otherwise you know well enough who hath been desirous to have them, and where they should be, as well looked unto as they can be in your own house, and more to their good and less to my charges: I mean for the girls with my lady of Huntington, and my lady of Warwick, with whom also you told me you were willing to leave them. They are not so young now, but that they may well be from their mother. Mary is almost ten, and Kate almost eight; and though I cannot find fault hither unto with their bringing up, yet I know now every day more and more, it will be fit for them to be out of their father's house. For here they cannot learn what they may do in other places; and yet, perhaps, take such humors, which may be hurtful for them hereafter. But you will want persuaders not to let them to go from you, who think they shall lose some of their own interest, if they were not about the children. But there is not anything that makes me speak so much as the experience I have of the dangerousness of the air here, especially for young children, who have been accustomed to good air; and truly if you do bring them over, if anything happens amiss to any of them, you shall hereafter not have your will more in it.

from a letter from Sir Thomas Sydney to his wife

. . . AND GARDENS

Sir Francis Bacon's range of interests was inexhaustible. The following excerpt is taken from one of his most beautiful essays.

God Almighty first planted a Garden. And indeed it is the purest of human pleasures. It is the greatest refreshment to the spirits of man, without which buildings and palaces are but gross handyworks, and a man shall ever see that when ages grow to civility and elegancy, men come to build stately sooner than to garden finely, as if gardening were the greater perfection. I do hold it, in the royal ordering of gardens, there ought to be gardens for all the months in the year, in which severally things of beauty may be then in season. For December and January and the latter part of November, you must take such things as are green all winter: holly, ivy, bays, juniper, cypress trees, yew, pineapple trees, fir trees, rosemary, lavender, periwinkle, the white, the purple, and the blue, germander, flags, orange trees, lemon trees, and myrtles, if they be stoved, and sweet marjoram, warm set. There followeth, for the latter part of January and February, the mezereon tree, which then blossoms, *crocus vernus*, both the yellow and the gray, primroses, anemones, the early tulippa, *hyacinthus orientalis*, charmairis, fritellaria. For March, there come violets, specially the single blue, which are the earliest, the yellow daffodil, the daisy, the almond tree in blossom, the peach tree in blossom, the cornelian tree in blossom, sweetbriar. In April follow the double white violet, the wallflower, the stock gillyflower, the cowslip, flower-de-luces, and lilies of all natures, rosemary flowers, the tulippa, the double peony, the pale daffodil, the French honeysuckle, the cherry tree in blossom, the dammascene and plum trees in blossom, the white thorn in leaf, the lilac tree. In May and June come pinks of all sorts, specially the blush pink, roses of all kinds, except the musk, which comes later, honeysuckles, strawberries, bugloss, columbine, the French marigold, *flos Africanus*, cherry tree in fruit, ribes, figs in fruit, rasps, vine flowers, lavender in flowers, the sweet satyrion with the white flower, herba muscaria, *lilium convallium*, the apple tree in blossom. In July come gillyflowers of all varieties, musk roses, the lime tree in blossom, early pears and plums in fruit, genitings, quadlins. In August come plums of all sorts in fruit, pears, apricots, berberries, filberds, musk melons, monks-hoods, of all colors. In September come grapes, apples, poppies of all colors, peaches, melocotones, nectarines, cornelians, wardens, quinces. In October and the beginning of November come services, medlars, bullaces, roses cut or removed to come late, hollyoaks, and such like. These particulars are for the climate of London, but my meaning is perceived, that you may have *ver perpetuum* ["constant blossoming"], as the place affords.

And because the breath of flowers is far sweeter in the air (where it comes and goes like the warbling of music) than in the hand, therefore nothing is more fit for that delight than to know what be the flowers and plants that do best perfume the air. Roses, damask and red, are fast flowers of their smells, so that you may walk by a whole row of them and find nothing of their sweetness; yea though it be in a morning's dew. Bays likewise yield no smell as they grow. Rose-

143

mary little, nor sweet majoram. That which above all others yields the sweetest smell in the air is the violet, specially the white double violet, which comes twice a year, about the middle of April and about Bartholomew-tide. Next to that is the musk rose. Then the strawberry leaves dying, with a most excellent cordial smell. Then the flower of the vines; it is a little dust, like the dust of a bent, which grows upon the cluster in the first coming forth. Then sweet briar. Then wallflowers, which are very delightful to be set under a parlor or lower chamber window. Then pinks and gillyflowers, specially the matted pink and clove gillyflower. Then the flowers of the lime tree. Then the honeysuckles, so they be somewhat afar off. Of bean flowers I speak not, because they are field flowers. But those which perfume the air most delightfully, not passed by as the rest, but being trodden upon and crushed, are three; that is, burnet, wild thyme, and water mints. Therefore you are to set whole alleys of them, to have the pleasure when you walk or tread.

For gardens (speaking of those which are indeed prince-like, as we have done of buildings), the contents ought not well to be under thirty acres of ground, and to be divided into three parts: a green in the entrance; a heath or desert in the going forth; and the main garden in the midst, besides alleys on both sides. And I like well that four acres of ground be assigned to the green, six to the heath, four and four to either side, and twelve to the main garden. The green hath two pleasures: the one, because nothing is more pleasant to the eye than green grass kept finely shorn; the other, because it will give you a fair alley in the midst, by which you may go in front upon a stately hedge, which is to enclose the garden. But because the alley will be long and, in great heat of the year or day, you ought not to buy the shade in the garden by going in the sun through the green; therefore you are, of either side the green, to plant a covert alley, upon carpenter's work, about twelve foot in height, by which you may go in shade into the garden. As for the making of knots or figures with divers colored earths, that they may lie under the windows of the house on that side which the garden stands, they be but toys; you may see as good sights many times in tarts. The garden is best to be square, encompassed on all the four sides with a stately arched hedge. The arches to be upon pillars of carpenter's work, of some ten foot high and six foot broad, and the spaces between of the same dimension with the breadth of the arch. Over the arches let there be an entire hedge of some four foot high, framed also upon carpenter's work, and upon the upper hedge, over every arch, a little turret with a belly, enough to receive a cage of birds, and over every space between the arches some other little figure, with broad plates of round colored glass gilt for the sun to play upon. But this hedge I intend to be raised upon a bank, not steep but gently slope, of some six foot, set all with flowers. Also I understand that this square of the garden should not be the whole breadth of the ground, but to leave on either side ground enough for diversity of side alleys, unto which the two covert alleys of the green may deliver you.

For the ordering of the ground within the great hedge, I leave it to variety of device, advising nevertheless that whatsoever form you cast it into, first, it be not too busy or full of work. Wherein I, for my part, do not like images cut out in juniper or other garden stuff; they be for children. Little low hedges, round like welts, with some pretty pyramids, I like well; and in some places fair columns upon frames of carpenter's work. I would also have the alleys spacious and fair. You may have closer alleys upon the side grounds, but none in the main garden. I wish also in the very middle a fair mount with three ascents and alleys, enough for four to walk abreast, which I would have to be perfect circles, without any bulwarks or embossments, and the whole mount to be thirty foot high; and some fine banqueting house, with some chimneys neatly cast, and without too much glass.

For fountains, they are a great beauty and refreshment, but pools mar all, and make the garden unwholesome and full of flies and frogs. Fountains I intend to be of two natures: the one that sprinkleth or spouteth water; the other a fair receipt of water, of some thirty or forty foot square, but without fish or slime or mud. For the first, the ornaments of images gilt or of marble, which are in use, do well, but the main matter is so to convey the water as it never stay, either in the bowls or in the cistern; that the water be never by rest discolored, green or red or the like, or gather any mossiness or putrefaction. Besides that, it is to be cleansed every day by the hand. Also some steps up to it and some fine pavement about it doth well. As for the other kind of fountain, which we may call a bathing pool, it may admit much curiosity and beauty, wherewith we will not trouble ourselves; as that the bottom be finely paved, and with images; the sides likewise; and withal embellished with coloured glass, and such things of lustre; encompassed also with fine rails of low statues. But the main point is the same which we mentioned in the former kind of fountain, which is that the water be in perpetual motion, fed by a water higher than the pool, and delivered into it by fair spouts, and then discharged away under ground by some equality of bores, that it stay little. And for fine devices, of arching water without spilling and making it rise in several forms (of feathers, drinking glasses, canopies, and the like), they be pretty things to look on, but nothing to health and sweetness.

For the heath, which was the third part of our plot, I wish it to be framed, as much as may be, to a natural wildness. Trees I would have none in it, but some thickets made only of sweetbriar and honeysuckle and some wild vine amongst; and the ground set with violets, strawberries, and primroses. For these are sweet, and prosper in the shade. And these to be in the heath, here and there, not in any order. I like also little heaps, in the nature of mole-hills (such as are in wild heaths), to be set, some with wild thyme; some with pinks; some with germander, that gives a good flow to the eye; some with periwinkle; some with violets; some with strawberries; some with cowslips; some with daisies; some with red roses; some with lilium convallium; some with sweet-williams red; some with bear's-foot, and the like low flowers, being withal sweet and sightly. Part of which heaps are to be with standards of little bushes pricked upon their top, and part without. The standards to be roses, juniper, holly, berberries (but here and there, because of the smell of their blossom), red currants, gooseberry, rosemary, bays, sweetbriar, and such like. But these standards to be kept with cutting, that they grow not out of course.

from Essays or Counsels, Civil and Moral

Like the English in every age, the Elizabethans loved their gardens. Householders in the slums clung to their plots despite pressures to sell, while the wealthy planted gardens with elaborate fancies like this maze of hedges.

THE REALM OF ENGLAND

Elizabethan England, that "other Eden," was not quite the garden of perfection hymned by Shakespeare and depicted by such painters as Joris Hoefnagel, a Flemish traveler whose *Wedding Feast at Bermondsey* appears at right. Although the sixteenth century was a time of social and economic advancement for the middle classes, a considerable portion of the lower social orders—those farm workers, artisans, and laborers who were dependent on fixed incomes—was reduced to beggary by inflationary living costs and the enclosure of common lands. Overpopulation was a major problem; unemployment, unknown in feudal times, was widespread; hundreds of farming villages were ruined by the profiteers who converted good cropland to pasture to capitalize quickly on the expanding wool trade; and the diet of the peasantry was more wretched than it had ever been. Even the affluent suffered a variety of maladies directly traceable to the decline of farming and a resultant scarcity of fruits and vegetables.

Still, Elizabeth's England was as paradisiacal a realm as the times were capable of producing. On balance the nation prospered; the government was stabilized and relative peace prevailed; the old rigidities were replaced by a more fluid social structure; merit superseded birth as the criterion for preferment; great houses were built; the yeomanry flourished; an exuberant national literature was willed into being; and a quickening of the spirit was felt everywhere.

146

COUNTRY PLEASURES

Physically, Elizabeth's England must have seemed another Eden. Even London was a far more bucolic place than cities of comparable size on the Continent (Bermondsey, shown on the preceding page, lay just outside the city's limits), and the other English "cities" were really little more than country towns. Although the sun shone seldom, the climate was soft—except in the dead of winter, when servants' noses were "red and raw" and the parson's sermon could hardly be heard above the coughing of his flock. Most of life was lived out of doors. Villages and farms were self-sufficient, and hunting, hawking, and angling added variety to the monotonous diet of bread, mutton, and ale, while providing healthy diversion for the countryman. Other outdoor diversions such as shin-kicking matches, cudgel play, and a particularly uninhibited brand of football were somewhat more detrimental to the physical well-being of the participants.

In the tapestry detail at right, a mounted hunter rides off in search of a boar while his companions seek smaller game. The fisherman in the foreground prepares to deposit his catch in a creel. Above, a young man takes his ease in an enclosed garden. The enigmatic device hanging from the tree may have been meant to symbolize the youth's poetic interests.

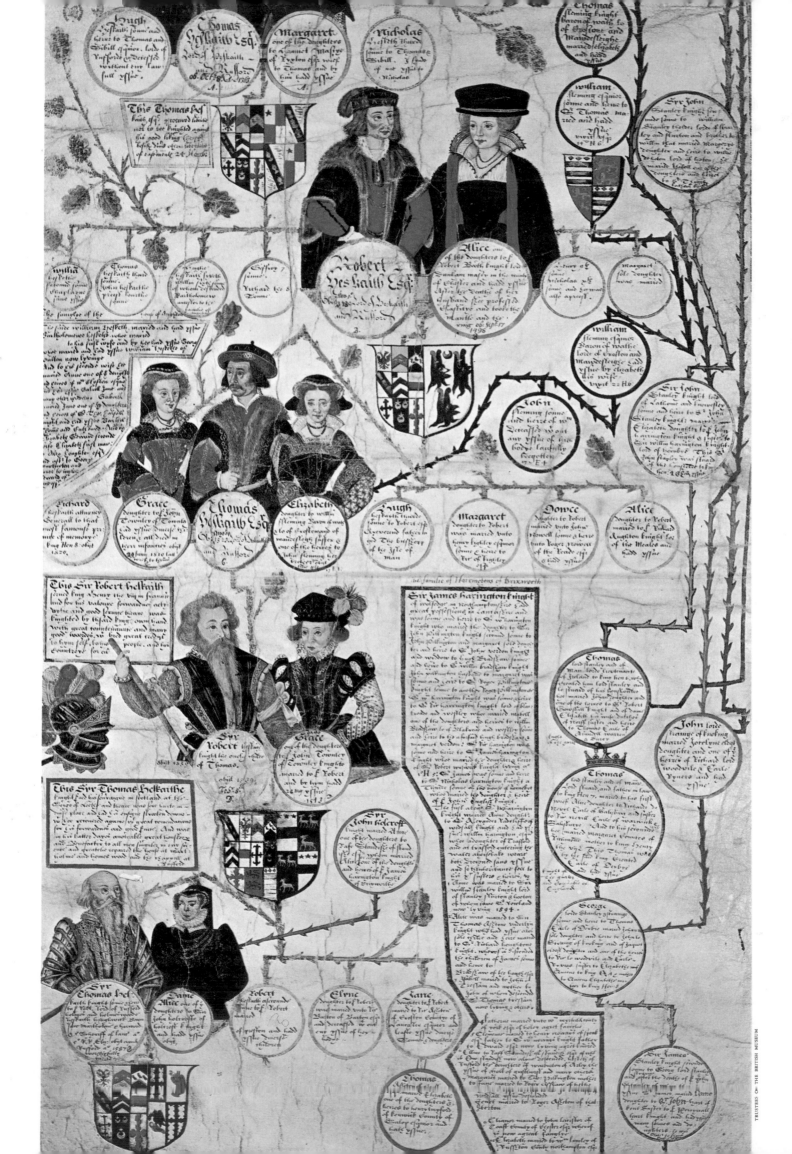

THE RISING MIDDLE CLASS

Elizabeth inherited a changed English social structure along with her crown. The commercial classes had prospered while the great feudal families were divested of their powers. A new nobility had been created: a nobility not of ancient lineage but of newly acquired wealth. During the reign of Henry VIII, when loyalty to the crown had been rewarded with deeds to land, feudal and monastic estates were taken over by a rising middle class. Social distinctions blurred as middle-class land speculators married their children to indigents of noble birth, and the herald's office made a lucrative business of "discovering" forgotten pedigrees and armorial bearings in old registers.

To ensure family continuity in an age of high infant mortality and short life expectancy, women were expected to bear children early and often. The twin sisters (at top) display their first-born delivered the same day. The embroidery above shows a mother of thirteen daughters. Opposite, an ornate genealogy testifies to the importance of pedigrees for the rising Elizabethan gentry.

Februarye, sol in pisses

Jf winters weather weareth out of mynde
All pleasures past of lustie sommers game
And nipping could enforceth man to fynde
Great ease by fyre through warmnesse of ẙ same

Behould what desier, man have to the fier

An Elizabethan yeoman, his family, and dog warm themselves at the fire.

This hurtlesse beast with meeke moode yelds his woll
And skin. to cloth our naked clotte of claye
He giues his flesh to feede our bellies full
Nought for him selfe he bringe but for our staye

June

Cancer

mayd. milke cleane

A primitive form of sheep dip guarded against potentially ruinous epidemic diseases.

THE YEOMANRY

Although he was still considered the "nerve and sinew" of the realm, the English yeoman of the sixteenth century was no longer the humble, steadfast bumpkin who had drawn the longbow at Crécy, Poitiers, and Agincourt. As one of his number put it, ". . . our progenitors and forefathers were at the beginning but plain and simple men and women and of small possession and ability, yet have they little by little so run their course that we are come to much more possessions, credit, and reputation than any of them had." Legally a yeoman was still one who derived an annual income of at least forty shillings from freehold land. Through cautious husbandry, conservative investment, and land enclosure, however, and by charging exorbitant rents to tenant farmers, many yeomen had acquired considerable wealth and social position by the beginning of Elizabeth's reign.

The' Southgate'

Both the fishing industry and the port towns along the English coast prospered as a result of Elizabeth's two-day-a-week ban on the consumption of meat. One such port was the ancient walled Norfolk town of Yar-

The Ne

mouth (shown in the sixteenth-century painting above), which, as can be seen from its cows, its milkmaids, and its windmills, was not altogether dependent upon the flourishing fishing industry for its subsistence.

Two couples make hay while the sun shines.

THIS BLESSED PLOT, THIS EARTH

The Elizabethan era was not only a time of social, political, and economic change in England but of physical change as well. In Sussex the oak forest that had once covered the entire county was gradually leveled, to be replaced by an industrial landscape of iron foundries and glassworks. Elsewhere, land-hungry speculators were engaged in reclamation projects designed to convert vast tracts of morass, or "moss land," into usable acreage. Immense flocks of sheep browsed the rolling countryside in ever-increasing numbers as woolgrowers, intrigued by the prospect of quick profits and minimal labor costs, turned arable soil into pasture land. The old-style communal farms, consisting of three sprawling fields—one planted in barley, one in wheat, and one lying fallow— were being rapidly converted to private properties enclosed by hedgerows. Hay, because it could be grown on grazing lands and required little care, became a major crop.

The photograph at right, taken in Suffolk, shows a bit of countryside that has not changed greatly since Elizabeth's time. Pasture lands (foreground) gave sheep easy access to water.

ENGLISHMEN'S CASTLES

The nature of English domestic architecture changed drastically during the Tudor era, particularly during the peaceful and prosperous years of Elizabeth's reign. The manor house was no longer conceived of as a fortress but as a dwelling place of beauty and comfort. Terraces and formal gardens replaced the drawbridge and moat, and the narrow loopholes of old-style feudal houses gave way to wide latticed windows and decorative oriels. Even in regions where stone was easy to come by and extensively used, massive, impregnable walls were no longer much in evidence. Lighter, more graceful substances—brick in the clay-rich eastern counties, timber and plaster in the west—were the preferred building materials. The black-and-white half-timbered house became a ubiquitous feature of the Elizabethan landscape. Many of these houses were quite literally fit for a queen—a queen who might honor their owners with a visit during a royal progress. Rooms were richly furnished and paneled or hung with brilliant tapestries; ceilings were patterned in deep relief; and staircases were broad and stately, with elaborately carved wooden balustrades.

Various types of plaster-and-timber construction are seen in a gentleman's residence, Little Moreton Hall, opposite, the manor house in the woodcut above, and in the village cottages at right. At top right is a North Country castle bedroom.

OVERLEAF: *A detail from a sixteenth-century tapestry map shows part of the county of Middlesex with London visible at right, and the royal palace of Hampton Court at bottom center.*

STAINES
MAGNA

CHALFVIT
S. PETERS

PINNER

HARLEFORD

ICKNAM

RISLIP

KIMSBV

DENHAM

FVLMER

HARROW

MIDDEL

NHAM

VXBRIDGE

NORTHOLT

SEXIA

HIRE

WERHAM

HAIS
COWLEY

VVRVFORD

SOVTHOLT

STOKE
POGES

DRATON

HORVOOD

FARMSVORTH

LANGLEY

HARLINGTON

EATON

VPTON

OX

HESTON

COLBROKE

CRANFORD

DATCHET

STANVEL

HOWNSL

HORTON

BEDSVNT

WINDSOR

ASHFORD

SW

WAVRBVRY

FEETHAM

OLDE
WINDSOR

HAVVORTH

LITTLETON

EGHAM

LALAM

SVNBVRY

EGE

SVNNINGHILL

THORP

SHEP

SHEPERTON

HAMPTON

TV

FINCHLEY

HORNSEY

TOTNAM

HIGAT

NEWINGTON

PANCRAS

WILSDON HAMPSTED ISLINGTON HAKENEY

PADDINGTON

S. GILES

ACTON

PARS KENSINGTON LONDON

ELING

HAMERSMITH

BRAINFORD CHISWICKE CHELSEY LAMBETH

FULLAM SOUTHWARK

KENINGTON

BATTERSEY

BARNES CLAPHAM CAMBERWEL

SHENE MORTLACKE

WORTH PUTNEY WANSWORTH

RICHMONT STRETHAM

TOUTING BECK

WIMBLTON

MERTON TOWTING GRAVENEY

MITCHAM

COURT

KINGS TON MORDON

5

THE ORDEAL OF FRANCE

A jousting knight at a festive tournament did for the Holy Roman Emperor what all his armed men had been unable to accomplish during forty years of Hapsburg-Valois rivalry: he destroyed France as an international power. On June 30, 1559, the broken lance of a jousting opponent pushed through the royal armor and severely injured the brain of Henry II of France. In ten days the king was dead. Three years later France was torn by the first of nine monstrous civil and religious wars, during which the kingdom was scourged by foreign and private armies that burned, maimed, and tortured in the name of divine justice. For almost forty years France was to bleed until humanity became so sickened at the sight of butchery that "peace without God" seemed preferable to "war for Him." During the ordeal, religious paranoia and the actions of desperate men strained to the breaking point the bonds of political stability, but France was destroyed not so much by religious anarchy, which was common to all Europe, as by the rot that was eating away the heart of the French monarchy. In 1533 the Valois dynasty was united with the equally decadent Italian House of Medici. The consequences were fatal: the union produced the four ailing and degenerate sons of Henry Valois and Catherine de Médicis.

Catherine de Médicis was born in 1519, the year Charles V of Spain was elected Holy Roman Emperor. An orphan at five days and from birth a pawn in the diplomatic designs of her Medici cousin Pope Clement VII, Catherine was raised in the spirit of the Italian Renaissance, where patience and calculation were the qualities most likely to ensure survival. At

eight she was swept up in the Florentine revolution, and her fate was openly debated by the city fathers, some of whom suggested that she be chained naked to the city walls and raped by the republican soldiers. Catherine survived the revolution with her virginity intact and her matrimonial usefulness to the pope unmarred, and in 1533 Francis I of France was lured into accepting Clement's fourteen-year-old ward as the bride of his second son, Henry, duke of Orleans. Within months of the marriage, it became painfully apparent that the French monarch had bought an Italian pig in a poke. The Holy Father had no intention of living up to his side of the bargain and risking war with the emperor to win Milan, Parma, and Urbino for France. Without these cities Catherine had nothing to her credit, not even noble blood; and from the start the marriage was regarded as a misalliance and the princess looked upon as a Florentine shopkeeper's granddaughter. When her husband became heir apparent in 1536, Catherine's position at court worsened. Henry became infatuated with the lovely Diane de Poitiers, and the princess continued to lack fecundity—the one quality that might have compensated for her bourgeois vulgarity.

For ten years Catherine was tolerated, and for ten years she remained barren. Then, beginning in 1544, she became a mother seven times over, giving birth in rapid succession to Francis, Elizabeth, Claude, Charles, Henry, Margaret, and Hercules (who was rechristened Francis after the death of his older brother). Eventually an extraordinary trinity evolved: the slow-witted and obstinate royal husband, his sorceress-mistress who at fifty retained the looks of

A tapestry detail shows Catherine de Médicis with Henry of Navarre and a court dwarf.

a Venus, and Catherine, the queen. Diane de Poitiers' domain was the king's bedchamber, from which she wielded immense political power; Catherine ran the household and had to be content with turning the court into "a veritable earthly paradise," where, exclaimed one ecstatic admirer, ladies shone "like stars in the sky on a fine night." Like most earthly paradises this one was not perfect. Henry II was indecisive and easily influenced, the treasury was empty, and the court was torn by aristocratic factiousness that verged on anarchy.

The lengthy struggle between France and the empire had made a mockery of royal finances, and by 1559 both Valois France and Hapsburg Spain were bankrupt. The peace between them, signed at Cateau-Cambrésis, was diplomatic recognition of the fact that not even the riches of the Spanish Indies or the suffering of French peasants could continue to finance wars that were beginning to approach modern dimensions. By mid-century, cannons that had formerly measured three to four feet had grown into ten- and twenty-foot monsters and had to be drawn by teams of twenty horses. Armies had swollen to 60,000 and 80,000 soldiers—insatiable beasts compared to the companies of knights and bowmen who had fought at Agincourt and Crécy. At the battle of St. Quentin, in 1557, a Spanish force of 60,000 men smashed a French army of equal size, leaving 3,000 Frenchmen dead on the field and taking 6,000 prisoners. It was this defeat that induced France to sue for peace and Spain to accept the offer in 1559, for neither country could continue financing wars that were costing 300,000 livres a month. When Henry II of France died, his treasury was faltering under a war debt of 40 million livres. Theoretically the crown's income came to 12 million livres annually, but its actual income was probably only half that sum, and the interest owed on the royal debt, which varied between twelve and sixteen per cent, consumed every available sou.

On the principle that the king of France could tax as much as he wanted, the main French source of revenues, the taille, rose steadily until peasants fled their land or feigned poverty, and merchants and artisans saw their profits eaten up by wars that benefited only the nobility. Even so, the sums collected did not suffice, and the king turned to selling existing offices and creating new ones for future sale. This prevented a complete financial collapse, but it cost the crown its control over the administrative and judicial organs of state. Purchasers of offices could not be dismissed very easily, and they regarded their posts as profitable, private sinecures, not as public trusts. Courtiers sold influence, judges sold justice, bureaucrats sold favors. Rogues grew rich, upright men were disgusted, and almost everybody lost confidence in a government that was rapidly moving from mere inefficiency into blatant corruption.

Economic nemesis descended in 1557, when not even eighteen per cent interest rates could tempt international bankers to rescue the French crown, and Henry had to break his most solemn and regal promise and declare himself bankrupt. In the wake of fiscal chaos came a political crisis that attacked the very basis of royal power, for the class worst hit by the economic crash was that section of society traditionally most loyal to the crown—the lesser nobility. Throughout the century, wartime deficit spending and the wealth of the New World, coming into Europe by way of Spain, had been producing an inflationary cycle: the value of the livre dropped fifty per cent, and rents from land failed to keep abreast of the rising cost of living. Social pressure required nobles to maintain lavish hospitality and wear costly apparel, and men and women were known to carry their entire estates on their backs. In the past, war had provided a form of outdoor relief for the nobility, but in 1559 peace came, and they were overwhelmed by the clamor of their creditors. In desperation they turned away from a bankrupt monarchy and toward the great feudal magnates instead.

The most dangerous of all social partnerships was taking shape: the great lords, already restless under the crown and bristling with family vanity, were being joined by lesser folk who looked to them for protection and in return were willing to man their private armies, wear their livery, and support their feudal brawling. The age of liveried retainers and baronial war lords had returned to France. The duke of Montmorency, constable of France, arrived at court in 1560 with eight hundred horsemen, and in an emergency he was able to muster twice that number. The duke of Guise was recognized as an uncrowned king, so great was his feudal and political following; and the House of Navarre controlled the allegiance of a host of vassals who would provide military service if it became necessary. Even the king's own army, which had a nominal strength of twelve thousand cavalrymen and sixteen thousand infantry, was little more than a conglomeration of feudal retainers, supported by royal taxes but wearing the uniform of various commanders who regarded the troops under their control as their personal henchmen.

High society and the political configurations at court were dominated by three private dynasties—Guise, Bourbon, and Montmorency. The insatiable pride of the Guises was accepted as appropriate to their exalted position in baronial society, and their irresponsibility was excused because they were descended from Saint Louis and Charlemagne. They were possessed of immense feudal holdings, scattered gleanings from the great days of the dukes of Burgundy situated along the borders of France, the Lowlands, and the empire. The family included two cardinals, a queen regent of Scotland, a grand prior of France, and François, duke of Guise, perhaps the most distinguished soldier of the day. Fear of the other great lords had led the French crown to favor the partly foreign and princely dynasty of Guise, and François and his brother Charles, cardinal of Lorraine, were dominant figures at the court of Henry II. Cultured and devious, Charles aspired to wear a papal tiara while his brother grasped at the crown of France.

Equally dangerous but less brilliant than the Guises were the Bourbons, heirs to the Valois throne in the unlikely eventuality that all four of Henry's sons should die without issue—as indeed they did in time. The titular chief of the clan was Anthony of Navarre, a man possessed of little except his royal blood and an aggressively Calvinist wife whose dearest wish was to convert her husband. The hotheaded leader of the family was Anthony's younger brother, Louis, prince of Condé, a hunchbacked, belligerent, and penurious young man who had nothing to lose and everything to gain from conspiracy and rebellion. Hatred of the Guises, not conviction, drove Condé into the Calvinist camp, and his conversion to the new faith inaugurated in France the dangerous union of baronial gangsterism and spiritual discontent.

The Montmorencys were government aristocrats, servants of the crown. The entire family held high office: Anne, duke of Montmorency, was constable of France; his son François was marshal of the kingdom, governor of Paris, and lieutenant general of the Ile-de-France; another son, Henry, count of Damville, became governor and uncrowned king of Languedoc; and Gaspard de Coligny, his nephew, was admiral of France. Their house was religiously divided: the constable remained a devout Catholic, his nephew, the admiral, a rough, masterful, Bible-quoting man, became an equally staunch Huguenot.

The entire realm was divided among the three families, and scarcely a gentleman of France was not in some way beholden to one or another of them for a pension, a sinecure at court, a suit favorably settled at law, or a marriage with a fat dowry. At Paris, that "sun and moon of France," the baronial chieftains met in the glitter of Catherine de Médicis' court, where the constable advised peace with Spain, the duke of Guise counseled war, and the Bourbons

Catherine's entertainments were as elaborate as her intrigues. A 1582 engraving shows a bosky court ballet.

SERVICE PHOTOGRAPHIQUE, BIBLIOTHÈQUE NATIONALE

fluttered aimlessly, urging nothing but their distinguished rank and princely blood. As the years passed, it became apparent that the Guises were gaining the upper hand. Mary Stuart, that delightful child queen of Scotland, was a niece of the Guise brothers, and her marriage to the heir apparent of France was a major victory for their house. François alone of the great barons of the court had escaped defeat during the war with Spain and England and emerged in 1558 as the liberator of Calais from three centuries of English tyranny. Unexpectedly the Peace of Cateau-Cambrésis brought the Guises to the zenith of their power; for it was during a tournament held in honor of the Peace and wedding of the king's daughter Elizabeth to Philip of Spain that Henry II received the fatal splinter.

For a year the Guises ruled through Mary Queen of Scots, who had become queen of France upon

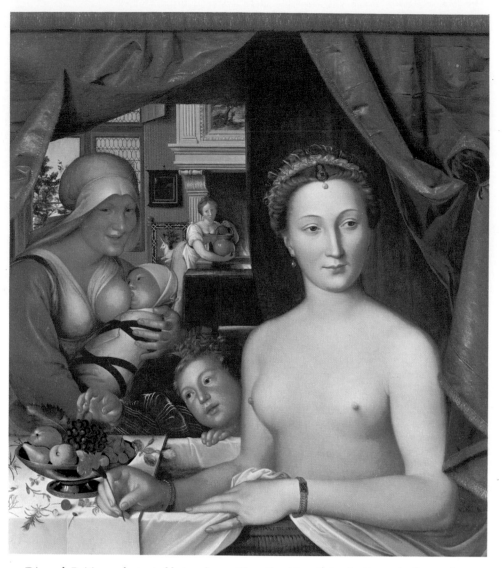

Diane de Poitiers, who probably posed—at fifty—for this painting by François Clouet, clung to her beauty, and by mixing sex with political expediency, to a precarious position at court.

Henry's death, and through her fifteen-year-old husband, Francis II, who did what his wife's uncles told him to do. The dowager queen, Catherine de Médicis, was even more in eclipse than before, and the Bourbon and Montmorency factions were eased out of important positions at court. The cardinal was a consummate diplomat and politician, and the duke a splendid soldier, but neither was a statesman capable of rising above family and factional concerns.

They rapidly became unpopular throughout the country and were held responsible for all the evils besetting France. Worse yet, they drove the Huguenot minority to desperation, for the duke, if not his brother, clamored for the blood of the heretics and the absolute triumph of the Catholic Church. If necessary, he said, he "was quite ready to sacrifice his life for that purpose." Guise's words were prophetic. In 1563 he was struck down by a Protestant assassin, and almost thirty-five years of bloodshed were necessary to assure the victory of Catholicism.

By 1560 Calvinism in France had reached dangerous proportions. Overtaxed merchants, underpaid bureaucrats, bankrupt noblemen, and disgruntled princes of the blood all found outlets for their disenchantment in the Huguenot faith. With the government crippled by dissension, ruinous inflation, and mounting violence, provincial feudalism began to merge with the hierarchical organization of the Huguenot Church. Each Huguenot consistory had its feudal patron who acted as captain and defender of the flock, each colloquy or presbytery had its great nobleman and colonel, and each provincial synod had its *chef général*. On all sides—at court, in the country, and in the hearts of men—there was a steadily growing willingness to risk civil war and revolution. That war did not in fact break out in 1560 was the result of accident, for just when the controversies between Guises and Bourbons and Catholics and Huguenots were spilling over into armed action, the young king, Francis II, died of an abscessed ear, and the government was taken over by Catherine de Médicis as regent for her nine-year-old son, Charles IX. Patience, cunning, and the sickness of her Valois offspring had finally given the queen what her bourgeois heart had long coveted above all else—political power.

Catherine de Médicis was no beauty. She inherited most of the least enviable characteristics of her family: bulging eyes, heavy lips, greasy skin, a sharp and sloping nose, spreading hips, a ravenous appetite, and a passion for intrigue. "A lady of masculine proportions," a contemporary called her. Yet she had great charm and zest. She doted on court gossip, she had a passion for grand receptions and bustling activity, and she built exquisite palaces and filled them with all the sumptuous gaiety that only regal rank and mercantile private means could afford. She ate prodigiously and suffered from gout and indigestion, but "she exercised enough for two," loved to dance, shoot, and hunt, and she was the first lady to ride sidesaddle with a leg hooked around the pommel instead of sitting sacklike with both feet resting on a board placed against the horse's flank. She rode far and fast and surrounded herself with forty to fifty maids of honor, her notorious *escadron volant* of court beauties who excelled in equestrian style as well as in the gorgeousness of their apparel. Catherine knew well how to use sex to her advantage, and her flying squadron of lovely and approachable goddesses was one of her most effective political weapons.

Catherine, as her enemies took pleasure in pointing out, owed her wealth to trade and her birth to Italy. The cabinet of deadly poisons and love potions that she was rumored to possess never actually existed, but to the English and French Catherine's birthplace remained by reputation the land of Machiavellian devilry, what the English satirist Thomas Nashe described as "the academy of man-slaughter, the sporting place of murder, the apothecary shop of poison for all nations." The new regent was undoubtedly an admirer of Machiavellian diplomacy, but her deviousness was always mitigated and often negated by her motherly approach to politics. She delighted in power, but loved gossip even more; she endeavored to preserve the integrity of France, but doted on her children above all other interests. She was, as the Venetian ambassador said, "a clear and intelligent businesswoman," but she could always be enticed by the promise of a crown or a kingdom for one of her many offspring. She invariably confused principles of state with palace politics, and she ruled by a policy of calculated indiscretions mixed with the artless flutterings of a mother hen.

Catherine was a tireless but ineffectual political and diplomatic manipulator, for she never really understood the quality of her opponents. She brilliantly maneuvered to grasp the regency on the death of her eldest son and jockeyed both Guise and Bourbon into accepting her control over the government of Charles IX, but her idea of ruling France was to move her couch into the king's bedchamber. What could not be solved by a bedside chat, a midnight supper, the suggestion of perfume, or the hint of marriage was beyond her intelligence. Her statesmanship tended to be little more than cloying maternalism, her boundless energy was no substitute for real ability, and her methods, though rational, were invariably shortsighted.

In December, 1560, however, it appeared as if Catherine might indeed be the savior of the kingdom and do for France what Elizabeth was doing for England—persuade court factions and rival religions to live in peace. Catherine was more experienced than her regal sister across the Channel, but she was a dowdy middle-aged forty-one compared to Elizabeth's vital twenty-seven; she was a foreigner and a plebeian; and, most important of all, she never possessed the magic that could melt the chilly heart of treason, charm Catholics and Protestants into contentment, and envelop every action in the mantle of greatness. Nevertheless she accomplished a miracle: she persuaded Anthony of Bourbon to renounce his claim as the ranking prince of the blood and forego the regency; she argued the duke of Guise into remaining at court and accepting "a policy of pity" toward the Calvinists; and she brought Huguenots and Catholics together in a national conference to establish a doctrinal solution that would be acceptable to both faiths. Even Henry of Navarre, whose success was so closely dependent upon the frustration of Catherine's dynastic dreams

HERSCHEL LEVIT

Chenonceaux castle, where Henry II established his ménage à trois, *was extended to bridge the river Cher in* 1560.

Henry III

Charles IX

Francis II

and who ultimately replaced her three Valois sons upon the thrones of France, wondered what the poor woman could "have done with her husband dead and five small children upon her hands, and two families, our own and the Guises, who were scheming to seize the throne." Navarre and most later observers were agreed that Catherine de Médicis might indeed have done worse.

The queen's purpose was to pour balm on troubled consciences and smooth the ruffled pride of courtiers. Unfortunately she lacked the authority and the magnetism to maintain her influence over a quarreling court, and her "policy of pity" was little more than a clever stopgap, devoid of principle and reflecting only political necessity. Calvinists and Catholics throughout Europe maintained without reservation the creed: "one doctrine, one discipline, one religion." They merely quarreled over the content of such a monolithic faith. The queen regent's willingness to compromise on points of faith had all the disadvantages of a policy of appeasement. The Huguenots did not want concessions; they demanded total victory, and they viewed the end of persecution and the crown's effort to achieve a broad theological solution as signs of weakness and as an invitation to make further demands.

The results of the religious conference were disastrous, for the Huguenots claimed victory for themselves and promptly increased their demands. They had discussed theology on equal terms with bishops, and they now demanded the right to worship on equal terms with Catholics. In every bailiwick and town of France the Huguenot Church moved into the open, proving itself to be just as bigoted as the intolerance against which it was rebelling. At Castres in 1560 Calvinists had been a tiny, persecuted, and imprisoned minority, holding their services in secret and enduring the fury of the populace. In February, 1561, by government order all Protestants were liberated from jail; by April they were

holding services in public before audiences of six hundred; by the end of the month academy students from Geneva were flocking into the town; on June 5, Protestants for the first time dared ignore the order to decorate their houses in honor of Corpus Christi Day; in August the first Huguenot funeral service took place; in September elections gave the Calvinists control over the city government; and in October both Catholic and Protestant services were being held in all the town churches.

The crisis at Castres came in December and January. Friar Claude d'Oraison was preaching when a fervent Protestant in the congregation shouted that he was a liar. The Huguenot was promptly hustled out of church, but that same evening his coreligionists in the town took up arms, seized the friar, and expelled him from the district. On January 1, 1562, Catholicism was formally abolished, and in the following month, when a monk was discovered celebrating Mass in secret, he was seized, dressed in his sacerdotal robes, placed backward on a donkey, and paraded through the streets of Castres. The monk was then presented with a consecrated wafer and asked whether he was ready to die at the stake for his idolatry. The poor man was not, and only his robes were consigned to the flames. Throughout France a Huguenot dialectic was forming, and within five years the young king, Charles IX, would have occasion to complain to Coligny: "Not so very long ago you were content with being tolerated by the Catholics, but now you demand equality! Soon you will want the power for yourselves alone, and will wish to drive us out of the country!" Except for the implied disloyalty to the person of the sovereign, most Huguenots in their hearts could not have denied the king's accusation.

If Catherine's moderation gave encouragement to the Protestants, it drove the Catholics to fury. For every Huguenot aggression Catholics answered in kind. In Paris, when Calvinists pillaged the Church of St. Médard, enraged Catholics in turn burned the Protestant meetinghouse. Protestantism was so much in the ascendant at court that Catholics feared that the queen mother and king himself might be won to the devil's cause. Mounting religious frenzy began to seize men's minds, destroying the power of custom, loosening the bonds of obedience, and elevating monsters of human cruelty and selfishness into instruments of God's purpose.

Exactly what Catherine had worked hardest to prevent was taking place: France was being polarized into two armed and hostile religious camps. In April, 1561, Catholic factions overcame their differences, and Constable Montmorency and François, duke of Guise, joined forces in an effort to stem the Huguenot tide and save the French government from John Calvin. By October each party—Huguenot and Catholic—was secretly making ready its weapons, and in March the inevitable occurred: one of a series of appalling atrocities committed by partisans of both religions during the winter of 1562 exploded into civil war. On March 1, two hundred horsemen under the command of the duke of Guise discovered in a barn near Vassy, in the duke's domain, a band of some five hundred Protestants at worship. Soldiers and churchgoers exchanged impassioned words, insults led to blows, and Guise was hit on the nose by a rock. At that moment the soldiers unsheathed their swords and the massacre of Vassy began. Reports vary, but probably about thirty Huguenots were killed and more than one hundred were wounded. When word of the slaughter reached Paris, the hotheaded Huguenot prince of Condé sent out a call to arms and war began.

The first civil war was the culmination of a steady drift toward violence. It broke out at that moment when it was easier to act than to think, to kill than to negotiate. In the provinces anarchy went unchecked. Protestants were busy pillaging and profaning Catholic churches and putting idolaters to the sword. Catholics were equally brutal in their campaign against the poison of heresy. The governor of Guyenne, Blaise de Montluc, hanged every Huguenot who came his way and announced that "one man hanged is a better example than a hundred killed." Montluc typified the leaders on both sides—men who preferred to begin with the execution and argue the case afterwards.

As early as 1559 the English ambassador Nicholas Throckmorton wrote Elizabeth: "Now is the time to spend money and it will never have been better spent." In 1562 the English decided the time to act had arrived; at Hampton Court Elizabeth signed a treaty with Coligny and Condé to part with one hundred thousand crowns and to dispatch a six-thousand-man army to support the Protestant cause in exchange for the port of Le Havre. At the end of the war Le Havre was to be given back to France, and England was to get Calais. If the Huguenots were willing to sell the realm of France for the sake of the kingdom of God, and if the price was right, Gloriana was delighted to cooperate.

The war, however, decided nothing except that France would never go Protestant and that Elizabeth had underestimated the cost of intervention. The first civil war came to an end when the leaders of both sides were either killed or captured: Guise fell to the assassin's blade; Anthony was killed in battle; Condé and the Constable Montmorency were captured. On the principle that captives are reasonable peacemakers, Catherine urged Condé and Montmorency to negotiate peace, and a treaty between them was signed in March, 1563. The results satisfied no one except the queen mother. Limited liberty of worship was accorded the Huguenots, a concession that infuriated the Catholics and failed to appease the Protestants; Calvinists were irritated by having their faith prohibited in the city of Paris; and the Guise family failed to obtain satisfaction for the death of François of Guise. They did have the doubtful pleasure of seeing his assassin, a fanatical young Huguenot nobleman, pulled to pieces by four wild horses; but they continued their personal

Gaspard de Coligny is shown flanked by his brothers Odet (left), who converted him to Protestantism, and François.

MUSEE CONDE, CHANTILLY; GIRAUDON

vendetta against Coligny, whom they deemed morally responsible for the murder.

The only positive result of the settlement was a lesson to Elizabeth of England not to meddle in French affairs. The moment peace was signed, Catherine gathered an army of forty thousand men and forty cannons and moved on Le Havre. If Queen Elizabeth, she said, would not return the city "to us willingly, God will enable us to take it by force." Gloriana never returned anything willingly, but in this case the siege was short and the English defense of the city inglorious.

Victorious over Elizabeth, and with all her French generals either dead or humiliated, Catherine emerged as the sole victor of the war, but again her triumph proved hollow. The queen's solution to the ills that beset France was to set out in January, 1564, on a triumphal progress. She traveled with her young son, who received the accolades of both Protestants and Catholics, and with her squadron of alluring goddesses, whose smiles, it was hoped, would banish the bitter memory of war. The full bankruptcy of Catherine's policy was revealed in the shallowness of her own words. "They all danced together," she told the duchess of Guise, "Huguenots and papists alike, and so happily" that she had great hope of a permanent reconciliation.

Although Catholics and Protestants might dance together, they had in fact only one thing in common: the darkest suspicion of the queen mother. Hers was the fate of all inveterate schemers, for, as one English observer said, "she had too much wit for a woman, and too little honesty for a queen." Philip of Spain called her *Madame La Serpente* and wrote that he trusted "neither her leagues nor her marriages." Calumny and rumors, bred of distrust for an Italian queen, found ready audience in both religions. The queen, Catholics said, preferred heretics to faithful and godly subjects; she might at any moment barter the safety of the Catholic Church for the sake of a golden crown for one of her many children. Protestants whispered that she was planning to cut the throats of all godfearing Huguenots, delaying only until they were lulled into a sense of security by her empty promises.

During the autumn of 1567 distrust led to the renewal of war that was to last with but one interruption for almost three years. The fury with which Frenchman tore at Frenchman was worse than in the dreadful days of the Hundred Years War. Protestants stormed a Catholic monastery and forced the monks to hang each other; cities that had been induced to open their gates by the offer of honorable terms of surrender were put to the sword; at Orleans Huguenot captives were burned en masse in prison by Catholic mobs; at Auxerre crowds pulled to bits one hundred fifty Calvinists and threw the pieces into the sewer; at Foix Protestants slaughtered one hundred twenty papists, and Catholics retaliated by killing seven hundred Calvinists. The temper of the times was epitomized by the revenge that Henry, duke of Guise, took when his enemy, the prince of Condé, was captured in battle and then killed. In retaliation for his father's murder he ordered his men to place the prince's naked body on the back of a donkey and expose it to the public view. On both sides men lived only for hatred, and so many unspeakable atrocities were committed that the Venetian ambassador wrote that he could not better describe the state of the kingdom "than by comparing it to a leg, an arm, or any other member attacked by gangrene; when the doctor, having cauterized a wound, thinks that his task is finished, he sees another one opening beside it."

Toleration was born in the horrors of war. For a few men, such as Montaigne, liberty of conscience became a principle and guide to life, but most Frenchmen adopted it from grim necessity. Slowly, in the face of barbarism and outrage, a small group of men determined that "a man does not cease to be a citizen for being excommunicated." A thousand times, Montaigne said, he had retired to bed expecting to be "betrayed or murdered before morning," hoping only that death, when it came, would be "done without terror or lingering" torture. Life was intolerable under such conditions, and merchants and nobles, peasants and artisans began to argue that secure homes were more important than quiet consciences, and the repose of the kingdom more desirable than the salvation of their souls. The politiques, as the disciples of such belly wisdom were called, grew in number with every act of vengeance and mayhem. Eventually, when enough men on both sides had demanded the end of war, peace was concluded at St. Germain in August, 1570. The Catholics had triumphed in all battles, but the Protestants won the peace. Liberty of conscience and freedom of worship were assured to all Huguenots throughout the realm except in Paris and its environs; Protestants were made eligible for all public offices, and they received as guarantees of the government's good faith the possession of four cities—La Rochelle, Montauban, Cognac, and La Charité. Catholics were horrified by the terms of the settlement, and Montluc complained that the enemy had everywhere been destroyed by force of arms but now had "triumphed by means of their diabolical writings."

Despite Catholic protests, Catherine was satisfied with the Peace of St. Germain, for it allowed her

TEMPLE DE LYON, NOMMÉ PARADIS.

The Huguenots of Lyons were permitted by the ruling Catholics to build a temple in the city. An anonymous sixteenth-century painting shows a service in progress in its oval interior.

to pose as the leader of a new alliance of Catholic politiques and moderate Huguenots. In characteristic Medici fashion she planned a series of marriages to win allies for her policies and crowns for her children. Her second son, Henry, duke of Anjou, was to marry that aging champion of Protestantism, the thirty-seven-year-old Elizabeth of England, and her daughter Margaret was designated as the bride of young Henry of Navarre, who was now titular head of the Huguenot party and the Bourbon heir to the throne.

The queen's ambassadors failed to come home with the virgin bride, even though they also offered Elizabeth Catherine's youngest son, the duke of Alençon, when it became evident that she wasn't interested in the duke of Anjou; but they did achieve a major diplomatic triumph when England gave up more than three hundred years of cherished francophobia and joined France in a defensive alliance against Spain. The Treaty of Blois, in 1572, was a token of a fundamental change in the structure and

balance of European diplomacy. As the power of France and the dynastic ambitions of monarchs receded, the might of Spain and the affairs of God loomed larger. Once, armies had marched as conquerors with no other purpose than capturing booty and enhancing the glory of kings; now they marched as liberators and instruments of God's glory. Elizabeth of England and Catherine of France were of the old school; they preferred to keep diplomacy the concern of men, not of angels, and they regarded with the deepest misgivings Philip of Spain's argument that when dealing with heresy "it was better to go and put out the fire in a neighbor's house than to wait for it to spread to one's own." Both queens agreed that at all costs the affairs of their respective kingdoms must be solved without benefit of Spanish troops, and in both countries there were men who urged that the best defense against Spanish good intentions was to encourage the rebellion that had recently broken out in several provinces of the Netherlands, where the Spaniards were con-

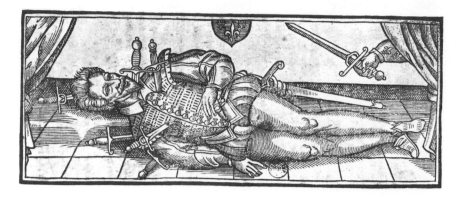

A French woodcut shows the assassination of Henry, duke of Guise, which took place in Henry III's palace at Blois.

fronted with a major social and religious revolution.

In June, 1572, Coligny was again called to court, this time to help arrange the marriage of Henry of Navarre to Catherine's daughter Margaret. Though the marriage negotiations moved smoothly, the queen again miscalculated, for Coligny began to exercise an inordinate influence over the neurotic and impressionable Charles IX. In the eyes of the queen mother he was committing the one crime that could be neither forgiven nor ignored: he was stealing the affections of a son who until that moment had listened to no one but his mother. "After God," Charles had said, "the queen, my mother, is the one to whom I have the greatest number of obligations." As usual, Catherine's solution was expedient but tragically myopic. Coligny, she decided, would have to go, and the obvious instrument of assassination was the Guise family's blood feud with the admiral.

The staging of murder was complicated by the approaching wedding of Protestant Navarre and Catholic Margaret, which had been set for August 18, 1572, and by the decision of the Huguenot nobility to attend in force. On both sides tension mounted: Paris was stoutly Catholic and viewed the growing number of visiting Protestant nobles and their henchmen with fear and hatred; Navarre and his young cousin, Duke Henry, entered the city with eight hundred cavalry; and the roads to Paris were crowded with some five thousand Huguenots determined to view the wedding. The queen mother was worried lest Coligny and Condé were plotting to kidnap the king, and the Protestants were filled with anger at Catherine's refusal to intervene in the Netherlands. Under conditions guaranteed to explode at the slightest spark, Catherine went ahead with her plans to dispatch the admiral. The results were catastrophic. On August 22, as Coligny was walking down a narrow alley, his assassin shot at him from a small window. What saved the admiral's life was the accident of his bending down to adjust his shoe. The bullet ripped open his arm and smashed his hand. At this outrage to their leader, every Huguenot in the city was up in arms. Protestants crowded into Coligny's residence, shouting: "That arm shall cost thirty thousand other arms!" And the admiral indignantly demanded an immediate audience with the king.

Charles IX was the one weak link in the queen's design. He was unaware of his mother's plans and told Coligny that he was "determined to have justice done on such a scale that it shall be a warning to every man in my kingdom." If the king carried out his threat, his own mother would be implicated; and at this moment Catherine lost her head. In her panic she chose to take literally the Huguenot threat to demand thirty thousand arms in vengeance for what Guise had done to Coligny, and she decided to have all the Huguenot leaders, so conveniently assembled in Paris, massacred. It remained only to win over her son. After pleading with him for hours she triumphed, and a beaten and furious Charles turned and cried: "Well then . . . let it be so. But kill them all, that no one will be left to reproach me afterwards."

The signal for bloodshed was given early on the morning of August 24, the feast of Saint Bartholomew. It had been decided to spare the Huguenot princes of the blood, Navarre and Condé, but no other nobleman was to escape. If Catherine intended to murder the Calvinist leaders only, her plans tragically miscarried, for the moment the bells tolled, the citizens of Paris rose up and shouted, "The Huguenots! The Huguenots! Death to the Huguenots!" Some of the victims were stabbed, some were hanged, some were drowned, some were thrown from windows and rooftops, and Henry, duke of Guise, personally supervised the death of Admiral Coligny. Paris, said one shocked observer, "was like a conquered city," and the Seine ran red with blood. Killing and butchery spilled over into the provinces, bringing the grisly total of deaths to an estimated 10,000; including 1,000 at Orleans, 800 at Lyons, and possibly 4,000 in Paris.

Despite the torrent of blood, St. Bartholomew's Day achieved little except to divide further a kingdom that was already falling apart. The Catholic world applauded. Philip of Spain announced that the deed "has given me one of the greatest joys of my life," and wrote young King Charles that the extermination of the hateful heretic would be his "greatest title to glory." The pope had a medal issued to commemorate the victory of God over Satan, and His Holiness ordered Rome to be illuminated for three nights in token of the triumph. If ardent

Catholics viewed the massacre as a particularly holy act, Protestant Europe regarded it as one of unmitigated infamy. Elizabeth of England, dressed in the deepest mourning and accompanied by her full Council, listened in icy silence to the French ambassador's efforts to justify the slaughter. In Calvin's Switzerland, in the Netherlands, and in Lutheran Germany, Protestants were aghast. Gruesome and generally inaccurate details were published: Charles IX was accused of having used Huguenots for target practice, shooting them down from his window in the Louvre, and William of Orange wrote that the French king would never be able to wash the red stain from his bloody hands. Even Ivan the Terrible of Russia, who was no stranger to savagery, wrote a letter of protest.

After Catholic applause and Protestant shudders had died away and the bloody gutters of Paris had been washed clean, the queen mother was able to take stock. The inventory was far from satisfactory. From the blood of the aristocratic martyrs sprang an invigorated and republican Huguenot Church that openly advocated regicide and war. In destroying the aristocratic leadership of Calvinism, Catherine had created a worse danger to the state, for the Huguenot party became democratic and theocratic and came to consider monarchy as well as Catholicism incompatible with godliness. In the south, where some Huguenot nobles survived and remained strong, feudal provincialism, sustained and encouraged by religious hatred, achieved its ultimate purpose: independence. After the St. Bartholomew's Day Massacre France was broken in two. The province of Languedoc went republican, setting up a council of state, an assembly of deputies, and provincial councils, establishing its own laws and fiscal machinery, and levying its own taxes upon Catholics and Protestants alike.

The governor and virtual king of Languedoc was a Catholic, Henry, count of Damville, second son of the old constable, and his support of the Huguenots represented still another result of the events of St. Bartholomew's Day, for Damville was a member of the politique party and a cousin of the murdered Coligny. The slaughter represented everything he and his party had striven to avoid. Moderate Catholics were outraged, and the politiques wondered when their own turn might come. St. Bartholomew's Day and the queen's policy had driven the politiques and the Huguenots into union, and Damville announced publicly his willingness to follow the direction of the new Huguenot leaders.

Final retribution, regarded by the Protestant world as divine in origin, came when Charles IX was stricken by a combination of remorse and congenital tuber-

culosis. After St. Bartholomew's Day he began to change, visibly to die. He hung his head constantly and dared look no man in the eye. At twenty-four he looked sixty-four. His hands began to tremble; he was plagued with hideous nightmares; and in the end he was little more than a living skeleton. He died on May 30, 1574, the worn-out scion of an exhausted house. His final word was a suitable and tragic summation of his life: a moment before he died he mumbled, "Mother." Catherine, in her efforts to save herself and her son's throne, had helped to destroy the one child who had been totally dependent on her, and into his place stepped Henry III, the child she feared and loved the most, and the Valois king who destroyed himself and everything the queen had worked to protect in his determination to escape his mother's stifling affection.

The years between 1572 and 1576 were filled with fighting and political anarchy. Navarre reported to a friend that "we carry daggers and wear coats of mail and very often breastplates under our cloaks. I am only waiting for the opportunity to have a little fighting, for I am told that they are plotting to kill me and I want to steal a march on them." Everyone was waiting for the opportunity to kill, and when the occasion did come, they took full advantage of it. The kingdom was in arms, justice dead, France divided, the exchequer empty, and the court so im-

A detail from a painting done by a Huguenot survivor depicts the massacre of Protestants on St. Bartholomew's Day.

poverished that the king often had scarcely enough money to purchase his dinner. Anything was preferable to continued war, but peace could only be purchased by total capitulation to the Huguenots and politiques. In the end Henry III and Catherine had no choice but to accept their terms, and the Peace of Monsieur was signed in May, 1576. The government officially apologized for St. Bartholomew's Day; Protestants were once again granted complete liberty of worship throughout the kingdom, and four additional surety cities were placed under their control.

With a perversity born of bad luck and worse judgment, the queen continued to take one step after another that only created more pressing problems. From 1576 on, the Valois throne was crushed between two political-religious forces for whose existence Catherine herself was in large measure responsible. From the start her aim had been to hold the balance between two equal parties and thus preserve the security of France and the throne of her sons. After 1576 the crown was too weak to control its own creations. Catherine's consummate duplicity might possibly have postponed the fate of the Valois dynasty, but after the humiliation of the Peace of Monsieur, the gouty and aging pilot was dropped. Henry cast off his mother's tutelage and set off to rule his kingdom alone.

Everything about the king, wrote the papal legate, is contradictory. Henry was a skeptic, yet he scourged and mortified his flesh. He could be every inch a monarch if he chose, but more often he elected to play the degenerate. He was avid for excitement, yet constitutionally incapable of enduring it. He surrounded every thought with a coating of verbiage so thick that none knew whether he spoke profound wisdom or merely gabbled without meaning. He sensed with uncanny accuracy the truth about men and politics, but he was incapable of acting upon his own instincts, for, as he confessed, "nobody else would agree with me and I may possibly be wrong." Henry suffered from constant headaches, an infected ear, and a maddening itch brought on by chronic eczema. Occasionally there were spells of frantic activity during which he drenched his body in perfume, festooned himself with ribbons and earrings, and painted his face with a mask of rouge and powder, from which his sick and sunken eyes peered. He surrounded his royal person with effeminate young men who wore their hair in elaborate curls and spent their time in gaming, drinking, and dancing. On one occasion he arranged a banquet served by the beauties of the court dressed as men in garments of green silk; another time he assumed feminine attire and attended a ball with his bodice cut low and his

neck adorned with "a pearl necklace and three linen collars." Long after he was mercifully dead, the duke of Sully remembered those days. "I shall never forget," he said, "the fantastic and extravagant equipage and attitude in which I found this prince in his cabinet: he had a sword at his side, a Spanish hood hung down upon his shoulders, a little cap, such as collegians wear, upon his head, and a basket full of little dogs hung to a broad ribbon about his neck." Such was the last Valois king of France.

While the state faltered under the rule of a prince of Sodom and his "court of silk and blood," Catholics, under the leadership of Henry of Guise, took matters into their own hands. The Peace of Monsieur was regarded as a disgrace to France and an insult to God, and Catholics joined together in a Holy

Members of the Catholic Holy League, shown here marching through the streets of Paris, controlled all the large cities of France and won the active support of Philip II of Spain.

MUSÉE CARNAVALET; ARTS GRAPHIQUES DE LA CITÉ

League dedicated to the extermination of heresy. The League openly sought military aid from Spain and deliberately appealed to every variety of provincial and feudal greed. Once again France fell prey to open warfare, and neither the kingdom nor the king had anything to gain, no matter which side won. Fortunately the war lasted less than a year. By 1577 the Holy League had forced the Huguenots to accept a more limited form of freedom to worship.

Though the Catholics again triumphed in war, whatever hopes they may have had for the future vanished when the king's youngest brother, Francis, died and Protestant Henry of Navarre became heir to the throne. The youngest of Catherine's children had originally been created duke of Alençon, but on Henry III's succession to the throne he became duke of Anjou. He was one of those turbulent and improbable characters who keep appearing in history. After his older brother had failed at the task, he tried to win Elizabeth's hand in 1572 in a whirlwind courtship; he was consumed with pathological hatred for his brothers; he openly conspired to snatch the succession from Henry when Charles IX died in 1574; and he tried his hand at treason by joining the politique-Huguenot alliance in open war against his mother and brother. Anjou was a chronic pest, the master of five duchies, the possessor of four hundred thousand crowns yearly, and a man obsessed with a passion to become a king. In 1577 Henry III found an opportunity to send his difficult and unstable brother to make trouble for someone else. Unofficially he and Catherine urged Francis to

In honor of his warlike exploits Henry IV is shown on this medallion as Mars greeting a figure representing victory.

A Bourbon family portrait shows Henry IV with his wife and children. The boy in the foreground, wearing a hat and long skirt, is the dauphin, later Louis XIII.

176

find himself a crown in the Netherlands, where both the Catholic and Calvinist subjects of Philip of Spain were in full-scale revolt. Unfortunately Anjou was no more successful at war than he had been at winning Elizabeth's hand in marriage (several years after his first attempt he had tried again), and he was disastrously defeated in battle by the Netherlanders themselves, the very people he had come to protect. Three years later, in 1584, at the age of thirty, he died of the Valois sickness, hemorrhage of the lungs.

His death upset the political applecart. Throughout France primitive passions welled to the surface again, and Catholics, motivated by greed, fear, and idealism, were seized by the determination to preserve France from the horror of a heretic king. The dynastic aspirations of Henry, duke of Guise, the religious policy of the papacy, the absolute conviction of the Jesuits, the international interests of Spain, and the irrational fear of tens of thousands of Frenchmen who disciplined their children and terrified themselves with stories of sinister Huguenots rising up in the dead of night to murder good Catholics in their beds—all these were in accord: Henry of Navarre must never be king of France.

Anjou was dead scarcely three months when Catholic demagogues whipped the Holy League into action again. To priest, monk, and prior, the League was an instrument of God's ultimate victory, and humble men joined its ranks as if they were going on a crusade. At least two men viewed it from a more worldly perspective, however. There is little doubt that the duke of Guise was dazzled by the prospect of succeeding to the throne once Henry III was dead, and he used the League in an effort to win a crown. Don Bernardino de Mendoza, the resident Spanish ambassador at Paris and undoubtedly the best informed man in France, was equally sanguine. Mendoza was welcomed in the innermost circles of the Holy League. He was the valued friend and paymaster of both the duke and the fanatically revolutionary Committee of Sixteen, the secret left wing of the League. As the man who controlled the League's purse strings, Mendoza also called the tune, which became increasingly Spanish in tempo. Spanish interests demanded that Henry of Navarre be barred from the throne and that France be broken by civil war. The might of Spain had been ordained as the means by which all Europe would be won back to the Catholic fold, and if heresy were to be exterminated in the Netherlands and England, Valois France must be kept pure in faith and helpless in diplomacy.

In July, 1585, the League demanded of a bankrupt and helpless Henry III that he revoke all edicts of toleration toward heretics and ban Protestants from the land. By September the pope had proclaimed Henry of Navarre a relapsed heretic, incapable of lawfully succeeding to the throne, and in October, much to Mendoza's satisfaction, the bitterest and most extraordinary of all the French religious wars broke out. The War of the Three Henrys was fought by Navarre for survival, by Guise for a kingdom, and by Valois because he had no other choice. By the winter of 1585–86 the League had three armies in the field, all heavily financed by Spain: one to destroy Henry of Navarre, one to handle an army of thirty-five thousand Germans marching to the aid of their Protestant brethren in France, and one to guard the king. As the conflict progressed, it became increasingly apparent that Henry III was not the master of his army, but its prisoner, and that Henry, duke of Guise, was king of Catholic France in all but name. With well-deserved pride Mendoza reported to Philip in Madrid that "events here could hardly have gone more happily for Your Majesty's affairs."

By 1588 the war among the three Henrys had been reduced to a struggle between Henry of Guise, who sought to maintain his control of the kingdom and who coveted the crown of France, and Henry of Valois, who possessed neither a son nor a realm, but who was determined to keep his crown and bequeath what little he possessed to his legal, if heretical, heir, Henry of Navarre. The climax came in May on the Day of the Barricades. At the invitation of the revolutionary Committee of Sixteen, who controlled the city's government, and in open defiance of the king's command, Duke Henry entered Paris. Henry III, in self-defense, mobilized the Swiss guards. Rumors spread that he was planning a Catholic St. Bartholomew's and the murder of the duke. The citizens of Paris instantly flew to arms, barricaded the streets, and pelted the king's troops with filth and debris. The monarch fled in panic, leaving Henry "king of Paris" and virtual dictator of northern France. A month later Henry III gave his official recognition to political reality. He dismissed his ministers, surrendered the substance of power to the League, promised to change the succession, and in return was permitted the hollow satisfaction of calling himself king of France. Henry's capitulation was not complete, however. The Swiss guards remained, and the ministers he had dismissed had been more loyal to the queen, his mother, than to him. It was symptomatic of the violence of the age that yet another murder was deemed necessary and acceptable to solve a political problem. Almost immediately the king began to arrange the carefully staged elimination of his rival.

The end came like the conclusion to a Shakespearean tragedy. On December 23, 1588, Henry,

duke of Guise, was murdered in the anteroom to the sovereign's bedchamber while Henry, king of France, hid behind the curtains. The next day the cardinal of Guise was struck down by assassins. The double murder produced the ultimate irony of almost thirty years of religious horror. Catholic fanaticism erupted, Paris revolted, the Holy League demanded vengeance and threatened regicide, and a badly frightened Henry III was forced into open alliance with his cousin of Navarre and the hated heretics in order to save his toppling throne. In the end the inevitable happened: on August 1, 1589, the chain of murders was completed when a young Dominican monk Jacques Clement, convinced that God had instructed him to deliver the Mother Church from such a monstrous monarch, set out to kill the king. He asked for an audience, and as Henry stood before him, he drove a knife into the king's stomach. The monk was dead almost before Henry knew what had struck him, but murder had been done, and within hours the last of the Valois line died. Protestant Henry of Navarre was now monarch of a realm that was swept by hatred and social revolution and overrun by foreign armies.

Catherine de Médicis must be given her share of responsibility for the death of her son, even though she was already seven months dead at the time of the assassination. She had taught her children the art of survival in an age of religious madness, but ultimately her own art destroyed everything that she held most dear—her offspring, her house, her adopted realm. As the Florentine ambassador said, she was always "prudent and very experienced in matters of this world," yet she never knew "what remedy to apply to so many present ills nor to the ills to come." Surely she had more than her share of ills, but just as surely she had the morals and the instincts of a Machiavellian diplomat, which hardly accorded with her love for her children or fitted into a world where kings and commoners were willing to sacrifice men and kingdoms to religious conscience. There is a legend that when the Guise brothers were murdered at the command of her son, Cardinal Bourbon reproached her, saying, "Ah! Madam, this is your doing. It is you who are killing us all!" She did not deny the charge; instead she whimpered, "I can bear no more. I must go to bed." Less than a month later, in January, 1589, she was dead, aged seventy, and eight hundred thousand écus in debt. Even in death she failed to attain the grandeur that had so persistently eluded her in life. Her body was inadequately embalmed and had to be buried in haste in the shallow grave of a provincial church, and thereafter, as one contemporary observed, no one paid any "more notice to her than to a dead goat."

EMPIRES OF THE EAST

Europe was not the only part of the world that experienced a golden age in the sixteenth century. The period was a time of astonishing development and creativity throughout the entire eastern hemisphere. From England to Japan societies radiated new energies and capabilities. Men moved about the globe with ever-greater freedom, and there was an inevitable cultural exchange. In some cases the exchange was hostile, yet even war fostered the dissemination of ideas. More often, however, influences spread through commercial channels. The Japanese and Portuguese immediately established a rapport, and their trade of everything from clothing styles to words went far beyond the stipulations of their commercial agreements. An important new development was the Atlantic slave trade, which brought greater power to already thriving African kingdoms and exerted a profound effect on the history of both American continents. Monarchs everywhere were alert to the importance of international contacts. Ivan the Terrible of Russia eagerly courted the European powers to promote trade and benefit from technical advances. Moscow's Cathedral of St. Basil, whose bizarre towers are shown at right, is characteristic of the age; built by Ivan, it is purely Russian in inspiration, yet it was erected with the aid of Italian architects.

178

EMMA LANDAU

JAPAN AND THE WEST

When the Portuguese made their way to Japan in the middle of the sixteenth century, they found the first Asians for whom they had respect. At the time Japan, like the European countries, was emerging from feudalism to become a more unified national state. The Japanese realized immediately how much the Portuguese could teach; they even welcomed Christianity, seeing it as a type of Buddhism. The Portuguese in turn were eager to acquire Japanese silver and copper and were flattered by the intelligent interest the Japanese showed in them. By 1600 European firearms and fortress designs had enabled a few warriors to consolidate power and unify the country, and the introduction of new crops and a growth in trade had made the island kingdom prosperous.

The Portuguese became fashionable in Japan during the late sixteenth century. The Japanese adopted Portuguese games, dress, and words, and learned European technical skills. Screens like this, which shows citizens of both nations mixing on a large ship, became very popular.

A WORLD APART

When the first Portuguese ships arrived on the coast of China in the year 1514, Ming Dynasty officials permitted the visitors to land and trade their goods. But by 1522 the Chinese had to bar the Portuguese from the country, for more often than not the foreigners, considering all pagans fair game, had chosen to plunder and murder rather than trade. Twenty years later the Chinese relented; trading their pottery and silks had been extremely profitable and European technology and scientific learning were irresistible. After 1600 the emperor warily allowed trade with the Dutch, Spanish, and English; but these Europeans behaved no better than the Portuguese had. It was only the weakness of the Ming Dynasty, which had to turn to the Europeans for military support, and the fact that missionaries arriving at the end of the century somewhat ameliorated the impression made by their merchant countrymen, that kept China from being sealed off from the West again.

A painting on silk depicts a spring morning in the emperor's palace; the empress, attended by her handmaidens, has her portrait painted. At left is a figure of a Taoist sage, one of the small ivory carvings for which Ming Dynasty sculptors are famous.

6

GOD'S OBVIOUS DESIGN

"If death," wrote the Spanish viceroy in Naples, "came from Spain, we should all live to a very great age." Like the mills of the gods Philip of Spain ground slowly, and when death finally came to the king of Spain, it was quietly told to wait while His Most Catholic Majesty discussed with his ministers and priest every particular of his impending funeral, ordered great bolts of black cloth to shroud his palace, and demanded that his coffin be brought to the bedside to make sure it was the proper size for his putrid and withered body. Just as Philip the Prudent could not die without ensuring that his corpse would fit perfectly its final resting place, so for forty years he could not live without scrutinizing with agonizing care every detail of the government of his vast domain. When his father, the Emperor Charles, gouty and sick of heart, resigned the immense burden of his many realms to Philip, not a king but a prince of pedants mounted the throne of Spain and shouldered the weight of the largest empire the world had ever seen.

The magnitude of Philip's failure, the martyrdom of an entire kingdom to his unselfish but vainglorious vision of a Europe purged of heresy and united in the ample bosom of the Mother Church, has led scholars to speculate on the character of a monarch who hid himself in a cell twelve feet square as his empire grew ever larger, who dressed himself in the severest black as the gold of the Indies poured into his coffers, and who sought the quiet of his study as Spanish arms won victories for God and Church on land and sea. There is something terrifying about the words used to describe the king: *solitary, reserved,*

dispassionate, cold, imperturbable are the adjectives most often employed by apologists and critics alike. The anecdotes about his iron self-restraint are numerous. One is told about a young and nervous clerk who ruined an evening's work when he inadvertently poured ink, not sand, on one of the king's letters. With superhuman patience Philip carefully explained: "*That* is the ink. *This* is the sand." During his lifetime Philip buried seventeen of his family, but he never showed sorrow, and he ordered his priests to render thanks to God on the occasion of each funeral. The most celebrated story told is probably untrue, but it is in keeping with the king's character. When a frightened secretary brought news of the disaster of the Armada, Philip barely interrupted the motion of his pen to remark: "I give thanks to God by whose hand I have been so endowed that I can put to sea another fleet as great as this we have lost whenever I choose."

Even in his fanaticism Philip was without enthusiasm, which made his words to one of the Inquisition's victims, Don Carlos de Seso, more monstrous than if they had been spoken in anger. The occasion was the magnificent auto-da-fé of October, 1559, staged by the inquisitor general to celebrate the king's happy return to Spain and to demonstrate to the world Philip's determination never to "live to be a king of heretics." The celebration was held in the great square of Valladolid, opposite the Cathedral of St. Francis, where before an audience of two hundred thousand Philip took a mighty oath to defend the holy Catholic faith with all the strength of his empire. Then to the tolling of the bells, twenty-

Philip II *of Spain as portrayed by Titian*

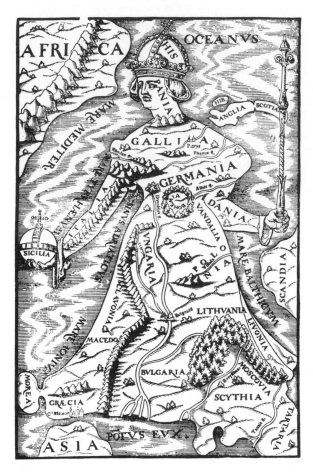

Political realities supersede geographical accuracy in this sixteenth-century map showing Spain as Europe's head.

the rock upon which Philip built the administrative system of his empire.

Spain and its dependencies were governed by an administrative pyramid with a royal council of state near its peak and twelve regional and departmental councils at its base. The lesser units, such as the councils of Castile and of the Indies, or the Inquisition, exercised immense authority, but the council of state was little more than a debating forum that the king kept divided into opposing factions and used only as a source of information and as a place in which to test his ministers. Philip the Prudent never sought the unanimous advice of his council, for that would have smacked of conciliar control. Instead, he confronted every minister with his opposite number. If half the council followed the lead of one member, the duke of Alva, and espoused a policy of strong action, Philip was at pains to see that the other half was of the opinion of an opposing councilor, the prince of Eboli, who stood for mildness, diplomacy, and caution. Philip listened to both men with endless patience, but his ultimate purpose was to ensure that every policy urged by the one would be criticized by the other. Information, not advice, was the king's obsession, and he read an ambassador's passing comment about English insects as avidly as he did Mendoza's political analysis.

"It is well to consider everything," Philip once said, and he sedulously followed his own dictum. Government by annotation was the result. No detail was trifling enough to be delegated, no report long enough to warrant abridgment. Mountains of papers arrived daily from Aragon and Naples, Milan and the Netherlands, Mexico and Peru, Africa and the Indies. The duke of Alva in Antwerp, Bernadino de Mendoza in London or Paris, Cristobal de Moura in Lisbon, and Francisco de Toledo in Lima dutifully reported to their master, and he as faithfully read, corrected, and annotated everything they wrote. With stupefying industry Philip filled the margins of their reports with his spidery handwriting, laboriously noting that a Latin scribe had spelled *quasi* with a double *s*, commenting upon a detail of government, or curtly dismissing some opinion with which he disagreed.

The result was endless, infuriating delay; but that hardly mattered to Philip, for patience was a virtue that he shared with Elizabeth of England. Philip's statement that "time and I are a match for any two" was more than a passing expression of his belief that delay resolved all things, it was the essence of his life. Every petition, every memorandum from the council, every ambassador's report followed a carefully prescribed path and was eventually added to the great heap of documents that weighted down

five condemned heretics received judgment. Thirteen escaped with imprisonment and penance; the rest were sentenced to burn alive, but ten of them, who chose to die as Catholics, were mercifully strangled before being consumed in the fire; the two who refused to recant endured the agony of the stake. One of these was Carlos de Seso, who accused the king of inhumanity and barbarism. Philip's flat and epicene voice answered: "If my son were as evil as you are, I myself would fetch the wood wherewith to burn him."

Throughout his life Philip acted only after most painstaking deliberation, but once a decision was made he moved with the inexorable conviction of a man at peace with God. Philip's conscience was no servant to ambition, and he always maintained that his royal office placed upon him a burden far greater than that of other men, for God expected more of kings than of subjects and more of the king of Spain than of any other king. The entire structure of his government was designed to give Philip the time and the information to make decisions for himself. His father, the emperor, had warned him to depend on none but yourself," and that advice became the king's desk and consumed his waking hours. Everything that the king handled had to be in precise and proper form, and Philip was loath to read any letter that did not, as custom demanded, address him simply as "Sir" and conclude with the words "God guard the Catholic person of Your Majesty." Without time to deliberate, without the security of system, without every scrap of information by which to arrive at certainty, Philip was as helpless as a pedant without facts or a bureaucrat without organization. Only when every *i* had been dotted and every *t* crossed, did the king finally make up his mind.

Philip's somber palace outside Madrid stands as a monument to the man and the golden age of Spain. The Escorial is a savage and sinister pile of gray stone in a setting that only El Greco could have captured in paint. Part monastery, part mausoleum, and part mansion for a ruler possessed of a clerical turn of mind and consumed by a messianic ideal, the Escorial is a mirror of the king who built it and the empire that sustained it. Long before Philip came to the throne, he had pictured to himself just such a massive hiding place, safe in that "land of rocks

and saints." His father, when in Spain, had lived in the exquisitely cool and arabesque rooms of the caliphs of Granada and later had built himself a superbly impractical palace in the best Renaissance style. But the son sought not a home but a tomb, not the grandeur of Rome nor the miracle of Moslem artistry but a Christian citadel and hermitage.

In one task alone Philip would tolerate no delay; he could not wait to see his dream translated into the granite of the Sierra de Guadarrama. Massive, fortresslike walls formed an enormous structure that was 675 feet long and 530 feet wide and almost 100 feet high, split by narrow and unfriendly windows; their appearance belied the luxury within the Escorial. Every region of Philip's empire contributed to the fulfillment of the royal vision: from Milan came silver chalices and gold candelabra, tapestries were provided by Antwerp and Brussels, an infinite variety of woods were imported from the New World. From Spain itself came marble of the Sierra Nevada and steel of Toledo; and Venice—outside Philip's domain—sent paintings by Titian and Tintoretto to decorate the walls.

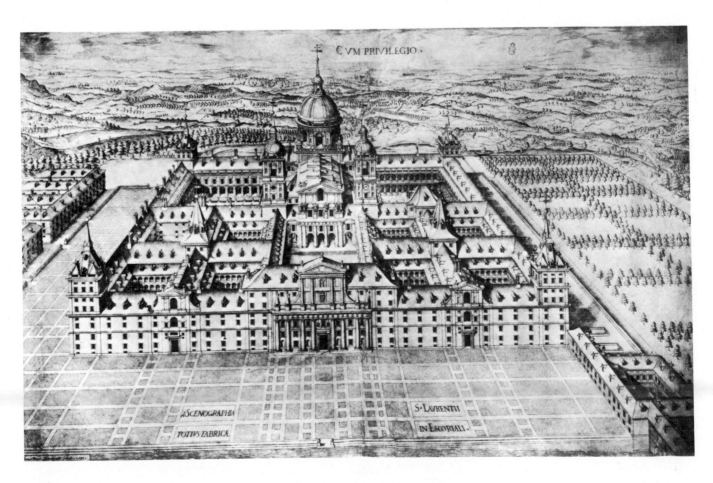

Philip's great new palace and monastery, the Escorial, shown here in a contemporary print, takes its name from El Escorial ("the slag heap"), the hamlet that it dominates.

Les estampes y el sumario de el Escorial, EDITORIAL TECNOS, MADRID, 1954

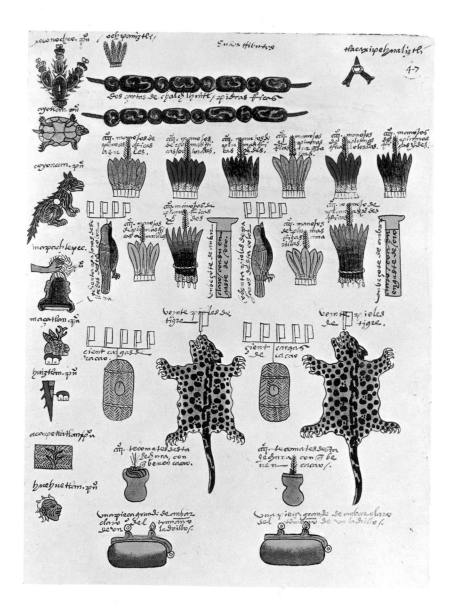

Pages from an Aztec Codex (above and opposite) itemized tribute exacted from subjugated Mexican tribes.

before the high altar of Saint Lawrence. In lonely eminence, God's lieutenant on earth wrapped himself in the mantle of divinity and meditated upon the heavy responsibilities of kings.

Philip allowed himself a single luxury: as monarch of twenty-seven kingdoms and an empire upon which the sun never set, he could indulge his collector's instinct, and even before the Escorial was finished, the king had turned it into a vast library and reliquary. Books, manuscripts, relics, oddities, and rarities poured in from agents all over the world. Philip had been educated in the Renaissance tradition of learning; his library with its thirty thousand volumes and four thousand manuscripts was no less precious to him than the shelves upon which were placed in rich settings the arm of Saint Lawrence, two bones of the apostles Philip and James, and the remains of Saint Justus and Saint Pastor. Every facet of Philip's character found expression in the Escorial —his coldness, his pedantry, his magpie instinct, his austerity, his passion for privacy, and above all, his sense of divine mission. For all his golden locks, Hapsburg chin, and Germanic complexion, Philip was the perfect Spaniard. He was at home in the land of Ignatius Loyola and Saint Theresa and her barefooted Carmelites, where every man's soul was his castle and the Lord walked "among the pots and pans."

Spain had been the product of a Christian vision come true; it had been won by blood and faith. Spanish soldiers had hurled back the onslaught of Islam and had carved out a kingdom for God. A handful of Spanish conquistadors, stout of heart and strong in faith, had performed miracles and had toppled the empires of the New World. Philip belonged to such a Spain, for his image of himself as the instrument of God's glorious design was no more fantastic than Loyola's will to sainthood, Saint Theresa's determination to reform the Church, Cortes' dream of empire, or Don Quixote's romantic chivalry. In Spain fantasies like the Escorial or Don Quixote's windmills had a way of coming true. When Philip, in August, 1559, determined to return to his kingdom of miracles after the death of his wife Mary Tudor and accept his destiny as the chosen leader of the forces of the Counter-Reformation, he believed that he would be able to make another fantasy come true and restore the Church to power throughout Europe.

On October 25, 1555, the Emperor Charles, with tears in his eyes, had announced his decision to abdicate and spend his remaining days in the Spanish monastery of Yuste. Early the following year he resigned his Spanish dominions to Philip and later assigned his imperial crown to his brother, Ferdinand. At fifty-six the "greatest emperor that the Christian world had ever seen," as his wife persisted in calling

Even working in haste it took twenty-one years to construct and furnish a palace that would conform exactly to the king's demanding tastes. Philip gathered the riches of his empire not only for his personal satisfaction but also to honor God and Saint Lawrence, whose grisly martyrdom had inspired the architectural plan and after whom the great church of the Escorial was named. Saint Lawrence had died on a gridiron and Philip's palace was laid out accordingly. At the center of the grid was placed the monastery church, hidden, except for its great dome, by the towering walls of monastic cells and royal apartments. In vaults beneath the church rested the family coffins filled with Hapsburg bodies; alongside the church was located Philip's bedchamber, equipped with a shuttered peephole through which the king could look out on the Hieronymite monks in prayer him, was white-haired and exhausted, his hands so arthritic that he could scarcely open a letter and the pain so terrible that he prayed for death. A rich diet of pickled partridges, eel pies, sardines, Rhenish wine, and iced beer may have shortened his life, but it was his constant effort to discipline an empire as quarrelsome as a pack of wolves that had made Charles old beyond his years. Thirty-six years of ceaseless peregrinations had taught him three things about his empire: heresy had to be tolerated in Germany, fortune was a woman who loved not an old man, and his ramshackle dominions would be more orthodox in their faith and more manageable in their proportions if divested of the German states and freed from imperial responsibility.

Even without the imperial dignity, Philip's titles were impressive beyond measure. He was ruler of the three kingdoms of Spain (Castile, Aragon, and Navarre), lord of Burgundy and the Netherlands, archduke of Milan, sovereign of Naples and Sicily, monarch of the Indies, and until Mary's death, king of England as well. England had been regarded by his father as absolutely essential to the dynastic interests of the Hapsburgs in their struggle against Valois France. The island kingdom completed the encirclement of France, secured the Channel route between Spain and the Netherlands, and ensured a constant flow of unfinished wool cloth to the markets of Flanders. So important was the English alliance that in 1554 the Emperor Charles had bestowed his only legitimate son upon the aging and ailing Mary Tudor. Philip had dutifully accepted the possessive caresses of his neurotic wife and had suffered exile in a land of heretics and barbarians, who unmercifully insulted and cheated his entourage. As long as the Valois threat continued and there remained any real hope of an heir by Mary, Philip stayed close to England, but by 1557 it was painfully evident that his queen's pregnancies were the fictions of a disordered mind, and it was apparent that France, after its defeat at St. Quentin, could easily be persuaded to sue for peace. By the time Mary died in November, 1558, Philip was prepared to view the event as a blessed liberation that relieved him of the responsibility of rescuing Calais for the English, and freed him to sign the peace of Cateau-Cambrésis and marry Elizabeth Valois of France.

The French marriage brought unexpected blessings, for it was during the celebration of the wedding by proxy that Henry II of France, the bride's father received the fatal injury to his head. By default, Philip became the colossus of Europe: France was ruled by a sickly boy king and his greedy uncles; the Emperor Ferdinand was rendered almost impotent by the Lutheran princes of Germany; and

Tribute goods collected by the Aztec emperor and later by the Spaniards included costumes, skins, and jade beads.

England was exposed to the doubtful charms and tender government of a virgin queen. August, 1559, seemed a good time for the king to return to Spain to begin transforming the land of his birth into a "fortress, strength, treasure, and sword" of God. Even the famous astrologer Nostradamus considered the moment to be propitious.

Colossus though he was, Philip faced a formidable task. The soldiers of Satan, by their many triumphs among the Protestant princes of the empire, had left his father a broken man and Germany a dying and divided realm. Scotland and England had both fallen into the devil's grasp, and in France the heretics waited impatiently to bathe the kingdom in blood. Everywhere heresy marched triumphant and unchecked, and Philip heard with alarm of the discovery of Protestant cells in Spain itself, in Seville

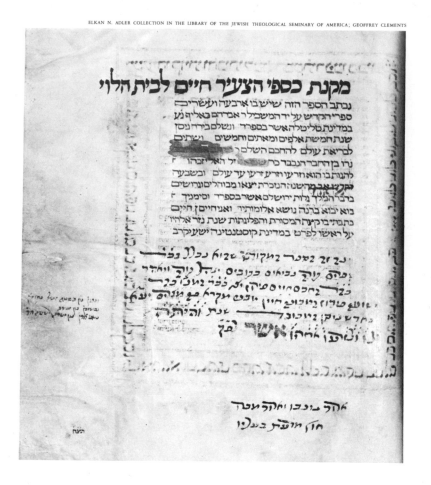

מקנת כספי הצעיר חיים לבית הלוי

The page above is from a Hebrew Bible manuscript written in Toledo in 1492, the year Jews were expelled from Spain. Possession of such books by a Marrano—a descendant of the converted Jews who remained in the country—was considered ample evidence of heresy by the Spanish Inquisition.

and Valladolid. By chance the Inquisition had been alerted to the growing peril: Calvinist propaganda intended for a heretical priest had been delivered accidentally to another cleric of the same name. That worthy ecclesiastic read with shock about the inefficacy of good works and viewed with horror a picture of the pope giving thanks to the devil. He immediately took the book to the Inquisition. A swift and thorough heresy hunt ensued, and a series of autos-da-fé was administered as an antidote to Protestantism before the poison could infect disgruntled nobles and susceptible merchants.

Spaniards were shocked that even a few hundred disciples of evil had crept into a land "so Catholic, so firm, and so true." In no other country in Europe was unity of faith and state so intimately and emotionally linked and the Inquisition held in such reverence. The *Suprema*, which governed the Inquisition, was thought of as God's special agency for preserving purity of creed and served as the king's effective instrument for maintaining his authority over Church, aristocracy, and citizenry. Each auto-da-fé increased the prestige and power of the Inquisition, and no one was too insignificant or too

lofty to escape its scrutiny. Even an archbishop, Bartolomé de Carranza, of Toledo, was quietly whisked away in the dead of night by order of the *Suprema* and vanished from sight. The charge of heresy against him was grounded on sentences torn out of context, and his secret trial dragged on for seventeen years. It is difficult to judge men who strove to detect deviations of faith with the aid of red-hot pincers and stretched men upon the rack in order to force Satan to reveal his presence in them. Yet the twentieth century is no stranger to heresy hunts. Then, as now, it was argued that all men must be formed from a single ideological mold, for only thus would it be possible to be sure of friends and recognize enemies. Ideas, unless carefully expurgated, were considered dangerous, and deviation in thought, it was said, bred confusion and doubt, the inevitable harbingers of treason and ultimate defeat.

Had Protestantism been the sole consideration of the Spanish Inquisition, the office would have withered away for lack of work. What inspired the *Suprema* to unrelenting vigil and convinced good Spaniards that it was "guided by God for His praise and honor" was the constant fear in every Catholic heart of Moriscos and Marranos—Christian Moors and Christian Jews. As French Catholics saw Huguenots in their nightmares and English Puritans read with horrified fascination of the atrocities committed by Jesuits and inquisitors, so Spaniards were brought up on grisly tales of Catholic children kidnapped and educated in the Jewish faith, of girls sold into Moorish slavery, and of secret and satanic rites practiced high in the mountains surrounding Granada.

Fiction born of hysteria and reports based on reality can be difficult to disentangle. After the fall of Granada, in 1492, the Moors had been forced to choose between Christianity and exile. Most chose to convert, but their conquerors still eyed them with deep suspicion, noting that they remained Moorish in dress, language, and custom. The people of Granada worked on feast days, observed Fridays more carefully than Sundays, practiced circumcision, and married according to the Islamic rites. The day of reckoning had been postponed by Morisco money, which persuaded the government not to enforce laws that had been decreed against Moorish dress and culture, but in 1567 Philip determined upon the total Christianization of such doubtful subjects. His decision, the result of great deliberation, was typical; he concluded that both conscience and national policy demanded strong action. Arabic was outlawed, Moorish books, both innocent and pernicious, were destroyed, Islamic customs and dress were forbidden, and during all Fridays, Church holy days, and marriage celebrations, every Moorish family was ordered to keep its doors open so that all the world could inspect the sincerity of its Catholicism. Faced with cultural annihilation the Moriscos rebelled. Christian men, especially priests, were butchered, and women and children were sold as slaves to the Barbary pirates in exchange for arms. Moorish atrocities were countered with Spanish reprisals and the entire province of Granada was put to the sword.

War in the high sierras was much more than a civil insurrection by an oppressed minority; it was another battle in the great crusade that wrested Spain from the infidel. Granada was regarded as the weak spot through which Islam might re-enter and again conquer the peninsula. The threat was no figment of wild Spanish imagination. The Ottoman empire was at its apogee, and with its support the Moors might be enabled to reassert their independence in Granada. In 1560 a Spanish fleet had been nearly destroyed at Los Gelves and the western Mediterranean opened up to Turkish expansion; Suleiman the Magnificent had died in 1566 while his armies were hammering at the gates of Vienna; and the new sultan, Selim II, was urged to send an army to liberate the Moriscos and reconquer Spain. Fortunately for Philip, Turkish attention was diverted towards a struggle with Venice over the island of Cyprus; even so the Moriscos received eight hundred trained soldiers from Algiers and a steady flow of arms and volunteers from their Moorish brethren in North Africa.

Treason and heresy in Granada and Moslem power in North Africa and the Mediterranean were equally dangerous, and Philip set about the task of exterminating one and repelling the other. During 1570 Granada was overrun by Spanish troops, and the Morisco menace was destroyed once and for all. The entire Moorish population was transported to other parts of Spain and the province repopulated with Spaniards of untarnished blood and unimpeachable orthodoxy. Thenceforth any adult male of Moorish descent found within ten leagues of the province of Granada was executed, and any female was sold into slavery. The price of victory had been heavy—sixty thousand Spaniards killed and an entire province turned into a desert—but purity of faith and the security of the kingdom were worth the cost. Spain had to be made safe for Christianity at home before it could begin the battle against the menace of Islam abroad.

A union of Venice, the papacy, and Spain to form a holy league was the necessary preliminary to victory over the infidel in the Mediterranean, but such a union took months of hardheaded negotiation to achieve. The Venetians hated the Spaniards and

A 1520 relief shows the baptism of Moslem women. Later, when Philip found that the Moriscos of Granada were only nominal Christians, he rigidly suppressed Moorish customs.

deeply mistrusted the papacy, and the pope's fear of Spanish hegemony was almost as great as his need for Spanish troops in the battle against heresy. It galled the Holy Father unspeakably when he discovered that his Spanish champion treated him more like a palace priest than like the supreme judge of Christendom. Fourteen years earlier Philip had been at open war with the ferocious and bitterly anti-Spanish Paul IV, and his troops had marched against banners consecrated by the Vatican. The king of Spain had regarded the Council of Trent as a conclave "in which the devil was working and plotting," and not until Spanish influence had triumphed over both French and papal interests did he look favorably upon its decrees. Even Henry VIII might have envied Philip his ecclesiastical arrogance, for that Most Catholic Monarch taxed, disciplined, and governed his Church without papal interference, and at the same time interfered so much in the affairs of Rome that Pius IV, the gentlest of pontiffs, once shouted in rage: "If the king wants to be king in Spain, I want to be pope at Rome." In the end, however, necessity prevailed over dissension. A Spanish, Venetian, and papal fleet of six great

galleasses—each of them bearing 44 cannons—203 galleys, and 100 transport ships, carrying a total of 28,000 soldiers, sailed to the rescue of Cyprus in September, 1571, a month after that Greek island had been overrun by the Turkish troops of Sultan Selim II.

Once Philip had determined upon war he was willing to chance all in God's service, and the fleet was ordered to seek out the navy of the Sublime Porte and destroy it no matter what the risk. Christian met infidel in the Gulf of Lepanto, in waters controlled by the Turks, where defeat would have meant annihilation and mastery of the entire Mediterranean by the Ottoman empire. The battle was as much a clash of religions as of vessels. As the Turkish navy, in every way equal to the allied fleet, advanced, every Moslem sailor shouted his scorn and hatred of the enemies of Allah. When the moment came for Don John, Philip's illegitimate half brother and commander of the Christian armada, to give the order to engage the Turks, a crucifix was raised aloft on every mast, and the sailors and soldiers of the allied navy knelt in adoration.

The commanders of the two fleets met in the

Turkish janizaries (above) engage the Spanish during Philip's greatest victory, the battle of Lepanto—one of the last decisive naval engagements fought at close quarters.

thick of battle, where the pride of the sultan's janizaries clashed with the pick of the Spanish legions. Twice Don John's soldiers boarded Ali Pasha's flagship and twice they were repulsed by a torrent of arrows and bullets, but on the third attack the Turkish admiral was struck down by a Spanish musket. In triumph Don John ordered Ali Pasha's head impaled upon a lance for both navies to behold. Christian cheers and Catholic crosses were raised high and the banners of Allah were pulled down on vessel after vessel. Of the sultan's 300 ships of war, 117 were captured and 133 were destroyed. A mere 50 escaped to fight again. Of his forces, 8,000 infidels were sent to their Moslem reward, and 8,000 more were captured; and 10,000 Christian galley slaves were liberated.

In the words of Miguel de Cervantes Saavedra, who had fought at Lepanto, the Spanish victory was "the noblest occasion that past or present ages have seen or future ones may hope to see," and a disillusionment to all nations who believed that the Turks were invincible upon the sea. Pope Pius danced with ecstasy at the news and showered biblical thanks upon Don John, proclaiming "there was a man, one sent from God, whose name was John." The great campanile of Venice sounded the fervent thanks of all Christendom, and the lofty arches of St. Mark's echoed with the *Te Deum*. But in the Escorial there was only quiet acceptance of God's will and the ceremonial presentation of the captured sanjak, the great standard of the sultan. The banner was bestowed on the monks of the Escorial in solemn recognition of the Spanish contribution to victory and of God's manifest favor toward his champion.

Lepanto marked a turning point for Spain and its messianic monarch. By 1571 the Philip of legend had begun to emerge—black, cheerless, touched with necrophilia, and suffering in stoic silence the pains of asthma, kidney stones, and gout. More and more the king's mind turned away from the infidel, whose continued existence for eight hundred years seemed to indicate a respectable role in "God's ultimate design," to the more poisonous problem of heresy within the Christian flock. Spain itself had been made safe from Allah without and Satan within, but elsewhere the devil marched unopposed. If Philip were to be the good shepherd and to realize his dream of a Catholic and orthodox Europe, he would have to exterminate heresy in his own Dutch provinces and win England and Scotland back to the fold of the Roman Church.

Philip had begun to change in the years immediately preceding Lepanto. His court had not always been devoid of pomp and circumstance. He had inherited from his father an enormous entourage of

A broadside reporting the battle of Lepanto depicts the Turkish commander Ali Pasha before and after his defeat.

one thousand five hundred persons, and his house had been filled with life and laughter while his French wife and his son lived. In 1568, however, death struck a double blow. In July, Don Carlos, heir to all of his father's possessions, died under circumstances that have provided the theme for partisan novels and high romance ever since, and two months later Elizabeth Valois, the only one of Philip's wives who had given him happiness, followed her stepson to the grave. The story of Don Carlos is so wrapped in legend that fiction and truth are hopelessly mixed. The picture of the king that emerges reveals Philip at his most insensate—so coldly stoic that any sympathy for him is almost destroyed, although he must have suffered agonizingly before acknowledging the fact that his son was mad.

Don Carlos was misshapen in mind and body. His back was hunched, his body dwarfed, and at eighteen he weighed only seventy-six pounds. He was a sadist and a paranoiac, roasting rabbits alive and torturing his horses to hear them scream. He found sexual satisfaction in whipping girls, and it was while chasing his steward's daughter or some other young unfortunate that he fell down a flight of stairs and severely injured his head. His life was saved by a painful and delicate operation, trepanning, which involved cutting a hole through his skull to relieve the pressure on his brain. For good measure, his father insisted on placing the withered corpse of the saintly cook of a Franciscan convent in bed with his son, and he always maintained that not surgery but the odor of sanctity had saved the infante's life.

Despite the Franciscan chef, Don Carlos never fully recovered. From sadism he moved on to periods of homicidal mania, during which he endeavored to murder anyone who thwarted him. He grew to hate his father and delighted in giving away state secrets. Finally he attempted flight to Germany. Philip could not risk having his only son fall into the hands of his enemies. Don Carlos, even mad and deformed, was a potential tool in the dynastic schemes of the sovereigns of Europe. The king had no choice but to convert the infante's apartment into a prison. In the early hours of January 19, 1568, Philip entered his son's rooms and personally

supervised the nailing up of doors and windows, directing that thenceforth no man should speak or write to his heir. Six months later Don Carlos was dead. Some said it was suicide; some insisted it was natural death brought on by the prince's habit on hot nights of sleeping naked on a bed of ice; some whispered that it was murder ordered by a father who had detected the taint of heresy in the infante and who could never forgive his son's incestuous lust for the queen, Elizabeth Valois. Whatever the cause, Don Carlos' death, followed so closely by that of the queen, filled Philip's life with anguish. Thenceforth he lived in mourning, increasing the hours of his labor and turning his thoughts more and more to the problem of exterminating heresy in the Netherlands.

The situation in the Netherlands had always been difficult. Even under Philip's father, fat Burgundian burghers and sly Flemish artisans had been jealous of their municipal liberties and suspicious of the emperor's Spanish son. Heresy had found a fertile breeding place in this country of fleshy Rubens females and scrubbed and tidy Vermeer kitchens. At first the language of heresy had been limited to the relatively quiet tones of Lutheranism, but by 1566 the streets of Antwerp, Brussels, and Amsterdam were ringing with the strident voice of Calvinism. Charles had directed the most brutal edicts against his heretical subjects and had introduced the Inquisition to the Netherlands; but he had always preferred a live taxpayer to a dead Protestant, and during his reign the Inquisition had remained inactive, though heretics had not.

Philip faced a serious decision: the choice between an orthodox realm or a prosperous people. For the first eight years of his rule he accepted his father's policy. The Netherlands was the economic jewel of his empire. It consisted of seventeen provinces, half industrial, half commercial, part French, but all rich and held together in a loose union under the power of the Hapsburg throne and the authority of a States-General, which was little more than an assembly of ambassadors who disliked one another almost as much as they loathed Philip and his Spanish ways. Antwerp was a city of one hundred thousand and boasted a bourse "for the use of all merchants of whatever land or language." It was the focal point of the European money market, the center of the spice trade with the Indies, and the magnet that attracted the gold and silver of the New World. Louvain, after Paris, was the leading university of northern Europe; Brussels was the source of the most prized tapestries in all Europe. The ports of the northern provinces of Holland and Zeeland harbored some five thousand sail-

Despite his usual chilliness, Philip was a devoted father and doted on his daughters, portrayed here by Coello.

ing vessels, which were beginning to monopolize the oceanic trade routes.

Treason and rebellion were cherished, historic traditions in the Netherlands, as the kings of France, the dukes of Burgundy, and the Hapsburgs of Germany all had learned to their sorrow. Towns were jealous of their ancient rights, proud and impoverished nobles resented any encroachment upon their independence, merchants were reluctant to finance the dynastic wars of Hapsburg princes, and clerics feared any rational reorganization of the ecclesiastical muddle of bishoprics and benefices. The Walloons of the south detested the Dutch-speaking north, the apprentices and journeymen of Ghent and Bruges could always be inflamed to violence, and nearly everyone, from Prince William of Orange to the weavers of Arras, feared the presence of the Inquisition and despised the Spanish soldiers who tramped the streets of Brussels and Antwerp.

In the spring and summer of 1566, social, religious, and political discontent, which had been bubbling and seething for five years, erupted into revolution. The lesser nobles bound themselves together to demand the abolition of the Inquisition and force Philip to promise that he would consult the States-General on all matters of religion. When Philip's regent submitted to the so-called Request and granted religious toleration, the Calvinist minority incited the masses to violence and religious hysteria. In August, 1566, four hundred churches and monasteries were looted, tombs were broken open, statues of saints smashed, and the gold pillaged from the high altar of Antwerp Cathedral. Monks and nuns were beaten and dispossessed; Catholic homes were sacked; and revolution and religious ecstasy engulfed town after town. At first Philip showed surprising restraint in the face of defiance and heresy, but if he were ever to fulfill his vow to maintain the Catholic faith with all his strength and possessions, the king could not permit treason and godlessness to go unpunished. By the summer of 1567 Philip's "duty as a Christian prince" left him no choice but to dispatch the duke of Alva and twenty thousand troops—half of them Spanish—to Brussels, where, should it prove necessary, they were ordered to write God's will in blood.

Alva's soldiers were crusading Catholics who hated the Dutch for their civilian habits, bourgeois greed, and religious laxity. The duke himself believed in immediate and terrible retribution and never doubted that his troops would swiftly settle a revolution led by common apprentices and heretic priests. "I have tamed men of iron," he boasted, "and shall I not be able to tame these men of butter?" Alva did in a year what all the prayers and ser-

Even Philip's limitless patience was sorely tried by his only son, the depraved and deformed Don Carlos, whom Coello seems to have flattered outrageously in this portrait.

mons of the Calvinists had been unable to do: he united all elements and provinces in hatred of Philip. A special court, the bloody Court of Troubles, enforced his law upon nobles and wealthy merchants as well as on peasants and tradesmen. Aristocratic privileges, sacred rights, and ancient laws were swept aside with a flick of the duke's sword, and thousands were tried with military efficiency and executed without mercy. To judicial murder Alva added economic strangulation: he imposed a crushing tax of ten per cent on the sale of movable goods and five per cent on the transfer of land. The result was to drive merchants, tradesmen, manufacturers, and aristocrats to further insurrection.

For four years the rebellion was limited to the northern provinces—the present-day territory of the Netherlands—where privateers, the famous Sea Beggars, carried on an immensely profitable war of piracy against Spanish shipping. At first they operated out of English ports, but in 1572 the Beggars seized the coastal city of Brielle and won control of northwestern provinces of Holland and Zeeland. Safe behind a morass of bogs, canals, estuaries, and shallow broads, they were secure on land from Alva's Spanish legions and triumphant on the high seas, where the profits of piracy and commerce were to finance a war that lasted more than thirty years and that laid the foundations for Dutch naval and maritime supremacy in the seventeenth century.

The Dutch Sea Beggars found in William the Silent, prince of Orange, possibly the only man in the Netherlands who had the vision, determination, and reputation to keep the revolt alive. How he earned the title of "Silent" is difficult to say. Certainly William was neither quiet nor taciturn, but he seems to have possessed a considerable talent for keeping his thoughts to himself. He was a master at masking feudal ambitions behind patriotic sentiments and associating his own dynastic designs with Dutch dislike of Philip's autocratic methods. The hero of the Netherlands may have had feet of clay, but he was a great leader of men and the successful champion of principles to which Dutchmen of every class and prejudice could adhere. Patient, practical, and imperturbable, he discovered the formula that ultimately united the seven quarreling provinces of the north into a nation. He called upon his countrymen "to restore the whole fatherland to its old liberty and prosperity out of the clutches of the Spanish vultures and wolves." It is little wonder that Philip placed a bounty on the prince's head and offered a reward of twenty-five thousand écus to any man who could devise a way to rid Europe of this "enemy of the human race."

In the winter of 1576 William the Silent almost succeeded in uniting the entire Netherlands when Catholics and Calvinists, Dutch and Walloons were shocked into a single community by the sight of Alva's troops putting Antwerp to the sword. November was bitterly cold and cheerless, and Spanish soldiers had been without pay for months. They rose in rebellion and turned upon the fat war profiteers, the rich merchants, and the idle citizens of Antwerp, in a mutinous attempt to reimburse themselves through plunder. During the "Spanish fury," the city was sacked, its women raped, and seven thousand of its inhabitants killed. Throughout the southern Netherlands, horrified Catholics put aside their fear of Calvinists and northern rebels and joined with Holland and Zeeland in the Pacification of Ghent, resolving to fight together to liberate the entire land from Spanish misrule.

Despite the Spanish atrocities at Antwerp, Philip managed to salvage a portion of his Flemish inheritance and to frustrate William of Orange's hope of total victory. Alva was replaced; he was succeeded first by Don John and then in 1578 by the king's most able diplomat and warrior, Alexander Farnese, duke of Parma. Parma won back the southern and Catholic provinces by combining brilliant military tactics with such diplomatic finesse that he soon had Catholics once again hating Calvinists more than Spaniards. Prince William met his match in this Spaniard, whose sense of military timing was unsurpassed and whose calculated moves and use of terrain made William's military efforts look amateurish. Parma was a pick and shovel general, spending more time digging ditches and diverting streams than drilling his men in the use of pike and musket. Yet it was he who transformed Spain's undisciplined and cumbersome army, gleaned from every hamlet of Europe, into an effective fighting force that was not to lose a major battle for the next century.

Spanish successes in the Netherlands might never have been so impressive had not religious and linguistic dissension allowed Parma to drive a wedge between the north and the south. Protestants in the central and southern provinces looked with envy on their brothers in God who had won dictatorial control in Holland, and they unwisely rushed to establish the kingdom of God's elect in the southern regions too. In 1578 a Calvinist coup d'état took place in Ghent, and worried Catholics began to ask themselves whether they had driven Spanish troops out the front door only to let the soldiers of Satan in the back. By 1579 religious discord had wrecked William of Orange's dream of unifying the Netherlands, and each half of the country went its separate way. The south formed itself into the Catholic Union of Arras, the north into the Union of Utrecht.

In this English satirical painting, Philip's bovine mount, representing the Netherlands, reacts emphatically to the attentions of the duke of Alençon (left). Other interested parties are the duke of Alva (milking the cow), William of Orange, and Queen Elizabeth.

Divided, the Netherlanders could not resist, and step by step, village by village, canal by canal, the Spaniards inched northward. In desperation the seven northern provinces took the monumental step of renouncing their allegiance to Philip and proclaiming their independence in 1581, with William of Orange as hereditary stadholder.

Prince William never lived to see Holland fully independent, for three years later, in July, 1584, he was killed by a French fanatic, Balthasar Gérard. In the following year Antwerp fell to Parma, and all well-informed sources in Europe assured Philip that his Dutch ulcer had been drained of its infection and that the final phase of the war against Holland would be completed within a year. Diplomatic and military pundits reckoned, however, without the interference of Elizabeth of England.

The sixteenth century was no stranger to the fine distinction between hot and cold war. In fact both Elizabeth and Philip preferred intrigue, diplomatic assassinations, and the quiet fostering of domestic strife to open warfare. Such measures were safe and cheap, and they could always be denied with diplomatic grace. Brinkmanship was an honored art long before the great powers of the twentieth century gave it new meaning in an age of atomic warfare. Ever since 1568 Elizabeth had been calmly and not very secretly offering aid and comfort to Philip's rebellious and heretical subjects. Of course, Philip was doing exactly the same for Elizabeth, but that is the story of another chapter. Elizabeth had sanctioned the seizing of a Spanish treasure ship laden with bullion for Alva and his unpaid troops, had given haven to Dutch Sea Beggars and allowed them to dispose of their loot through English commercial channels, and had permitted English volunteers and English capital to strike a blow for God in support of the Netherlands revolt.

In their frustration Spanish military strategists probably overestimated the amount and effectiveness of Elizabeth's help, but English aid to the Dutch was a handy excuse for Spanish failures. As

In this allegorical statuette the duke of Alva is beset by a tangle of serpents representing three of Spain's problems: the pope, Elizabeth, the Protestant elector of Saxony.

early as 1577 Philip's regent in the Netherlands, Don John, had excused his inability to stem the revolt on the grounds that "the only remedy for the disorders of the Netherlands is that England should be ruled by someone devoted to Your Majesty. If the contrary case prevails it will mean the ruin of these countries and their loss to your crown." In 1585, when Elizabeth committed the unpardonable diplomatic sin of bringing her unfriendly activities out into the open by sending a small army of five thousand foot and one thousand horse soldiers to the Lowlands, Philip reluctantly concluded that his half brother had spoken the truth. The king of Spain knew England better than most of his advisers, and he feared war with that barbaric race "as a burned child dreads the fire." But Elizabeth gave her brother sovereign no choice. If the dream of Philip's lifetime was to be fulfilled, the Great Enterprise had to be set in motion. The destruction of a heretical queen of England would be but the first step in the ultimate spiritual reunification of Europe.

Philip was never sanguine about his prospects of success. From the start he was aware of the terrible risks involved but content that God's will should be done. Actually the vision of re-establishing a medieval Christian empire was not as fantastic as it may seem. Many Christians viewed the prospect as one devoutly to be desired; Protestants and Catholics alike gave lip service to the ideal; and the chances of success after 1585 were probably greater than they had ever been since the time Luther posted his defiance on the doors of Wittenberg Church in 1517. Spain, that pillar of the Church and champion of Catholicism, stood at the apex of its military, moral, and economic strength. The riches of the Spanish Indies, which had been worth 213,400 pounds between 1503 and 1505, rose during the five years from 1580 to 1585 to a golden flood of 16,890,000 pounds. No monarch commanded revenues equal to Philip's. The *alcabala* alone—the ten per cent sales tax on all Spanish goods—realized 585,000 pounds, while the kingdom of Castile regularly contributed over 1,400,000 pounds a year to finance "God's obvious design." Spanish soldiers—the mainstay of Philip's army—were the best in the world, toughened in a climate that was "nine months' winter and three months' hell," and so convinced of their own invincibility that it was said that in battle they "postponed fear" to another day. The reputation of Spanish arms was no myth: Parma and his iron legions had seen to that, and the fall of Antwerp encouraged even the cautious Philip to believe that Castilian pikemen and Aragonian musketeers could perform miracles.

Spain was equally triumphant and invincible

upon the high seas. Lepanto had been a combined Christian victory, but Spanish ports had supplied half the ships and three fourths of the manpower. In 1582 Spanish naval prowess was again confirmed when twenty-five Spanish men-of-war and two thousand troops, under the command of the marquis of Santa Cruz, destroyed a French fleet of sixty great ships and seven thousand men. Impressed by this feat, Philip was inclined to trust Santa Cruz's assurance that he could handle anything the English might send against him.

Diplomatically Spain stood on a pinnacle. From Malta to Warsaw, from Buda to Antwerp, Catholicism was triumphant. The infidel was in obvious confusion under the corrupt successors of Suleiman the Magnificent. France was impotent, held ransom to the wishes of Spain by the art of Mendoza and the greed of the Guise family. The prince of Orange was dead and the return of the Netherlands to Spain seemed imminent; Antwerp was held by Parma, and his disciplined troops were ready to move northward into Holland or westward into England at a sign from the Escorial. Most important of all, Philip had inherited the treasures of the Portuguese empire, and for the first time had the ports and facilities to outfit an Atlantic fleet to sail against that arsenal of heresy and haven of rebels—Britain.

Ironically it was a Christian defeat at the hands of the infidel that gave Philip his chance to take over the impressive wealth and trade of his Iberian neighbor and to complete the unification of the peninsula. In August, 1578, at Alcazarquivir, King Sebastian of Portugal was killed and his troops massacred by the emperor of Morocco. At once Philip pressed his claims to the Portuguese throne. Tact, diplomacy, bribery, the influence of the Jesuits, and a carefully planned invasion of the country won still another crown for the king of Spain. In July, 1580, he entered his new kingdom preceded by a small army, which had such stringent orders not to pillage the land that the duke of Alva ran short of ropes with which to hang the offenders. For the first time in nine hundred years the Iberian peninsula was united under a single monarch; for the first time in history a single empire encircled the earth. In the western hemisphere Brazil joined New Spain and New Castile to bring all of South and Central America under Spanish control. In Africa Portuguese trading and supply stations gave Spain a claim to thousands of miles of coastline and a route to the Far East. In Asia Philip fell heir to Goa, Malabar, and Macao and the heavy Portuguese spice galleons sailing from those ports. Even more important to the destinies of Europe were the quiet coastal towns of Portugal with their docks and shipwrights,

and the great port of Lisbon with its protected harbor where an entire armada could safely anchor. Spain now had a wide vista to the west and the three thousand miles of rolling gray Atlantic, and Philip could seriously consider building a Catholic armada that would cleanse the seas of Dutch Sea Beggars, English pirates and heretics, and open England to the brutal mercies of Parma's troops.

The king of Spain had more than men and money at his command. Philip's mission was not his own; it was shared by ten million Spaniards, who had been brought up on the heroic exploits of conquistadors in America, crusaders in Granada, and the magnificent Spanish victories at Pavia, Lepanto, and Antwerp. As Ignatius Loyola had willed himself to be a saint by the power of his imagination, so all of Spain dreamed of a divine venture in which Castilian hidalgos, Catalan priests, and the peasants of Aragon would carry forward the banner of God. Spanish morale was sustained by a fairy tale that everyone from the grand inquisitor to the herdsmen of Navarre believed would some day come true. Miguel de Cervantes Saavedra was not alone in his Castilian conviction that faith and courage could transform romance into reality, fiction into truth; all of Spain agreed with him. Cervantes knew all about the unembellished realities of life. He had accompanied his father on that impecunious and itinerant physician's travels; he had fought beside Spanish veterans in Italy and had been wounded at Lepanto; he had lived as a slave in Algiers and served time in a Spanish prison; yet Cervantes could still rejoice in Spain's Great Enterprise and cheer the Armada on its way. Don Quixote and all of Spain somehow contrived never to look foolish even when mistaking windmills for dragons.

Ruinous inflation and indebtedness, an overtaxed and artificial economy, a mortgaged empire, a population in which thirteen per cent of the families paid no taxes and did no work and another twenty-five per cent of the adult males wore clerical garb—all this was reality. But who can blame Philip in his land of miracles if he saw himself as the chosen instrument of the Lord and if he agreed with Mendoza writing from distant Paris: "I pray Your Majesty will hasten the Enterprise of England to the earliest possible date, for it would seem to be God's obvious design to bestow upon Your Majesty the crowns of these two kingdoms."

Had Philip and Mendoza been as successful in the tactics of cold war in London and Edinburgh as they were in Paris and Brussels, the contrast between Gloriana's successes and Catherine de Médicis' failures might not have been so great, and the age might have belonged to Philip, not to Elizabeth.

THE SPANISH EMPIRE

"The sun never set on the dominions of the king of Spain and at the slightest movement of that nation the whole earth trembled." Thus did one Spanish historian sum up the might and magnitude of the empire of Philip II. At the height of Philip's reign that empire encompassed not only the entire Iberian peninsula, the Netherlands, Franche Comté, the Balearic Islands, Sicily, Sardinia, and the better part of the Italian mainland but most of the known New World, stations along the coast of Africa, and trade settlements at seaports in India and the Far East. Besides being the greatest imperial power in history, Spain was a thriving industrial power. The production of wool, felt, jewelry, leather, soap, ceramics, gloves, and armor brought prosperity to the people and a virtual end to unemployment. Such places as Seville, Valladolid, La Mancha, Granada, and Segovia were busy mercantile centers. Toledo, on the other hand, although still a manufacturing city renowned throughout Europe for the quality of its tempered steel—especially for its sword blades—was made the headquarters of the Inquisition, and gradually became the spiritual heart of the Spanish empire. A stronghold of mysticism, it attracted the somewhat mystical El Greco, who settled there in the 1570's, after a brief stay in Madrid, and painted the world-famous landscape view of the town (right) toward the end of Philip's reign.

210

anchois de Binero

Dame Constance de Binero

Dame Blanche de Binero.

Docteur Cacalla

Alfonse Perez

Dame mencia de figneroa

Don Pierre Sarmiento

Don Loys de Roxas

Dame anne Henriaues

In this German engraving of an auto-da-fé the condemned, wearing depictions of the gates of Hell on their robes, are flanked by officers urging repentance. The effigy borne on a pole represents either an escapee or an accused heretic who died during torture. (Coffins containing bones of the dead were burned beneath the appropriate effigies.) Sentences were read on an open stage (above banner) and executed outside the city.

By 1540, when a bored Hernando Cortes retired to Spain, Mexico had been thoroughly subjugated. The once-proud Aztecs—their downfall brought about by gold artifacts like the ornament shown at right —were reduced to the manufacture of export ware, and their temples (above) were replaced by Catholic churches. The paintings at top, by a native artist, show Indians working gold and feather handicrafts.

THE WEALTH
OF THE INDIES

When Philip came to the throne in 1566, Spain was in control of much of the New World, and the conquistadors—that raffish, quarrelsome, often illiterate band of fortune hunters, who had sacked the Indies "to serve God and His Majesty, to give light to those who were in darkness, and to grow rich, as all men desire to do"—had been replaced by stodgy bureaucrats and cautious merchants. The discovery of silver mines in Mexico and Peru in the 1540's had increased transatlantic shipping enormously, and some sixty-five ships cleared Seville yearly for the western hemisphere. They carried supplies for the growing European population there, and returned with silver that was to prove far more important to the Spanish economy than Aztec and Inca gold ever was.

UNION WITH PORTUGAL

When King Sebastian of Portugal died without issue in 1578, Philip of Spain was able to realize a long-cherished dream. A strong show of force by the Spanish army in 1581 quickly discouraged his only serious rival, and Philip acceded to the Portuguese throne. Union with Portugal not only assured the Spanish empire of the most powerful navy afloat but provided it with the safe Atlantic harbors that were so vital to its New World trade. Moreover, the union enabled Spain to take over the Portuguese slave trade, thereby providing much-needed labor for its agricultural and mining enterprises in America. For Portugal too the union began as a happy one: Philip scrupulously observed the articles of concession that guaranteed his new subjects control of their internal affairs, and an influx of Spanish bullion stabilized the tottering Portuguese economy. Only Philip's interminable, wasteful wars in the Netherlands spoiled the chances of lasting Iberian prosperity.

AMACAO.

In 1582 a small Spanish and Portuguese force from Lisbon engaged a powerful fleet sent by Catherine de Médicis to take the Azores. A resounding victory over the French at the battle of Terceira (right) encouraged Philip in his ill-fated plan to send an expedition against England. The sixteenth-century engraving above shows Portuguese vessels anchored at the Chinese port of Macao.

A CITY TRANSFORMED

The Catholic city of Brussels, capital of Brabant and seat of the Spanish governors of the Netherlands, was a glittering adornment to Philip's empire at the time of his succession. A center of the wool, lace, and tapestry trades since the Middle Ages, the city had long been celebrated for gaiety, sophistication, and luxury. By 1561, when the Willebroek Canal was completed, providing Brussels with access to the sea and avenues to further profit, the burghers of the city were as prosperous as any people in Europe except possibly the merchants of Antwerp. All this changed, however, with the appointment of the fanatical duke of Alva as captain general (and later governor) of the Netherlands. Alva set up the notorious Court of Troubles at Brussels, executed a large number of rebels there and in the provinces, and drew a curtain of Spanish gloom over the city's life.

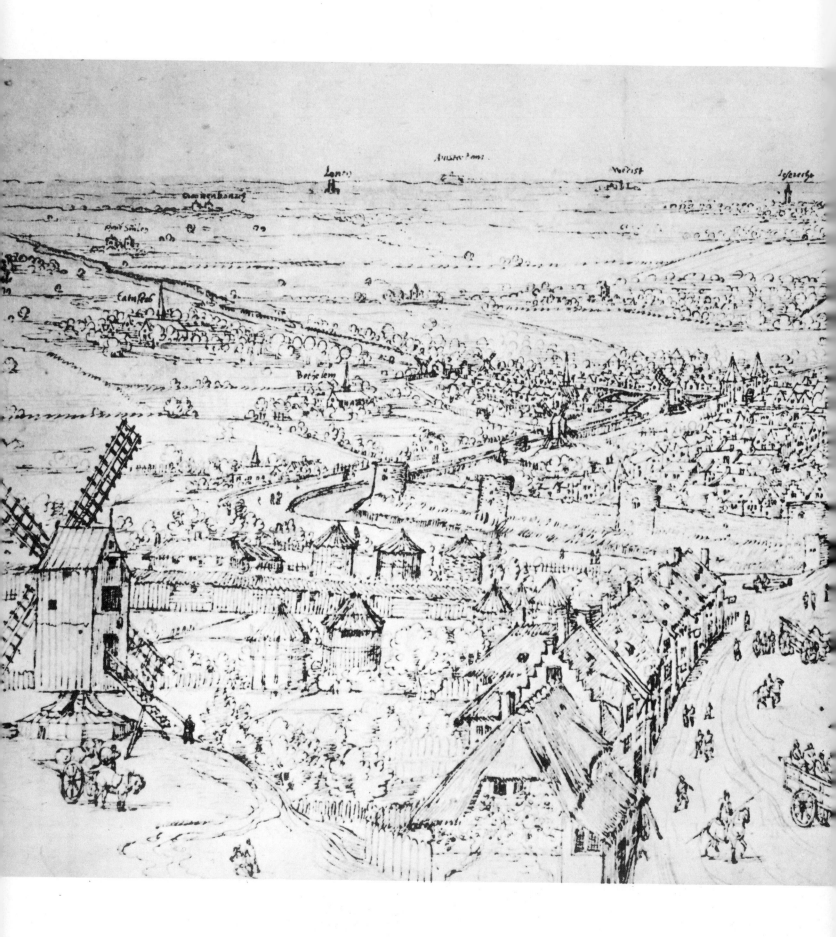

REVOLT IN THE NETHERLANDS

The war with France that ended with the Peace of Cateau-Cambrésis in 1559 had seriously depleted the Spanish exchequer, and to Philip II the rich Netherlands—industrial in the south and mercantile in the north, with Antwerp as a geographical and financial hub—seemed the best place to recoup his losses. The Low Countries were taxed excessively during the early years of Philip's reign, and Spanish rule, never very popular, was soon bitterly resented. Philip's problems were exacerbated by his importation of foreign governors, Spanish troops, and the Spanish Inquisition. All this, together with the discontent of Dutch and Walloon nobles, deprived of their patronage, and the merciless policies of the duke of Alva, set the stage for rebellion in the Netherlands. By 1566, only seven years after representing Philip at Cateau-Cambrésis, William of Orange had organized the Dutch rebels and was raising an army in defiance of Alba. Ten years later, he united the Netherlands with the Pacification of Ghent.

The city of Utrecht, where the seven provinces of the North Netherlands united for their common defense in 1557, is depicted at left in a pen-and-ink drawing by the sixteenth-century artist Antonius van den Wyngaerde. The arms of the province of Utrecht (above) were adorned with peacock feathers, the symbol for pride.

OVERLEAF: *A detail from a painting by an unknown sixteenth-century artist shows a portion of the market place on Antwerp's principal thoroughfare. Spanish troops stationed in the Netherlands antagonized the burghers by making plain their contempt for trade, heresy, and the Dutchman's notorious love of drink.*

7

PLOT AND COUNTERPLOT

Sixteenth-century diplomacy had most of the more insane qualities of the Mad Hatter's tea party. Periodically everybody changed seats, but the same old dirty plates remained; ambassadors never meant what they said, but somehow always said what they meant; the riddles of diplomacy were as bewildering as any concocted by the March Hare; and Elizabeth, Mary of Scotland, and Catherine de Médicis were as extraordinary in their diplomatic tastes as any three sisters who lived in a treacle well. For all his shrewdness and secret sources of information, Philip of Spain remained a baffled stranger in this wonderland of international politics. He could never fathom the mind of Catherine, perhaps because it was so deceptively shallow. He regarded Mary as an emotional and thoroughly unreliable female; and he agreed wholeheartedly with his ambassador who reported Elizabeth to be a woman possessed of "a hundred thousand devils," who fooled nobody with her idle chatter about becoming a nun and passing her days in quiet prayer.

Diplomats were as concerned with the pedigrees of monarchs as they were with terms of trade. Society took seriously Philip's claims on behalf of his daughter, Isabella Eugenia, to the thrones of England and France; Elizabeth thought Mary of Scotland's defiant display of the heraldic arms of England on her escutcheon worthy of a diplomatic protest; and English ambassadors regarded it as an insult to be invited to eat with cutlery flaunting such armorial pretensions. Heraldry and the birthrights of kings were more than window dressing left over from a bygone age. They were the only recognizable guidelines for life in a European family of adolescent states. The emerging nations, jealous of their sovereignty and fearful for their internal security, were endeavoring to formalize their relations with each other. Diplomatic procedure remained in its infancy and its vocabulary had yet to be established; consequently statesmen had to make do with the language of heraldry and dynasty.

Ambassadors as the accredited representatives of nation-states successfully maintained the inviolability of their persons, but they were usually regarded and often behaved as if they were common spies. The principal interest of diplomats was not peace but information, and every resident ambassador in Europe had a carefully organized and well-paid network of informers. The wealthier the kingdom he represented, the more secret his sources of information, for only the great powers could afford the sums necessary to discover the truth about monarchs, the plots of councilors, and the secret plans of state. Guerau de Spes, the Spanish ambassador in London, had a spy on the Privy Council, and Mendoza, his successor, had an agent in the principal secretary's household. If the information concerned the sovereign, no detail was too trivial to escape the watchful eyes of a diplomat, and Mendoza's spy in the royal laundry even took careful note of Elizabeth's menstrual periods.

In an age that still judged loyalty to kin, to region, and to God to be as commendable as allegiance to the crown, ambassadors found a ready

Mary Queen of Scots is depicted with her son, the future James VI, shortly before her forced abdication.

audience for their tempting proposals and a fertile ground in which to plant the seeds of treason and discord. All men had their price, though the purchase was not always reckoned in silver. Throughout Europe men sought a chance to strike a blow for their faith. As a consequence, diplomatic residences in Antwerp, London, Paris, and Amsterdam became the resorts of malcontents, and ambassadors became the provocateurs of treason. Mendoza in London or Paris, Parma's spies in every city of the Netherlands, and Sir Nicholas Throckmorton at the court of Catherine de Médicis spun their webs of intrigue in the best cloak-and-dagger tradition. Secret messages were written in invisible ink that reappeared when the letter was immersed in water; dispatches were invariably in cipher; information was concealed in hollow heels and trick bottle stoppers, or was tucked away in codpieces or in the linings of trunks; and couriers rode swiftly through the night disguised as dentists, priests, and merchants.

In defense monarchs occasionally jailed or evicted ambassadors, but such actions generally had unpleasant diplomatic repercussions. Usually it was safer to watch their activities, plant agents in their houses, and hoodwink them with a regular supply of erroneous information, fake traitors, and fabricated conspiracies. In 1571, during the Ridolfi plot to murder Elizabeth, Sir John Hawkins completely fooled the Spanish ambassador by offering, as part of the government's web of counterespionage, to betray the English navy to Spain. De Spes' assurance to his master that "I can discover nothing suspicious about it" is simply further confirmation that Philip was wise not to believe the sanguine opinions of his gullible ambassadors in England.

The constant fear of the assassin's knife added a macabre note to European diplomacy. Elizabeth's councilors were driven to distraction by the queen's total unconcern for even the most elementary precautions for her personal safety. Regicide was a tricky philosophical and moral problem, but the extremes of both faiths endorsed it on the grounds that good might come from evil, and that the godless sovereign was an enemy to the human race. Moreover, political murder was quick and efficient. Remove the vigorous leadership of kings, and the "state doth whole default, the realm is rent in twain in such a loss." The death of Henry II in France was grisly proof of this, and Europe abounded with men anxious to prove it in England as well. Lord Burghley was deeply aware that Elizabeth's crown was "not like to fall to the ground for want of heads that claim to wear it," and he prepared a careful report on "certain cautions for the queen's apparel and diet," warning her to eat nothing that was not

prepared and tasted by the royal cooks, to use no perfumes presented by strangers, and to keep her laundry and wardrobe under guard.

For the first ten years of Elizabeth's rule the "calm and quiet season" prevailed, and though the diplomatic configurations were kaleidoscopically varied, Spain remained safely in a quandary, France in the throes of civil discord, Scotland in the convulsions of Calvinist revolution, and England in the hands of a benevolent deity who arranged to have an embarrassed and unhappy Philip continue as the champion of his heretical sister-in-law. The king of Spain's dilemma was England's greatest safeguard. Mary Queen of Scots was beyond a doubt Elizabeth's legal heir, and in the eyes of many Catholics she was the rightful ruler of England. But Mary was also a Guise, a member of that acquisitive and predatory clan that had so successfully merged its own destinies with those of France. Throughout crisis and reprisal, plot and counterplot, Philip could never convince himself that he did not prefer heretical Elizabeth, free of French influence, to Catholic Mary, with her French sympathies and Guise uncles.

For almost two decades Philip permitted his artful sister-in-law to throw dust in his eyes, and accepted her ardent assurances that her heresy was nothing but political necessity. He turned the other cheek to the most blatant provocations by English pirates; he read with cold reserve the optimistic reports of ambassadors who urged their intricate plots to rescue Mary and unseat Elizabeth; and he refused to be stampeded into war with the country that lay athwart his sea lanes to the Netherlands. It was not until 1577, when the Guise family was brought into the Spanish orbit, that Philip's awful perplexity was resolved. Only then could he begin seriously to consider means to rid the Catholic world of the foul, heretical, and unlawful queen of England.

Ultimately every diplomatic move somehow involved Mary of Scots, who bedeviled the international scene with her charm, her intrigues, her idiocy, and her claims to Elizabeth's throne. Success did not become the enchanting dowager queen of France. Time and again she proved herself to be petty, deceitful, and self-centered; but Mary was magnificent in defeat, and all her defects were invariably forgiven her. No gown became her half so well as the cloak of adversity; no colors could set off the golden red hair, the great dark eyes with their hint of tears, or the heart-shaped lips as did the black of mourning and the scarlet of martyrdom. By any normal standard she was detestable; as a lady in distress, who could offer her prince valiant the crowns of Scotland and England, she was irresistible and exercised a fascination that brought a host of men

A contemporary map (with north on the right) shows Mary's kingdom of Scotland; her subjects—for the most part Calvinists—were never reconciled to the rule of the Catholic queen.

far worthier than she ever was to their graves.

From the moment of Francis II's death in 1560, misfortunes beset his seventeen-year-old widow. Her Guise uncles sought a brilliant new marriage for their royal niece, and there was much talk of the nine-year-old Charles IX and of the dwarfed and deranged fifteen-year-old Don Carlos of Spain. Catherine de Médicis, however, refused to have Mary Stuart as her daughter-in-law for a second time. Nor would she countenance having the lordly Guises linked to Spain, and she threatened Philip with an English alliance if he married his son to Mary. Catherine made it clear that Mary's usefulness lay in her claim to the English throne and that her place was among the chilly lochs and cheerless hills of Scotland, where the Catholic faith was in grave peril and the French party had been destroyed by the force of English arms and by John Knox's blasts upon his Calvinist trumpet.

At one time French interests and culture had predominated at Edinburgh, and Scotland had viewed France as its "auld ally" in the agelong war against the English. James V, that ill-starred, melancholic sovereign, had died in 1542, shamed by the spectacle of his Scottish soldiers floundering in a bog in their panic to escape an English army. His widow, Mary of Guise, ruled as regent for the week-old Mary Stuart, and six years later the child queen was whisked off to Paris to be brought up French in anticipation of her marriage to the dauphin of France.

The Scottish clans soon learned to dislike French intervention as much as they had feared and detested English domination. Discontented nobles found in Calvinistic Protestantism a faith that sanctioned their distaste for French interference and provided a godly excuse for liberating Church lands from a government that was controlled by a foreign Catholic power. The new faith, with its severity and rigid righteousness, was peculiarly congenial to these clannish souls independent in their highland fastnesses. John Knox had been preaching against the enemies of "Christ Jesus and his holy evangel" in Scotland with varying results since 1545. He had been forcibly exiled to France and had spent nineteen months in the galleys, where the "grudging and murmuring complaints of the flesh" sharpened

231

John Knox

both his faith and his temper. After a sojourn at that "perfect school of Christ," Geneva, the Moses of Scotland returned in 1559 to his homeland, where he began to preach a doctrine that found a congenial audience among lairds frustrated both by a French regent and by a Church that seemed to be little more than a corrupt tool of the crown.

Scottish nobles, steeped in the ways of feudal anarchy and independence and convinced by the hard logic of Knox's sermons, were quick to act and banded together to protect the perfect faith and to oppose the queen regent and her French court and policy. In 1557 they convened to form the Congregation of the Lord, a combined Church, army, and parliament of the rebellious faithful. By the summer of 1559 Protestant lairds were in full revolt against Mary of Guise and the French alliance, but it was gradually borne in upon ardent reformers and militant Scottish clans that victory would never be won by God's elect without the assistance of the queen of England.

Relations between Elizabeth and the Scottish rebels were complicated by Gloriana's repugnance for John Knox, whom she had never forgiven for his tactless blasts against the "monstrous regiment of women" who ruled on earth. Reluctantly Knox assured the queen that his wrath had been directed toward her sister, Mary Tudor, and the regent of Scotland, and that Elizabeth was obviously an exception to an otherwise perfectly valid rule. William Cecil and the English Council wisely considered such a grudging apology to be insufficient and

warned the Scottish Protestants that if they wanted English arms and gold they had better muzzle Mr. Knox. As always Elizabeth was reluctant to commit herself or her troops to a course of action from which there was no retreat, but the lairds of the congregation gave her no choice. They were so consistently worsted in battle that Elizabeth was forced to send both her army and navy to Scotland. Ultimately, with the help of British arms and the timely death of the regent, Mary of Guise, the English and Protestant factions triumphed. By the Treaty of Edinburgh, in 1560, French troops were withdrawn, and England and Scotland joined hands in a community of interests for the first time in three hundred years. Their strongest bond was a mutual fear of the young queen, Mary, who returned from France on a chill and misty day in August, 1561, to rule a nation of rebels and heretics.

Mary landed full of determination to please, but if she thought that Gallic charm and Stuart guile could return her errant kingdom to the Catholic and French fold, she was tragically mistaken. Knox remained dour and unconvinced: "The very face of Heaven," he grumbled, "did manifestly speak what comfort was brought into this country with her—to wit, sorrow, dolor, darkness, and all impiety." "If there be not in her a proud mind, a crafty wit, and an indurate heart against God and his truth, my judgment faileth me." In the end, however, it was not religion but dynastic ambition that proved her undoing, for Mary was anxious to exchange her bleak Scottish kingdom for the warmth and luster of Elizabeth's throne. No queen possessed of the granite stubbornness of the Stuarts and educated in the Renaissance brilliance of the French court would ever be satisfied with the crown of Scotland if that of her "dear sister, so tender cousin, and friend" lay within her reach. She bombarded every capital of Europe with matrimonial proposals, schemes to carry forward the Catholic faith, and plans to inherit, by force, if necessary, the Tudor crown.

As far as Elizabeth was concerned, the only completely safe solution was for Mary to remain a maiden queen. Relations between the two ladies became chillier with every new marriage scheme. Elizabeth not only endeavored to frustrate her cousin, she insulted her by making the unbelievable suggestion that Mary should marry that soiled hero of the English court, Robert Dudley, who was suspected of having murdered his wife in the hope of marrying Elizabeth. Mary was furious at such a proposition; she sought a great match, not the worn paramour of a rival queen.

Mary's ultimate choice of a husband was diplomatically ill considered, and destroyed forever any possibility of happiness either as wife or queen. Henry Stuart, Lord Darnley, was the "beardless and lady-faced" grandson by a second marriage of Mary's own grandmother, Margaret Tudor. He was three years the queen's junior, stupid, vicious, and effeminate, but Mary viewed him as "the lustiest and best-proportioned long man" she had ever seen. On July 29, 1565, Mary defied Elizabeth and married the one man guaranteed to antagonize both the English because of his Tudor connections, and the Scottish because he was Catholic. "Woe worth the time," wrote the English ambassador, "that ever the Lord Darnley set foot in this country!" The time of woe descended with unexpected speed. It did not take Mary long to realize the truth about the man she had married primarily for his Tudor blood and his closeness to Elizabeth's throne, and within a year and a half a double murder had been committed.

Mary of Scotland's marriage to a nobleman, even one of Darnley's ancient lineage and royal blood, underscored the wisdom of Elizabeth's determination to remain single. It is possible that Mary too often disregarded the medieval warning to wives: "Take care thou dost on no account say to him, 'my advice is better than thine'"; but the real trouble lay with Darnley himself. He proved to be a drunken, degenerate, and vainglorious malcontent with neither emotional stability nor moral fiber. He coveted the crown matrimonial and the right to succeed Mary on the throne. When she wisely refused to grant his wish, he sulked and blamed the pernicious influence of the queen's very private amanuensis, the Italian David Rizzio, a bass in the royal quartet and the object of Mary's affections. It was "Seigneur Davie" who dined alone with the queen, read to her, played cards with her till two in the morning, and who shared not only her confidence but, as gossip reported it, her bed as well. Darnley regarded himself as a cuckolded husband and an impotent sovereign, and he determined to have his revenge.

Lord Darnley set about organizing all those who detested Rizzio for his influence and lowly birth or sought to limit the queen's authority. On a Saturday night in March, 1566, Darnley's henchmen surrounded Holyrood House, and Darnley and Lord Ruthven broke into the queen's chambers where Mary and Rizzio were at supper. They demanded that Rizzio join them in the anteroom, and when he hid behind the queen's skirts and refused to move, they dragged him shrieking from the room and cut him to pieces with fifty-six thrusts of sword and dagger. Mary, six months pregnant, was at her emotional best. She demanded to know why Darnley had perpetrated such a wicked deed, "considering that I took you from low estate and made you my

husband." To the rest of the company she cried out: "I will think upon a revenge." She ordered Rizzio's body to be buried in the royal chapel and gave the dead secretary's office to his eighteen-year-old brother. With gold and fair promises she set about undermining the alliance of those who had hated Rizzio, and laid her plans for revenge upon her husband.

Had the queen planned only the quiet murder of her spouse, she might have kept her throne, for Scotland abounded with men who loathed Darnley, but Mary Stuart mixed love and homicide in proportions fatal to her crown and reputation. From her infatuation with the weak and vicious Darnley, she fell headlong in love with James Hepburn, the earl of Bothwell, as bad-tempered, impetuous, oversexed, and politically inept a hero as ever tried to rescue a damsel in distress. It was the earl who performed the murder of Darnley, carried off the queen in a carefully prearranged "rape," and finally married her in a Protestant rite. The queen's guilt as a murderer, if not as an adulteress, is open to debate; her innocence has been passionately argued for the last four hundred years. Mary may not have known specifically about the conspiracy to lure Darnley to his death, but she certainly must have guessed that some sort of scheme was afoot, and she lent herself as bait to the trap. Her husband had been in Glasgow convalescing from an attack of smallpox, and Mary rushed off in wifely fashion to nurse him and to bring him back to Edinburgh, where he was lodged in a small house in Kirk o' Field, outside the city gates. On February 9, 1567, the queen conveniently remembered a promise to attend a wedding and failed to sleep that night in her husband's house. Early on the morning of the tenth, the city was rocked by an immense explosion; Lord Darnley, his house, and a good part of Kirk o' Field had gone up in dust.

The public was deeply shocked by the news, but Mary might yet have saved herself had she been willing to sacrifice her lover. Instead she ran away with the earl of Bothwell, proclaiming that she would "go with him to the world's end in a white petticoat ere she [would] leave him." The sixteenth century could condone murder in a queen, but not impropriety. Mary was acting like a guttersnipe, and the streets of Edinburgh rang with the cry, "Burn the whore!" In June she was imprisoned, forced to abdicate in favor of her thirteen-month-old son, and persuaded to acknowledge the regency of her half brother, the earl of Moray. Bothwell escaped to Denmark, where he died some years later. Scotland had not heard the last of its Stuart queen, however: less than a year later she managed an utterly roman-

A Nicholas Hilliard miniature, painted shortly after Mary's execution, shows the queen of Scotland lying in bed.

tic escape and within weeks had collected an army of six thousand enthusiastic supporters. Enthusiasm, unfortunately, proved no match for the discipline and training of Moray's troops, who encountered Mary's army at Langside, near Glasgow. In forty-five minutes the battle was over and so was the queen's career in Scotland. Three days later, on May 16, 1568, Mary fled to England, arriving on Elizabeth's doorstep just in time to participate in the first determined effort to remove Gloriana from her throne.

The moment Mary crossed the border and became the embarrassing and difficult "guest" of her Tudor cousin, Elizabeth discovered, as the archbishop of Canterbury remarked, that she had "the wolf by the ears." She dared not send Mary home, where barbarian Scots might venture to execute their divine-right monarch; she feared equally to give her rival sanctuary in England, where Mary was certain to become the magnet for every species of malcontent. The "calm and quiet season" was over for Elizabeth, for the same social, economic, and religious tensions that were tearing France apart were slowly loosening the ties of loyalty in England as well. English Catholics were hearkening to the quickened tempo of religious hysteria across the Channel, and Puritans were beginning to murmur that "no papist can be a good subject." Once again there were uneasy stirrings in the northern shires, where the word of a Percy, a Neville, or a Darcy was dearer to con-

servative hearts than the most weighty command of a Tudor queen. The days of private armies had passed, but local influence and patriotism remained strong, and the northern earls were restive as domesticated aristocrats. In the north Mass was still celebrated despite royal statutes and proclamations, and the parish clergy stubbornly resisted the best efforts of reforming bishops to purge them of their idolatrous ways. The return of the good old days, when men were true to their faith and to their overlord and free from interfering bureaucrats and prying Protestants, was a dream for which men in the northern counties were still willing to risk the gallows.

More was brewing in the north than old-fashioned feudal rebellion: now traitors looked to Rome and Madrid for aid in destroying the English Jezebel. Their cause was linked to the success of the entire Counter-Reformation, and their conspiracies coincided with the mounting rift between England and Spain. As early as 1566 Elizabeth and Philip had grievances against one another. Gloriana insulted her brother-in-law by sending as her resident ambassador to Madrid a married cleric who lacked both good breeding and good birth. When Philip indignantly ordered him home, Elizabeth was outraged by such arrogance. The same year English ports were opened to Dutch Sea Beggars—rebels, pirates, and heretics, Philip called them—and English money and volunteers were sent to foster rebellion in the Spanish Netherlands. By 1568 the cold war was warming up. Elizabeth condoned piracy against Spanish ships in the Caribbean and the Channel, and when Philip retaliated in September, 1568, by almost annihilating Sir John Hawkins' third slave-trading expedition to the New World, the two nations seemed on the brink of war.

In December, 1568, Philip's patience all but broke. A Genoese merchantman, heavily laden with gold loaned to Spain for the payment of Alva's troops in the Netherlands, was confiscated when it put into an English port to escape Dutch pirates. Elizabeth promptly seized the bullion and impudently renegotiated the loan with the Italian bankers. Outraged, Philip placed an embargo on English shipping to the Netherlands, and Elizabeth countered by freezing Spanish assets in England. At this propitious moment Mary Stuart sent a message to the Spanish ambassador "that if his master will help me, I shall be queen of England in three months, and Mass shall be said all over the country."

Mary, with her French ways and Highland wit, was proving to be a most unwelcome guest in England. She stole every heart, with a tear-stained smile for one, a diamond ring for another, and a well-phrased promise to all who dreamed of riches and of high office. Mary could offer anyone what Elizabeth Tudor kept only for the crowned heads of Europe—the hope of matrimony and the vision of a throne. The man who was "brought abed" by such a dream was the duke of Norfolk, Elizabeth's cousin and the ranking peer of the realm. Thomas Howard, fourth duke of Norfolk, was a simple man, unable to perceive the folly of his actions, though intelligent enough to proceed cautiously. He should have known better. It was not by accident that he was England's sole remaining duke, for the Tudors never looked kindly on too much princely blood or feudal independence, and the life expectancy of a member of the Norfolk house was not great. His great-grandfather, the duke of Buckingham, had been executed for treason in 1521; his grandfather had been imprisoned and his father executed for the same offense in 1546. His cousins, Anne Boleyn and Catherine Howard, had fared no better as the wives of Henry VIII. But Stuart smiles blinded him to Tudor scowls, and he allowed himself to be talked of as a prospective husband for the woman who might yet unite the thrones of England and Scotland.

By the spring of 1569 the devil's brew had reached the boiling point. The earls of Westmoreland and Northumberland were armed and waiting in the north; Guzman de Silva, the Spanish ambassador in London, was busy plotting with Catholics and court factions; courtiers opposed to William Cecil were looking hopefully toward Mary and Norfolk; a papal anathema declaring Elizabeth a heretic and divesting her of her divinity was being prepared at Rome; Philip had written to Alva to ascertain the cost and effort required to unseat Elizabeth and restore the queen of Scots to her rightful throne; and Mary was waiting expectantly at her residence at Tutbury to be rescued by an army of gallant heroes. Had Philip been less cautious, had Alva been willing to risk his disciplined troops in England, had the papal thunder been better timed, had the feudal lords in the north been slightly more powerful, had Norfolk been more courageous and de Silva's assassination plots better conceived, the Elizabethan age might have ended in civil and international war. As it was, the wheel of fortune still turned in Elizabeth's favor. The queen lived and her enemies were once again confounded.

England and Spain approached war, then hurriedly retreated, for both Elizabeth and Philip were reluctant to commit their countries to the final ordeal of arms. A rising in the north was crushed during the winter of 1569–70, and eight hundred feudal tenants paid with their lives for their devotion to a dying way of life. The hum of the spinning wheel

A painting executed in London in memory of Lord Darnley and later sent to Scotland shows Mary Stuart's murdered husband and his family, praying for revenge beside his tomb.

235

One of a series of engravings, A Thankful Remembrance of God's Mercy, *illustrated in full on page 333, shows several famous Catholic plots against Elizabeth's throne.*

and the ring of the coal miner's pike were slowly drowning out the voice of the feudal magnate. Almost as an afterthought, Pius V ineptly issued the long-deferred bull of excommunication against Elizabeth in February, 1570. His anathema fell on deaf ears; at home the queen was closer to the hearts of her subjects than ever before; abroad Philip was too preoccupied with rebellion in the Netherlands and Turkish penetration in the Mediterranean to put teeth into an otherwise harmless papal threat. The only consequence of the proclamation was to darken the lives and burden the hearts of good English Catholics who, until Elizabeth was excommunicated, could at least remain loyal to the queen without violating their consciences.

Though triumphant, Elizabeth was still saddled with her Stuart cousin, who seemed to thrive on adversity and derive renewed hope from every defeat. Councilors advised the queen that she had taken to her heart "the daughter of sedition, the mother of rebellion, the handmaid of iniquity, and the sister of unshamefastness." Yet Elizabeth persisted in viewing Mary as an anointed queen who must be treated with respect and, if possible, restored to the throne of Scotland. Unfortunately Mary Stuart never learned from experience. She sat placidly among her ladies, her nimble fingers embroidering exquisite needlepoint and her fertile mind spinning clever conspiracies, the central theme of which was always Elizabeth's death. Even her own brother-in-law, Charles of France, was moved to exclaim: "Ah! the poor fool will never cease until she loses her head."

The same words might have been said about Norfolk, who had learned nothing about the dangerous consequences of treason when he escaped with only a brief term in prison and a warning after the fiasco of the northern rebellion. Within a year both the duke and the exiled queen were irresponsibly enmeshed in one of the more brainless conspiracies of the century, concocted by the ebullient Roberto di Ridolfi, a Florentine banker in London and a secret agent of the pope. In its final form the plot proposed that Alva land at Portsmouth with ten thousand troops and march on London, where Norfolk would seize the queen, rescue Mary Stuart and marry her, and restore the Catholic faith. Everyone except Alva was taken in by the polished and enthusiastic Italian, and even Philip put aside his Cassandralike

236

fears for dreams of success. Ridolfi's intrigues fared no better than the more realistic plans of the northern earls. Norfolk was arrested for a second time and finally executed in June, 1572; the Spanish ambassador was unceremoniously shipped back to Spain, and Elizabeth gave up any pretense of dealing with Mary Stuart as a sister queen and blood cousin. Mary was imprisoned in Sheffield Castle at a cost to Elizabeth of fifty-two pounds a week, but most Englishmen continued to complain that she still was not treated for what she was—"a monstrous and huge dragon" of sedition.

There is no doubt that had Elizabeth listened to her Parliament, Mary of Scotland would have died in 1572. Loyal Englishmen were convinced that she was an immoral and dangerous female, and they were determined to "cut off her head and make no more ado about her," but Elizabeth could not bring herself to execute a divinely ordained sovereign. To do so was impolitic (it would set a dangerous precedent) and immoral (Mary was one of God's lieutenants on earth). So Mary Stuart lived on another fifteen years, surrounded by English spies but still possessed of a queen's household and always confident that some new plot might yet succeed.

For ten of those years there was relative quiet in Sheffield: just the usual letters to Philip, the pope, the duke of Guise, and Mary's son, King James of Scotland, all successfully smuggled out of the castle, and all urging her friends and relatives to strike a blow for God and the Stuart cause. Around 1581 the tempo of international intrigue began to quicken as Mary gained renewed hope from abroad. The house of Guise had moved into the Spanish orbit, and Philip was beginning to consider seriously the militant advice of his new ambassador in London, Bernardino de Mendoza, who inaccurately reported that England was in such a state that "if even so much as a cat moved the whole edifice would crumble down in three days." The ambassador was not a man who let nature take its course, and in 1583 he plotted with a young English Catholic, Francis Throckmorton, to raise the Catholic gentry, rescue Mary, and assassinate Elizabeth. When Throckmorton was arrested he did not long withstand interrogators, who twisted the handle of the rack to give emphasis to their questions. In the end the tortured man, revealing every detail of the conspiracy to Secretary Walsingham, could only whisper, "Faith broken, honor lost." Throckmorton died on the scaffold, Mary's mild imprisonment gave way to a closer watch and less friendly jailers, and Mendoza, to his lasting indignation, was ordered home as a common disturber of the peace. "Tell your mistress," he haughtily informed the English guard

who saw him off at Dover, "that Bernardino de Mendoza was born not to disturb kingdoms but to conquer them!"

The Spanish ambassador's defiance was in accord with the prevailing wind from the Escorial. England had to be conquered and punished. If the assassin's knife could not reach Elizabeth, then Parma's troops would have to assume the task so necessary to God's purpose. In London the queen's ministers were justifiably frightened. William of Orange had been murdered in his own house at Delft in June, 1584. Six months later the Privy Council got wind that a Doctor William Parry, reformed burglar, ex-spy, and member of Parliament, planned to assassinate Elizabeth with a bullet blessed by Rome. In August, 1585, Parma's troops swept into Antwerp. It seemed inevitable that next they would either strike northward against a demoralized and ill-led Dutch and English army or, if Philip gave the order, move against that sink and source of all heresy and sedition, England itself.

As war grew steadily closer and the plots to murder the queen grew more desperate, patriotic feeling in Parliament and the Privy Council exploded into a terrible anger against Mary Stuart. It seemed monstrous that the cankered heart of treason should go unpunished, that an avowed adulteress, murderer, and archliar should continue to live. Years earlier, John Knox had warned that "if ye strike not at the root, the branches that appear to be broken will bud again." To angry Puritans, frightened ministers, and loyal Englishmen, it was clear that Mary of Scotland was the root of all evil. The problem was how to make Elizabeth see her cousin for what she really was—a common traitor. The mantle of her divinity had to be torn aside, so that even Elizabeth would no longer believe her cousin's regal and pious assurances of innocence.

In the end, the queen of Scotland was destroyed by her own insatiable passion for intrigue and caught by her own cunning. First the trap had to be laid, then baited. Mary was moved to Chartley House, in Essex, where all means of communication with the outside world were closed, save one. The exception appealed to Mary's fondness for mystery. Her letters were smuggled in and out of Chartley House in waterproof packages slipped through the bungholes of beer kegs. News from abroad arrived in the French ambassador's diplomatic pouch and was sent on to Mary, but before it was placed in the beer kegs it was deciphered, read, and copied by Elizabeth's principal secretary, Francis Walsingham. The system satisfied everyone: Mary was lulled into a false feeling of security and received secret news from Europe for the first time in years; Walsingham learned everything Mary read or wrote and waited patiently for his victim to enmesh herself in still another plot; and the astute brewer was handsomely paid by both Mary and Walsingham and received an inflated price for his beer as well.

Walsingham did not have to wait long for the unsuspecting flies to walk into his parlor. First a priest named John Ballard entered. He assured Mary that sixty thousand Spanish soldiers were waiting to rescue her, and informed Philip that an equal number of Catholics would rush to arms once Parma's troops landed in England. Then came Anthony Babington, who gave his name to the plot; and finally John Savage, who had taken a great oath to kill Elizabeth. All that Walsingham needed was written evidence that Mary Stuart was a party to the conspiracy. On July 17, 1586, she fell into the trap and wrote Babington expressing her fervent approval of what he and his colleagues proposed to do. Walsingham had all the evidence he required. The assassins were promptly rounded up, Mary's two secretaries were arrested, and Elizabeth was persuaded to permit the trial of her cousin for attempted murder.

When Mary Stuart stood trial for her life before thirty-six commissioners on October 11, Puritans and privy councilors had achieved their purpose: the legal prosecution of a divine-right sovereign and her condemnation as a public menace to the Tudor crown. As usual, however, Mary of Scotland stole the show with an infuriating and infectious performance. She haughtily denied all knowledge of the Babington plot; she passionately protested that queens could not be tried by anyone except God Himself; and when her enemies had done their worst, she dismissed the damning evidence with a smile, saying: "God forgive you lawyers, for you are so sore fellows. God bless me and my cause from your laws, for it is a very good matter that they cannot make seem bad."

The demand for Mary's life now reached a crescendo, and Parliament, without a dissenting vote, petitioned the queen that Mary of Scotland be executed. Still Elizabeth hesitated. She had lived with Mary for so long that to put her hand to her cousin's death warrant was like ordering the execution of a part of herself. Who knew what terrible events might descend from heaven in retribution for destroying an anointed queen? How would James VI of Scotland react to the execution of his mother? What would Henry III of France do to avenge the death of his sister-in-law? And the greatest mystery of all—What about that leaden colossus, the king of Spain? In vain Elizabeth's councilors assured her that to James the hope of succeeding to the crown of England was more important than his mother's

life, that Henry III cared nothing for his hysterical relative, and that Philip was no more dangerous to England as Mary's avenger than he had been as her rescuer. Still the queen held back, and she dropped broad hints that if Mary had to die then it would be best to have her choked with a pillow or silenced with poison. She ordered her secretary to write Mary's jailer to inquire whether he would perform the task, but Sir Amias Paulet's Puritan conscience would have none of it. He wrote back refusing to "make so foul a shipwreck of my conscience as to shed blood without law or warrant." Elizabeth dared procrastinate no longer, and on February 1 she called for pen and ink and signed the death warrant, but even then she side-stepped the responsibility of sending it to Fotheringay, where Mary was imprisoned. After signing it, she threw it to the floor, and when her Scottish secretary, William Davison, asked her pleasure, she answered vaguely that the document should be taken to the Lord Chancellor to be sealed and recorded. The Privy Council well knew the queen's ways, and Burghley, Walsingham, Leicester, and others quietly dispatched the warrant to Fotheringay without further ado.

Execution was done on a cold Wednesday morning in February. The great hall at Fotheringay was cleared of its tables and chairs and turned into a death chamber. In the center, opposite a blazing log fire, was placed a three-foot-high wooden platform, draped in black cloth, upon which stood a straight-backed chair and the axing block. Late, as usual, and dressed in black velvet with a lace kerchief at her throat and a white veil over her auburn-gold locks, Mary entered the hall, walked serenely to the scaffold, and seated herself on the chair to listen to the reading of the warrant signed by her royal cousin. *Stubborn* and *disobedient* were the words used. No one doubted the first, but many thousands, including Elizabeth herself, wondered whether a divine-right queen could justly be called disobedient, and if so, to whom?

Even at the eleventh hour, the dean of Peterborough sought to win Mary from her faith and tactlessly urged her to repent, for "the hand of death," he said, "is over your head, and the axe is put to the root of the tree." The queen calmly bid him be silent. "Peace, Master Dean, you have nothing to do with me, nor I with you." The supreme moment had arrived, and no one knew better than Mary Stuart how to play her part or how becoming was the red of martyrdom. The black velvet cloak fell from her, and she knelt ready for death in bodice and petticoat of scarlet silk. Twice the axe struck, and Mary Stuart's head tumbled to the wooden floor. The executioner reached down to grasp the severed

In the watercolor above, Mary, holding a crucifix and surrounded by courtiers and official witnesses, kneels before her executioner in the great hall of Fotheringay Castle.

head by the hair and hold it aloft, and as he swung his grisly burden high, he shouted: "God save the queen." Suddenly the romantic legend was shattered, and the truth was revealed for all to see: in his hand the executioner held not a head but a golden wig, and on the floor rolled the cropped, white-haired head of the queen of Scotland.

Londoners went mad with joy at the news and came close to burning the city to the ground in a frenzy of bonfires and merrymaking. The good citizens believed that a new era had begun in which all men would live without fear now that the source of so much evil had been destroyed. Elizabeth knew otherwise, and she wept and raged at her Council and vowed to have poor Davison's head in revenge. How many of those tears were sincere, how many politic, no one can say. Doubtless many were shed for diplomatic reasons: Henry III had lost a sister, James VI a mother, and it behooved Elizabeth to weep at a tragedy ostensibly committed without her knowledge and against her will. She grieved that she had ever signed the warrant, and passionately assured the crowned heads of Europe that she had had no intention of executing it. Still other tears were directed in fury at councilors who had failed to do

away with Mary Stuart in her sleep, and who had now confronted the queen with a public execution and an international scandal. Finally a few tears must have fallen for a sister queen, a dead cousin, and an old rival.

For all the charm that had incited Norfolk, Babington, Throckmorton, and a host of others to treason, for all her regal blood and royal titles, Mary Stuart remained a pawn on the international chessboard, and her death did not affect the final conclusion of the game one whit. Long before Mary died, the king of Spain had made up his mind that his Great Enterprise was God's will, and that once he had won England, the Netherlands would fall too, for it was "God's obvious design" that he should "lay down the law for the whole world." Elizabeth, too, had come to recognize that the paths of England and Spain must meet in violence, and in her heart she believed, with navigator John Davys, that Englishmen were the saved people, predestined to "give light to all the rest of the world." The odds had been taken, the sides drawn, and Europe waited and speculated on which of them, Elizabeth of England or Philip of Spain, would prove to be the shining messenger of the Lord.

THE NOBLE VOICE

"Not marble, nor the gilded monuments/Of princes, shall outlive this powerful rime," wrote Shakespeare, in verse that was characteristic of the confident Elizabethan age. The lines were accurate as well. The sonnet from which they come, like so much of the work of Shakespeare and his contemporaries, will endure as long as the English language is spoken. For the Elizabethan poets produced a rich and melodious body of work, which at its best is unsurpassed by the literature of any other nation or age.

The Elizabethans were fortunate in living at a time when styles were becoming more sophisticated, and writers could experiment with novel forms and meters that had been brought to their attention by the revival of interest in classical poetry. The development of printing gave poets a wide audience, and the growth of London's population provided an appreciative and discriminating public for the city's numerous playwrights. The very language that the writers worked with was changing too, in part as a result of their own efforts. The subject matter, the diction, and the vocabulary of the age's poetry were exalted, but they were not completely divorced from real life, for lovers in England still lived in a flowery and pastoral landscape. It is this landscape of Elizabethan poetry—with its nightingales and larks and gardens of lilies, its nymphs with pearly teeth and golden tresses—that was to provide a setting for English poetry for centuries thereafter; and long after poets had moved on to more austere scenes, it still epitomized the poetic for English-speaking people. The Elizabethan poets placed far more than flowers and nymphs in this memorable landscape. The dramatists found room there for "sad stories of the death of kings" and amusing tales of rogues and buffoons; and poets wrote of failure as well as of success in love. Selections from the work of some of the great Elizabethan poets and playwrights, and a sampling of the various forms in which they wrote, appear in the anthology on the following pages.

The figure of tragedy, opposite, is taken from the first edition of Ben Jonson's plays.

THE FALL OF RICHARD II

The Elizabethans' political philosophy—their horror of rebellion and belief in the divine election of kings—pervades Act II, Scene II of Shakespeare's Richard II. The scene begins with the king's return from Ireland to a country racked with rebellion and ends with Richard certain that his troubled reign has finally come to a close.

The Coast of Wales. A Castle in view.

Flourish: drums and trumpets. Enter King Richard, the Bishop of Carlisle, Aumerle, and Soldiers.

KING RICHARD: Barkloughly Castle call they this at hand?

AUMERLE: Yea, my lord. How brooks your Grace the air,
After your late tossing on the breaking seas?

KING RICHARD: Needs must I like it well: I weep for joy
To stand upon my kingdom once again.
Dear earth, I do salute thee with my hand,
Though rebels wound thee with their horses' hoofs:
As a long-parted mother with her child
Plays fondly with her tears and smiles in meeting,
So, weeping, smiling, greet I thee, my earth,
And do thee favor with my royal hands.
Feed not thy sovereign's foe, my gentle earth,
Nor with thy sweets comfort his ravenous sense;
But let thy spiders, that suck up thy venom,
And heavy-gaited toads lie in their way,
Doing annoyance to the treacherous feet
Which with usurping steps do trample thee.
Yield stinging nettles to mine enemies;
And when they from thy bosom pluck a flower,
Guard it, I pray thee, with a lurking adder
Whose double tongue may with a mortal touch
Throw death upon thy sovereign's enemies.
Mock not my senseless conjuration, lords:
This earth shall have a feeling and these stones
Prove armed soldiers, ere her native king
Shall falter under foul rebellion's arms.

CARLISLE: Fear not, my lord: that power that made you king
Hath power to keep you king in spite of all.
The means that heaven yields must be embrac'd,
And not neglected; else, if heaven would,
And we will not, heaven's offer we refuse,
The proffer'd means of succor and redress.

AUMERLE: He means, my lord, that we are too remiss;
Whilst Bolingbroke, through our security,
Grows strong and great in substance and in friends.

KING RICHARD: Discomfortable cousin! know'st thou not
That when the searching eye of heaven is hid
Behind the globe, and lights the lower world,
Then thieves and robbers range abroad unseen,
In murders and in outrage bloody here;
But when, from under this terrestrial ball
He fires the proud tops of the eastern pines
And darts his light through every guilty hole,
Then murders, treasons, and detested sins,
The cloak of night being pluck'd from off their backs,
Stand bare and naked, trembling at themselves?
So when this thief, this traitor, Bolingbroke,
Who all this while hath revell'd in the night
Whilst we were wandering with the antipodes,
Shall see us rising in our throne, the east,
His treasons will sit blushing in his face,
Not able to endure the sight of day,
But self-affrighted tremble at his sin.
Not all the water in the rough rude sea
Can wash the balm from an anointed king;
The breath of worldly men cannot depose
The deputy elected by the Lord.
For every man that Bolingbroke hath press'd
To lift shrewd steel against our golden crown,
God for his Richard hath in heavenly pay
A glorious angel: then, if angels fight,
Weak men must fall, for heaven still guards the right.

Enter Salisbury.

Welcome, my lord: how far off lies your power?

SALISBURY: Nor near nor further off, my gracious lord,
Than this weak arm: discomfort guides my tongue
And bids me speak of nothing but despair.
One day too late, I fear me, noble lord,
Hath clouded all thy happy days on earth.
O! call back yesterday, bid time return,
And thou shalt have twelve thousand fighting men:
To-day, to-day, unhappy day too late,
O'erthrows thy joys, friends, fortune, and thy state;
For all the Welshmen, hearing thou wert dead,
Are gone to Bolingbroke, dispers'd, and fled.

AUMERLE: Comfort, my liege! why looks your Grace so pale?

KING RICHARD: But now, the blood of twenty thousand men
Did triumph in my face, and they are fled;
And till so much blood thither come again
Have I not reason to look pale and dead?
All souls that will be safe, fly from my side;
For time hath set a blot upon my pride.

AUMERLE: Comfort, my liege! remember who you are.

KING RICHARD: I had forgot myself. Am I not king?
Awake, thou sluggard majesty! thou sleepest.
Is not the king's name twenty thousand names?
Arm, arm, my name! a puny subject strikes
At thy great glory. Look not to the ground,
Ye favorites of a king: are we not high?
High be our thoughts: I know my uncle York
Hath power enough to serve our turn. But who comes here?

Enter Sir Stephen Scroop.

SCROOP: More health and happiness betide my liege
Than can my care-tun'd tongue deliver him!

KING RICHARD: Mine ear is open and my heart prepar'd:
The worst is worldly loss thou canst unfold.
Say, is my kingdom lost? why, 'twas my care;
And what loss is it to be rid of care?
Strives Bolingbroke to be as great as we?
Greater he shall not be: if he serve God
We'll serve him too, and be his fellow so:
Revolt our subjects? that we cannot mend;
They break their faith to God as well as us:
Cry woe, destruction, ruin, loss, decay;
The worst is death, and death will have his day.

SCROOP: Glad am I that your highness is so arm'd

To bear the tidings of calamity.
Like an unseasonable stormy day
Which makes the silver rivers drown their shores,
As if the world were all dissolv'd to tears,
So high above his limits swells the rage
Of Bolingbroke, covering your fearful land
With hard bright steel and hearts harder than steel.
White-beards have arm'd their thin and hairless scalps
Against thy majesty; and boys, with women's voices,
Strive to speak big, and clap their female joints
In stiff unwieldy arms against thy crown;
Thy very beadsmen learn to bend their bows
Of double-fatal yew against thy state;
Yea, distaff-women manage rusty bills
Against thy seat: both young and old rebel,
And all goes worse than I have power to tell.

KING RICHARD: Too well, too well thou tell'st a tale so ill.
Where is the Earl of Wiltshire? where is Bagot?
What is become of Bushy? where is Green?
That they have let the dangerous enemy
Measure our confines with such peaceful steps?
If we prevail, their heads shall pay for it.
I warrant they have made peace with Bolingbroke.

SCROOP: Peace have they made with him, indeed, my lord.

KING RICHARD: O villains, vipers, damn'd without
    redemption!
Dogs, easily won to fawn on any man!
Snakes, in my heart-blood warm'd, that sting my heart!
Three Judases, each one thrice worse than Judas!
Would they make peace? terrible hell make war
Upon their spotted souls for this offense!

SCROOP: Sweet love, I see, changing his property,
Turns to the sourest and most deadly hate.
Again uncurse their souls; their peace is made
With heads and not with hands: those whom you curse
Have felt the worst of death's destroying wound
And lie full low, grav'd in the hollow ground.

AUMERLE: Is Bushy, Green, and the Earl of Wiltshire dead?

SCROOP: Yea, all of them at Bristol lost their heads.

AUMERLE: Where is the duke my father with his power?

KING RICHARD: No matter where. Of comfort no man speak:
Let's talk of graves, of worms, and epitaphs;
Make dust our paper, and with rainy eyes
Write sorrow on the bosom of the earth;
Let's choose executors and talk of wills:
And yet not so—for what can we bequeath
Save our deposed bodies to the ground?
Our lands, our lives, and all are Bolingbroke's,
And nothing can we call our own but death,
And that small model of the barren earth
Which serves as paste and cover to our bones.
For God's sake, let us sit upon the ground
And tell sad stories of the death of kings:
How some have been depos'd, some slain in war,
Some haunted by the ghosts they have depos'd,
Some poison'd by their wives, some sleeping kill'd;
All murder'd: for within the hollow crown
That rounds the mortal temples of a king
Keeps Death his court, and there the antick sits,
Scoffing his state and grinning at his pomp;

Allowing him a breath, a little scene,
To monarchize, be fear'd, and kill with looks,
Infusing him with self and vain conceit
As if this flesh which walls about our life
Were brass impregnable; and humor'd thus
Comes at the last, and with a little pin
Bores through his castle wall, and farewell king!
Cover your heads, and mock not flesh and blood
With solemn reverence: throw away respect,
Tradition, form, and ceremonious duty,
For you have but mistook me all this while:
I live with bread like you, feel want,
Taste grief, need friends: subjected thus,
How can you say to me I am a king?

CARLISLE: My lord, wise men ne'er sit and wail their woes,
But presently prevent the ways to wail.
To fear the foe, since fear oppresseth strength,
Gives in your weakness strength unto your foe,
And so your follies fight against yourself.
Fear and be slain; no worse can come to fight:
And fight and die is death destroying death;
Where fearing dying pays death servile breath.

AUMERLE: My father hath a power; inquire of him
And learn to make a body of a limb.

KING RICHARD: Thou chid'st me well. Proud Bolingbroke,
    I come
To change blows with thee for our day of doom.
This ague-fit of fear is over-blown;
An easy task it is, to win our own.—
Say, Scroop, where lies our uncle with his power?
Speak sweetly, man, although thy looks be sour.

SCROOP: Men judged by the complexion of the sky
The state and inclination of the day;
So may you by my dull and heavy eye,
My tongue hath but a heavier tale to say,
I play the torturer, by small and small
To lengthen out the worst that must be spoken.
Your uncle York is join'd with Bolingbroke,
And all your northern castles yielded up,
And all your southern gentlemen in arms
Upon his party.

KING RICHARD: Thou hast said enough.
[To Aumerle.] Beshrew thee, cousin, which didst lead me
    forth
Of that sweet way I was in to despair!
What say you now? What comfort have we now?
By heaven, I'll hate him everlastingly
That bids me be of comfort any more.
Go to Flint Castle: there I'll pine away;
A king, woe's slave, shall kingly woe obey.
That power I have, discharge; and let them go
To ear the land that hath some hope to grow,
For I have none: let no man speak again
To alter this, for counsel is but vain.

AUMERLE: My liege, one word.

KING RICHARD: He does me double wrong,
That wounds me with the flatteries of his tongue.
Discharge my followers: let them hence away,
From Richard's night to Bolingbroke's fair day.
Exeunt.

THE DEATH
OF FAUSTUS

Christopher Marlowe's The Tragical History of Doctor Faustus *ends with a powerful soliloquy in which Faustus mourns having sold his soul to the Devil, who is coming at midnight to take him away. The Latin line that appears in the soliloquy, "O lente, lente, currite noctis equi," means "Run slowly, slowly, steeds of the night."*

The clock strikes eleven.
FAUSTUS: Ah, Faustus,
Now hast thou but one bare hour to live,
And then thou must be damn'd perpetually!
Stand still, you ever-moving spheres of Heaven,
That time may cease, and midnight never come;
Fair Nature's eye, rise, rise again and make
Perpetual day; or let this hour be but
A year, a month, a week, a natural day,
That Faustus may repent and save his soul!
O lente, lente, currite noctis equi!
The stars move still, time runs, the clock will strike,
The Devil will come, and Faustus must be damn'd.
O, I'll leap up to my God! Who pulls me down?
See, see where Christ's blood streams in the firmament!
One drop would save my soul—half a drop! ah, my Christ!—
Ah, rend not my heart for naming of my Christ!—
Yet will I call on him!—O, spare me, Lucifer!—
Where is it now? 'T is gone; and see where God
Stretcheth out his arm, and bends his ireful brows!—
Mountain and hills, come, come and fall on me,
And hide me from the heavy wrath of God!
No! no!—
Then will I headlong run into the earth!—
Earth, gape!— O no, it will not harbor me!—
You stars that reign'd at my nativity,
Whose influence hath allotted death and hell,
Now draw up Faustus like a foggy mist
Into the entrails of yon lab'ring cloud,
That when you vomit forth into the air,
My limbs may issue from their smoky mouths,
So that my soul may but ascend to Heaven.
The watch strikes.
Ah, half the hour is past! 'T will all be past anon!
O God,
If thou wilt not have mercy on my soul,
Yet for Christ's sake, whose blood hath ransom'd me,
Impose some end to my incessant pain;
Let Faustus live in hell a thousand years,
A hundred thousand, and at last be sav'd!—
O, no end is limited to damned souls!
Why wert thou not a creature wanting soul?
Or why is this immortal that thou hast?
Ah, Pythagoras' metempsychosis! were that true,
This soul should fly from me, and I be chang'd
Unto some brutish beast! All beasts are happy,
For, when they die,

Their souls are soon dissolv'd in elements;
But mine must live, still to be plagu'd in hell.
Curs'd be the parents that engend'red me!
No, Faustus, curse thyself, curse Lucifer,
That hath depriv'd thee of the joys of Heaven.
The clock strikes twelve.
O, it strikes, it strikes! Now, body, turn to air,
Or Lucifer will bear thee quick to hell!
Thunder and lightning.
O soul, be chang'd into little water-drops,
And fall into the ocean—ne'er be found!—
My God, my God, look not so fierce on me!
Enter Devils.
Adders and serpents, let me breathe awhile!—
Ugly hell, gape not!—Come not, Lucifer!—
I'll burn my books!—Ah, Mephistophilis!
Exeunt Devils with him.

VOLPONE, THE
MOUNTEBANK

Ben Jonson's comic hero Volpone is a champion confidence man, tricking his friends out of their money and women out of their virtue. Here in a scene from Act II of Volpone—*set in Venice—he erects his stand as a patent medicine salesman in front of his beloved Celia's home to catch a glimpse of her. His extravagant sales pitch follows.*

VOLPONE: I protest I and my six servants are not able to make of this precious liquor so fast as it is fetch'd away from my lodging by gentlemen of your city, strangers of the terra firma, worshipful merchants, ay, and senators, too: who, ever since my arrival, have detained me to their uses by their splendidous liberalities. And worthily. For what avails your rich man to have his magazines stuff'd with *moscadelli*, or of the purest grape, when his physicians prescribe him, on pain of death, to drink nothing but water cocted with aniseeds? O health! health! the blessing of the rich! the riches of the poor! who can buy thee at too dear a rate, since there is no enjoying this world without thee? Be not then so sparing of your purses, honorable gentlemen, as to abridge the natural course of life . . .

For, when a humid flux, or catarrh, by the mutability of air, falls from your head into an arm or shoulder, or any other part, take you a ducat, or your *cecchine* of gold, and apply to the place affected; see what good effect it can work. No, no; 'tis this blessed *unguento*, this rare extraction, that hath only power to disperse all malignant humors that proceed either of hot, cold, moist, or windy causes . . .

To fortify the most indigest and crude stomach, ay, were

it of one that, through extreme weakness, vomited blood, applying only a warm napkin to the place, after the unction and fricace;—for the *vertigine* in the head, putting but a drop into your nostrils, likewise behind the ears, a most sovereign and approv'd remedy; the *mal caduco*, cramps, convulsions, paralyses, epilepsies, *tremor cordia*, retir'd nerves, ill vapors of the spleen, stoppings of the liver, the stone, the strangury, *hernia ventosa*, *iliaca passio*; stops a *dysenteria* immediately; easeth the torsion of the small guts; and cures *melancholia hypocondriaca*, being taken and applied according to my printed receipt. (*Pointing to his bill and his glass.*) For this is the physician, this the medicine; this counsels, this cures; this gives direction, this works the effect; and, in sum, both together may be term'd an abstract of the theoric and practic in the Aesculapian art. 'Twill cost you eight crowns. . . .

No more.—Gentlemen, if I had but time to discourse to you the miraculous effects of this my oil, surnamed *oglio del Scoto*, with the countless catalogue of those I have cured of th' aforesaid, and many more diseases; the patents and privileges of all the princes and commonwealths of Christendom; or but the depositions of those that appear'd on my part, before the signiory of the Sanità and most learned College of Physicians; where I was authorized, upon notice taken of the admirable virtues of my medicaments, and mine own excellency in matter of rare and unknown secrets, not only to disperse them publicly in this famous city, but in all the territories that happily joy under the government of the most pious and magnificent states of Italy. But may some other gallant fellow say, "Oh, there be diverse that make profession to have as good, and as experimented receipts as yours." Indeed, very many have assay'd, like apes, in imitation of that which is really and essentially in me, to make of this oil; bestow'd great cost in furnaces, stills, alembics, continual fires, and preparation of the ingredients (as indeed there goes to it six hundred several simples, besides some quantity of human fat, for the conglutination, which we buy of the anatomists); but when these practitioners come to the last decoction—blow, blow, puff, puff, and all flies in fumo. Ha, ha, ha! Poor wretches! I rather pity their folly and indiscretion, than their loss of time and money; for those may be recovered by industry; but to be a fool born, is a disease incurable. For myself, I always from my youth have endeavor'd to get the rarest secrets, and book them, either in exchange or for money; I spared nor cost nor labor where anything was worthy to be learned. And, gentlemen, honorable gentlemen, I will undertake, by virtue of chemical art, out of the honorable hat that covers your head, to extract the four elements; that is to say, the fire, air, water, and earth, and return you your felt without burn or stain. For, whilst others have been at the *balloo* I have been at my book; and am now past the craggy paths of study, and come to the flow'ry plains of honor and reputation. . . .

You all know, honorable gentlemen, I never valu'd this *ampulla*, or vial, at less than eight crowns; but for this time, I am content to be depriv'd of it for six; six crowns is the price, and less in courtesy I know you cannot offer me; take it or leave it, howsoever, both it and I am at your service. I ask you not as the value of the thing, for then I should demand of you a thousand crowns; so the Cardinals Montalto, Fernese, the great Duke of Tuscany, my gossip, with divers

other princes, have given me; but I despise money. Only to show my affection to you, honorable gentlemen, and your illustrious state here, I have neglected the messages of these princes, mine own offices, fram'd my journey hither, only to present you with the fruits of my travels. . . .

Well, I am in a humor, at this time, to make a present of the small quantity my coffer contains; to the rich in courtesy, and to the poor for God's sake. Wherefore now mark: I ask'd you six crowns; and six crowns, at other times, you have paid me; you shall not give me six crowns, nor five, nor four, nor three, nor two, nor one; nor half a ducat; no, nor a *m[o]ccinigo*. Six—pence it will cost you, or six hundred pound—expect no lower price, for, by the banner of my front, I will not bate a bagatine,—that I will have, only, a pledge of your loves, to carry something from amongst you, to show I am not contemn'd by you. Therefore, now, toss your handkerchiefs, cheerfully, cheerfully; and be advertised, that the first heroic spirit that deigns to grace me with a handkerchief, I will give it a little remembrance of something beside, shall please it better than if I had presented it with a double pistolet. . . .

Celia, at the windo[w], throws down her handkerchief.

Lady, I kiss your bounty; and, for this timely grace you have done your poor Scoto of Mantua, I will return you, over and above my oil, a secret of that high and inestimable nature, shall make you for ever enamor'd on that minute wherein your eye first descended on so mean, yet not altogether to be despis'd, an object. Here is a powder conceal'd in this paper, of which, if I should speak to the worth, nine thousand volumes were but as one page, that page as a line, that line as a word; so short is this pilgrimage of man, which some call life, to the expressing of it. Would I reflect on the price? Why, the whole world is but as an empire, that empire as a province, that province as a bank, that bank as a private purse, to the purchase of it. I will only tell you: it is the powder that made Venus a goddess, given her by Apollo, that kept her perpetually young, clear'd her wrinkles, firm'd her gums, fill'd her skin, color'd her hair; from her deriv'd to Helen, and at the sack of Troy unfortunately lost; till now, in this our age, it was as happily recover'd, by a studious antiquary, out of some ruins of Asia, who sent a moiety of it to the court of France (but much sophisticated), wherewith the ladies there now color their hair. The rest, at this present, remains with me, extracted to a quintessence; so that, whereever it but touches, in youth it perpetually preserves, in age restores the complexion; seats your teeth, did they dance like virginal jacks, firm as a wall; makes them white as ivory . . .

A WOMAN KILLED WITH KINDNESS

Thomas Heywood's A Woman Killed with Kindness *is a tragedy, but one of a far different nature from* Hamlet *or* Lear. *Here it is a household, not a kingdom, that is wrecked. Scene* IV *of Act* IV *depicts the hero, Frankford's, discovery of his wife's infidelity. He punishes her by dooming her to exile, in which she pines away and dies of a broken heart, but not before receiving a deathbed forgiveness.*

Enter Frankford and Nicholas.

FRANKFORD: Soft, soft. We have tied our geldings to a tree,
Two flight-shoot off, lest by their thundering hoofs
They blab our coming. Hear'st thou no noise?

NICHOLAS: Hear? I hear nothing but the owl and you.

FRANKFORD: So; now my watch's hand points upon twelve,
And it is just midnight. Where are my keys?

NICHOLAS: Here, sir.

FRANKFORD: This is the key that opes my outward gate;
This is the hall door; this, my withdrawing chamber;
But this, that door that's bawd unto my shame,
Fountain and spring of all my bleeding thoughts,
Where the most hallowed order and true knot
Of nuptial sanctity hath been profan'd:
It leads to my polluted bedchamber,
Once my terrestrial Heaven, now my earth's hell,
The place where sins in all their ripeness dwell.—
But I forget myself; now to my gate!

NICHOLAS: It must ope with far less noise than Cripplegate,
  or your plot's dash'd.

FRANKFORD: So; reach me my dark lantern to the rest.
Tread softly, softly.

NICHOLAS: I will walk on eggs this pace.

FRANKFORD: A general silence hath surpris'd the house,
And this is the last door. Astonishment,
Fear, and amazement beat upon my heart,
Even as a madman beats upon a drum.
Oh, keep my eyes, you Heavens, before I enter,
From any sight that may transfix my soul;
Or, if there be so black a spectacle,
Oh, strike mine eyes stark blind; or, if not so,
Lend me such patience to digest my grief,
That I may keep this white and virgin hand
From any violent outrage, or red murder.
And with that prayer I enter.

Exit.

NICHOLAS: Here's a circumstance, indeed!
A man may be made a cuckold in the time
He's about it. An the case were mine,
As 'tis my master's, 'sblood! (that he makes me swear!),
I would have plac'd his action, enter'd there;
I would, I would!

Enter Frankford.

FRANKFORD: Oh! oh!

NICHOLAS: Master! 'Sblood! Master, Master!

FRANKFORD: O me unhappy! I have found them lying
Close in each other's arms, and fast asleep.
But that I would not damn two precious souls,
Bought with my Savior's blood, and send them, laden
With all their scarlet sins upon their backs,
Unto a fearful judgment, their two lives
Had met upon my rapier.

NICHOLAS: Master, what, have you left them sleeping still?
Let me go wake 'em.

FRANKFORD: Stay, let me pause awhile.—
O God, O God, that it were possible
To undo things done; to call back yesterday;
That Time could turn up his swift sandy glass,
To untell the days, and to redeem these hours.
Or that the sun
Could, rising from the west, draw his coach backward,
Take from th' account of time so many minutes,
Till he had all those seasons call'd again,
Those minutes, and those actions done in them,
Even from her first offense; that I might take her
As spotless as an angel in my arms.
But, oh! I talk of things impossible,
And cast beyond the moon. God give me patience;
For I will in, and wake them.

Exit.

NICHOLAS: Here's patience perforce.
He needs must trot afoot that tires his horse.

*Enter Wendoll, running over the stage in a night-gown, [Frankford]
  after him with his sword drawn; the maid in her smock stays his
  hand and clasps hold on him. He pauses for a while.*

FRANKFORD: I thank thee, maid; thou, like an angel's hand,
Hast stay'd me from a bloody sacrifice.
Go, villain; and my wrongs sit on thy soul
As heavy as this grief doth upon mine.
When thou record'st my many courtesies,
And shalt compare them with thy treacherous heart,
Lay them together, weigh them equally—
'Twill be revenge enough. Go, to thy friend
A Judas; pray, pray, lest I live to see
Thee, Judas-like, hang'd on an elder tree.

Enter Mistress Frankford in her smock, night-gown, and night-attire.

MISTRESS FRANKFORD: Oh, by what word, what title, or what
  name,
Shall I entreat your pardon? Pardon! oh,
I am as far from hoping such sweet grace,
As Lucifer from Heaven. To call you husband,—
O me, most wretched, I have lost that name;
I am no more your wife.

NICHOLAS: 'Sblood, sir, she swoons.

FRANKFORD: Spare thou thy tears, for I will weep for thee;
And keep thy count'nance, for I'll blush for thee.
Now I protest I think 'tis I am tainted,
For I am most asham'd; and 't is more hard
For me to look upon thy guilty face
Than on the sun's clear brow. What, would'st thou speak?

MISTRESS FRANKFORD: I would I had no tongue, no ears, no
  eyes,

No apprehension, no capacity.
When do you spurn me like a dog? when tread me
Under feet? when drag me by the hair?
Though I deserve a thousand thousand-fold
More than you can inflict—yet, once my husband,
For womanhood, to which I am a shame,
Though once an ornament—even for His sake,
That hath redeem'd our souls, mark not my face,
Nor hack me with your sword; but let me go
Perfect and undeformed to my tomb.
I am not worthy that I should prevail
In the least suit; no, not to speak to you,
Nor look on you, nor to be in your presence;
Yet, as an abject, this one suit I crave;
This granted, I am ready for my grave.

FRANKFORD: My God, with patience arm me.—
    Rise, nay, rise,
And I'll debate with thee. Was it for want
Thou play'dst the strumpet? Wast thou not suppli'd
With every pleasure, fashion, and new toy,
Nay, even beyond my calling?

MISTRESS FRANKFORD: I was.

FRANKFORD: Was it, then, disability in me;
Or in thine eye seem'd he a properer man?

MISTRESS FRANKFORD: Oh, no.

FRANKFORD: Did I not lodge thee in my bosom?
Wear thee in my heart?

MISTRESS FRANKFORD: You did.

FRANKFORD: I did, indeed; witness my tears, I did.—
Go, bring my infants hither.—

Two children are brought in.

                              O Nan, O Nan,
If neither fear of shame, regard of honor,
The blemish of my house, nor my dear love,
Could have withheld thee from so lewd a fact;
Yet for these infants, these young, harmless souls,
On whose white brows thy shame is character'd,
And grows in greatness as they wax in years—
Look but on them, and melt away in tears!—
Away with them; lest, as her spotted body
Hath stain'd their names with stripe of bastardy,
So her adulterous breath may blast their spirits
With her infectious thoughts. Away with them.

The children are taken out.

MISTRESS FRANKFORD: In this one life, I die ten thousand
    deaths.

FRANKFORD: Stand up, stand up; I will do nothing rashly.
I will retire awhile into my study,
And thou shalt hear thy sentence presently.

MISTRESS FRANKFORD: 'Tis welcome, be it death. O me,
    base strumpet,
That, having such a husband, such sweet children,
Must enjoy neither! Oh, to redeem my honor,
I would have this hand cut off, these my breasts sear'd;
Be rack'd, strappado'd, put to any torment.
Nay, to whip but this scandal out, I would hazard
The rich and dear redemption of my soul.

He cannot be so base as to forgive me,
Nor I so shameless to accept his pardon.
O, women, women, you that yet have kept .
Your holy matrimonial vow unstain'd,
Make me your instance; when you tread awry,
Your sins, like mine, will on your conscience lie.

*Enter Cicely, Spigot, all the serving men, and Jenkin,
    as newly come out of bed.*

ALL: O, Mistress, Mistress! What have you done, Mistress?

NICHOLAS: What a caterwauling keep you here.

JENKIN: O Lord, Mistress, how comes this to pass? My master is run away in his shirt, and never so much as call'd me
to bring his clothes after him.

MISTRESS FRANKFORD: See what guilt is! Here stand I in this
    place,
Asham'd to look my servants in the face.

*Enter Master Frankford and Cranwell; whom seeing,
    she falls on her knees.*

FRANKFORD: My words are regist'red in Heaven already.
With patience hear me. I'll not martyr thee,
Nor mark thee for a strumpet; but with usage
Of more humility torment thy soul,
And kill thee even with kindness.

CRANWELL: Master Frankford—

FRANKFORD: Good Master Cranwell. —Woman, hear thy
    judgment.
Go make thee ready in thy best attire;
Take with thee all thy gowns, all thy apparel;
Leave nothing that did ever call thee mistress,
Or by whose sight, being left here in the house,
I may remember such a woman by.
Choose thee a bed and hangings for thy chamber;
Take with thee every thing which hath thy mark,·
And get thee to my manor seven mile off,
Where live; 'tis thine; I freely give it thee.
My tenants by shall furnish thee with wains
To carry all thy stuff within two hours;
No longer will I limit thee my sight.
Choose which of all my servants thou lik'st best,
And they are thine to attend thee.

MISTRESS FRANKFORD: A mild sentence.

FRANKFORD: But, as thou hop'st for Heaven, as thou believ'st
Thy name's recorded in the book of life,
I charge thee never after this sad day
To see me, or to meet me; or to send,
By word or writing, gift or otherwise,
To move me, by thyself, or by thy friends;
Nor challenge any part in my two children.
So farewell, Nan; for we will henceforth be
As we had never seen, ne'er more shall see.

MISTRESS FRANKFORD: How full my heart is, in my eyes
    appears;
What wants in words, I will supply in tears.

FRANKFORD: Come, take your coach, your stuff; all must
    along.
Servants and all make ready; all begone.—
It was thy hand cut two hearts out of one.

Exeunt.

THE SONNET

There were, according to one curious estimate, more than a million sonnets written during the sixteenth century, most of them about love. Fortunately, the great majority, by poets whose talents failed to match their passion, has failed to survive. The twelve sonnets that are presented here include poems by Edmund Spenser, Sir Philip Sidney, and Shakespeare, the three great English masters of the form, and an engaging satire on mooning lovers by John Davies of Hereford.

Edmund Spenser

Is it her nature or is it her will,
To be so cruel to an humbled foe?
If nature, then she may it mend with skill,
If will, then she at will may will forego.
But if her nature and her will be so,
That she will plague the man that loves her most:
And take delight t' increase a wretch's woe,
Then all her nature's goodly gifts are lost.
And that same glorious beauty's idle boast,
Is but a bait such wretches to beguile:
As being long in her love's tempest tossed,
She means at last to make her piteous spoil.
O fairest fair let never it be named,
That so fair beauty was so foully shamed.

Edmund Spenser

Sweet is the rose, but grows upon a brere;
Sweet is the juniper, but sharp his bough;
Sweet is the eglantine, but pricketh near;
Sweet is the fir-bloom, but his branches rough;
Sweet is the cypress, but his rind is tough;
Sweet is the nut, but bitter is his pill;
Sweet is the broom-flower, but yet sour enough;
And sweet is moly, but his root is ill.
So every sweet with sour is tempered still,
That maketh it be coveted the more;
For easy things, that may be got at will,
Most sorts of men do set but little store.
Why then should I account of little pain,
That endless pleasure shall unto me gain?

Edmund Spenser

My love is like to ice, and I to fire;
How comes it then that this her cold so great
Is not dissolved through my so hot desire,
But harder grows the more I her entreat?
Or how comes it that my exceeding heat
Is not delayed by her heart frozen cold:
But that I burn much more in boiling sweat,
And feel my flames augmented manifold?
What more miraculous thing may be told
That fire which all things melts, should harden ice:
And ice which is congealed with senseless cold,
Should kindle fire by wonderful device?
Such is the power of love in gentle mind,
That it can alter all the course of kind.

Sir Philip Sidney

O joy too high for my low style to show!
O bliss fit for a nobler state than me!
Envy, put out thine eyes, lest thou do see
What oceans of delight in me do flow!
My friend, that oft saw through all masks my woe,
Come, come, and let me pour myself on thee.
Gone is the Winter of my misery:
My Spring appears: O see what here doth grow!
For Stella hath, with words where faith doth shine,
Of her high heart given me the monarchy.
I, I, oh I, may say that she is mine,
And though she give but thus conditionly
This realm of bliss, while virtuous course I take,
No kings be crown'd but they some covenants make.

Sir Philip Sidney

Stella, think not that I by verse seek fame
Who seek, who hope, who love, who live but thee;
Thine eyes my pride, thy lips mine history:
If thou praise not, all other praise is shame.
Nor so ambitious am I as to frame
A nest for my young praise in laurel tree:
In truth I swear, I wish not there should be
Graved in my epitaph a poet's name.
Ne, if I would, could I just title make,
That any laud thereof to me should grow,
Without my plumes from others' wings I take:
For nothing from my wit or will doth flow,
Since all my words thy beauty doth indite,
And Love doth hold my hand and makes me write.

William Shakespeare

Some glory in their birth, some in their skill,
Some in their wealth, some in their body's force;
Some in their garments, though new-fangled ill;
Some in their hawks and hounds, some in their horse;
And every humor hath his adjunct pleasure,
Wherein it finds a joy above the rest:
But these particulars are not my measure;
All these I better in one general best.
Thy love is better than high birth to me,
Richer than wealth, prouder than garments' cost,
Of more delight than hawks or horses be;
And having thee, of all men's pride I boast:
Wretched in this alone, that though mayst take
All this away, and me most wretched make.

William Shakespeare

Like as the waves make towards the pebbled shore,
So do our minutes hasten to their end;
Each changing place with that which goes before,
In sequent toil all forwards do contend.
Nativity, once in the main of light,
Crawls to maturity, wherewith being crown'd,
Crooked eclipses 'gainst his glory fight,
And Time that gave doth now his gift confound.
Time doth transfix the flourish set on youth
And delves the parallels in beauty's brow,
Feeds on the rarities of nature's truth,
And nothing stands but for his scythe to mow:
And yet to times in hope my verse shall stand,
Praising thy worth, despite his cruel hand.

William Shakespeare

Since brass, nor stone, nor earth, nor boundless sea,
But sad mortality o'ersways their power,
How with this rage shall beauty hold a plea,
Whose action is no stronger than a flower?
O! how shall summer's honey breath hold out
Against the wrackful siege of battering days,
When rocks impregnable are not so stout,
Nor gates of steel so strong, but Time decays?
O fearful meditation! where, alack,
Shall Time's best jewel from Time's chest lie hid?
Or what strong hand can hold his swift foot back?
Or who his spoil of beauty can forbid?
O! none, unless this miracle have might,
That in black ink my love may still shine bright.

Bartholomew Griffin

Fair is my Love that feeds among the lilies,
The lilies growing in that pleasant garden
Where Cupid's Mount that well belovèd hill is,
And where that little god himself is warden.
See where my Love sits in the beds of spices,
Beset all round with camphor, myrrh, and roses,
And interlaced with curious devices
Which her apart from all the world incloses!
There doth she tune her lute for her delight,
And with sweet music makes the ground to move,
Whilst I, poor I, do sit in heavy plight,
Wailing alone my unrespected love;
Not daring rush into so rare a place,
That gives to her, and she to it, a grace.

George Gascoigne

You must not wonder, though you think it strange,
To see me hold my louring head so low;
And that mine eyes take no delight to range
About the gleams which on your face do grow.
The mouse which once hath broken out of trap,
Is seldom 'ticèd with the trustless bait,
But lies aloof for fear of more mishap,
And feedeth still in doubt of deep deceit.
The scorchèd fly, which once hath 'scaped the flame,
Will hardly come to play again with fire:
Whereby I learn that grievous is the game
Which follows fancy dazzled by desire:
So that I wink or else hold down my head,
Because your blazing eyes my bale have bred.

Samuel Daniel

Let others sing of knights and paladins
In agèd accents and untimely words,
Paint shadows in imaginary lines,
Which well the reach of their high wits records:
But I must sing of thee, and those fair eyes
Authentic shall my verse in time to come,
When yet the unborn shall say, "Lo, where she lies,
Whose beauty made him speak that else was dumb."
These are the arks, the trophies, I erect,
That fortify thy name against old age;
And these thy sacred virtues must protect
Against the dark and Time's consuming rage.
Though the error of my youth in them appear,
Suffice they show I lived, and loved thee dear.

John Davies

If there were, oh! an Hellespont of cream
Between us, milk-white mistress, I would swim
To you, to show to both my love's extreme,
Leander-like,—yea! dive from brim to brim.
But met I with a buttered pippin-pie
Floating upon 't, that would I make my boat
To waft me to you without jeopardy,
Though sea-sick I might be while it did float.
Yet if a storm should rise, by night or day,
Of sugar-snows and hail of caraways,
Then, if I found a pancake in my way,
It like a plank should bring me to your kays;
Which having found, if they tobacco kept,
The smoke should dry me well before I slept.

IMMORTAL SPENSER

The verses below, on "mutabilitie," appear at the end of Edmund Spenser's great philosophical allegory, The Faerie Queene. Along with the excerpt from the Epithalamion, which was written on the occasion of his marriage, they display the poetic power that made his contemporaries consider "Immortal" Spenser England's greatest poet. Both excerpts retain the original spelling.

from The Faerie Queene, Book VII

Then forth issewed (great goddesse) great Dame Nature,
With goodly port and gracious majesty,
Being far greater and more tall of stature
Then any of the gods or powers on hie:
Yet certes by her face and physnomy,
Whether she man or woman inly were,
That could not any creature well descry:
For, with a veile that wimpled every where,
Her head and face was hid, that mote to none appeare.

That, some doe say, was so by skill devized,
To hide the terror of her uncouth hew
From mortall eyes, that should be sore agrized;
For that her face did like a lion shew,
That eye of wight could not indure to view:
But others tell that it so beautious was,
And round about such beames of splendor threw,
That it the sunne a thousand times did pass,
Ne could be seene, but like an image in a glass. . . .

In a fayre plaine upon an equall hill
She placed was in a pavilion;
Not such as craftes-men by their idle skill
Are wont for princes states to fashion:
But th' Earth her self, of her owne motion,
Out of her fruitfull bosome made to growe
Most dainty trees, that, shooting up anon,
Did seeme to bow their bloosming heads full lowe,
For homage unto her, and like a throne did shew. . . .

And all the earth far underneath her feete
Was dight with flowres, that voluntary grew
Out of the ground, and sent forth odours sweet;
Tenne thousand mores of sundry sent and hew,
That might delight the smell, or please the view;
The which the nymphes from all the brooks thereby
Had gathered, which they at her foot-stoole threw;
That richer seem'd then any tapestry,
That princes bowres adorne with painted imagery. . . .

This great grandmother of all creatures bred,
Great Nature, ever young yet full of eld,
Still mooving, yet unmoved from her sted,
Unseene of any, yet of all beheld,
Thus sitting in her throne, as I have teld,
Before her came Dame Mutabilitie;
And being lowe before her presence feld,
With meek obaysance and humilitie,
Thus gan her plaintif plea, with words to amplifie:

"To thee, O greatest goddesse, onely great,
An humble suppliant loe! I lowely fly,
Seeking for right, which I of thee entreat,
Who right to all dost deale indifferently,
Damning all wrong and tortious injurie,
Which any of thy creatures doe to other
(Oppressing them with power, unequally)
Sith of them all thou art the equall mother,
And knittest each to each, as brother unto brother.

"To thee therefore of this same Jove I plaine,
And of his fellow gods that faine to be,
That challenge to themselves the whole worlds raign;
Of which the greatest part is due to me,
And heaven it selfe by heritage in fee:
For heaven and earth I both alike do deeme,
Sith heaven and earth are both alike to thee;
And gods no more then men thou doest esteeme:
For even the gods to thee, as men to gods, do seeme.

"Then weigh, O soveraigne goddesse, by what right
These gods do claime the worlds whole soveraity,
And that is onely dew unto thy might
Arrogate to themselves ambitiously:
As for the gods owne principality,
Which Jove usurpes unjustly, that to be
My heritage, Jove's self cannot deny,
From my great grandsire Titan unto mee
Deriv'd by dew descent; as is well knowen to thee.

"Yet mauger Jove, and all his gods beside,
I doe possesse the worlds most regiment;
As, if ye please it into parts divide,
And every parts inholders to convent,
Shall to your eyes appeare incontinent.
And first, the Earth (great mother of us all)
That only seems unmov'd and permanent,
And unto Mutability not thrall,
Yet is she chang'd in part, and eeke in generall.

"For all that from her springs, and is ybredde,
How-ever fayre it flourish for a time,
Yet see we soone decay; and, being dead,
To turne again unto their earthly slime:
Yet, out of their decay and mortall crime,
We daily see new creatures to arize,
And of their winter spring another prime,
Unlike in forme, and chang'd by strange disguise;
So turne they still about, and change in restlesse wise."

from The Epithalamion

Wake now, my love, awake! for it is time;
The Rosy Morne long since left Tithones bed,
All ready to her silver coche to clyme;
And Phoebus gins to shew his glorious hed.
Hark! how the cheerefull birds do chaunt theyr laies
And carroll of Loves praise.
The merry Larke hir mattins sings aloft;
The Thrush replyes; the Mavis descant playes;
The Ouzell shrills; the Ruddock warbles soft;
So goodly all agree, with sweet consent,
To this dayes merriment.
Ah! my deere love, why doe ye sleepe thus long?
When meeter were that ye should now awake,
T' awayt the comming of your joyous make,
And hearken to the birds love-learnèd song,
The deawy leaves among!
Nor they of joy and pleasance to you sing,
That all the woods them answer, and theyr eccho ring.

My love is now awake out of her dreames,
And her fayre eyes, like stars that dimmèd were
With darksome cloud, now shew theyr goodly beames
More bright then Hesperus his head doth rere.
Come now, ye damzels, daughters of delight,
Helpe quickly her to dight:
But first come ye fayre houres, which were begot
In Joves sweet paradice of Day and Night;
Which doe the seasons of the yeare allot,
And al, that ever in this world is fayre,
Doe make and still repayre:
And ye three handmayds of the Cyprian Queene,
The which doe still adorne her beauties pride,
Helpe to addorne my beautifullest bride:
And, as ye her array, still throw betweene
Some graces to be seene;
And, as ye use to Venus, to her sing,
The whiles the woods shal answer, and your eccho ring.

Now is my love all ready forth to come:
Let all the virgins therefore well awayt:
And ye fresh boyes, that tend upon her groome,
Prepare your selves; for he is comming strayt.
Set all your things in seemely good aray,
Fit for so joyfull day:
The joyfulst day that ever sunne did see.
Faire Sun! shew forth thy favourable ray,
And let thy lifull heat not fervent be,
For feare of burning her sunshyny face,

Her beauty to disgrace.
O fayrest Phoebus! father of the Muse!
If ever I did honour thee aright,
Or sing the thing that mote thy mind delight,
Doe not thy servants simple boone refuse;
But let this day, let this one day, be myne;
Let all the rest be thine.
Then I thy soverayne prayses loud wil sing,
That all the woods shal answer, and theyr eccho ring.

Harke! how the Minstrils gin to shrill aloud
Their merry Musick that resounds from far,
The pipe, the tabor, and the trembling Croud,
That well agree withouten breach or jar.
But, most of all, the Damzels doe delite
When they their tymbrels smyte,
And thereunto doe daunce and carrol sweet,
That all the sences they doe ravish quite;
The whyles the boyes run up and downe the street,
Crying aloud with strong confusèd noyce,
As if it were one voyce,
Hymen, iö Hymen, Hymen, they do shout;
That even to the heavens theyr shouting shrill
Doth reach, and all the firmament doth fill;
To which the people standing all about,
As in approvance, doe thereto applaud,
And loud advaunce her laud;
And evermore they Hymen, Hymen sing,
That al the woods them answer, and theyr eccho ring.

Loe! where she comes along with portly pace,
Lyke Phoebe, from her chamber of the East,
Arysing forth to run her mighty race,
Clad all in white, that seemes a virgin best.
So well it her beseemes, that ye would weene
Some angell she had beene.
Her long loose yellow locks lyke golden wyre,
Sprinckled with perle, and perling flowres atweene,
Doe lyke a golden mantle her attyre;
And, being crownèd with a girland greene,
Seeme lyke some mayden Queene.
Her modest eyes, abashèd to behold
So many gazers as on her do stare,
Upon the lowly ground affixèd are;
Ne dare lift up her countenance too bold,
But blush to heare her prayses sung so loud,
So farre from being proud.
Nathlesse doe ye still loud her prayses sing,
That all the woods may answer, and your eccho ring.

251

THE POPULAR MUSE

Along with the age's major poetry, the Elizabethans produced thousands of widely circulated ballads, most of them anonymous. Many were printed as broadsides—like the example shown on the facing page—and sold by traveling peddlers. The ballad below commemorates the earl of Essex's famous expedition to Cadiz (Cales) in 1596.

The Winning of Cales

Thomas Deloney

Long the proud Spaniard
    advanced to conquer us,
Threat'ning our Country
    with fire and sword,
Often preparing
    their Navy most sumptuous,
With all the provision
    that *Spain* could afford,
Dub, a dub, dub,
    thus strikes their Drummes,
Tan ta ra ra, tan ta ra ra,
    English men comes.

To the Seas presently,
    went our Lord admirall,
With Knights couragious,
    and Captains full good,
The Earl of *Essex*,
    a prosperous Generall,
With him prepared,
    to passe the salt flood:
Dub a dub, etc.

At Plimouth speedily,
    take they ships valliantly:
Braver ships never
    were seen under sails:
With their fair coulers spred,
    and streamers ore their head:
Now bragging Spaniards
    take heed of your taile:
Dub a dub, dub, etc.

Unto *Cales* cunningly
    came we most happily
Where the Kings Navie
    securely did ride,
Being upon their backs,
    peircing their Buts of Sacks,
Ere that the Spaniard
    our comming descrid
Tan ta ra ra ra, English-men comes

bounce abounce, bounce abounce
Off went our Guns.

Great was the crying,
    running and riding,
Which at that season
    was made in that place;
Then Beacons were fired,
    as need then required:
To hide their great treasur
    they had little space:
Alas they cryed,
    English men comes.

There might you see the Ships,
    how they were fired fast:
And how the men drowned
    themselves in the Sea,
There might you hear them cry,
    wail and weep piteously:
When as they saw no shift
    to escape thence away,
Dub a dub, etc.

The great *Saint Philip*,
    The pride of the Spaniards,
Was burnt to the bottom
    and sunk in the sea,
But the *Saint Andrew*,
    and eke the *Saint Matthew*,
We took in fight manly,
    and brought them away.
Dub a dub, etc.

The Earl of *Essex*,
    Most valiant and hardy,
With horsemen and footmen,
    marcht towards the Town.
The enemies which saw them,
    full greatly affrighted,
Did fly for their safegard,
    and durst not come down.
Dub a dub, etc.

Now quoth the noble Earl,
    courage my Soldiers all,
Fight and be valiant,
    and spoyl you shall have,
And well rewarded all,
    from the great to the small:
But look that Women
    and Children you save,
Dub a dub, etc.

The Spaniard at that sight,
    saw 'twas in vain to fight:
Hung up their flags of truce,
    yeelding the Town:
We marcht in presently,
    decking the walls on hie,
With our English coulors,
    which purchast renown:
Dub a dub, etc.

Entring the houses then
    of the richest men,
For Gold and Treasure
    we searched each day:
In some places we did finde
    pies baking in the Ovens,
Meat at the fire roasting,
    and men ran away.
Dub a dub, etc. . . .

When our brave Generall
    saw they delayed time,
And would not ransom
    the Towne as they said:
With their faire Wainscots,
    their Presses and Bedsteds,
Their Ioynt-stooles and Tables,
    a fire we made:
And when the town burnt in a flame,
With tan ta ra, tan ta ra ra,
From thence we came.

A comparison of the life of Man,
Concerning how fickle his estate doth stand,
Flourishing like a Tree, or Vine, or dainty flower,
Or like a ship, or raine, that's turn'd each houre.
To the tune of   Sir Andrew Barton.

As I lay musing all alone,
Great store of things I thought vpon,
And specially of mans estate,
And how hee's subject vnto Fate.

First Ile compare him to a tree,
Which you sometimes all greene may see,
But suddenly his leaues doe fall
That he was beautify'd withall.

The Tree likewise is knowne by's fruit
Better then by his fine greene sute,
He may show comely to the eye,
Yet his fruit may tast bitterly.

So men sometimes make a faire showe,
All fresh and greene they seeme to growe,
But when the winter of griefe and thrall
Doth on them seize, their greene leaues fall.

But for the difference of mens fruit,
I must indeed be something mute,
But those that grow like Cedars tall
Yield little fruit or none at all.

Yet doe they flourish fresh and greene,
Much like the pleasant sommer Queene:
They are bedect with fragrant flowers,
And they doe dwell in stately Towers.

But as the Tree is great and tall,
The great and mightier is his fall:
And as he falls, so doth he lye,
Untill the builder him apply.

What though a man haue store of wealth,
It cannot him assure of health,
By his fruits he must sure be try'd,
Either condemn'd or justify'd.

Againe, a man is like a Vine,
That from the earth doth flourish fine,
Adorn'd with natures ornament.
With store of Grapes to giue content

But with a knife, or such a thing,
The Vine is soone set a bleeding,
And then those Grapes will soone decay,
And piningly will wast away.

Even so stands the life of man,
If that his blood from him be drawne.
Then suddenly his life doth yield,
And vnto death he is compell'd.

Man flourisheth even like a flower,
Which liues and dyes within an houre,
He growes perhaps vntill his prime,
Or he may dye in's budding time.

He may chance liue till hee is old,
And bide the brunt of Winters cold,
But then hee'l lose the smell and shew,
And will no more be worth the view.

So many men dye in their prime,
And some dye in their budding time:
But he that liues the longest life,
Shall find but sorrow, care, and strife.

Mans life is like a ship o'th Seas,
Which is sometimes as Fortune please,
Sometimes in safety, yet not still so,
Even as proud Boreas blasts doe blow.

When Winds are still, and weather's faire,
Then Mariners are free from care;
But when as stormes make dark the skye,
Then must each man his labour plye.

. . . on Love

Love and death—then as now—were prime concerns of the poet. Donne's elegy presents one Elizabethan view of love; Marlowe's romantic plea of the passionate shepherd another. Elizabethan fascination with death increased during the last decades of the queen's reign. Most of these poems were written at the end of the sixteenth century or in the early period of King James' reign.

To His Mistris Going To Bed

John Donne

Come, Madam, come, all rest my powers defie,
Until I labour, I in labour lie.
The foe oft-times having the foe in sight,
Is tir'd with standing though he never fight.
Off with that girdle, like heavens Zone glistering,
But a far fairer world incompassing.
Unpin that spangled breastplate which you wear,
That th'eyes of busie fooles may be stopt there.
Unlace your self, for that harmonious chyme,
Tells me from you, that now it is bed time.
Off with that happy busk, which I envie,
That still can be, and still can stand so nigh.
Your gown going off, such beautious state reveals,
As when from flowry meads th'hills shadow steales.
Off with that wyerie Coronet and shew
The haiery Diademe which on you doth grow:
Now off with those shooes, and then safely tread
In this loves hallow'd temple, this soft bed.
In such white robes, heaven's Angels us'd to be
Receavd by men; Thou Angel bringst with thee
A heaven like Mahomets Paradice; and though
Ill spirits walk in white, we easly know,
By this these Angels from an evil sprite,
Those set our hairs, but these our flesh upright.
  Licence my roaving hands, and let them go,
Before, behind, between, above, below.
O my America! my new-found-land,
My kingdome, safeliest when with one man man'd,
My Myne of precious stones, My Emperie,
How blest am I in this discovering thee!
To enter in these bonds, is to be free;
Then where my hand is set, my seal shall be.
  Full nakedness! All joyes are due to thee,
As souls unbodied, bodies uncloth'd must be,
To taste whole joyes. Gems which you women use
Are like Atlanta's balls, cast in mens views,
That when a fools eye lighteth on a Gem,
His earthly soul may covet theirs, not them.
Like pictures, or like books gay coverings made
For lay-men, are all women thus array'd;
Themselves are mystick books, which only wee
(Whom their imputed grace will dignifie)
Must see reveal'd. Then since that I may know;
As liberally, as to a Midwife, shew
Thy self: cast all, yea, this white lynnen hence,
[Here] is no pennance, much less innocence.
  To teach thee, I am naked first; why then
What needst thou have more covering than a man.

The Passionate Shepherd
To His Love

Christopher Marlowe

Come live with me and be my Love,
And we will all the pleasures prove
That hills and valleys, dales and fields,
Or woods or steepy mountains yields.

And we will sit upon the rocks,
Seeing the shepherds feed their flocks
By shallow rivers, to whose falls
Melodious birds sing madrigals.

And I will make thee beds of roses
And a thousand fragrant posies;
A cap of flowers, and a kirtle
Embroidered all with leaves of myrtle.

A gown made of the finest wool,
Which from our pretty lambs we pull;
Fair-linèd slippers for the cold,
With buckles of the purest gold;

A belt of straw and ivy-buds
With coral clasps and amber studs:
And if these pleasures may thee move,
Come live with me and be my Love.

The shepherd swains shall dance and
                                        sing
For thy delight each May morning:
If these delights thy mind may move,
Then live with me and be my Love.

The Nymph's Reply
To The Shepherd

Sir Walter Raleigh (?)

If all the world and love were young,
And truth in every shepherd's tongue,
These pretty pleasures might me move
To live with thee and be thy Love.

Time drives the flocks from field to fold,
When rivers rage and rocks grow cold;
And Philomel becometh dumb;
The rest complains of cares to come.

The flowers do fade, and wanton fields
To wayward winter reckoning yields:
A honey tongue, a heart of gall,
Is fancy's spring, but sorrow's fall.

Thy gowns, thy shoes, thy beds of roses,
Thy cap, thy kirtle, and thy posies
Soon break, soon wither, soon forgotten,
In folly ripe, in reason rotten.

Thy belt of straw and ivy buds,
Thy coral clasps and amber studs,
All these in me no means can move
To come to thee and be thy Love.

But could youth last, and love still
                                        breed,
Had joys no date, nor age no need,
Then these delights my mind might move
To live with thee and be tny Love.

. . . on Death

BRITISH MUSEUM

Fear No More

William Shakespeare

Fear no more the heat o' the sun,
    Nor the furious winter's rages;
Thou thy worldly task hast done,
    Home art gone, and ta'en thy wages:
Golden lads and girls all must,
As chimney-sweepers, come to dust.

Fear no more the frown o' the great;
    Thou art past the tyrant's stroke:
Care no more to clothe and eat;
    To thee the reed is as the oak:
The scepter, learning, physic, must
All follow this, and come to dust.

Fear no more the lightning-flash,
    Nor the all-dreaded thunder-stone;
Fear not slander, censure rash;
    Thou hast finished joy and moan:
All lovers young, all lovers must
Consign to thee, and come to dust.

No exorciser harm thee!
Nor no witchcraft charm thee!
Ghost unlaid forbear thee!
Nothing ill come near thee!
Quiet consummation have;
And renownèd be thy grave!

On My First Son

Ben Jonson

Farewell, thou child of my right hand, and joy!
My sin was too much hope of thee, loved boy;
Seven years thou wert lent to me, and I thee pay,
Exacted by thy fate, on the just day.
Oh, could I lose all father now! For why
Will man lament the state he should envy—
To have so soon 'scaped world's and flesh's rage,
And, if no other misery, yet age?
Rest in soft peace, and, asked, say here doth lie
Ben Jonson his best piece of poetry:
For whose sake, henceforth, all his vows be such
As what he loves may never like too much.

A Religious Use of Taking Tobacco

Robert Wisdome

The Indian weed witherèd quite,
Green at morn, cut down at night,
    Shows thy decay;
    All flesh is hay:
Thus think, then drink Tobacco.

And when the smoke ascends on high,
Think thou behold'st the vanity
    Of worldly stuff,
    Gone with a puff:
Thus think, then drink Tobacco.

But when the pipe grows foul within,
Think of thy soul defiled with sin.
    And that the fire
    Doth it require:
Thus think, then drink Tobacco.

The ashes that are left behind,
May serve to put thee still in mind
    That into dust
    Return thou must:
Thus think, then drink Tobacco.

A Song

Anonymous

Hey nonny no!
Men are fools that wish to die!
Is't not fine to dance and sing
When the bells of death do ring?
Is't not fine to swim in wine,
And turn upon the toe
And sing hey nonny no,
When the winds do blow,
And the seas do flow?
Hey nonny no!

A Dirge

John Webster

Call for the robin-redbreast and the wren,
Since o'er shady groves they hover
And with leaves and flowers do cover
The friendless bodies of unburied men.
Call unto his funeral dole
The ant, the field-mouse, and the mole,
To rear him hillocks that shall keep him
                                                              warm
And, when gay tombs are robbed, sustain
                                                        no harm;
But keep the wolf far thence, that's foe to
                                                                  men,
For with his nails he'll dig them up again.

The Shrouding

John Webster

Hark, now everything is still,
The screech-owl and the whistler shrill,
Call upon our dame aloud,
And bid her quickly don her shroud!
Much you had of land and rent;
Your length in clay 's now competent:
A long war disturbed your mind;
Here your perfect peace is signed.
Of what is 't fools make such vain keeping?
Sin their conception, their birth weeping,
Their life a general mist of error,
Their death a hideous storm of terror.
Strew your hair with powders sweet,
Don clean linen, bathe your feet,
And (the foul fiend more to check)
A crucifix let bless your neck:
'Tis now full tide 'tween night and day;
End your groan, and come away.

255

ELIZABETHAN SONGS

*"Music and sweet poetry" were, as one Elizabethan poet wrote, sister
and brother; one god, Apollo, reigned over both. Poets were accustomed to write lyrics that were to be set to music; and many wrote
words and music both, like Henry VIII, whose famous song "Pastime
with Good Company" appears below, with other songs of the period.*

Henry VIII

Pastime with good company
I love, and shall until I die.
Grudge who lust, but none deny,
So God be pleased, thus live will I.
      For my pastance,
      Hunt, sing, and dance,
      My heart is set;
      All goodly sport
      For my comfort,
      Who shall me let?

John Fletcher (?)

Orpheus with his lute made trees,
And the mountain tops that freeze,
  Bow themselves when he did sing:
To his music plants and flowers
Ever sprung; as sun and showers
  There had made a lasting spring.

Every thing that heard him play,
Even the billows of the sea,
  Hung their heads and then lay by.
In sweet music is such art,
Killing care and grief of heart
  Fall asleep, or hearing, die.

John Fletcher

Do not fear to put thy feet
Naked in the river sweet;
Think not leech, or newt, or toad,
Will bite thy foot, when thou hast trod:
Nor let the water rising high,
As thou wad'st in, make thee cry
And sob; but ever live with me,
And not a wave shall trouble thee!

Thomas Campion

When to her lute Corinna sings,
Her voice revives the leaden strings,
And doth in highest notes appear
As any challenged echo clear.
But when she doth of mourning speak,
Even with her sighs the strings do break.

And as her lute doth live or die;
Led by her passion, so must I.
For when of pleasure she doth sing,
My thoughts enjoy a sudden spring;
But if she doth of sorrow speak,
Even from my heart the strings do break.

Shakespeare

Take, oh, take those lips away,
  That so sweetly were forsworn;
And those eyes, the break of day,
  Lights that do mislead the morn:
But my kisses bring again,
             Bring again;
Seals of love, but sealed in vain,
             Sealed in vain.

Ben Jonson

Come, my Celia, let us prove,
While we can, the sports of love;
Time will not be ours for ever,
He, at length, our good will sever.
Spend not then his gifts in vain:
Suns that set may rise again;
But if once we lose this light,
'Tis with us perpetual night.
Why should we defer our joys?
Fame and rumor are but toys.
Cannot we delude the eyes
Of a few poor household spies?
Or his easier ears beguile,
Thus removèd by our wile?
'Tis no sin love's fruits to steal,
But the sweet thefts to reveal;
To be taken, to be seen.
These have crimes accounted been.

Francis Beaumont or John Fletcher

Lovers, rejoice! your pains shall be rewarded;
The god of love himself grieves at your crying;
No more shall frozen honor be regarded,
Nor the coy faces of a maid denying.
No more shall virgins sigh, and say "We dare not,
For men are false, and what they do they care not."
All shall be well again; then do not grieve:
Men shall be true, and women shall believe.

Lovers, rejoice! what you shall say henceforth,
When you have caught your sweethearts in your arms,
It shall be accounted oracle and worth;
No more faint-hearted girls shall dream of harms,
And cry they are too young; the god hath said,
Fifteen shall make a mother of a maid:
Then, wise men, pull your roses yet unblown:
Love hates the too-ripe fruit that falls alone.

Anonymous

The silver swan, who living had no note,
When death approached, unlocked her silent throat,
Leaning her breast against the reedy shore,
Thus sung her first and last, and sung no more:
Farewell all joys! O death, come close mine eyes;
More geese than swans now live, more fools than wise.

Francis Davison

The sound of thy sweet name, my dearest treasure,
  Delights me more than sight of other faces:
A glimpse of thy sweet face breeds me more pleasure
  Than any other's kindest words and graces.

One gracious word that from thy lips proceedeth,
  I value more than others' dove-like kisses:
And thy chaste kiss in my conceit exceedeth
  Others' embraces, and love's chiefest blisses.

A singer, a lutenist, and a high-spirited young man with a horn present an alfresco concert.

THE
WORLD OF
LONDON

By 1585 London, with some 250,000 inhabitants, was the largest city in Europe, its most important trade and banking center, and perhaps the most exciting place on earth. It was the magnet that annually drew thousands of swains and maids from farms and villages all over England and merchants from all over the world. London really belonged to businessmen, those who had sought and made their fortunes in the city, and with their fortunes, London's own; but the businessmen themselves lionized aristocrats who clustered around the royal court and the few newcomers who were fortunate enough to have clambered from nowhere into its dazzling atmosphere. The vast majority of citizens lived in the teeming suburbs outside the walls of London, on the fringe of the world of the court, the mercantile classes, and the intellectual and artistic community. In the course of Elizabeth's reign these suburbs turned from rural villages into hideous urban slums. Despite the slums, the continuous din, the dirt, and physical dangers that ranged from cutpurses to outbreaks of the plague, there was an endlessly varied offering of opportunity and acquaintance, scenery and entertainment. At right, a detail from a hand-colored version of a famous view (see overleaf) shows one center of the city's life, busy London Bridge, which citizens considered "the glory of London." Structures along its sides made it a shopping and dwelling place as well as one of England's main thoroughfares.

S. Dunston inde eaſt.

Alhallowes Berking

Lion Kay

The most accurate representation of Elizabeth's London is this engraving by Cornelis Visscher, done a few years after the queen's death. On the following pages details from it illustrate various aspects of the town. London grew alongside the Thames, and the river remained the heart of the city. Because the streets were narrow, unpaved, and impossibly congested, the river became the town's main road. A nobleman wishing to get from his

home in the fashionable area located on the far bank at top left, to Cheapside, the elegant shopping district behind St. Paul's, or to the theatres across the river, would board a boat tied to his stairs and proceed to a dock near his destination. Watermen prided themselves on their skill at the exceedingly dangerous game of shooting swift currents under London Bridge, but their patrons preferred to walk around and catch another boat.

261

After dining at a tavern, Londoners went to the Globe.

Ben Jonson

William Shakespeare

TAVERN WITS

The food in London's taverns was not only cheap, it was good, and a wide selection of imported wines was available. There were rooms upstairs for private parties, and diversions of every sort in the taproom. A wonderful din permeated the air: patrons' voices droned; waiters and hostesses shouted to the drawers orders for sack and ale; gamers loudly invoked the services of lady luck; and there was always music in the background. Women were welcome in most taverns "and counted it a great honor to be taken there . . ." one chronicler wrote. "If one woman only is invited, then she will bring three or four other women along and they gaily toast each other." But the most important element of tavern life was the camaraderie. Tavern habitués formed unofficial clubs; often "members" simply gathered for a good time, but many taverns became places in which to conduct business or discuss important matters with companions of similar interests. Two neighboring, elegant taverns in Cheapside competed for the patronage of London's brilliant intellectual circle. The Mitre won the devotion of a few of the town's wits; but the Mermaid was more popular. At the Mermaid's tables on any particular evening actors, dramatists, and poets—Shakespeare, Jonson, Donne, Fletcher, Beaumont—might be found drinking, gossiping, and talking shop.

William Kemp, a famous comedian

This woodcut illustrated a ditty: merrily showing how to drive the cold winter away

Francis Beaumont

John Donne

John Fletcher

Christopher Marlowe (?)

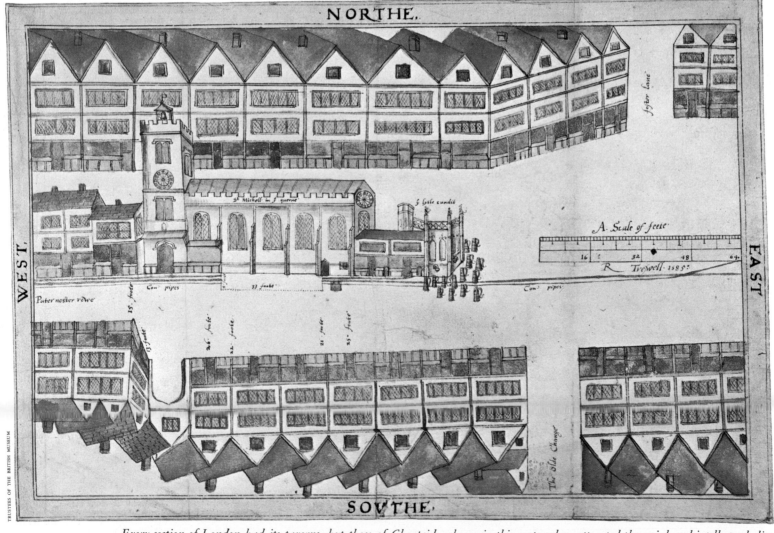

Every section of London had its taverns, but those of Cheapside, shown in this watercolor, attracted the social and intellectual elite.

Merchant ships were a common sight on the Thames.

CITY MERCHANTS

At heart London was bourgeois. The majority of its citizenry had been attracted to the town by the opportunity to learn a trade (even the nobility apprenticed younger sons) and establish independent businesses. The proximity of the court, with its need for services, entertainment, and luxury goods, brought wealth to one group of successful businessmen, and the vast population provided support for many others. The shopkeepers gave London its essential character, but the city actually owed most of its prosperity to foreign commerce based on a system of associations to which the crown granted monopolies for trading in certain parts of the world. Time after time members of the trading companies (usually prosperous merchants) risked their money on trading voyages; in the last decades of Elizabeth's reign speculation became the rage of the city. Anyone who could put together at least a few shillings bought an interest in the latest trade venture to Russia or the Levant. The nobility were often heavily involved, but control of England's thriving economy was always in the hands of the middle class. So, appropriately enough, was control of London's government. Chosen by and from among the members of the twelve great trade guilds, the lord mayor and the Common Council ruled with virtual autonomy. Any suggestions that came from the crown were phrased as requests and couched in terms of great respect.

SEPTENTRIO NORTH

DIEV ET MON DROYT

FORTVN A MY

ORIENS EAST

St. Thomas Greshem Knight at his owne costs and charges to the ornament and publike vse of this Royall citie of London, caused this place from the fondacion to be erected the VII. of Iune. Anno MDLXVI. And is full ended An. MDLXIX.

MERIDIES SOVTH

The Royal Exchange, built by Thomas Gresham, was a symbol of London's dominance of world trade.

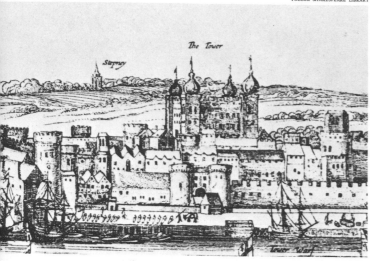

The courts placed culprits in the Tower of London.

THE THIRD UNIVERSITY

Sixteenth-century England had become "so litigious a world" that a son possessed of a legal education was almost a necessity for a family with fortune and property. Sons of the wealthy and the wellborn flocked to London to the famous Inns of Court and Inns of Chancery, which together formed an unofficial university for the study of law, "the third university of England." Their legal training served not only their families, it was of inestimable value to England also. Most members of Parliament, major officials, and judges were "graduates" of the Inns, and Inns of Court men became justices of the peace throughout England, providing valuable links between the queen and her countrymen. These justices were usually honest and efficient; their chief fault was their taste for London life, which more than once forced the queen to issue edicts ordering them to stay in their home districts. Their desire to visit London was understandable; life in the Inns was an idyll for the energetic, intelligent men who gathered there. Each Inn, which enclosed a beautiful garden, provided living quarters, a library, and a dining hall for its members, who were in touch not only with life at the law courts, government offices, and Parliament but also with the intellectual life of the city. Elizabethan literature and drama owed a great deal to enthusiastic members of the Inns. Many of the great playwrights were patronized by them, and Shakespeare himself wrote plays for showing in the Inn yards.

This trencher showing a lawyer was commissioned by one of the "graduates" of the Inns.

266

Elizabeth awarded her best men lucrative positions on prerogative courts like the Court of Wards (below), which met in Westminster.

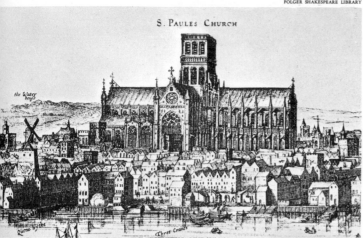

S. PAULES CHURCH

St. Paul's Cathedral dominated the city's skyline.

St. Paul's served as an employment agency, especially for servants like the two gentlemen's gentlemen shown in this detail from a contemporary manuscript. Valets stood in the part of the church known as Paul's or Duke Humphrey's Walk and haggled with prospective masters over the terms of service.

PRÆTOR

LIFE AT ST. PAUL'S

The principal gathering place of all London was St. Paul's Cathedral. People from every social class, from the lord mayor to the poorest apprentice, went there to meet friends, learn the latest gossip, and show off their finery. There were daily sermons, which were well attended, if not attended to, for strict concentration was not required; many in the audience walked around and talked until interesting announcements and newssheets were read, or the preacher began a provocative harangue against the government. But sermons—even entertaining ones—were the least of what Paul's had to offer. The cathedral and its grounds served as a trysting place, a park for strolling and chatting, and a market for all manner of goods and services. One observer caustically noted that the south alley of the nave was used "for usury and popery, the north for simony, and the horse fair in the middle for all kinds of bargains." Lawyers assigned themselves pillars where they met their clients, and tombs and the font were used as counters for the sale of groceries and spirits. The largest gallery of bookshops in England lined the churchyard, their names as colorful as their brightly painted signs: the Holy Ghost, the Bishop's Head, the Green Dragon. The view from the church tower was a main tourist attraction, and the tourists were among the chief interests of the cutpurses and thieves who mingled with the crowd. Amidst the hubbub, indigent gallants dallied hoping to receive an invitation to a meal or a drink.

Colorful processions added to the already lively scene at St. Paul's; above, the mayor and his entourage go by.

Homes of the wealthy lined the north bank of the Thames.

The lesser nobility, with their untitled fellows, became an upper middle class whose center was London. For them any place outside the city was purgatory. They resided in luxurious townhouses on the Thames near Westminster, living in a degree of comfort that even royalty had not known before. Most retained ancestral habits of hard work and diligence, but the sons of many rich fathers became idlers, spending their time at the barber having their lovelocks arranged and perfumed or at the tailor being outfitted in the fantastic costumes of the day. There was little emphasis on outdoor sports in London; gentlemen took exercise in the form of billiards or tennis or practice with rapier and dagger. They whiled away hours at cards, backgammon, and dice games. The ladies were accused by a contemporary observer of being "fond of taking it easy . . . They sit before their doors, decked out in fine clothes in order to see and be seen . . . They employ their time . . . visiting their friends and making merry. . ." Well-to-do couples entertained at lavish banquets featuring seafoods, meats, and game, served in sauces exotically flavored with ingredients like saffron and ambergris; dinner was often followed by the private performance of a play or singing and dancing. A typical London aristocrat was Sir Henry Unton, who commissioned the painting below depicting the important events of his life from birth (lower right corner) to his funeral (under his portrait). Over the scene of a banquet at which masquers and musicians entertain, Unton is shown as an ambassador in France, a general in the Netherlands, and a tourist in Italy.

A grim welcome greeted those crossing London Bridge.

A rich man spurns a ragged beggar.

THE CITY'S POOR

The lower class did not share in the new prosperity; the unemployed and artisans and laborers who lived on government-decreed fixed wages were the victims of a price inflation. Their numbers grew throughout Elizabeth's reign, for land hunger dispossessed thousands, who poured into London. "Great multitudes of people," wrote one observer, "were brought to inhabit in small rooms, whereof a great part are seen very poor . . . heaped up together . . . with many families of children and servants in one house or small tenement." Beggars were a common sight; hundreds appeared at one noble funeral hoping for the stipend customarily given to their kind on such occasions. Presumably a goodly proportion of beggars doubled as thieves, for a robber seemed to lurk in every shadow, especially in the slums. Schools for pickpockets and crooked gamblers had more applicants than they could accept. Officials whose duty was to check crime often aided it, and highwaymen and whores sometimes bribed their way into jail for a night or two to hide out from the prying eyes of the watch. "Proper" citizens reacted in two quite different ways. They passed more laws and harsher ones: some two hundred crimes warranted a death penalty. The severed heads of criminals swayed eerily atop London Bridge as a gruesome reminder of the wages of sin. The other reaction was surprisingly humane: poor laws were passed requiring each parish to provide work for the able-bodied. Hospitals and schools were built for the poor, and shelters opened for the unemployable.

A sham cripple, one of a band of coneycatchers, stands with his gang leader, who took part of each member's earnings.

272

Severe laws were passed against vagabonds. They were to be "grievously whipped" (below left) and branded on the ear. Second offenders were hanged; the two men attempting to break out of prison (above) received a like punishment. The watchman and ratcatcher (below) were ill paid but escaped the penalties of unemployment.

8

THE GREAT ENTERPRISE

A golden glow envelops the story of the defeat of the Invincible Armada, distorting, dramatizing, and immortalizing a battle that was actually unsatisfactory and untidy, although it was captained by heroes of Olympian proportions, who conquered the lumbering Goliath of Catholic Spain and won for Gloriana the command of the seas. Freedom triumphed over the overwhelming weight of tyranny, mere human courage prevailed against the soulless juggernaut, and a chosen few stood fast against a multitude. Alas, nothing is sacred to the scholar no matter how hallowed the myth, and the legend of those long August days and sleepless nights, when Philip's great ships swept up the Channel to visit the censure of God on a middle-aged female, has been sadly profaned by historians in their quest for truth. The elements can no longer be blamed for the Spanish defeat, for we know that the breezes blew Catholic as often as Protestant, and on two crucial occasions a shift in the wind saved the Armada from total destruction. The celebrated heroism of a handful of young men must be set against the known fact that Elizabeth's captains were seasoned veterans who sailed in vessels that were superior in maneuverability and in number to those of the enemy.

It is true that on inspection fact and fiction bear little resemblance to one another; yet the actual events of the summer of 1588 are no less extraordinary than the legend surrounding them. The story of the Armada still abounds with episodes of courage and endurance, and reality has added a note

rarely heard in mythology: the pathos of a venture upon which Spaniards embarked knowing full well that they had little chance of success unless God performed a miracle. Modern scholars have come to realize that the entire expedition was doomed from the very beginning.

From the start the Great Enterprise was grounded on the highly unlikely proposition that Philip's great ships, laden with men and arms, could rendezvous with the duke of Parma, reinforce his troops, and escort them from Flanders to England. All the logistic and strategic thinking that had gone into the Armada—the orders not to engage the enemy until the Channel was reached, the decision to anchor off Calais, the proportions of cannon balls to musket shot, of sailors to soldiers, of men to animals—was based on a false assumption. Parma knew it and begged for time to seize a deepwater port before the fleet sailed. Parma's adversaries, the Dutch seamen, who navigated with ease in their flyboats through a maze of shoals, sand bars, and islands, knew it. Even Philip knew it, for Luis Cabrera de Cordoba, who reported Parma's warnings, bluntly informed the king: "It is going to be impossible for the duke of Parma's ships ever to meet the Armada." Spanish oceangoing galleons were too deep in draught to approach Dunkirk, he said, and Dutch coastal sloops could prevent Parma's barges from ever leaving the harbor. Echoing the duke's own opinion, Cabrera asked a crucial question: "Why not give it up now and save much time and money?" Why not, indeed!

The answer lay deep within the mind of the man who secluded himself behind the granite walls of the Escorial. The Armada did not spring fully armed from the brow of Philip the Prudent; it was the work of a mind incapable of great imaginative bounds, a brain that inched, never leaped, to a conclusion. The decision to invade England was made only after every other possibility had been thoroughly considered and dismissed. The heretical poison that Elizabeth was spreading throughout Christendom could be stopped only at its source, by the invasion of an island protected by the rolling breakers and capricious breezes of the Atlantic. Philip, better than anyone on his council, knew the risks involved: the uncertainty of wind and current, the improbability that devout English Catholics would rush to arms, the appalling odds against victory in a naval engagement fought five hundred miles from home and in waters where every cove and eddy were familiar to the enemy. Philip had turned to the best advice available anywhere in Europe. Don Alvaro de Bezán, marquis of Santa Cruz and Admiral of the Ocean Sea, had urged the king first to destroy English naval power in the Channel and then to seize the island at his leisure. The cost of such an operation was too great, however, for the admiral had demanded 510 sailing vessels, 40 galleys, six galleasses, 94,000 men, and provisions for eight months. The king realized the economic absurdity of his plan and sought the opinion of the duke of Parma, who suggested that an army of 34,000 infantry and cavalry might conceivably be ferried across from Flanders in a single night if complete surprise could be achieved. Even Philip regarded the element of surprise as "hardly possible." So from among a half-dozen impossibilities, a theoretically feasible scheme was devised: a much smaller navy would be assembled at Lisbon, large enough to terrify the English but designed more to convoy Parma's barges to the Thames estuary than to engage an English fleet. This plan was to be the instrument of God's victory and the endeavor to which Philip and the entire Spanish empire bent every effort.

God's will never burst upon Philip like a beacon in the night, for the king did not presume to know God's purpose. Yet it seemed manifest that the Lord must desire the destruction of the English Jezebel. If the Armada was the only way of achieving a purpose so obviously in accord with the divine design, then God could be depended upon to sustain the faithful and give them victory. The mathematical odds meant nothing when fighting shoulder to shoulder with the Lord. Lepanto had been clear proof of that. When Philip planned the fleet that destroyed Moslem sea power, he had no clear notion of how victory could be achieved so far from Spain and so deep within Islamic waters. He had been content to labor quietly in the Lord's vineyard, and it had been sufficient that his Christian fleet was dedicated to a holy purpose. Philip the Prudent had been willing to risk all on a single engagement against the infidel at the battle of Lepanto. Now, seventeen years later, he was satisfied once again to leave the details of victory to God.

Caught up in his sense of mission, he began to lose sight of the distinction between fact and fancy. It was enough that God's Armada should sail. Such questions as how Parma's barges and Sidonia's great galleons could meet and what wind would drive the attacking Dutch flyboats back to Flushing could safely be left to Providence. Nor was Philip's confidence entirely misplaced. The age of miracles had not passed, and during the hair-raising moments when the Catholic Armada was within inches of running aground upon the sands of Dunkirk, there were wonders aplenty. The only trouble was that God failed to give Spanish sailors and soldiers anything more than valor with which to defend ships that were technologically outdated, as obsolete in relation to their English opponents as bombers are in comparison with intercontinental missiles.

The real tragedy was that the Armada was the very best fleet of its kind. Upon it had been lavished the riches of the Indies, the ceaseless labors of shipwrights, victualers, ironmongers, and carpenters, and the fervent prayers of an entire kingdom. For its 2,431 heavy guns and long-muzzled culverins, 123,790 cannon balls had been transported to Lisbon from every province of Philip's empire. Unheard of quantities of powder and shot for small arms were piled high on the wharves. Salt fish and hard biscuits were brought in from Andalusia, hemp and tar from the Baltic, and oil from southern Italy. Almost every race and nationality—Castilian peasants, French adventurers, Moorish slaves, Italian mercenaries—were packed into ships that had been begged, borrowed, built, and stolen in every corner of Europe. On paper, at least, the Armada was indeed invincible.

Once he had determined that this fleet was to be God's sword "for the triumph of His cause," Philip could not wait to see it forged, sharpened, and made ready to strike. Yet setbacks, delays, dishonesty, and disasters hindered every step of the way. Disease and malnutrition attacked mariners and landsmen while the Armada lay in harbor, fouling its own berth and consuming meat, fish, and hardtack as fast as they could be brought in by oxcart and barge. Ships expected to be seaworthy fighters turned out to be hulks, their rigging rotten, their hulls sprung, and their crews peasant boys more accustomed to the plow than the topsail. In desperation Philip deluged his captains with instructions and wrote endlessly to the shipyards at Algeciras, the naval arsenal at Lisbon, and the military warehouses at Barcelona, worrying them with a single theme: "Success depends mostly upon speed. Be quick!" Creaking and groaning in every joint, the Spanish military colossus made ready while Philip buzzed, nagged, and fretted in his impatience to launch his Great Enterprise.

Then on April 29, 1587, a disaster struck the Armada that delayed its sailing for a year. Sir Francis Drake, with twenty-five of the queen's stoutest and fastest ships, appeared among the moored galleys and merchantmen, the loaded freighters and galleons being refitted in Cadiz harbor. Santa Cruz's own warship was in port, newly launched, tied up, and waiting for armaments and stores; so were sixty other vessels, possibly half of them were being readied for the great fleet gathering at Lisbon. Sir Francis arrived with instructions "to impeach the joining together of the king of Spain's fleets," and once in the harbor, the terrible Drake was like a fox in a chicken coop. Throughout the night he systematically scuttled or burned some thirty vessels, paying scant heed to the Spanish cannonade from the forts of Cadiz, and brushing off the ineffectual darts and sorties of the swift but lightly armed Spanish galleys. "The loss," said Philip, "was not very great, but the daring of the attempt was very great indeed." The loss was to be greater than the king imagined, for Drake had just begun. From Cadiz he swept up the Spanish and Portuguese coasts, pillaging shipping and plundering fishing villages. Mean and petty work it may have been, but when the Armada finally sailed, the fish supply was meager and inferior, the barrels leaked, and the food was spoiled. Sir Francis Drake had played havoc with the Andalusian fishing industry and had destroyed the supply of well-seasoned barrel staves and iron hoops set aside to make kegs for the food and water that would keep men and animals alive on the long voyage from Lisbon to Calais.

By May, 1588, the Armada was finally ready. Ships had been tarred, caulked, and freshly painted, supplies had been stored away, galleons and merchantmen had been rebuilt to conform to the traditional Spanish idea of warships as floating castles, crews had been assigned, soldiers taken aboard, and Medina Sidonia, the captain general of the fleet, was reasonably satisfied that everything humanly possible had been done to organize a naval host that spoke six different languages and consumed its supplies even faster than they rotted in damp holds and

Philip II of Spain

leaky barrels. There were 19,290 Castilian and Portuguese soldiers, 8,350 sailors, 1,000 gentlemen volunteers from every noble household in Spain, 600 monks, priests, and chaplains, innumerable servants, physicians, surgeons, ordnance experts, and over 2,000 Turkish, Moorish, and heretic slaves, who labored at the oars of the light galleys and the heavy galleasses, packed into a fleet that numbered 130 sails and weighed less in total tonnage than the present-day liner the *Queen Mary*.

The fighting heart of the Armada was the twenty Portuguese and Castilian galleons, great lumbering fortresses carrying up to fifty-two guns, their main timbers four and five feet thick. They were built high in the stern and wide in the beam to give their musketeers an elevated platform from which to rake the enemy with gunshot and to cast grappling hooks to prevent his escape. In addition to the clumsy galleons, which rolled, plunged, and required a mild hurricane to move them, there were four Italian galleasses, each mounting fifty guns and rowed by three hundred slaves. They were larger, heavier, and more seaworthy than the light-oared Mediterranean galleys, yet they could outmaneuver the galleons and match their firepower. The second line of the Armada consisted of forty merchantmen and carracks, some of them so large that "the ocean groaned under their weight," and all of them armed primarily to defend themselves from Barbary pirates and Moslem corsairs. The largest of the merchantmen, the Portuguese East Indiamen, were gigantic tubs, slow, seaworthy, and practical. They had been refitted and rearmed and constituted a fighting force almost as formidable as the galleons. No fleet could do without its pinnaces, the light, nimble sloops that were the eyes, ears, and maids of all work of the navy. Medina Sidonia had managed to collect thirty-four of these useful vessels. This vast assemblage was expected to escort some two dozen supply ships, laden with men, horses, and siege guns for Parma's invading army, vessels that could not defend themselves in a fight but that would contribute to the awful majesty of the Armada.

The man who sailed in command of a fleet "wonderful, great, and strong" was peculiarly unfit for his position, not because he was a self-confessed landlubber who easily caught cold, was always sick at sea, and had begged Philip not to place him in command of "so important an enterprise," but because Don Alonso Pérez de Guzmán, duke of Medina Sidonia, was not a man who could call forth miracles. Efficiency, loyalty, calmness, affability, and honor were qualities that the duke possessed in abundance; he was, in fact, a splendid and soothing chief of staff, but the very virtues for which Philip selected him as the successor to that grizzled old seadog Santa Cruz ultimately destroyed him. Medina Sidonia was the product of generations of aristocratic breeding; his house had long since been squeezed dry of any vitality, and all that remained was dignity. The duke was personally dedicated, hard working, and invariably did the right thing. Throughout the disaster of the Armada, there is scarcely a decision that he made for which he can be condemned. As a Christian he was magnificent, as an admiral he was blameless, but as a leader of men he was a total failure, for Medina Sidonia could not inspire in his subordinates that extra ounce of nerve, that wild belligerence, and the endurance that in the end wins battles and performs miracles.

In one quality alone, the new Admiral of the Ocean Sea was well suited to his command: he was a nobleman of deep and unfanatical devotion, emphatically believing that the Armada was sailing on a divine mission, and the men who worked the guns and climbed the rigging were embarking on a crusade to restore the true faith to England and liberate the tens of thousands of faithful Catholics who had suffered privation and suppression at the hands of the heretics. The papal excommunication against Elizabeth had been reissued, and it was

now the holy duty of the Armada to enforce that sentence against a queen who was branded "an incestuous bastard, begotten and born in sin of an infamous courtesan, Anne Boleyn." The list of Elizabeth's great transgressions was disgustingly long. She was a profaner of the sacraments, persecutor of the faithful, suppressor of the old nobility, protector of profligates and licentious minions, prostituter of God's Word, torturer of innocent priests, who were systematically torn upon the rack and dismembered in public, murderer of the cousin who was lawfully entitled to her crown, and finally a scourge of God and the shame of womanhood. The destruction of such a foul and monstrous dragon of heresy could not be accomplished in a spirit of revenge or conquest. It could only be achieved in righteousness, and officers and men, sailors and soldiers were ordered to confess and hear Mass before setting sail. Gambling and swearing were outlawed, prostitutes were forbidden on board, and no unclean thing or person was allowed to accompany so sublime a venture. Medina Sidonia himself, passing through lines of kneeling crusaders, bore to the Armada the holy standard of the fleet from the high altar of the cathedral of Lisbon.

Throughout the fleet, every seaman and soldier thrilled to a sense of moral superiority, which more than compensated for the sour taste of military inferiority. It was not too much to count on God's help against barbarous, heretical people who made no account of soul or conscience, disobeyed Him, disregarded the saints, and mocked the pope. "So we are sailing against England," said one Spanish sea captain, "in the confident hope of a miracle" that will send "some strange freak of weather" or will deprive "the English of their wits." Without a miracle, he added, the heretics would knock the Armada "to pieces with their culverins." These words were not intended as a grim prophecy but as a straightforward statement of the consequences of not having God on one's side. When the fleet finally took to sea, Spanish confidence was just as firm as that of the enemy, but it was of a different brand. It was based on the inability of an entire realm to entertain seriously the possibility that a mission supported by the Church and the entire heavenly hierarchy could be defeated; English confidence was grounded on an equally sublime conviction that their cause was just and on the knowledge that their ships, captains, and tactics were superior to those of the enemy.

The English had good cause to be confident. It was no idle dream when Sir Francis Drake bragged to Walsingham that he doubted "not but ere it be long so to handle the matter with the duke of Sidonia as he shall wish himself at St. Mary Port among his orange trees." The English had the best navy afloat and the most dreaded and celebrated captains in Europe, especially *El Draque*, Drake "the Dragon," whose vanity was without equal but who was not overstating the case when he said he knew what great fear his name inspired all along the coast of Spain. His reputation alone was worth the mightiest galleon in the queen's navy.

When Elizabeth's subjects prayed to God to "set a wall" about England and "evermore mightily defend it," they might also have raised their voices in thanks to the queen's father, old King Henry. It was he who had built the dockyards from which Elizabeth's great ships slipped into the sea, and it was he who had reorganized the admiralty so that a navy existed, at least on paper, even in peacetime. By 1588 England had eighteen heavy men-of-war, built according to the revolutionary and imaginative notions of Sir John Hawkins, the treasurer of the navy, and the shipwrights of Bristol, Portsmouth, and Plymouth. Pumps had been improved, rigging modified, hawsers lengthened, but the most basic change was in the shape and proportions of the hulls. Reflecting a new approach to naval war and the function of the galleon in battle, the English did away with the towering superstructure of the traditional warship, and streamlined their vessels by increasing their length, cutting down on their width, and leveling off their deck lines. The lofty castles at bow and stern, which added so to a ship's weight and made them so difficult to sail, were discarded; and the pit, or center, where reserve contingents of soldiers huddled, protected by the thick sides of the galleons, was planked over to make two new decks for heavy, ship-destroying guns. The new silhouette was the technological expression of a tactical revolution that no longer treated the sailing vessel as a means of conducting land war at sea, but as an instrument of destruction suited to the ocean. Sink the enemy, rather than capture him like some fortress: this was the aim of English sea captains in their trim warships that could outpoint, outmaneuver, and outsail anything the Spanish had afloat.

Along with the new hull design came the introduction of lighter but more numerous guns that

A detail from a sixteenth-century painting shows one of the Armada's heavily armed, many-oared galleasses in action. Spanish troops and a priest (right) stand amidships.

279

The inexperienced duke of Medina Sidonia (top left) commanded the Armada. Sir Francis Drake (top right), England's finest captain, served under Lord Admiral Charles Howard (above), who led the English fleet.

could hurl a nine-pound shot half a mile. Spanish guns were heavier and could heave a thirty-pound ball with indifferent accuracy about a quarter of a mile if the nine-foot barrel did not happen to explode. On both sides naval gunnery was still in its infancy. The amount of powder, the strength of the barrel, and the timing of the charge in synchronization with the roll of the ship were largely matters of guesswork, and neither fleet had any real idea of how many cannon balls would be needed to sink a galleon or at what range a nine-pound shot hurled at high velocity or a thirty-pounder thrown less violently would penetrate the thick timber of a man-of-war. The Spanish thought of their massive cannons as siege guns. They assumed that the real work would be done by popguns or mortars designed to destroy men, not ships, but they had nevertheless brought with them what they imagined to be an overabundance of heavy ammunition—fifty rounds per cannon. The English carried fewer cannon balls, and Drake was evidently willing to meet the enemy with only thirty rounds per gun, even though English tactics called for staying well away from the Spanish ships with their deadly musketeers and grappling hooks, and using their own greater mobility and longer-range culverins to fire broadside after broadside into the Armada. The English, however, were prepared to experiment with new methods of war and could always replace their cannon shot; the Spanish could do nothing but close in and attempt to board the enemy. When instead they received salvos of iron fired at long range, they could answer only with guns that could not reach the enemy and ammunition that could not be replaced.

The fundamental problem for the English was not how to win the battle but how to maintain a fleet in readiness against an enemy whose exact time of arrival was unknown and whose plans were uncertain. On this point Elizabeth and her seadogs clashed. Drake's advice, sent from Cadiz in 1587, had been explicit: "Prepare in England strongly and most by sea!" Elizabeth was equally insistent: ships were financial monsters and she was too poor to feed them. Her army in Holland, that "sieve that spends as it receives to little purpose," was eating up 126,000 pounds a year; she had raised another 50,000 pounds with which to pay a German army to invade France and destroy the Catholic duke of Guise; and she had promised to scrape together still another subsidy to keep Henry of Navarre from total bankruptcy. It was costing the queen at least 12,000 pounds a month to feed, arm, and pay a fully mobilized fleet, and all this had to be done on a yearly peacetime income of 250,000 pounds. In the circumstances, it is little wonder that Lord Burghley sourly observed that "a man would wish, if peace cannot be had, that the enemy would no longer delay, but prove, as I trust, his evil fortune," or that Gloriana constantly maintained the fiction that she was not and had no intention of ever being at war with Spain, and that her greatest desire was to see Philip's rebellious Dutch subjects returned to their true allegiance once again. Neither Philip nor the queen's sea captains agreed with her or believed her, but at least such a pretense allowed Elizabeth to keep her fleet in mothballs and to spare her war chest. Except for full mobilization resulting from a false alarm in December, 1587, the thrifty sovereign kept her fleet in dock, partly decommissioned and only half staffed, thus saving herself over 2,000 pounds a month. Even during the summer of 1588, when she finally permitted full mobilization of a fleet of about 200 ships, she complained that the cost was bankrupting her.

The queen's worries did not end with finding the fourteen shillings a month that it took to feed and pay a single seaman or with collecting the stores of food for a fleet that ate up most of its provisions before even venturing out of harbor. Despite half measures and penny pinching, Elizabeth's naval arm remained strong; the greatest danger was from the unknown enemy lurking within the kingdom, the nightmare of a Catholic fifth column, wherein lay hid "the secret treasons of mind and heart."

Everyone was aware of the rottenness of the home defenses: English cities were unwalled, ungarrisoned, and defenseless; stout English yeomen had grown soft and fat during decades of peace and possessed neither the strength nor the training to draw the longbows that had gained victory at Agincourt and at Crécy; the magnates of the north still secretly nourished a fondness for medieval attitudes; and most serious of all, no one knew how many silent allies of the pope lurked in English homes. Possibly three hundred of Cardinal William Allen's seminary priests still crept from their priest holes and cellars to strengthen the Catholic faithful in their determination and to perform the miracle of the Mass. Twenty thousand copies of the cardinal's inflammatory writings, assuring the flock that the day of liberation was near, were being read and circulated from one Catholic house to the next.

How many sympathetic readers there were was the crucial question. Cardinal Allen hopefully estimated that two-thirds of the population were, in their secret hearts, loyal to the Holy Church, and English exiles in Europe lived on a roseate dream of a rich and prosperous land where sturdy Catholic peasants would rise up at a signal from Rome or Madrid and deliver "Catholic friends and brethren from the damnable and intolerable yoke of heresy." Two thirds, one half, one third, the number meant little on an island sustained by boisterous xenophobia and darkly suspicious of anyone who did not admire all things English. If even the small voice of conscience could speak louder than loyalty to crown and country, as it so often did in France, then, despite the government's efforts to round up leading Catholics and to root out with axe and rack the Jesuit spies and seminary priests, there was no real defense against the danger of religious hysteria.

But Elizabeth thought otherwise. She was willing to gamble that her subjects were more English than popish and that in a showdown patriotism would prove stronger than faith. She was right, but at the time no one could be certain, and the warriors who sailed to meet Philip's crusaders did so with the fear that their houses might at any time be burned down behind their backs.

The two fleets sighted one another for the first time off Dodman Point during the early evening of July 30, the English sails sparkling in the red glare of the setting sun, and the Spanish galleons appearing like black silhouettes in the fading light. The long haul from Corunna, where the Armada had refitted after leaving Lisbon, had been made in just under ten days. The weather was difficult, as it had been all that summer, and five Spanish ships—four unseaworthy galleys designed for Mediterranean waters and a seven-hundred-sixty-eight-ton converted merchantman—had failed to reach the rendezvous off the Lizard. Though Medina Sidonia's fleet had already been reduced to one hundred twenty-five sails, Charles Howard, the English Lord Admiral, had nowhere near that number in readiness. A cautious queen, who did not trust her Dutch allies, had insisted that five galleons and thirty merchantmen and pinnaces under Lord Henry Seymour should patrol the approaches to Dunkirk and Nieuport lest Parma make a sudden dash in his barges for the English coast. Fourteen great galleons and possibly fifty other vessels under Vice-Admiral Francis Drake were stationed at Plymouth, but only fifty-four English ships had been able to slip out against the wind to confront the Armada in open water; the rest of Howard's navy was victualing and arming in various Channel ports.

Given time, the Lord Admiral could collect a grand fleet of some two hundred vessels, which he proudly described as "the best ships in the world"; Hawkins' eighteen sleek galleons, weighing between three hundred and seven hundred tons, seven smaller galleons, one hundred fifty merchantmen of varying sizes, and possibly thirty pinnaces and light frigates. It was these figures that determined

for both sides the nature of the running fight up the Channel. Sidonia had orders not to engage such a formidable enemy unless conditions were favorable or the English forced a fight. Howard's design was to test his strength against the Spanish by a series of running broadsides and wait until he could marshal a numerically superior fleet. Until the crucial battle off Gravelines, when the Lord Admiral's ships had been joined by Seymour's five galleons, the action from Eddystone up through the Channel to Calais was a noisy gun duel of swift English seadogs circling an infuriated Spanish bull.

The Armada was indeed a bull. It had rushed into the arena expecting to find matadors flourishing red capes and ceremonial swords, and picadors on heavily padded horses, and had imagined that it would engage an ancient and worthy enemy who fought according to the rules. It had anticipated a relatively fair fight in which men were often killed and occasionally, almost by divine dispensation, the bull was granted its life. On such terms the Armada had been willing to fight and if need be to die. Instead, it encountered English galleons, armed with long-range guns, that refused to play the game and sought to kill without honor or mercy.

On the morning of July 31, Medina Sidonia was alarmed to discover that the English had gained the weather gauge during the night, having slipped out from Plymouth well to the lee of the Spaniards. Many naval historians consider this feat to have been the decisive maneuver of the week-long engagement, for thereafter Howard never really lost the advantage of position. The move may have been decisive, but it was no great feat; it was merely por-

Although a contemporary painter shows English and Spanish ships firing at oar's-length range, it is improbable that any part of the battle was fought at such close quarters.

tentous evidence that Hawkins' newly designed vessels could tack well into the eye of the wind and achieve any position they chose. In answer to the English maneuver the duke ordered his fleet to battle stations and placed his squadrons in a perfectly executed crescent formation, his strongest galleons clustered at the point of each horn, his troop carriers and clumsier merchantmen in the center. Then he unfurled and hoisted high in the morning breeze the sacred banner of the Armada. Stitched on one side were the imperial arms of Spain and the figure of the crucified Christ, on the other the image of the Madonna and the words: "Arise, oh Lord, and vindicate Thy cause." At a signal from the admiral's flagship "every man in the fleet knelt down and prayed our Lord to give us victory over the enemies of His faith." Howard

countered with a piece of chivalric nonsense, sending his sloop, the *Disdain*, to deliver his personal challenge to the duke. There was a fundamental difference, however, between the two gestures: for the Spanish it was the traditional way of fighting, secure in the guardianship of heaven; for the English it was mere heraldic posing before getting down to the serious matter of sinking the enemy.

The Spanish, in their dangerously strong defensive crescent, expertly handled vessels named after the celestial host the *San Marcos, San Mateos, San Felipe, San Juan, San Lorenzo, San Martin,* and *Nuestra Senora del Rosario.* They waited with confidence for the gaily colored enemy fleet—the red-painted *White Bear,* the black-and-white *Bonaventure,* the brown *Lion,* the green-and-white *Revenge*—to commence the attack. The English, however, had no in-

283

tention of facing almost certain death by sailing between the deadly prongs of the crescent and engaging in a general melee of grappling and boarding. Instead, they approached, wheeled off, and, firing four shots to the enemy's one, raked the Armada with burst after burst of cannon shot. The entire encounter was nothing more than an extensive gunnery practice, neither side doing the other any harm, for Howard never came close enough either to risk the timber-splitting, Spanish thirty-pounders or to permit his own nine-pounders to penetrate the Spanish hulls.

Thoroughly frustrated, both sides gave up the fight, and Medina Sidonia proceeded majestically up the Channel, with Admiral Howard worrying the Spaniards from behind and adding ship after ship to his own fleet as both forces approached Calais. On the evidence of the first few days of battle, the English were increasingly alarmed that the Armada might meet Parma after all, and there seemed to be nothing they could do to prevent it. The Spanish, plagued by bad luck and unable to come to grips with a swift and nimble enemy, were equally concerned. One great ship, the forty-six-gun *Rosario*, carrying fifty-five thousand gold ducats and four hundred eighteen sailors and soldiers, fouled its neighbor, broke its own bowsprit, lost its foremast, and fell into the hands of the English. There is a legend that another ship blew up when a Spanish captain caned a master gunner for insubordination, and the gunner, in a rage, thrust a flaming linstock into the stern powder magazine and then leaped through a porthole into the ocean. The story made good copy everywhere and grew with each telling, but it is probably grounded on nothing more substantial than the fact that there was an explosion on another ship, the *San Salvador*, which like the *Rosario* fell into the hands of the English squadrons.

Between Eddystone and Calais the unsatisfactory and indecisive battle of July 31 was repeated three times over. Throughout the week the Spaniards' discipline and morale remained as impressive as ever, even if their supply of cannon balls was running desperately low and they had inflicted no damage on the enemy. The English were still unable to stop the Armada, and their cannonading continued to bounce harmlessly off the thick sides of the Spanish men-of-war. If the laurels of victory had been handed out on August 6, the decision might have been given to Medina Sidonia, who had brought his fleet, as instructed, safely to anchor off the Calais Roads to wait for a chance to rendezvous with Parma, encamped thirty miles away at Dunkirk. Reports of Spanish successes were already spreading

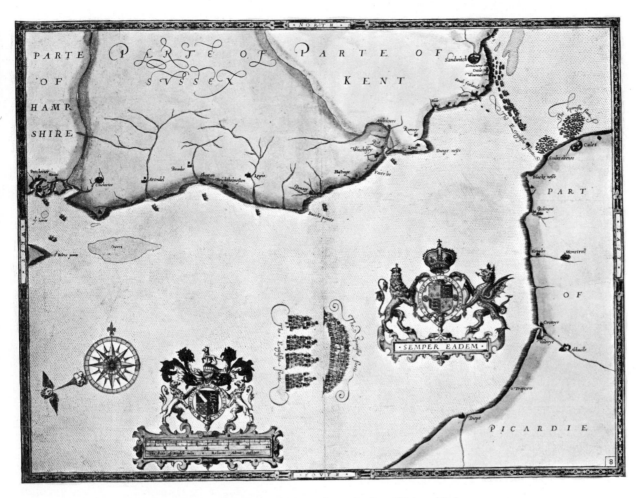

The three charts opposite show, from top to bottom: the Armada gathering off Lizard Point as a scout from Plymouth surveys the situation; the English fleet leaving Plymouth; and the contending forces off the Dorset coast. Above, the two fleets approach Calais and anchor there.

in every capital of Europe; they were followed by marvelously embellished and brilliantly detailed stories of Drake being captured while trying to board the *San Martin* and of the English fleet sunk or fleeing in panic for shelter. Mendoza, who could scarcely restrain his eagerness for news, was sufficiently convinced by the early rumors to order kindling for a huge victory bonfire in the courtyard of his Paris residence. Had he known the truth that was slowly being borne upon Medina Sidonia, he might have hesitated to spend his money; on the day the ambassador ordered his wood, the balance of war shifted decisively and disastrously against the Spanish fleet.

On Sunday morning, August 7, Medina Sidonia was told by couriers from Parma that the Great Enterprise was hopeless and the fleet doomed. Parma's troops and barges were bottled up at Dunkirk, where the harbor was too shallow to receive the duke's heavy galleons, and the Armada, its stores spoiling, its ammunition expended, and its water barrels leaking, had passed the point of no return. The wind and a superior English fleet prevented any

chance of retreat through the Channel, and ahead lay the treacherous and uninviting waters of the North Sea. Whether the thousands of doomed men on board realized the terrible truth is doubtful, for their courage remained high and they continued to have confidence in divine intervention. Not even faith, however, could withstand the unnerving sight of eight blazing fire ships driving down on the fleet during the early hours of August 8.

The possibility that the enemy might resort to fire to dislodge the Armada from its anchorage was only to be expected. Fire at sea was the gravest menace faced by men and ships, and Medina Sidonia had ordered every galleon to mark well its anchor and be ready to slip, but not cut, its cable, in order to side-step the fire ships if they should penetrate the ring of pinnaces stationed to intercept them and tow them harmlessly to shore. What the duke was unable to guard against was hysteria in his own ranks. To the dread of fire at sea was added a fearful rumor: the English had hired Federigo Giambelli, the satanic Italian inventor of the hell-burner. These infernal monsters had floated down

285

on Parma's bridges and waterworks during the siege of Antwerp, had blown to smithereens hundreds of men and months of bloody effort, and had almost saved the city. What the Spanish ships saw drifting toward them on the early morning tide were not Giambelli's floating bombs but something just as awesome—eight small frigates, their rigging and tarred decks afire and their white-hot cannons spiked and primed to explode and add molten metal and flaming debris to the floating inferno. The pinnaces were unable to intercept all of these deadly vessels, "spurting fire and their artillery shooting" and sounding like Giambelli's hellburners, and Spanish nerve, strained by sleepless nights and exhausting days of inconclusive fighting, finally snapped. Against orders most of the captains cut their cables and ran for it. The Armada was no longer a fighting machine but a formless throng of ships headed for certain destruction at the hands of the English or on the sandy shoals of the Flemish coast. Next morning only five ships remained in position, having obeyed Medina Sidonia's orders to slip cable and return to their anchorage. The rest were scattered up and down the coast, and one of the cumbersome giant galleasses, rudderless, had run aground. Like a beached whale, it was lying helpless on the sandbar off Calais harbor.

The decision to panic the Spanish fleet from its berth was a reflection of the swelling confidence within the English fleet. For a week, captains and seamen had been testing their galleons and new naval tactics against an enemy that remained medieval and Mediterranean in its military thinking. What they had learned was both heartening and alarming. Ship for ship Howard's galleons were better manned, better gunned, and better constructed than the Spanish ones, but it was also apparent that English nine-pound culverins could do Medina Sidonia's heavy battleships no real harm unless Howard was willing to close the range and risk Spanish heavy artillery. This the Lord Admiral was now prepared to do, for Seymour's squadron had joined him the previous evening, and at last he had a decided numerical superiority. At daybreak on August 8, English trumpets called the queen's fleet to action.

Somehow, despite the treacherous sands of the Dunkirk bar and the English sea wolves at his heels, Medina Sidonia got his fleet back into its familiar crescent formation, but it was a sorry shadow of the Armada that had sailed from Corunna. Pinnaces, freighters, and a number of smaller merchantmen were still scattered up and down the coast, but twenty-five of the most powerful galleons and galleasses had recovered from the panic of the

night before and answered the admiral's call to battle stations. The odds were not as desperate as they appeared, for the English had no more than twenty-five men-of-war capable of handling the hard fighting core of the Spanish fleet. All day the battle raged. Drake's ships swept in close but never quite close enough for the Spanish to grapple and board them. The English delivered terrible broadsides and then veered off, to wheel about and let fly another salvo or to move on to the next enemy galleon.

For the first time the decks of the Spanish warships ran red with blood and even from a distance the English could see the gore dripping from scuppers and cannon hatches. With the four-foot oak walls and the lighter superstructures being smashed by English broadsides, men died as often from flying splinters as they did from gun and musket shot. Spanish gallantry was magnificent, but as cannon after cannon was hit or ran out of shot, there was little left with which to fight. The *San Mateo*, with

In this detail from a painting by H. C. Vroom, the Spanish San Martin *(left) engages the* Ark Royal *off the Isle of Wight as musketeers swarm up onto the forecastles.*

of food and ammunition had allowed the enemy to escape. Actually, however, the Spanish were mortally stricken, and Drake judged correctly that Parma and Medina Sidonia would never shake hands and that neither of them would "greatly rejoice at this day's service."

Medina Sidonia indeed had no cause to rejoice; his condition next morning turned out to be even worse than he had imagined. Not only had he been beaten in open battle off Gravelines and saved from total destruction only by a chance squall, but during the night three of his finest warships had been lost, one sunk and the others run aground to save themselves from sinking. More serious than leaking hulls and broken rigging was the wind that was driving the entire fleet to certain destruction on the shallow sandbars off Flushing. Then about noon the miracle for which nearly thirty thousand men had so fervently prayed was delivered. As the leadsmen called out the depth and sailors could almost feel the sand under their ships' keels, the wind suddenly boxed the compass and steadied at a point that allowed the Armada to slip past the Dutch coast in safety and sail on into the gray-green waters of the North Sea.

It might have been more merciful had God withheld his miracle and let the stricken monster die swiftly upon the sands of Zeeland. At least sailors and soldiers would have been spared a slow and agonizing death from cold and starvation, or the futile hours spent manning pumps and climbing rigging that ended only in catastrophe on the cliffs of Scotland and the heavy surf of the Irish coast. There was no question of returning to fight again, though the duke and all his captains vowed that they would stand and do battle if only the wind would shift. As it was, they had no choice but to be swept into the North Sea with Howard at their heels, and to endure the twenty-five-hundred-mile ordeal that would eventually bring only a few of them back home to Spain.

When Medina Sidonia was finally able to take stock, he found that the Armada was in greater peril of dying of thirst than of being destroyed by the English, who trailed behind at a respectful distance. The duke did the best he could for his exhausted, demoralized men. Horses and mules were cast overboard to save water, and every officer and man was reduced to a ration of a pint of water and half a pint of wine a day. In a desperate effort to restore discipline, twenty captains who had disobeyed the duke's orders during the disastrous battle off Gravelines were court-martialed and sentenced to hang.

Howard gave up the chase on August 12. Had he stayed on another two days he would have been

half its company dead and scarcely able to stay afloat, invited tormentors to stand to and fight like men, and when an English officer, judging the ship's condition to be hopeless, climbed the rigging of his own warship and offered terms of honorable surrender, he received a musket ball for an answer. As the English galleon backed away, the Spanish crew jeered at the heretics for being cowardly hens who dared not board and fight man to man.

In every action of the battle the story was the same—a magnificent Spanish fleet that begged to be allowed at least to die honorably. Time and again the crescent formation was broken only to be reformed, and when the last cannon was fired and the battle was over, Howard was still unaware of how desperate was Medina Sidonia's plight. The enemy, he reported, "consisteth of mighty ships and great strength," and all he had been able to do was "pluck their feathers little and little." Howard was depressed; a sudden rainstorm and his own shortage better able to guess the ultimate fate of the enemy, for on August 14, three Italian merchantmen dropped behind and vanished into the cold expanse of the North Sea. Each day, as the fleet ran northward before the wind, toward a point where it could turn west around the Orkney Islands, the Armada grew smaller as the slower and clumsier vessels dropped away into the fog. Each morning there was the sad ceremony of throwing the dead overboard, and by August 21, three thousand men were mortally ill. For two more weeks the battered galleons made no progress at all in their desperate efforts to tack against a perverse wind. Doggedly they tried to inch westward, far enough to avoid being swept by giant Atlantic rollers onto boiling surf and the sheer cliffs of the Blasket Islands off the Irish coast. Vessel after vessel was flung upon rock and sand to be pounded to pieces by tides and waves. Their crews drowned, and at Sligo, on a five-mile stretch of beach, Sir Geoffrey Fenton reported "eleven hundred dead bodies of men, which the sea had driven upon the shore."

So many lurid tales have been written about the savage doings on the Irish coast that it is impossible to say what really happened. Possibly it was true that as one of the immense Spanish galleons broke up on the rocks of the Blasket Islands a maddened nobleman struck down the pilot, screaming that he had wrecked the ship by treason and that of all the gentlemen and sailors on board only the pilot's son, who had lashed himself to a spar, survived. Possibly also, officers and noblemen, if they escaped drowning, were killed by Irish peasants for their finery, and possibly the prince of Ascoli, Philip's illegitimate son, was murdered for his silk stockings, satin doublet, and gold lace. It would probably be closer to the truth, however, to say that both aristocrats and commoners were butchered by order of Sir William Fitzwilliam, Elizabeth's lord deputy of Ireland.

More ships survived the agony than could humanly have been expected to: the amazing strength that allowed Medina Sidonia and his bleeding crews to bring home a limping squadron of some sixty-six sails bordered on the miraculous. Even this was a useless and tragic feat; half of the vessels never sailed again, and perhaps two-thirds of the men, still alive when the duke sighted Spain, died of disease, dysentery, and hunger within the month. One crew arrived home so sick and exhausted that it was unable even to lower sail and drop anchor, and ran its ship aground in the safety of Santander harbor.

In all, ten men-of-war had been lost: two captured by accident, three stranded on the Flemish and Calais beaches, and five sunk by the guns of the English. Another eleven, and possibly a dozen

freighters were demolished on the long flight home, partly because the winds and the immense surge of the Atlantic cast them on the jagged rocks of the Irish coast, but mostly because men dying of privation and exhaustion could not man their sodden, leaking ships. Twenty smaller vessels remain unaccounted for. Some authorities say they were "lost, fate unknown"; others claim that most of them eventually found their way back to Spain.

By the time the jubilant word of what had happened to Philip's proud vessels off the Irish coast had made its way to England, the supreme moment of Elizabeth's reign had passed and the long recessional had begun. When the Armada first approached the Lizard on July 29, and Captain Thomas Fleming of the pinnace *Golden Hind* rushed to report the news, interrupting Drake's immortal game of bowls on Plymouth Hoe, legend maintains that the old buccaneer dismissed him with the flamboyant statement: "We have time enough to finish the game and beat the Spaniards too." Whatever Drake may have actually said or felt, most Englishmen were less insensate about the approaching ordeal. Certainly by the time the game of bowls was finished, the chain of beacons had been lit, and within hours London and even distant York knew that the crisis was finally upon them.

No one could be sure that England's naval wall, however much it had been blessed by a Protestant deity, would be able to hold back the Catholic onslaught. Highly exaggerated reports trickling in from the Netherlands had it that Parma's legions were only awaiting Medina Sidonia's galleons and a favorable tide to commence the invasion of the island. The queen could not hope to muster an army to match Castilian pikemen and musketeers seasoned by years of hard fighting in and around Antwerp, but could only counter a mercenary Spanish army with the theory of a nation in arms. The responsibility of Elizabeth's subjects, from sixteen to sixty, to maintain themselves in fighting trim was built into English history, reaching even further back than Harold's ill-trained shire levies that broke and fled at the battle of Hastings. But an ancient and rusty obligation had now become a pressing patriotic duty. For centuries hired bands of semi-feudal retainers had been sent to fight on the Continent, but for the first time in over three hundred years the realm faced a serious threat of invasion. A creaky and decayed feudal system still worked to some degree, and members of the nobility rushed to offer their queen troops raised from among their own retainers and paid from their own purses. Lord Morley, though his estates were diminished, raised a company numbering 120 horse and foot soldiers;

Lord Dacre, despite the demands of his many creditors, did almost as well; and the wealthy earl of Pembroke attended upon the sovereign with 300 cavalry and 500 infantrymen.

The backbone of the queen's defenses, however, was no longer an antiquated feudal machine but a system of national musters, whereby the Tudor government endeavored to keep in military readiness at least a part of the kingdom's manpower. In March, 1573, a royal commission had taken a muster of all the shires and had found them woefully unprepared. Derbyshire reported it could provide 4,000 men but could afford to train only 500 in musketry and bowmanship. Other counties announced that they were too poor to organize any kind of militia. The same excuses, prevarications, and incompetence were again in evidence in 1577, and almost every shire claimed that the 320 pounds needed to train a company of 400 men was too great a load for their taxpayers to carry.

Fortunately, by the year 1588 the Privy Council had managed to whip the muster into reasonable shape, and the counties opened their pocketbooks as the emergency grew near. Essex reported a potential of 13,062 infantry and 300 horses, and promised almost 4,000 men fully armed with musket, shot, and pike. In shire after shire, the gentry, bullied and encouraged by the Privy Council, had taken over local defense. Despite feuds, confusion, and shortage of money, they had organized, at least on paper, an impressive national levy capable of putting into the field an army of 100,000 men. In actual fact, it was quite impossible to feed, arm, and discipline such a force, and older hands grumbled that almost every recruit was "rawly furnished, some lacking a headpiece, some a sword," and what equipment was available was "evil, unfit, or unbecoming." In July, 1588, the best the earl of Leicester, captain general of Her Majesty's forces, could collect and feed at his camp at Tilbury was an army of around 10,000. He complained bitterly when 4,000 men from Essex arrived without a barrel of beer or a loaf of bread among the lot, and he sourly announced that he was more "cook, caterer, and huntsman" than a captain general.

Whatever their fighting deficiencies may have been, Leicester's brave lads made a magnificent audience for the most dramatic moment of Gloriana's reign. On August 18, ten days after the Armada had fled northward before Howard's fleet, the queen determined to inspect her loyal troops, gathered in full war regalia, at Tilbury. She arrived with great white plumes in her hair and confidence in her heart, for the news from Howard, who had given up the chase near Scottish waters, was increasingly hopeful.

A commemorative medal, struck soon after the Armada's defeat, shows a victorious Elizabeth in ruff and finery.

It is true that Puritan Francis Walsingham complained about the "half-doing" that had bred "dishonor and leaves the disease uncured," but with the Armada limping home, almost destroyed, and not a single English ship lost, the disease for the moment did not seem very dreadful. The queen was always satisfied with half-doings; in fact she preferred them, and she was now ready to receive the accolades of her jubilant subjects and stout defenders. She spoke to throngs who were still dazzled by the famous red hair (now a wig), the ruddy and healthy complexion (now liberally helped by rouge pot and rice powder), and the "princely resolution" (made more majestic by a white velvet gown and more resolute by a silver breastplate). Gloriana carried her fifty-five years well and could still marshal words and command emotions that not even the dead hand of history can deprive of their splendor:

> "My loving people, we have been persuaded by some that are careful for our safety, to take heed how we commit ourselves to armed multitudes, for fear of treachery. But I assure you, I do not desire to live to distrust my faithful and loving people. Let tyrants fear. I have always so behaved myself that, under God, I have placed my chiefest strength and safeguard in the loyal hearts and good will of my subjects; and therefore I am come amongst you as you see, at this time, not for my recreation and disport, but being resolved, in the midst and heat of the battle, to live or die amongst you all, and to lay down for my God

For some time the English were not convinced the Armada had indeed been beaten, and thousands of volunteers massed at Tilbury, near London, to repel an invasion. Elizabeth is shown here riding to Tilbury, where she solemnly pledged: "I myself will take up arms."

and for my kingdom and for my people, my honor and my blood, even in the dust. I know I have the body of a weak and feeble woman, but I have the heart and stomach of a king, and of a king of England too and think foul scorn that Parma or Spain, or any prince of Europe should dare to invade the borders of my realm; to which, rather than any dishonor shall grow by me, I myself will take up arms, I myself will be your general, judge, and rewarder of every one of your virtues in the field. I know already for your forwardness you deserve rewards and crowns; and we do assure you, in the word of a prince, they shall be duly paid you."

Though the queen was as good as her word and paid her soldiers to the last farthing—which was more than Philip did for his crews when they crept home to Spain—her loving people felt that some-

how they had been deprived of their full quota of deserved "rewards and crowns." The romance of war had a sour ending, for the news of the Armada's fate was delayed, mercifully for Philip and infuriatingly for Elizabeth, who wanted above all else to decommission her fleet, dismiss her soldiers, and save her exchequer. Howard returned home triumphant, but men talked of might-have-beens, not of laurels won. They did not know that wind, rock, and water on the Irish coast were giving them a far greater victory than English guns could ever have hoped to achieve. The watch still had to be kept, for the war, so gloriously begun, first with the rape of Cadiz and then with the defeat of the Armada, did not end, but deteriorated into a costly and endless struggle in Holland, France, and Ireland. On the high seas Philip profited from defeat and learned how to defend his ports and treasure fleets. In Ireland, an English ulcer fostered by Spanish gold, consumed the queen's carefully hoarded revenues, loaded her government with debt, and destroyed a host of military reputations. Elizabethans had every right to feel that the Spanish beard had only been singed and that Philip's fighting strength and determination remained almost as great as ever.

It was a full generation after the defeat of the Invincible Armada that elderly Elizabethans—scornful of a Stuart king who feared his own shadow, driveled at the mouth, picked his nose, and closeted himself with pretty young men—began to look back upon the great days of '88 through a golden haze of nostalgia and to see an event of decisive and heroic proportions. Even today, from the comfort of our armchairs, it is difficult to evaluate an enterprise that could have ended only as it did—in catastrophe. The boast that Elizabeth's sea dogs, strong in their knowledge of a God who was aggressively English, saved northern Europe for Protestantism, guaranteed the independence of Holland, secured France for the Bourbon dynasty, and made England safe for the great age of Elizabethan literature rings hollow.

Shakespeare never made direct reference to the English triumph. From the start Parma questioned whether the conquest of England was necessary to the destruction of Holland and Zeeland, and urged Philip to direct all of his efforts against Dutch deepwater ports and ocean shipping. Only after bringing the Dutch to heel might Spain have chanced the invasion of an island protected by the finest navy in the world. In France it is difficult to imagine the course of history being very different had God wrought a miracle, bemusing English wits and destroying Dutch flyboats so that Parma and Medina Sidonia could meet and cross the Channel to England. Even had Henry III never dared to order the death of the duke of Guise or had escaped the assassin's blade, Henry of Navarre still remained the rightful heir to the throne. Besides, after more than thirty years of religious and feudal bloodshed, the demand for peace, grounded firmly on history and legality, could not have been long denied.

Yet when the analysts have finished their work, there remains something to be said for a victory that has become the touchstone of Protestant mythology, for the destruction of the Armada was an immensely significant event in the transition of Europe into the modern age. The medieval profile, with its longing for unity, orthodoxy, and theology, was smashed beyond recognition by the nimble galleons and deadly culverins of Howard's fleet. In England, love of that blessed isle allowed no place for loyalty to a European commonwealth, and as the Armada disappeared into the mist of the North Sea so also did the memory of the seamless medieval cloak of Christendom. Even in the English Jesuit college at Rome it was reported that English students cheered at the defeat of an armada that had never lost its Spanish flavor, though it sought to represent all Christendom and defend a medieval dream.

On board the ships of the Armada, history had also been made. Of valor there was an abundance, but in the final reckoning even courage became the senseless, arrogant histrionics of men and captains whom time and technology—and, it would seem, God as well—had passed by. Militarily and spiritually the Armada belonged to the feudal, crusading past. Years earlier King Philip's father had discovered that fortune was a woman who loved not old men, and now the son learned that she was no lover of old-fashioned ways.

As the capitals of Europe learned the full magnitude of the disaster, king, pope, and general grieved, each according to his nature. In Rome Sixtus V congratulated himself that he had not after all lent the king of Spain a million gold ducats. In Brussels Parma went straight to the most tragic aspect of the calamity: "What adds," he said, "more than I can here express to my grief at this disaster is that it was humanly impossible to remedy it, or aid in any way." In Madrid, Philip wrapped himself in the mantle of his faith and, true to his character, returned to work. "In God's actions," he said, "reputation is neither lost nor gained: it is best not to talk of it." Philip may have been right; yet even Sixtus V could not refrain from exclaiming upon the wonders of Elizabeth and the fearless Drake, who together had tweaked the nose of the Spanish colossus. In London the fanfare for Elizabeth was even less restrained, and heroic Englishmen "did nothing but talk of what a great queen she was and how they would die for her."

The queen had reached the autumn of her life by the year of the Armada and was content to sit by the fire and remember the soft, fresh face of Leicester and the great deeds of her beardless boys, but her realm was in a more daring and jubilant frame of mind. The decade of heroes had begun, and men of more than mortal stature pranced and quarreled around their goddess-queen. Gloriana was doubtless flattered that her titans were willing to go anywhere and try anything for queen and country, but she found them, as often as not, mischievous and irresponsible as a pack of schoolboys. The Olympian posing of Raleigh, Essex, and Drake may have added magnificence to her middle age and luster to the noble achievements of her reign, but their juvenile antics drove Elizabeth to distraction and were far better suited to the realm of poetry than they were to the serious business of war and politics.

THE ELIZABETHAN THEATRE

Nowhere was the exuberance and passionate intensity of sixteenth-century English life expressed more eloquently than in the Elizabethan theatre, where a motley company of part-time scholars, occasional actors, scapegrace brawlers, and inspired hacks reinvented a language and used it to create a literature of incomparable richness, variety, and power. Intoxicated with the potentialities of blank verse and the sound of their own words, such men as Marlowe, Jonson, Shakespeare, Webster, Beaumont, Fletcher, and Kyd (a scene from his *The Spanish Tragedy* is shown in the woodcut at right) transformed a medieval theatre of stilted morality and mystery plays into a vehicle of expression such as the world had not seen since the time of Sophocles. The great period of English drama is often called the age of Shakespeare, but it would have been a golden age even if Shakespeare had never existed; indeed, had Christopher Marlowe, Shakespeare's exact—and even more promising—contemporary, not died in a tavern brawl at twenty-nine, the age might have been his. Although bawdy and bloody, the drama of the sixteenth and early seventeenth centuries was intensely human, and if it was often excessive, the excesses of which it was guilty were natural in a generation spoken for by one of the characters in Ben Jonson's play *Volpone*: "Success hath made me wanton. I could skip/Out of my skin now, like a subtle snake,/I am so limber."

THE PLAYHOUSES

Physically, the Elizabethan theatre—which Shakespeare called "this wooden O"—was modeled along the lines of the uncovered innyards in which early strolling players performed. Located in the London suburbs because they were illegal in the city itself, firetrap playhouses like the Globe, the Curtain, and the Swan flew flags to announce performances and attracted boisterous, quarrelsome, highly critical audiences made up of loafers, fops, truant apprentices, court hangers-on, and women of questionable virtue. Those peacocks who could afford the best seats preened themselves onstage, often interrupting the action with extemporaneous performances of their own. The stage itself was no more than a simple platform projecting into the pit, where the poorer playgoers crowded together, standing and at the mercy of the elements. Costumes were elaborate but few props were used, and audiences were entreated by Shakespeare to "Think when we talk of horses that you see them,/Printing their proud hoofs i' the receiving earth." Feminine roles were played by boys—"squeaking Cleopatras" with oranges in their bodices—but if the language soared and the acting was good, audiences would accept Juliets, Rosalinds—even Helens of Troy—who in a few short years would turn into Tamburlaines and Falstaffs.

The Globe Theatre

The Swan Theatre around 1596 is seen in the drawing at left. Although the greatest Elizabethan plays were crudely produced, no expense was spared for court entertainment. Indeed, a single performance of a masque designed by the architect Inigo Jones might cost more than a manor house. Two masque costumes by Jones appear above.

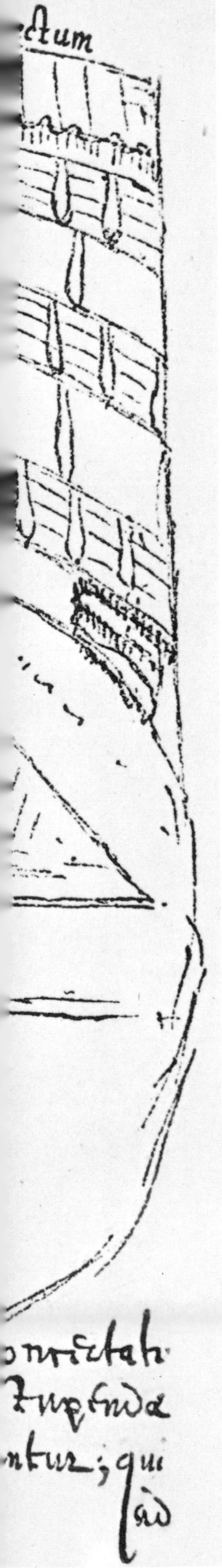

The Tragicall History
of the Life and Death
of Doctor F A V S T V S.

With new Additions.

Written by *Ch. Mar.*

Printed at London for *Iohn Wright*, and are to be sold at his shop without Newgate, 1624.

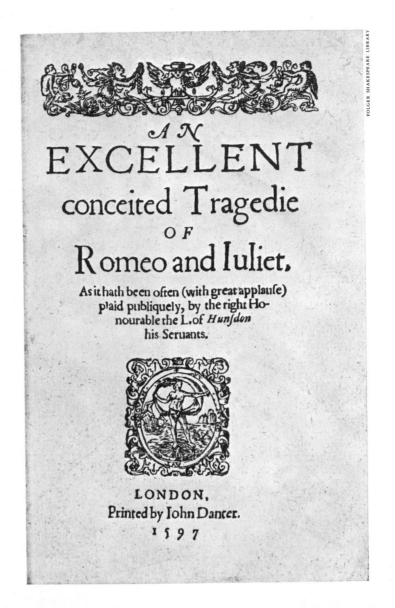

AN
EXCELLENT
conceited Tragedie
OF
Romeo and Iuliet.

As it hath been often (with great applaufe)
plaid publiquely, by the right Honourable the L. of *Hunfdon*
his Seruants.

LONDON,
Printed by Iohn Dancer.
1597

THE PLAY'S THE THING

With the notable exception of Ben Jonson, who spent much of his time chiding his colleagues for their lack of style or learning, the Elizabethan playwrights hardly concerned themselves with artistic immortality. Primarily, they were men of the theatre, determined to satisfy tough audiences with rousing, knockabout shows. Most of their plays were written quickly, often in order to meet a popular demand, and then sold to producers who doctored them as they saw fit. Preoccupied with the development of character, the choice of telling imagery, and the punning and byplay loved by the groundlings, playwrights had little time to work out elaborate story lines and literally begged, borrowed, or stole their plots wherever they could find them. (Of the three plays illustrated here, for example, only *The Maid's Tragedy* is not known to be based on an earlier plot.) Plays were circulated in manuscripts, which were often carelessly copied, and few attempts were made to publish them until they had proved their durability in the theatre. Indeed, Elizabeth herself was long dead before many plays produced during her lifetime were deemed worthy of publication.

The woodcut at left illustrates a scene from Christopher Marlowe's Doctor Faustus. *Faustus, standing within a magic circle, conjures up Mephistopheles. The scene at right, from Beaumont and Fletcher's* The Maid's Tragedy, *shows a favorite Elizabethan device, the girl (left) in male disguise. Above it is the first edition of* Romeo and Juliet.

Shakespere

COLLEGE OF ARMS

SHAKESPEARE OF STRATFORD

The towering figure in Elizabethan drama—and in all English literature—is, of course, William Shakespeare, the glovemaker's son who left his native Stratford for London around 1587. Soon after his arrival in the city Shakespeare went (or perhaps drifted) into theatre work, probably first as a play tinker, then as an actor, and finally as a full-fledged playwright. By 1592 he was well enough known—and popular enough—to provoke one of his university-trained rivals, Robert Greene, to complain of this "upstart crow, beautified with our feathers." In the course of his career Shakespeare wrote dozens of plays, thirty-eight of which survive, including one, *The Merry Wives of Windsor*, that was almost certainly written at Elizabeth's command. Around 1600 *Hamlet* was produced, ushering in a decade that brought unparalleled richness to the theatre and increasing affluence to Shakespeare himself.

Shakespeare, though popular with his London colleagues, was a countryman at heart and proud of his newly acquired family arms (upper left) and his status as "gentleman." Henry Peacham's drawing above, from a 1594 manuscript, is the earliest known Shakespearian illustration. It shows a scene from Titus Andronicus *in which Tamora begs for her son's life.*

Martin Droeshout sculpsit London.

To the Reader.

This Figure, that thou here seest put,
    It was for gentle Shakespeare cut;
Wherein the Grauer had a strife
    with Nature, to out-doo the life:
O, could he but haue drawne his wit
    As well in brasse, as he hath hit
Hisface; the Print would then surpasse
    All, that was euer writ in brasse.
But, since he cannot, Reader, looke
    Not on his Picture, but his Booke.

                      B. I.

Frontispiece for the first folio of Shakespeare's plays (1623), with a verse by Ben Jonson

299

Like his contemporaries, Shakespeare was not above cribbing plots from earlier sources, including Raphael
Holinshed's Chronicles of England, Scotland, and Ireland. Shakespeare based several plays on Holinshed, whose books were illustrated with woodcuts like this one of Macbeth, Banquo, and the three witches.

1602

Sr Walter Ralegh Knight Lord Warden of
the Staneries of the
& of the Isle of yarsey & ber M. Lieute
nant general of the Counties of Devonshyre & Cornwall

ÆTA· SÆ· 8

9

A DECADE OF HEROES

It is only proper to introduce a tale of heroes with traditional words: *Once upon a time* there lived a generation of men so exaggerated in their behavior and so flamboyant in their aspirations that not even the fearsome words of Marlowe's Faustus could describe the fiery zeal that consumed them.

Philosophy is odious and obscure;
Both law and physic are for petty wits;
Divinity is basest of the three . . .
'Tis magic, magic, that hath ravish'd me.

The magic that ravished them did not come, as did Faustus', from a bargain with the devil; it lay within them in the boundless self-confidence that led Raleigh to assert that "style is the man," and the playwright George Peele to shout: "King of a molehill had I rather be than the richest subject of a monarchy." One and all—Raleigh, Essex, Frobisher, Drake, Norris, Sidney, Grenville—were willing to "pay nature's debt with cheerful countenance," for they courted death and never feared it. The dynamism that urged them on was devoid of heavenly reward or hellish punishment. They asked of God only the chance to show their true mettle, forged in the fire of their egotism. The adventure of life, said Raleigh to his son, was "a troublesome bark," and it was up to each man to make good his "station in the upper deck; those that live under hatches are ordained to be drudges and slaves."

Whatever may be said against these heroes of Elizabethan England, they cannot be accused of dullness or slavishness. They spoke proudly and persistently of their duty to God and queen, but Elizabeth knew that neither the threat of prison nor the fear of hell could discipline her warriors, and in letter after letter, she was reduced to impotent rage and pleading. She was infuriated by Dudley's expensive and useless prancing about Holland and his peevish insistence on being styled governor general, and she angrily announced that she was "utterly at squares with this childish dealing." After Drake had embarked on the haphazard expedition of 1589, Elizabeth sought to prevent disobedience by warning him to beware lest vainglory "obfuscate the eyes of your judgment." The advice went unheeded, for, as the queen suspected, Sir Francis Drake and Sir John Norris "went to places more for profit than for service." They evaded their sovereign's orders to strike at warships and naval installations in northern Spain, and instead went looking for honor and plunder in an abortive attack on Lisbon. Elizabeth was particularly irritated with the entire venture since her favorite young courtier, the earl of Essex, had rushed to join the fray, announcing: "If I speed well, I will adventure to be rich; if not, I will not live to see the end of my poverty." Gloriana ordered her errant boy back to court and grimly reminded Drake and Norris: "As we have authority to rule, so we look to be obeyed."

Elizabeth might have spared herself the cost of the ink; she had endless authority, but when glory and gold were concerned she was rarely obeyed. To honor, her courtiers were willing slaves; to the standards of Tudor society and the wishes of their queen, they were often lighthearted rebels. Duty to themselves as a breed of men apart was the root and branch of their faith, and almost in anguish

The swashbuckling Sir Walter Raleigh is shown with his young son, Wat.

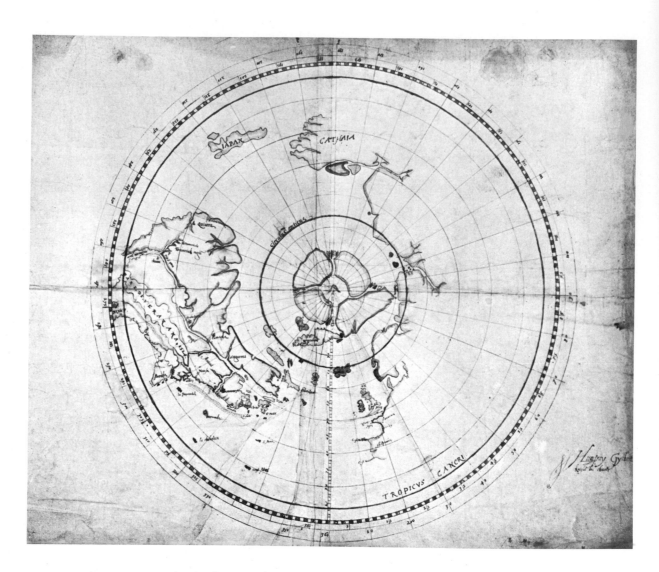

A polar map of 1582, drawn by Sir Humphrey Gilbert, tried—with more optimism than accuracy—to prove that a sea passage through America (left) provided access to China (top).

Essex cried out: "I am tied by my own reputation to use no tergiversation!"

Heroes, like saints, become grotesque caricatures when held up to the mirror of humanity. What is the normal man to think of the extraordinary behavior of Sir Richard Grenville during the last encounter of the *Revenge*? The occasion was one of the less glorious of Elizabeth's efforts to finance naval warfare with the profits of piracy. A small English fleet under Lord Thomas Howard—six galleons and a few auxiliary vessels bent on plundering the Spanish treasure fleet—was caught in 1591 by some fifty-five Spanish ships, including twenty of Philip's galleons of the Indian guard. Howard had been hovering off the Azores for months in fruitless expectation of the treasure *flota*, and had just begun filling his water kegs and resting his crew at Flores when the Spaniards swept in from the east and surprised the English at anchor. The admiral ordered his ships to run for it, and he managed to get five

of his vessels away to safety. Sir Richard Grenville in the *Revenge*, however, preferred to take on the enemy fleet singlehanded and smash his way through to the open sea. It remains a mystery whether Grenville's action was sheer bravado touched with madness, in which he regarded the war with Spain as a personal conflict between himself and Philip's empire, or a suicidal endeavor to save his comrades in arms by covering Lord Thomas Howard's retreat.

Whatever the truth, his defiance of the naval might of Spain has become one of the legendary feats of English history. For fifteen hours the *Revenge*, with only one hundred of its crew fit to fight, endured an agony of cannonading and musket fire that could end only in total destruction. Attacked by fifteen galleons in succession, at least one of which was three times the tonnage of the *Revenge*, Grenville fought until his ship was a slaughter house, running red with blood, riddled by eight

304

hundred cannon balls, its mast and rigging shot away, and almost every man dead or wounded. Finally, with no further chance of victory, he ordered the master gunner to blow up the *Revenge* with all aboard so that "nothing might remain of glory or victory to the Spaniards." Self-immolation may be a suitable death for heroes, but the crew, of a more pedestrian reasoning and more mortal clay, thought otherwise and insisted upon surrender. The Spanish presented amazing terms: common seamen would not be sent to row in the galleys but were promised safe passage to England, and officers would be kept in honorable captivity awaiting ransom. Grenville would accept no such terms. Although he was desperately wounded, there was still fight left in the old sea dog. His scorn was boundless; the *Revenge* had already sunk two Spanish galleons, and "the Spaniards," he said, "should never glory to have taken one ship of Her Majesty's." He had to be forcibly restrained from falling on his sword to escape capture. But finally he was overruled by his crew. The Spanish took him aboard and treated him with the respect due to the devil himself.

They did their best to save his life, but Grenville had no intention of living on in captivity or dying of his wounds. If we can believe the legend that surrounds the event—and it is unbelievable in any man but Grenville—he deliberately crushed his wine goblet at the first opportunity he had, and while his horrified hosts watched, methodically chewed up the pieces of glass. His last words were true to character: "Here die I, Richard Grenville, with a joyful and quiet mind, for that I have ended my life as a true soldier ought to do that hath fought for his country, queen, religion, and honor." When, a few days later, a hurricane swept down on both the flota and Philip's galleons and sank more than seventy ships, including the hulk of the *Revenge*, the Spanish understandably thought that Grenville had been in league with the devil and had called upon the elements to revenge his death. Without passing judgment upon Sir Richard's relations with the satanic forces, the twentieth century can only surmise that the ferocious old mariner was more fit for a padded cell than a naval command.

The same aura of wild fantasy surrounds the death of that literate Puritan and courtier-cum-adventurer Sir Humphrey Gilbert, who was lost at sea in 1583 on his return from an ill-starred effort to explore and colonize the coast of Newfoundland. Economic ruin faced Gilbert, for he had invested every penny he had in his vision of populating a new world. Yet his self-confidence never wavered. "Be of good cheer," he assured his men when they urged him to return to England, for God had given him

Sir Humphrey Gilbert

Sir Richard Grenville

special knowledge of the "inestimable good" to be achieved from the expedition and would help persuade the queen to lend him ten thousand pounds for further discoveries in distant lands. But Elizabeth had already noted that Sir Humphrey was a particularly unlucky commander, and this last voyage, when more than one hundred colonists were lost in a wreck on the uncharted coast of Nova Scotia, again proved her judgment correct.

When the little flotilla, sadly reduced to two ships but still confident of God's favor, sailed home, Sir Humphrey transferred his flag from the forty-ton bark, the *Golden Hind*, to the much smaller *Squirrel*, in part out of a sense of duty, but in part because he feared that men might say he was afraid of the sea. Even his admirers thought this gesture excessively rash and wondered that he should "prefer the wind of a vain report to the weight of his own life." Heroes, however, must live up to their reputations. The last that was ever seen or heard of the foolhardy commander was that he was sitting in the stern of his cockleshell craft, with a book in his hand, assuring his crew that they were "as near to heaven by sea as by land." Hours later, during a wild September storm, the *Squirrel* "was devoured and swallowed up of the sea."

It is easy to dismiss as mere madness the actions of heroes who behaved like a band of overgrown juvenile delinquents more suited for a house of correction than a hall of fame. Yet to do so is to miss the full flavor and true character of the age. Not only did Gilbert, Grenville, Essex, and the rest take themselves and their reputations seriously but so also did the world in which they lived. Represen-

Martin Frobisher made three arduous voyages to the Arctic and was knighted for his gallantry against the Armada.

tations of Drake's ruddy and belligerent features and tublike form hung in the portrait galleries of dozens of Protestant princes throughout Germany and Holland; the daredevil death of the thirty-two-year-old Sir Philip Sidney, who rode into battle without his steel cuisses because his commander was not wearing armor, was held up as an act of heroism becoming to a great poet; and Marlowe spoke for his generation when he wrote of the dreadful Tamburlaine that his honor consisted "in shedding blood."

The heroes of the sixteenth century were no deities fulfilling their boisterous destinies in Olympian isolation. Men like Grenville and Gilbert were not exceptions to the Tudor rule; they were simply magnified examples of it. Individually their actions are grotesque, but placed within the context of an age when exaggeration and violence were the central characteristics of life, their feats appear little more extraordinary than the actions of such lesser known contemporaries as the indefatigable Robert Carey, who won a two-thousand-pound bet by walking from London to Berwick in twelve days, or the nameless English soldier whose arm was torn off by a cannon ball at the siege of Ostend. Undaunted, the young man picked up the severed limb, returned with it to camp, and announced to his comrades: "Behold the arm which but at dinner helped its fellow." The sixteenth century believed, as did the eighteenth, in "bottom," that all but undefinable trait that unites stoicism with enthusiasm, histrionics with conviction, and foppery with toughness.

Violence, cruelty, and intensity were commonplaces of Tudor life. The endurance of Drake's tiny band that circumnavigated the globe in an epic voyage lasting three years must be set off against the discomforts and risks of normal existence. Imagine life as it actually was—a long agony of itches from skin diseases, lice, and fleas, a steady procession of toothaches, gout, stones, rheumatism, and bloodletting, and the constant fear of smallpox, sweating sickness, and the plague. Only the strong of body and stout of heart survived, and even they were hard put to withstand medical practices that were often more a test of the patient's fortitude than a cure for his sickness. The surgeon's saw without ether, the barber's tooth extractor without novocain, and the physician's potions without understanding were no less terrible than Spanish musket and cannon shot. The death of Don John, Philip's half brother, from a horrible combination of syphilis and some variety of the plague, was just as frightful as that of Sir Richard Grenville. The suffering of poor Lady Throckmorton at the hands of Doctor Atslow must have been comparable to that of the wretches on the *Revenge*. Lady Throckmorton had been hemorrhaging after the birth of a daughter, and Sir Arthur Throckmorton noted in his diary the treatment, with full clinical details. His good lady was wrapped in sheets soaked "in plantain water and vinegar of roses in equal quantities"; she was kept from all motion and both her arms were "tied very hard and sometimes loosed and tied again"; she was bled from both arms at frequent intervals for two or three days; and she was forced to "sit from her buttocks up to her navel in a deep bowl of cold water." The reader will be glad to know that not only did Lady Throckmorton survive her cure but that Doctor Atslow was later imprisoned for high treason and tortured on the rack—a mild punishment for what he prescribed for his unfortunate patients.

Men wore a tough hide of inhumanity and callousness that inured them to the sight of blind beggars trying to club a pig to death, or to the agonies of the condemned poisoner writhing in a pot of boiling oil, or the witch suffering on the stake, or the traitor strung up on the gallows and then, still living, cut down, castrated, and disemboweled. That good Christian gentleman, Master Phillip Stubbes, thought death not too great a penalty for swearing. If such a punishment, he conceded, were judged too severe, then he wished that offenders "might have a piece of their tongue cut off, or lose some joint," and if that still seemed too extreme, at the very least blasphemers should "be seared in the forehead or cheek with a hot iron [and] engraven with some pretty posy, that they might be known and avoided."

Every city and court of Europe was exposed to brawling, dueling, and histrionics. Raleigh delighted in the magnificence of his famous cloaks and his reputation for "perpetually differing"; George Clifford, earl of Cumberland, always wore in his hat a glove dropped one day by Elizabeth; Sidney, as he lay dying, gravely presented his cup of water to a common soldier with the words: "Thy necessity is yet greater than mine"; and Essex, sent to France at the head of an army to aid Henry IV against the Spaniards, arrived resplendent in orange velvet embroidered with gold and sprinkled with jewels, and with an entourage dressed in the same livery. As Raleigh said, it was style that made the man! Even in their personal lives the heroes of Tudor England lived by standards more suited to Valhalla than to the banquet hall. The story is told of how Raleigh and his son coined a bon mot by staging a family row at a dinner party. From the start Sir Walter was doubtful about his son's table manners, but the young man had promised to "behave himself mighty mannerly." The two Raleighs sat next to each other,

and halfway through the dinner young Wat suddenly remarked to the company: "I, this morning, not having the fear of God before my eyes but by the instigation of the devil, went to a whore. I was very eager of her, kissed and embraced her, and went to enjoy her; but she thrust me from her and vowed I should not, 'For your father lay with me but an hour ago'." Sir Walter was understandably outraged by his quarrelsome offspring's words and struck him "a damned blow over the face." In deference to his father, young Raleigh did not hit back but turned instead to his unsuspecting neighbor and struck the astonished gentleman, saying: "Box about: 'twill come to my father anon." "Box about" became a common saying in the seventeenth century.

Vainglorious buccaneers and gilded youths with "fierce dragons' spleens," wearing a lord's revenue on their backs, must have been irritating beyond measure to the merchant immersed in his accounts, to the bureaucrat insensate to romance, and to a queen who counted her change and constantly in-

Sir Philip Sidney, courtier, poet, and patron of the arts, died heroically at thirty-two in the war against Spain.

307

Imprisoned for a second time by James I, Raleigh spent years in the Tower working on this History of the World.

quired into the cost of glory. Most Englishmen, however, forgave them their idiocies because they were great. Man's fate on earth was boredom, pain, and death, and men welcomed the chance to enjoy life vicariously. They thrilled at Raleigh's boast that England could make the kings of Spain "kings of figs and oranges, as in old times," or at his bragging that one English warship could match forty Dutch, for such words lent verisimilitude to their dreams.

The cult of the individual was part of the European heritage. Although Renaissance emphasis on the worth of man may have given new brilliance to the actions of mankind, the medieval world also had thought in terms of the individual. Feudal society had always been willing to make allowances for the uncommon man. Saints had traditionally been a breed apart; their folly had been judged by standards applicable only to themselves and had been found to be a higher wisdom. By the same token heroes and geniuses in the sixteenth century were not judged as normal men were. Elizabeth forgave Essex for a degree of childishness and insolence that would have been ridiculed and punished in lesser men, and Pope Paul III thought it not unreasonable to excuse the boasted murders of Cellini

because, as he said: "Men unique in their professions, like Benvenuto, were not subject to the laws." Those proud, undisciplined, and extravagant conquistadors, who carved out an empire for Spain, lived by a code unique to themselves. Cortes persuaded his men on the beaches of Veracruz to burn their boats, cutting off their only means of escape, because, he said, such an act would be comparable to the "brave deeds done by heroes among the Romans." Bernal Diaz boasted that he had won nobility by fighting in twice as many battles as Caesar, and his claim was accepted by his contemporaries.

History, as the humble man knows, is reserved for the titans, those extraordinary men and women who achieve immortality by impressing their feats upon the memory of mankind; the rest of us must make do with heaven. But even among the Olympian host the historian must choose, and the remaining pages of the chapter are reserved for the adventures of but two Elizabethan heroes: Sir Walter Raleigh and Robert Devereux, earl of Essex.

Raleigh was "fortune's tennis ball," a knavish, witty, boisterous fellow, proud as the devil and impudent as Puck, who longed "to be able to sway all men's fancies, all men's courses," and who was hated above all others "in court, city, and country." Only Elizabeth could handle him, and she was among the few who seems to have liked this "tall, handsome, and bold man" who suddenly appeared at her court in the early months of 1582. The queen was willing to listen to his ready and persuasive tongue, but she never gave him a chance to "sway all men's fancies." She would dress Raleigh's shapely limbs in the orange uniform of the captain of her guard, but the door of the Privy Council remained closed to him.

Exactly how Raleigh came to Gloriana's attention is a mystery. He was born around 1552 and stemmed from an old and respected Devonshire family. Neither his carriage nor the company he kept endeared him to men in authority, for young Walter's insolent conviction of his own genius was matched only by the impudent rowdiness of his associates. His servants brawled with the London watch; Raleigh himself was twice jailed in 1580 for disturbing the peace, and he won a measure of renown for silencing a noisy tavern bully by filling the fellow's mouth with wax and tying his beard to his mustache. Despite his skirmishes with the law, he received a captaincy and the command of one hundred foot soldiers in 1580, and went forth to more glorious and bloody encounters against the nettlesome Irish rebels.

In Ireland Raleigh won notoriety by the violence and ruthlessness of his methods of waging war, and

In 1595, the year of his first expedition up the Orinoco River, Raleigh took time out to capture St. Joseph, Trinidad. He is shown here directing Spanish prisoners into boats.

he seems to have spent considerable time and energy criticizing his superiors, writing over their heads to the Council in London, and earning the dislike of the queen's lord deputy of Ireland. By spring, 1582, he was back in England and it was only then that he was introduced to the queen, perhaps through the favor of his half brother, Sir Humphrey Gilbert. If, as legend reports, Raleigh did spend his last farthing on a cape of wondrous grandeur, which he extravagantly sacrificed to keep Elizabeth dry-shod, the investment paid off handsomely, for by May, 1583, he had been granted the lucrative monopoly of licenses to sell wine. This eventually netted him the princely sum of one thousand two hundred pounds a year and permitted him to wear shoes reportedly worth "six thousand, six hundred gold pieces."

Though real power as a statesman continued to elude Raleigh, he was granted other lucrative monopolies: land and houses in England and Ireland, and in 1585, knighthood. In 1587 he was given the coveted post of captain of the guard, a position that daily brought him into contact with the queen. Elizabeth once asked him in some annoyance: "When will you cease to be a beggar?" The bare-

faced, but honest retort was typical of the man: "When your gracious majesty ceases to be a benefactor."

Raleigh was always something more than a piece of costly tinsel in Elizabeth's display of royalty. Gloriana doubtless admired her "Water," as she affectionately nicknamed him, for his dark beard, curly hair, and foppish elegance, but it was his quickness of mind and impertinence of speech that impressed her most; and much to the annoyance of the court, Elizabeth took him "for a kind of oracle, which nettled them all." There were few men in England who could gull their queen, but Raleigh did so when he boasted that he knew his tobacco so well that he could actually weigh the smoke. Elizabeth rose to the bait and wagered him that he could not make good his claim. Sir Walter simply weighed the tobacco, smoked it in his silver pipe, weighed the ashes, subtracted one from the other, and presented the queen with the answer. As she paid her debt Elizabeth wryly remarked that she had heard of men "who turned gold into smoke," but Raleigh was the first man she ever encountered "who had turned smoke into gold."

For five years Raleigh stood guard at the queen's

door, hated by all who begrudged him his riches and his closeness to Elizabeth. In 1587, however, another star was born, and Sir Walter discovered he had to reckon with an impudent lad of nineteen, the young earl of Essex, whose open face and soft, sensuous smile touched the heart of a middle-aged queen. Soon court gossip was reporting that Essex "hath chased Master Raleigh from the court and hath confined him into Ireland."

Certainly the young nobleman displaced the forty-year-old captain of the guard in his privileged position as royal confidant, but what ultimately destroyed Raleigh was his own conceit. Despite his virtuosity and imagination, Sir Walter was a sublime egotist, blind to the feelings of others, disdainful of the foibles of mankind, and insensitive and tactless in his criticism of convention. The animosity so often directed at him was largely of his own making. He was far too contemptuous of the shibboleths of polite society, and though the queen might find his barbed wit diverting, the ladies of the court could scarcely have been expected to take to their hearts a man who unflatteringly described them as witches who "could do hurt, but they could do no good." Raleigh knew well the proverb: "Slippery is the place next to kings." He himself had written "whoso reaps renown above the rest,/With heaps of hate shall surely be oppressed." But so long as Elizabeth smiled, the angry tongues and envious glances of

his fellow courtiers could do Raleigh no harm.

In 1592 Raleigh made the serious mistake of shocking Elizabeth, who held strict views on the proper sexual behavior of those attending upon a virgin queen. Rumor reported that Sir Walter had been "too inward with one of her majesty's maids"; and so he had, for Mistress Throckmorton had been undone and the unmistakable signs of pregnancy began to appear in the fall of 1591. In November Raleigh and his young mistress were secretly married, and on March 29 a son—Damerei Raleigh—was born. Incredible as it may sound, the earl of Essex stood godfather to the boy.

If Raleigh hoped to escape the queen's wrath by enlisting his rival's favor, he badly miscalculated. Despite the marriage and the blessing of Essex, Elizabeth took the view that one of her vestal virgins had been ravished. She was no prude, but she refused to countenance at her court the kind of sexual laxity prevalent at the court of that amorous sovereign, Henry IV of France. She withheld her fury for several months, but in August, 1592, the brash couple was dispatched to the Tower to meditate upon the consequences of incontinence. Raleigh's stay in the Tower lasted little more than a month, but his career at court was over.

The queen liked her courtly favorites to be of noble birth; with Raleigh she had made an exception, but in Essex she found the perfect Harlequin to her aging Columbine. The earl of Leicester, Essex's stepfather and Elizabeth's exasperating but beloved beau of yesteryear, introduced the young earl to court, where he attracted the queen's attention in 1586. Romantically handsome, irresistibly young, impetuously generous, carrying "on his brow either love or hatred," and never able to "understand concealment," Essex had the world at his feet. The queen sighed at the sight of so much promise and had to have her Essex in constant attendance. Together they played at cards and chatted until dawn, and Elizabeth put up with more sulking and more dangerous nonsense from this spoiled favorite than she ever had even from her "Robin," the earl of Leicester. Essex was "a great resenter." He complained about Raleigh and called him a knave, an upstart, and a vegetable of the court, and when Elizabeth still showed fondness for her "Water," he tried to steal off to the Netherlands to find solace in war. He petulantly insulted Charles Blount, who was presented by Elizabeth with a gold chess queen in recognition of his feats at the tilt. Blount appeared at court with his token tied by a crimson ribbon to his sleeve, and on spying it, Essex sneered in a loud voice: "Now I see every fool must have a favor."

The Sir Walter Raleigh Company, formed to promote the colonization of Virginia, adopted this emblem in 1588.

For all his trying ways, the earl of Essex must have had great magnetism to have charmed Elizabeth into giving him real responsibility. She allowed his passionate pleading to override her better judgment and sent him to France to lead an expeditionary force in support of Henry IV. The tiny army landed in August, 1591, with explicit orders to aid in the siege of Rouen and then return home after no more than two months. Rouen never fell; it was not even attacked until many months later; but Essex had a marvelous time. He outjumped the French king at a game of leapfrog, nearly fell into an ambush, challenged the governor of Rouen to personal combat, and lavishly bestowed knighthood upon twenty-four of his henchmen after apologizing for not having led them into battle, where they could have gained honor and earned their spurs. Elizabeth was understandably annoyed. She scornfully dismissed Essex's parading as "rather a jest than a victory," and ordered the errant commander home. The earl was amazed by such treatment and complained bitterly about being "blamed as negligent, undutiful, rash in going, slow in returning, undiscreet in dividing the horse from the foot, faulty in all things, because I was not fortunate to please."

It is difficult to say where Essex was more dangerous: at court, exercising his fatal charm and repairing his reputation in the queen's eyes, or abroad, handling the serious concerns of war and diplomacy as if they were sports designed to display his virtuosity and daring. With Leicester's death in 1588, Elizabeth turned emotionally and politically to his stepson, so like him in his surly pride and winsome ways. She needed a counterbalance to the two Cecils —old Lord Burghley and his son Robert—and she had hopes of transforming her divine juvenile into a court politician. Essex, although eager for power, had neither the patience nor the sagacity to develop into a statesman, however. Like Raleigh, Drake, and the other heroes, he lacked emotional stability and a sense of proportion. His idea of politics was to demand all sorts of offices and gifts for his friends, without regard for their qualifications or their acceptability to the queen, and when he was turned down he sulked and took it as a personal affront.

Essex must have been maddening and perplexing to his sovereign. At one moment he could dismiss politics with disarming candor as being beneath his dignity and intelligence, at the next he could be furious with Elizabeth for giving high offices to young Robert Cecil. Above all, the earl desired a chance for renown—not at court but in war. "Soldiers in peace," it was said, were "like chimneys in summer." In June, 1596, he finally got his opportunity when the wind blew fair and the queen's ships once

Robert Devereux, earl of Essex, is shown wearing the beard he grew during the Cadiz expedition of 1596.

again set sail on an expedition to Spain.

Here was the chance to win glory, achieve immortality, and relieve Philip of the fabulous riches of his empire. Seventeen of England's great galleons and merchantmen, accompanied by an armada of transports, pinnaces, and flyboats, and a disciplined army of six thousand—one third of them veterans of the Dutch wars—were being sent for a second time to harass Spanish naval power by a strike at Cadiz. Lord Howard of Armada fame and the inexperienced earl of Essex were given joint command; Raleigh was restored to partial favor, made vice-admiral, and placed on the five-man council of war authorized to advise the commanders. Such an expedition, led by the most famous captains of the older and younger generations, attracted an enormous number of volunteers; even John Donne went avoyaging in quest, one imagines, of more than inspiration for his poetry. The fleet's destination remained one of the few well-kept military secrets of the century, but it was quite apparent that some great enterprise was being planned against Spain.

Captains and sailors, generals and soldiers consciously put out of their minds the memory of a similar expedition under Sir Francis Drake, which

A 1603 drawing shows Drake's Golden Hind (right) *capturing a Spanish treasure ship off the coast of Ecuador.*

HULSIUS, 1603; NEW YORK PUBLIC LIBRARY, RARE BOOK ROOM

had set sail in 1589 with equally high hopes and had returned home a costly failure. It had netted one Spanish warship destroyed, plunder of only thirty thousand pounds, and had cost the lives of about half of the original company. Not even the death of Drake himself in February, 1596, a few months before the new fleet set sail for Cadiz, dampened enthusiasm for the expedition. Drake perished while he was fighting an outdated kind of war, his tactics appropriate to those wonderful and carefree days before Philip had learned to defend his treasure fleets and Caribbean ports. The old warrior had relied, as always, on lady fortune, and for once, she played him false. His night attack on Puerto Rico had been beaten back, his efforts to cross the Isthmus of Panama had ended in a rout, and no gold or treasure galleons had been discovered. Rather wearily the veteran pirate had assured his crew: "I will bring you to twenty places far more wealthy and easier to be gotten," but he never did; he died of dysentery instead, and true to form, in his last moments he rose and donned his armor, saying that he would face death like a soldier. Somewhere off the coast of Panama near Portobello his coffin was slipped into the sea.

The new enterprise was far more substantial than Drake's last voyages. A fleet of around one hundred twenty sails, under the daring Essex, the elegant

Raleigh, and the veteran Lord Admiral Howard, and blessed with a prayer written by the queen herself, was a very different matter. The volunteers who flocked to Plymouth thought of the 4,700 per cent profit made by those who had invested in Drake's famous voyage around the world or the even more fabulous treasures seized in 1592 when Sir Martin Frobisher captured the 1600-ton, seven-deck, thirty-two-gun Portuguese carrack, the *Madre de Dios*, carrying a 537-ton cargo of spices and precious jewels, silks, drugs, carpets, Chinese porcelain, ebony, and "elephants' teeth." The value of the cargo, even after the crew had plundered some 100,000 pounds worth of jewels, spices, plate, and gold, was estimated at 141,200 pounds, an impressive sum indeed when the greatest galleon in the queen's navy could be built, fitted, and manned for less than 5,000 pounds, a nobleman's estate purchased for 17,000 pounds, and an entire army raised for 40,000 pounds. The sailor who was lucky enough to find 320 "sparks of diamond" and "a collar of a threefold roll of pearl with six tags of crystal garnished with gold" had a king's ransom in his pocket. It was the dream of such riches that filled the heart of every officer, soldier, and sailor when the fleet finally set sail on June 3, 1596.

The second Cadiz expedition came close to being the most extraordinary feat of the century; for once, heroism, rampant individualism, and foolhardy histrionics paid off. From the start the gods were kind even to captains, who were inordinately touchy about rank and authority and who followed only those plans of action that happened to coincide with their own ideas. Before the fleet even sailed, Vice-Admiral Walter Raleigh and marshal of the army Sir Francis Vere had a row at dinner over precedence, and the younger and more hotheaded officers quarreled so openly that one of them, Raleigh's brother-in-law, had to be ordered from the table. Howard and Essex were suspicious of Sir Walter because they thought he had tried to persuade Elizabeth to give him sole command. The Lord Admiral was angered by the fact that the inexperienced earl of Essex had been made joint commander, and when Essex inserted his own signature above Howard's in a report to the queen, the Lord Admiral whipped out his knife and cut out the offending name because he "would have none so high as himself." "I see already," wrote one of the younger generation on board the fleet, "the fire kindled that must consume us inwardly"; but the depressing prediction proved false, and the damnable pride, the braggadocio, and quarreling that was so much a part of Elizabethan life for once proved a source of strength and won an outstanding triumph for the queen.

On Sunday morning, June 20, while the church bells of Cadiz rang out the alarm, the English approached the complicated and well-fortified harbor and discovered King Philip's entire West Indian fleet at anchor. Thirty-six loaded merchantmen, ready to set sail for the Caribbean, were awaiting their escorting galleons, which were being refitted at another port nearby. Only four huge galleons, known as the Apostles, and a small flotilla of other ships had been left behind to guard them. Cadiz itself was located at the tip of a five-mile-long spit of land, its ocean approaches defended by the high walls and cannons of Fort San Sebastian and its bay side protected by Fort St. Philip. Beyond the outer harbor was the inner one, Port Royal, six miles away, with an escape canal that led out into the sea some ten miles below Cadiz. When the English appeared, the smaller of the merchantmen scampered to the safety of the inner harbor, and the four Apostles, accompanied by several other large ships, anchored themselves, stem to stern, across the narrowest part of the harbor.

Howard refused to risk the queen's galleons against the combined fire of the Apostles and the heavy artillery of the land fortifications, but Raleigh was eager to proceed and pointed out that no one had decided "in what manner to fight" or "who should lead, and who should second." For once Essex agreed with him. After a great deal of wrangling over where and how to attack and who should have the honor of leading, the English commanders settled upon a plan suggested by Raleigh. The main attack was to be launched against the Apostles guarding the entrance to the harbor, and then Cadiz was to be attacked from the bay side of the peninsula. A whole day was wasted over these discussions, but on the twenty-first, with Raleigh in the van, since Elizabeth had issued explicit instructions that her Essex was not to risk his precious person no matter how much honor might be gained, the English fleet moved in on the four Spanish galleons—the *San Felipe*, the *San Andrés*, the *San Mateo*, and the *San Tomás*. The first two had been in on the death of Grenville's ship, the *Revenge*, and Raleigh headed straight for them resolved on retribution or, as he said, "to second her with mine own life."

What followed was a fairy tale come true. As the English squadrons approached and the Spanish guns began to thunder, Raleigh ordered his trumpeters to answer each salvo with a fanfare, "disdaining to shoot one piece at any one or all of those esteemed dreadful monsters." Once engaged with the Apostles, Essex, Raleigh, Vere, and Howard vied with one another to maneuver closest to the enemy's fire, and for three hellish hours each commander kept as

A miniature Golden Hind *surmounts a trophy of silver and coconut shell given to Drake by a grateful Elizabeth.*

careful an eye on his rival as he did on the enemy. Raleigh ended this piece of mad daring by warping his ship, the *Warspite*, close enough to the *San Felipe* to grapple and board her. Essex and Howard followed suit. When the Spanish saw the English closing in on them, they cut cable, intending to slip into the inner harbor at Port Royal, but wind, tide, fire, and panic destroyed them. All four giant galleons drifted aground; two were captured and two others went up in an inferno of roaring flames and exploding cannons. Even the hardened Raleigh was horrified by the sight and wrote that if "any man had a desire to see hell itself, it was then most lively figured."

The moment the four Apostles were routed, Essex ordered his troops ashore to establish a bridgehead and prepare a bivouac. With the earl in the lead boat, beating cadence on a drum, two thousand men made an unopposed landing. It was then discovered that the peninsula was only half a mile wide at the point of landing and that Cadiz could be cut off and attacked at once. Essex led his troops on the run for three miles over soft sand to Cadiz, scaled the walls of the city at the head of a company of three hundred men, and with some fifty soldiers fought his way to the central square. Sir Francis Vere, with a larger contingent, preferred a more orthodox entrance and broke through the gates of the city to join Essex in driving the Spanish forces into the citadel of St. Philip. By nightfall, except for the castle, Cadiz lay at the mercy of English troops, who by the rules of war could do as they pleased with the inhabitants and their possessions.

The usual scene of rape, wanton destruction, and slaughter, which was the fate of most sixteenth-century cities unfortunate enough to be captured in war, did not take place, for honor required mercy as well as heroism, and the English captains kept their men under unusual control. The city fathers were allowed to ransom their lives for one hundred twenty thousand ducats; more than one hundred of the wealthiest gentlewomen were ferried to safety and were permitted to take with them much of their jewelry and as many clothes as they could wear; and more than fifteen hundred priests, monks, and women were escorted out of the city and to the mainland. Only the Dutch regiments were anxious to put the citizens to the sword, and they were restrained by Raleigh and Essex.

Even so, Cadiz was pillaged, and contrary to the queen's command, every man was allowed to keep whatever he could grab: diamonds, jewelry, gold, silks—anything that glittered and caught the eye. Protestant sailors and soldiers strutted about in clerical vestments; the streets were cluttered with furniture, books, and bedding that had been cast out of windows in the frantic search for more portable and valuable loot; and everyone seemed to have forgotten the merchant fleet and the war galleys that lay huddled in the inner harbor. Troops assigned to guard the canal leading out of Port Royal hurried off to join the sack of Cadiz, and twelve of the galleys escaped into the open sea and made it safely up the coast to Rota. The tradesmen

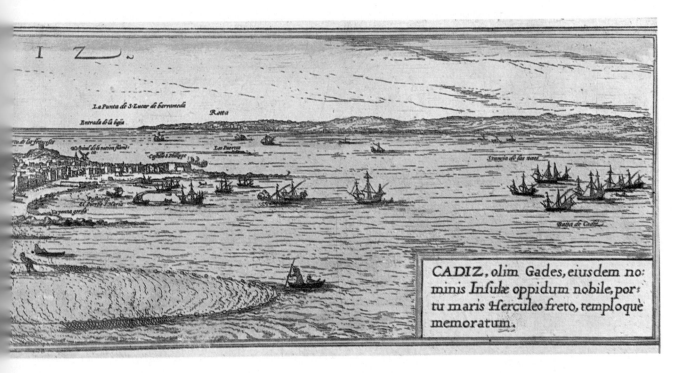

La Punta de S. Lucar de barrameda
Rotta
Entrada de la bçia

CADIZ, olim Gades, eiusdem no:
minis Insulæ oppidum nobile, por:
tu maris Herculeo freto, temploquè
memoratum.

This 1582 print shows Cadiz, with its snug harbor, dancing peasants, and fishermen. A few years later, when the English stormed in to capture the town, the scene was less idyllic.

of the city, presuming that the English had already secured the merchant fleet, offered to ransom it for two million ducats. Howard refused, demanding four million for the merchandise alone. While the Lord Admiral and the Spanish haggled, Howard's old enemy, Medina Sidonia, had his revenge upon the English in a way only a Spanish grandee could have conceived. With a splendid disregard for mercantile interests and a nobleman's contempt for trade, he ordered the burning of the entire fleet and its cargo, valued at eight to twelve million ducats.

The destruction of the merchant fleet restored a certain degree of chilly sanity to the English ranks. The leaders were worried about Elizabeth's reactions to such negligence, and Raleigh, Essex, and Howard each sent off special messengers in an effort to be first with their own highly colored versions of the victory. The Lord Admiral and Essex quarreled bitterly over whose fault the loss of the merchant fleet was, and they disagreed over the advisability of garrisoning and fortifying Cadiz. Essex was all in favor of staying on and nominated himself as the new governor of the city. He gave up this scheme after being voted down by the council of war, but he had the satisfaction of being the last Englishman to leave Cadiz before the fleet sailed homeward.

The returning heroes met with a very mixed reception at court. Elizabeth could not deny the magnitude of the victory: four of the largest galleons in the Spanish navy had been sunk or captured; thirty-six immense merchantmen, three ships loaded with ordnance and cannon shot for the war in Hol-

land, and an array of lesser craft had been burned with their cargoes; one hundred twenty thousand ducats had been paid in ransom, and the English carried home the president of the famous school of navigation at Seville in the vain expectation that he would fetch a handsome ransom. What irritated the queen was the inexcusable loss of the merchant fleet, the irresponsible and dangerously regal fashion in which Essex had cheapened the honor of knighthood by creating more than sixty knights, and the ill chance by which the West Indian treasure fleet, worth twenty million ducats, sailed into Lisbon harbor two days after the fleet had left the Spanish coast. Moreover, Elizabeth was outraged by the cavalier disregard of her orders that all plunder was to be regarded as crown property earmarked to help defray the cost of the expedition. Publicly she thanked her heroes: "Let the army know I care not so much for being queen, as that I am sovereign of such subjects"; and she allowed a popular celebration of the triumph, but limited it to London. Privately she raged at her military leaders and had her revenge upon Essex by forcing him to renounce most of his share of the plunder. Elizabeth was able to keep Raleigh's takings down to 1,769 pounds, but she could do little about the fortunes quietly pocketed by soldiers and sailors and even by her own agent, who had been sent with the fleet to look after the crown's interests. Where, Elizabeth wanted to know, was the 50,000 pounds she had invested in the venture? Essex, Raleigh, Vere, and the rest had acquired glory, but the queen had only an empty ex-

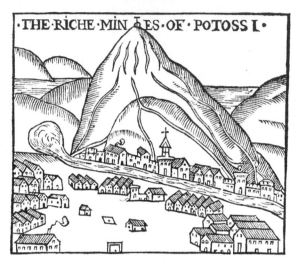

THE
DISCOVERIE AND CONQVEST
of the Prouinces of *PERV*, and
the *Nauigation in the South*
Sea, along that Coast.
And also of the ritche *Mines*
of *POTOSI*.

·THE·RICHE·MINNES·OF·POTOSSI·

❧ *Imprinted at London by* Richard Ihones. *Febru.6.1581.*

*Much of the silver coveted by the English came from Potosí,
Bolivia, shown here in the first printed view of the town.*

ZARATE, LONDON, 1581; NEW YORK PUBLIC LIBRARY, RARE BOOK ROOM

chequer, and as usual she didn't like it.

Brilliant as Raleigh's role had been at Cadiz, he
was never restored to full royal favor, though he
did regain the captaincy of the guard. Despite the
queen's annoyance at his irresponsibility, Essex remained the hero of the voyage and the queen's darling. Even so, the earl was not satisfied. Court life
did not become him. He lacked a graceful step both
in politics and on the ballroom floor. He had had to
share the honors with the old Lord Admiral Howard, and the queen persisted in turning down almost
every candidate he nominated for high office. Mo-
rosely he had to listen to the whispered truth that
he was able to get anything for himself but nothing
for his friends.

At nineteen Essex had been willing to sit at the
feet of his Faerie Queene in attitudes of courtly adoration, but by 1596 he had outgrown such love
tricks. He sought power commensurate with his
pride. He wanted a political party of his own, independent of royal favor like that of the French duke
of Guise. The beggar's role imposed on him by
Elizabeth galled his dignity; her constant rejections

insulted his ego. It seemed to Essex that only another brilliant feat of war could give him the mastery he desired at court, and he pestered Gloriana
for a sole command in yet another blow against
Spain. In June, 1597, he received his wish: the leadership of a fleet almost as large as the Cadiz expedition, and this time completely in the hands of young
heroes of "sweet conversation" and "greatness of
mind."

Great was Essex's optimism. One Dutch and
three English squadrons, totaling seventeen galleons, some seventy-five lesser vessels, and a picked
army of six thousand seasoned troops aboard twenty-
four transports, were assembled at Plymouth, with
precise orders to destroy the Spanish fleet gathering
at El Ferrol. Philip's naval resources were apparently
endless; during the winter of 1597 he had been able
to scrape together yet another armada, this time
under the experienced leadership of the *adelantado*,
or governor, of Castile, the nobleman whom Medina
Sidonia had once suggested as a captain more suitable than himself for the post of Admiral of the
Ocean Sea. Essex was instructed first to destroy the
king's fleet and naval installations "with the least
danger and loss of our people," and then to sail for
the Azores to intercept the treasure flota, seize the
island of Terceira, and establish a permanent English base there. From the start observers anticipated
nothing but evil for the voyage and gloomily predicted that the fleet at El Ferrol would not be
burned, the treasure flota would not be captured,
nor would the Azores be taken. Englishmen wondered whether the king of Spain and all his riches
were worth the risk of so many lives.

Such pessimism was quickly justified, for everything went wrong from the start. Essex, Raleigh,
and young Lord Thomas Howard commanded the
three English squadrons. Sir Francis Vere sailed as
marshal, but was chagrined to discover that the position of lieutenant of the land forces had been
given to Charles Blount, Lord Mountjoy. Essex tried
to mollify his most experienced army commander
by blaming the queen for this appointment, but
Vere suspected with reason that, since Blount belonged to the earl's following at court, it had been
made at Essex's request. For the first time the earl
was totally on his own; Howard proved himself the
better sailor, but cautiously stayed in the background, and Vere, by far the abler general, sulkily
refused to give advice.

The weather was as unreasonable and unman-
ageable as were the captains. On July 10, after weeks
of frustrating delay, the fleet sailed from Plymouth
with much fanfare, only to limp back about a week
later, having encountered heavy seas in which both

Raleigh and Essex came near to sinking. Howard rode out the fury of the gale and provokingly swept down the Spanish coast to the point of rendezvous off Corunna to wait for his chief. He returned on July 31 to discover Essex having his battered ships repaired and struggling to prevent discouraged and seasick gentlemen volunteers from deserting. Even Raleigh was moved to compassion by the earl's troubles and wrote to Cecil begging him "to work from Her Majesty some comfort to my Lord General, who, I know, is dismayed by these mischances even to death, although there could not be more done by any man upon the earth, God having turned the heavens with the fury against us, a matter beyond the power or valor, or wit of man to resist . . ."

Valor was of little avail against a perverse and maddening heaven. The wind continued to blow from the west, and the fleet remained harbor-bound until August 14, when Essex set sail, leaving behind a large part of the army. More than the weather was frustrating the Lord General. The fact of the matter was that neither the earl nor Raleigh wanted to obey the queen's explicit command to head for El Ferrol and destroy the Spanish fleet, for both men had their eyes on the plunder of the treasure flota. The burning of the Spanish fleet in port was out of the question with so few English troops available; and gales and contrary winds scattered the English ships, giving Essex an excuse for heading for the rich hunting ground of the Azores without even looking in at El Ferrol. Although the various elements of the English navy reached the Azores, riches and honor remained always just over the horizon. For Essex, bad luck, nervous dread of failure, and constant slights to his pride, seemed to be the only realities of a venture in which he almost invariably guessed wrong, failed to give adequate orders to his subordinates, and was forever chasing after mare's-nests.

They decided, while awaiting the treasure fleet, to attack the various islands of the Azores: Mountjoy was to head for St. Michael, the Dutch for Pico, Howard and Vere for Gratiosa, and Essex and Raleigh for Fayal. While Raleigh's squadron was taking on water, Essex suddenly rushed off to seek the fleet of the *adelantado*, who was reported to have left El Ferrol to meet and escort the West Indian fleet from the Azores to Spain. Hurriedly the earl ordered Raleigh to meet him at Fayal, but failed to mention the fact that he himself would not arrive there for several days. When Sir Walter's squadron reached its anchorage off Horta, he found no Essex, and to make matters worse, the people of Horta rapidly began to clear the town of all valuables and to disappear into the hills. For three days Raleigh waited while his men watched the dream

of plunder vanish before their eyes. The problem was again the sticky question of honor and command. Essex and Raleigh had been assigned to seize the island together. Moreover, the earl was the senior officer of the fleet and was expected to assume command and have the first bid at glory. Raleigh, on the other hand, had been left without instructions, and he did not regard himself as being inferior in authority to Essex. As he put it, he was one of the principal commanders of the fleet and as such was not subject to the queen's patents prohibiting captains from acting without orders.

If Raleigh's landing on Fayal had not so redounded to his honor, Essex might not have been so infuriated. Sir Walter led his men ashore in face of Spanish troops entrenched on the beach, forced his way into the town of Horta, and won immense renown by risking his life, first by walking nonchalantly across the field of fire without his helmet or armor and then by reconnoitering enemy territory. In this second venture he had asked for volunteers, but when no one spoke up he scornfully announced he would go himself. Donning his helmet and breastplate and accompanied by his cousin, Sir Arthur Gorges, he crawled forward against heavy Spanish musket fire. Both men were wearing gaily colored scarves that attracted the enemy's attention; bullets tore at Raleigh's clothing and a shot grazed Gorges' leg, but neither of the heroes would doff the conspicuous garments, being unwilling "to do the Spaniards so much honor" by removing their colors. Raleigh's charmed life remained impervious to Spanish shells, and both men won great esteem for one of the more senseless performances of the entire expedition.

Next morning, when Essex finally put in an appearance, the entire island, except the fort above the town, was in English hands, and a jubilant Raleigh rowed out to see his commander. He met with an icy reception, and some of the lesser officers around the earl actually urged him to court-martial and execute his disobedient vice-admiral. Eventually Thomas Howard made peace between the two men. Essex accepted a rather grudging apology from Raleigh for his unauthorized landing, and revenged himself by omitting all mention of Sir Walter's exploits in his official report to the queen.

Tension between the two leaders was not eased by the discovery that the Spanish in the fort had made off while the English captains bickered, taking with them almost everything worth plundering and leaving behind a Dutch and an English prisoner, each with his throat cut. Further acrimony was forestalled for the moment by a report of the approach of the treasure flota. Essex spread a cordon about the island of Terceira, with its heavily fortified port of Angra, but he was so worried that the Spanish fleet might elude him, he kept changing his position. Three hours after he had moved his ships, the entire West Indian fleet, rich with the treasures of the New World, majestically sailed to safety into Angra through the very place that Essex had evacuated. There was not even to be a consolation prize. A huge 1,800-ton carrack, which was almost trapped by Raleigh, escaped capture by running itself aground near the town of St. Michael. The Spaniards rushed out in small boats and rescued the crew and some of the cargo before burning the ship. Essex had gone off to seize the town of Villa Franca so as to approach St. Michael from the rear while Raleigh continued his blockade of the harbor. The army, however, discovered vast quantities of wine and melons at Villa Franca and failed to make the planned attack on St. Michael. Raleigh and the sailors all pointed out that if Essex and the army had done their part, the plunder of the great carrack would have fallen to the English.

As Essex cruised disconsolately and aimlessly about the Azores, reluctantly making up his mind to return home sans honor and sans profit to face the anger of the queen and the smiles of all his ill-wishers at court, England lay exposed to invasion by the fleet that Elizabeth had wanted to be burned at El Ferrol. Urged on by a dying Philip, who sought one last chance to achieve God's purpose against the heretics, the *adelantado* of Castile set sail from El Ferrol on October 9 with 136 ships, 4,000 sailors, and 9,000 soldiers. The Spanish planned to seize the Channel port of Falmouth for their base of operations, deposit a garrison there, and then turn out to sea again to await the arrival of Essex's fleet from the Azores. Whatever the merits or demerits of such a scheme—and certainly it had the advantage of catching the English totally unprepared—once again the heavens intervened: the autumn gales blew, and the winds dispersed the Spanish fleet as the English squadron swept homeward, each of its captains frantic to be first with his own version of the miserable failure.

The queen was thoroughly irked by her heroic children, and with good reason. She blamed Essex for having left her realm defenseless while he gallivanted without profit about the Azores, and she showed unusual self-restraint when she limited her criticism to the weary remark: "When we do look back to the beginning of this action which hath stirred so great expectation in the world and charged us so deeply, we cannot but be sorry to foresee already how near all our expectations and your great hopes are to a fruitless conclusion." Evidently Eliz-

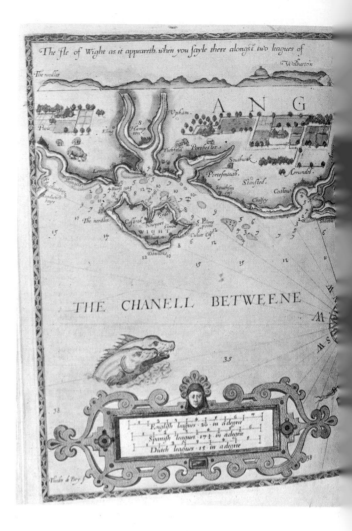

The English Channel ports, from which expeditions against Spain set sail, are shown on this 1588 chart.

abeth had finally learned the true worth of her Essex. She had known what to expect and had prepared herself for a "fruitless conclusion."

While Raleigh strutted like a peacock or withdrew into a mantle of cold contempt, and Essex alternated between spells of boyish enthusiasm and petulant temper tantrums, Elizabeth turned more and more to a nobleman of different mettle. Robert Cecil, the hunchbacked son of Lord Burghley, had received from his father some sound if sententious advice on how to succeed in the Elizabethan world. "Toward thy superiors," he warned, "be humble yet generous; with thy equals familiar yet respective; toward thy inferiors show much humility and some familiarity"; for "the first prepares the way to thy advancement; the second makes thee known for a man well bred; the third gains a good report which once gotten may be safely kept." Then the wise old Lord Treasurer drove home his lesson by examples from his son's generation. "Yet do I advise thee not to affect nor neglect popularity too much. Seek not to be E[ssex] and shun to be R[aleigh]."

The advice was well taken and carefully learned,

for Robert Cecil rose to be the principal minister of both Elizabeth and James I, whereas Essex and Raleigh consumed themselves, their fortunes, and ultimately their lives in the fires of their own megalomania. Essex, like Coriolanus, so forgot himself and his ordained place in society that he endeavored to usurp a function not properly his own: the right to rule. An inflated ego led him into treason during the twilight of the great queen's reign, but here we are getting ahead of our story.

Raleigh's destruction came more slowly. His fate was to live on after the Elizabethan age, a fallen Lucifer whose pride could not be suffered by contemporaries because it was sustained by extraordinary talent. Society might have accepted Sir Walter Raleigh's brilliant versatility—soldier and businessman, sailor and scientist, explorer and poet, colonizer and musician, shipbuilder and historian—but it could not stomach the damnable laughter with which he dismissed a world that had permitted him to excel.

> Tell potentates, they live
> Acting by others' action;

Not loved unless they give,
Not strong but by affection:
If potentates reply,
Give potentates the lie.

. . . .

Tell men of high condition,
That manage the estate,
Their purpose is ambition,
Their practice only hate:
And if they once reply,
Then give them all the lie.

. . . .

Tell zeal it wants devotion;
Tell love it is but lust:
Tell time it is but motion,
Tell flesh it is but dust:
And wish them not reply
For thou must give the lie.

. . . .

Tell physic of her boldness;
Tell skill it is pretention;
Tell charity of coldness;
Tell law it is contention:
And as they do reply,
So give them still the lie.

It was left for a Stuart king to strike off the head of the man who delighted in giving the lie to the very standards by which he chose to live.

Doubtless there was a fundamental rottenness about the final decade of Gloriana's reign, an artificiality that the tinsel of the court could conceal no more than cosmetics could hide the fact that the queen was growing old and ugly. Years later, after emotional exhaustion had set in and society had grown tired of its heroes, Raleigh looked back upon the heroic age and sadly confessed that "all is vanity and weariness." But Sir Walter added one last nostalgic comment: it had been "such a weariness and vanity that we shall ever complain of it and love it for all that." It had been good to be alive in those days when men had lived like gods. Humanity had enjoyed even its weariness and had gloried in the vanity of life, because the great feats of heroism had not been done solely for reasons of greed and egotism. Insatiable curiosity, the excitement of discovery, and above all imagination had urged Drake on around the world, had sustained Gilbert's dream of colonizing a new land, and had filled the heart of Essex. Lust for glory, plunder, and immortality drove them on, but so did the wonderful romance and secret fear of new worlds to conquer, new universes to comprehend, new gods to worship, and new horizons to lure them onward to "the discovery of things which were hidden from other men."

THE WORLD ENCOMPASSED

The sixteenth-century world was one of contrast and contradiction, one in which men of intellectual audacity called dogma into doubt and accepted only the evidence of their own observations—and then abandoned the results of their labors to toady to dogmatic authority. In an age when Copernicus dared challenge the wisdom of the ancients, other men of the highest intelligence applied the closest reasoning to problems—such as witchcraft—that existed only in their own superstition-ridden imaginations. While men like Francis Drake perpetrated appalling cruelties in the name of God, queen, and country, the queen herself could procrastinate indefinitely in an agony of soul-searching before ordering the death of a traitor. While men like Tycho Brahe made a modern science of astronomy, other, equally learned men soberly recorded the anatomical characteristics of such non-existent beings as mermen and "men whose heads do grow beneath their shoulders." Fortune hunters like Raleigh and his half brother, Sir Humphrey Gilbert, risked and lost all pursuing legendary cities of gold while others like Cortes and Pizarro calmly took possession of empires golden beyond men's imagining. The literature of the sixteenth century reflects the uneven temper of the times; Elizabeth herself could move the most hard-bitten members of Parliament to tears with an extemporaneous address from the heart, and James I, in a meticulously considered treatise on daemonic possession, could turn out some of the most turgid prose ever composed. Deeds of daring could be recorded as plainly as if they were merchants' inventories, and incidental descriptions of the terrain en route to those adventures could rival any descriptive writing in English. A selection of the writings and speeches of Elizabethan scientists, pseudo scientists, philosophers, adventurers, travelers, chroniclers, and statesmen appears on the following pages.

Elizabethan science was in part a quest for the unknowable. In this print two alchemists vainly try to distil the "elixir of life."

RALEIGH IN GUIANA

In 1595 Sir Walter Raleigh organized an expedition that he hoped would lead to El Dorado, the fabled city of gold supposedly hidden in the wilderness of Guiana. Raleigh was by then a tired, aging man, and the expedition foundered in its ascent of the Orinoco River. It returned to England the next year with only a few specimens of ore and the manuscript of Raleigh's The Discovery of Guiana. *The book, one of the greatest travel journals in English, was to remain the only real treasure the expedition produced. Here Raleigh describes life on the Orinoco.*

These Tiuitinas are a very goodly people and very valiant, and have the most manly speech and most deliberate that ever I heard of what nation soever. In the summer they have houses on the ground as in other places: in the winter they dwell upon the trees, where they build very artificial towns and villages, as it is written in the Spanish story of the West Indies, that those people do in the lowlands near the Gulf of Uraba: for between May and September the river of Orinoco riseth thirty foot upright, and then are those islands overflown twenty foot high above the level of the ground, saving some few raised grounds in the middle of them: and for this cause they are enforced to live in this manner. They never eat of any thing that is set or sown, and as at home they use neither planting nor other manurance, so when they come abroad they refuse to feed of aught but of that which nature without labor bringeth forth. They use the tops of palmettos for bread, and kill deer, fish, and porks for the rest of their sustenance; they have also many sorts of fruits that grow in the woods, and great variety of birds and fowl.

And if to speak of them were not tedious and vulgar, surely we saw in those passages of very rare colors and forms, not elsewhere to be found, for as much as I have either seen or read. Of these people those that dwell upon the branches of Orinoco called Capury and Macareo are for the most part carpenters of Canoas, for they make the most and fairest houses, and sell them into Guiana for gold, and into Trinidad for tobacco, in the excessive taking whereof they exceed all nations, and notwithstanding the moistness of the air in which they live, the hardness of their diet, and the great labors they suffer to hunt, fish, and fowl for their living in all my life either in the Indies or in Europe did I never behold a more goodly or better-favored people, or a more manly. They were wont to make war upon all nations, and especially on the cannibals, so as none durst without a good strength trade by those rivers, but of late they are at peace with their neighbors, all holding the Spaniards for a common enemy. When their commanders die they use great lamentation, and when they think the flesh of their bodies is putrified and fallen from the bones, then they take up the carcass again, and hang it in the cacique's house that died, and deck his skull with feathers of all colors, and hang all his gold plates about the bones of his arms, thighs, and legs. Those nations which are called Arawak which dwell on the south of Orinoco (of which place and nation our Indian pilot was) are dispersed in many other places and do use to beat the bones of their lords into powder, and their wives and friends drink it all in their several sorts of drinks.

For Raleigh, El Dorado was always just around the next bend in the river. He avidly collected—and passed along—the most outrageous travelers' tales of cities, even countries, that were built of pure gold.

All the vessels of his house, table, and kitchen were of gold and silver, and the meanest of silver and copper for strength and hardness of metal. He had in his wardrobe hollow statues of gold which seemed giants, and the figures in proportion and bigness of all the beasts, birds, trees, and herbs, that the earth bringeth forth: and of all the fishes that the sea or waters of his kingdom breedeth. He had also robes, budgets, chests, and troughs of gold and silver, heaps of billets of gold that seemed wood, marked out to burn. Finally there was nothing in his country whereof he had not the counterfeit in gold: Yea and they say the Incas had a garden of pleasure in an island . . . where they went to recreate themselves, when they would take the air of the sea, which had all kind of garden herbs, flowers and trees of gold and silver, an invention and magnificence till then never seen.

Raleigh harbored a lifelong hatred for Spain and seldom missed a chance to remark on Spanish perfidy. Nor did his eye for the ladies dim with advancing years; here he strikes a somewhat wistful note in telling of the restraint of his men in the face of temptation.

This Arawakan pilot with the rest, fearing that we would have eaten them, or otherwise have put them to some cruel death, for the Spaniards to the end that none of the people in the passage towards Guiana or in Guiana itself might come to speak with us, persuaded all the nations that we were maneaters and cannibals: but when the poor men and women had seen us, and that we gave them meat, and to every one something or other, which was rare and strange to them, they began to conceive the deceit and purpose of the Spaniards, who indeed (as they confessed) took from them both their wives and daughters daily and used them for the satisfying of their own lusts, especially such as they took in this manner by strength. But I protest before the majesty of the living God that I neither know nor believe that any of our company, one or other, by violence or otherwise, even knew any of their women, and yet we saw many hundreds and had many in our power, and of those very young and excellently favored which came among us without deceit, stark naked.

Nothing got us more love amongst them than this usage, for I suffered not any man to take from any of the nations so much as a pina or a potato root, without giving them contentment, nor any man so much as to offer to touch any of their wives or daughters: which cause so contrary to the Spaniards (who tyrannize over them in all things) drew them to admire Her Majesty, whose commandment I told them it was, and also wonderfully to honor our nation.

But I confess it was a very impatient work to keep the meaner sort from spoil and stealing when we came to their houses, which by cause in all I could not prevent, I caused my Indian interpreter at every place when we departed to know of the loss or wrong done, and if aught were stolen or taken by violence, either the same was restored, and the party punished in their sight, or else was paid for to their utmost demand. They also much wondered at us after they heard that we had slain the Spaniards at Trinidad, for they were before resolved that no nation of Christians durst abide their presence, and they wondered more when I had made them know of the great overthrow that Her Majesty's army and fleet had given them of late years in their own countries.

Raleigh recounts his activities as the queen's public relations man.

We then hastened away toward our purposed discovery, and first I called all the captains of the island together that were enemies to the Spaniards, for there were some which Berrio had brought out of other countries and planted there to eat out and waste those that were natural of the place, and by my Indian interpreter, which I carried out of England, I made them understand that I was the servant of a queen, who was the great cacique of the north, and a virgin, and had more caciques under her than there were trees in that island: that she was an enemy to the Castelani [Spaniards] to respect of their tyranny and oppression, and that she delivered all such nations about her as were by them opressed, and having freed all the coast of the northern world from their servitude had sent me to free them also, and with all to defend the country of Guiana from their invasion and conquest. I showed them Her Majesty's picture, which they so admired and honored, as it had been easy to have brought them idolatrous thereof.

Although Raleigh cut a flamboyant figure at court and in his various escapades, as a literary stylist he was considerably more restrained than most of his contemporaries and free of the bombast that characterized much of even the greatest Elizabethan literature. His straightforward descriptive passages, uncluttered with metaphor and classical allusion, are remarkably vivid and immediate.

Upon this river one Captain George that I took with Berrio told me there was a great silver mine, and that it was near the banks of the said river. But by this time as well Orinoco, Caroni, and all the rest of the rivers were risen four or five foot in height, so as it was not possible by the strength of any men, or with any boat whatsoever to row into the river against the stream. I therefore sent Captain Thyn, Captain Grenville, my nephew John Gilbert, my cousin Butshead Gorges, Captain Clarke, and some thirty shot more to coast the river by land, and to go to a town some twenty miles over the valley called Amnatapoi, and they found guides there, to go farther toward the mountainfoot to another great town, called Capurepana, belonging to a cacique called Haharacoa (that was a nephew to old Topiawari king of Arromaia our chiefest friend), because this town and province of Capurepana adjoined to Macareguarai, which was a frontier town of the empire: and the meanwhile myself with Captain Gifford, Captain Calfield, Edward Hancocke, and some half a dozen shot marched overland to view the strange overfalls of the river of Caroni which roared so far off, and also to see the plains adjoining and the rest of the province of Canuri: I sent also Captain Whiddon, W. Connocke, and some eight shot with them, to see if they could find any mineral stone alongst the riverside. When we run to the tops of the first hills of the plains adjoining to the river, we beheld that wonderful breach of waters, which ran down Caroni: and might from that mountain see the river how it ran in three parts, about twenty miles off, and there appeared from ten or twelve overfalls in sight, every one as high over the other as a churchtower, which fell with that fury, that the rebound of water made it seem as if it had been all covered over with a great shower of rain: and in some places we took it at the first for a smoke that had risen over some great town. For mine own part I was well persuaded from thence to have returned, being a very ill footman, but the rest were all so desirous to go near the said strange thunder of waters, as they drew me on by little and little, till we came into the next valley where we might better discern the same. I never saw a more beautiful country, nor more lively prospects, hills so raised here and there over the valleys, the river winding into diverse branches, the plains adjoining without bush or stubble, all fair green grass, the ground of hard sand easy to march on, either for horse or foot, the deer crossing in every path, the birds toward the evening singing on every tree with a thousand feverish tunes, cranes and herons of white, crimson, and carnation perching in the riverside, the air fresh with a gentle easterly wind, and every stone that we stooped to take up, promised either gold or silver by his complexion.

Despite ill health and a waning enthusiasm for the rigors of jungle life, Raleigh's curiosity about native life and customs remained lively. Here he describes an epic drinking bout staged by the Guianans.

Those Guianans . . . are marvelous great drunkards, in which vice I think no nation can compare with them and at the times of their solemn feasts when the emperor carouseth with his captains, tributaries, and governors, the manner is thus. All those that pledge him are first stripped naked, and their bodies annointed all over with a kind of white balm (by them called Curcas) of which there is great plenty and yet very dear amongst them, and it is of all other the most precious, whereof we have had good experience: when they are annointed all over, certain servants of the emperor having prepared gold made into a fine powder blow it through hollow canes unto their naked bodies, until they be all shining from the foot to the head, and in this sort they sit drinking by twenties and hundreds and continue in drunkeness sometimes six or seven days together . . .

all from The Discovery of Guiana *by Sir Walter Raleigh*

THE NEWFOUND-LAND EXPEDITION

In 1583 four English ships anchored at St. John's, Newfoundland, where Sir Humphrey Gilbert claimed the land in the queen's name. After some weeks spent gathering information about the country's natural resources, Gilbert set sail for England. The encounter with an aquatic "lion" (most probably a walrus), described here by Edward Hare, was thought a good omen, but the trip ended disastrously.

So upon Saturday in the afternoon of the thirty-first of August, we changed our course and returned back for England, at which very instant, even in winding about, there passed along between us and toward the land which we now forsook a very lion to our seeming, in shape, hair, and color, not swimming after the manner of a beast by moving of his feet, but rather sliding upon the water with his whole body (excepting the legs) in sight, neither yet diving under and again rising above the water, as the manner is of whales, dolphins, tunnies, porpoises, and all other fish, but confidently showing himself above water without hiding; notwithstanding, we presented ourselves in open view and gesture to amaze him, as all creatures will be commonly at a sudden gaze and sight of men. Thus he passed along turning his head to and fro, yawning and gaping wide, with ugly demonstration of long teeth and glaring eyes, and to bid us a farewell (coming right against the *Hind*) he sent forth a horrible voice, roaring or bellowing as doth a lion, which spectacle we all beheld so far as we were able to discern the same, as men prone to wonder at every strange thing, as this doubtless was, to see a lion in the ocean sea, or fish in shape of a lion. What opinion others had thereof, and chiefly the general himself, I forbear to deliver. But he took it for *bonum omen* . . .

With his little fleet reduced to only two ships, the Golden Hind *and the altogether inadequate* Squirrel, *Gilbert rashly chose the smaller vessel as his flagship. Hare describes the voyage's end.*

But when he was entreated by the captain, master, and other his well-willers of the *Hind* not to venture in the frigate, this was his answer. "I will not forsake my little company going homeward, with whom I have passed so many storms and perils." And in very truth he was urged to be so over hard by hard reports given of him that he was afraid of the sea, albeit this was rather rashness than advised resolution, to prefer the wind of a vain report to the weight of his own life. Seeing he would not bend to reason, he had provision out of the *Hind*, such as was wanting aboard his frigate. And so we committed him to God's protection and set him aboard his pinnace, we being more than three hundred leagues onward of our way home.

By that time we had brought the islands of Azores south of us; yet we then keeping much to the north, until we had got into the height and elevation of England, we met with very foul weather and terrible seas, breaking short and high,

pyramid-wise. The reason whereof seemed to proceed either of hilly grounds high and low within the sea (as we see hills and dales upon the land), upon which the seas do mount and fall, or else the cause proceedeth of diversity of winds, shifting often in sundry points, all which having power to move the great ocean, which again is not presently settled, so many seas do encounter together, as there had been diversity of winds. Howsoever it cometh to pass, men which all their lifetime had occupied the sea never saw more outrageous seas. We had also upon our mainyard an apparition of a little fire by night, which seamen do call Castor and Pollux. But we had only one, which they take an evil sign of more tempest. The same is usual in storms.

Monday, the ninth of September, in the afternoon, the frigate was near cast away, oppressed by waves yet at that time recovered; and giving forth signs of joy, the general sitting abaft with a book in his hand, cried out to us in the *Hind* (so oft as we did approach within hearing), "We are as near to heaven by sea as by land," reiterating the same speech, well beseeming a soldier resolute in Jesus Christ, as I can testify he was.

On the same Monday night, about twelve o'clock, or not long after, the frigate being ahead of us in the *Golden Hind*, suddenly her lights were out, whereof as it were in a moment we lost the sight, and withal our watch cried the general was cast away, which was too true; for in that moment the frigate was devoured and swallowed up of the sea. Yet still we looked out all that night and ever after, until we arrived upon the coast of England, omitting no small sail at sea, unto which we gave not the tokens between us agreed upon to have perfect knowledge of each other, if we should at any time be separated.

THE SEARCH FOR RICHES

In 1577 Sir Francis Drake embarked on a voyage, ostensibly of exploration but actually of piracy. Three years later, having circled the globe, he sailed into Plymouth Sound. This account of Drake's adventures off western South America was written by a crew member.

When Francis Drake had passed the Strait of Magellan, the first land he fell with was an island named Mocha, where he came to an anchor, and hosing out his boat, he with ten of his company went on shore, thinking there to have taken in fresh water. Two of the company going far into the island were intercepted and cut off by the Indians that inhabit the island, who, as soon as they saw our men come to anchor, thought they would come on land (as they did indeed), and laid an ambush of about one hundred Indians; and when our boat was fast on ground and all the men gone on land, the ambush broke out and set upon them, and before they could recover their boat and get her on float, they hurt all our men very sore with their arrows. Their names which went on shore were these following: Francis Drake, John Bruer, John Marten, Thomas Flud, Tom Bruer, great Nele a Dane, little Nele a Fleming, John Gripe, John Mariner, Gregory Rayment, and Diego a black Moor, which was Drake's man; of which company two, namely Tom Bruer and Tom Flud, were intercepted by the Indians and there lost, and great Nele the Dane, their gunner, and Diego the black Moor died of their wounds; the rest escaped their wounds and were cured. They stayed here but one day, but set sail toward the coast of Chile, where arriving they met with an Indian in a canoe near the shore, who thinking them to have been Spaniards, told that behind them, at a place called Santiago, there was a Spanish ship, for which good news they gave him diverse trifles. The Indian being joyful thereof went on shore and brought them two sheep and a small quantity of fish, and so they returned back again to Santiago to seek the Spanish ship (for they had overshot the place before they were ware); and when they came thither, they found the same ship and in her three Negroes and eight Spaniards; they of the ship, thinking Drake's to have been Spaniards, welcomed them with a drum and made ready a great barrel of wine of Chile to have made them drink; but when Drake's men were entered, one of them, whose name was Tom Moone, struck the Spanish pilot with his fist on the face, saying *"Abassho pirra,"* which is to say in English, "Go down, dog," and then the poor Spaniards being sore afraid went down into the hold of the ship, all saving one of them, who, leaping out at the stern of the ship swam on shore and gave warning to them of the town of their coming. When Drake had taken this ship and stowed the men under hatches, he took her boat and his own boat and manned them both with his men, and went to set upon the town of Santiago, having not passed eight or nine small houses, and coming on shore, he found all the people fled, and rifled their houses, and broke open a warehouse, wherein he found certain wine of Chile, which he brought with him into his ship; also he found there a chapel, which he rifled and took from thence a chalice of silver and two cruets of silver . . . and the altar cloth, all which he took away with him and brought them on board, and gave the spoil of that chapel to Mr. Fletcher, his preacher, at his coming on board; and then he set all of the men of the Spanish ship on shore, saving one John Grego, a Greek born, whom he took with him to be his pilot to bring him into the harbor of Lima. This Spanish ship Drake took along with him and rifled her, and found in her great store of wine of Chile, and about four hundred pounds weight of gold of Baldivia, which is a city and lies about four leagues from Santiago up into the land, from whence cometh the best gold of all Peru. This ship's name was the *Grand Capitayne.* So he carrying the *Grand Capitayne* along with him, arrived at a place called Coquimbo, where thinking to have watered, he sent fourteen of his men on land to fetch water. But they had not long arrived ere there came toward them to have intercepted them three hundred horsemen and two hundred footmen, Spaniards, very bravely furnished, whereby Drake's men were fain to wade into the sea a good space onto a rock and lay underneath the side thereof from the Spaniard; but one of their men being on that side of the rock next the Spaniard, thought to have shot at the Spaniards, and a Spanish horseman shot him through the head with his piece and slew him; and they shot diverse pieces at Drake's men that lay under the rock, but they could not come at them. Then at length the boat came on shore under the rock and set them on board, and so saved them from that danger. When they were gone on board, the Spaniards waded to the rock and set Drake's man on shore and cut out his heart, and cut off his head and stuck it upon a spears point and carried it away before them. These Spaniards were of a city called La Serena, a league distant from Coquimbo. When they were departed, Drake came with his boat on shore and buried his man's body without a head, and so made sail to depart, and at his departure the Spaniards came to the sea side with a flag of truce, but Drake would trust none of them, but set sail and bent his course toward a place called Arica, where he found in the harbor three small barks, and rifling them, he found in one of them fifty-seven slabs of fine silver weighing about twenty pounds weight each of them. These slabs were about the bigness of a brick bat each one of them, and one of the two other barks was set on fire by one Fuller and one Tom Marcks, and so burned to the very water. There were not in those three barks one person, for they mistrusting no thieves were all gone on shore. In this town of Arica were about twenty houses, which Drake would have set upon if he had had more company with him, but wanting company of pirates he departed hence, having still with him the *Grand Capitayne* of Santiago; but within one day after he was gone from this harbor of Arica, he cast off the *Grand Capitayne,* clapping her helm fast on the lee and let her drive seaward without any creature in her. From hence he sailed toward Lima, and by the way he met a small bark, and in her he found good store of linen cloth, whereof he took good store away to serve his own turn; and here he had news of the *Cacafoga,* which was gone toward Paita, after whom he bent his course. At his departure from the harbor of Lima he cut all the cables of the ships there and let them drive to seaward, and so made speed toward Paita, thinking there to have found the *Cacafoga,* but she was gone before he arrived there toward Panama, whom he still followed amain; but between Paita and Cape St. Francis he met with a bark laden with ropes and tackle for ships. This ship he rifled, and found in her about eighty-pound weight of gold, and he took out of her great quantity of ropes to store his own ship, and so let her go. The owner of this ship was a friar. He found also in her a great crucifix of gold, and certain emeralds near as long as a man's finger. From this robbery following still after the *Cacafoga,* he overtook her at Cape St. Francis, whom he had long wished for. In his journey he promised that whosoever should overtake her should have his chain of gold for his labor. This did John Drake descry on St. David's Day, being the first of March, about eight of the clock; and in the boarding of her he shot down her mizzenmast, and so entered her, and found in her about eighty-pound weight of gold, and thirteen chests full of royals of plate, and so much silver as did ballast the *Golden Hind.* In her return into England this ship he carried with him three or four days, and then he unladed her and let her depart; the pilot's name was Don Francisco, who had two cups of silver gilt clean over, to whom Drake said at his departure as followeth: Seignior Pilot, you have two cups and I must needs have one of them, which the Pilot yielded unto willingly, because he could not choose.

all from Voyages and Documents *by Richard Hakluyt*

CORTES IN MEXICO

The conquistador Bernal Diaz del Castillo served in the New World under five commanders. Late in the sixteenth century, when he was in his eighties, he recalled vividly Cortes' Mexican conquest of 1519.

Gazing on such wonderful sights, we did not know what to say, or whether what appeared before us was real, for on one side, on the land, there were great cities, and in the lake ever so many more, and the lake itself was crowded with canoes, and in the causeway were many bridges at intervals, and in front of us stood the great city of Mexico, and we—we did not even number four hundred soldiers! and we well remembered the words and warnings given us by the people of Huexotzingo and Tlaxcala, and the many other warnings that had been given that we should beware of entering Mexico, where they would kill us, as soon as they had us inside.

Let the curious readers consider whether there is not much to ponder over in this that I am writing. What men have there been in the world who have shown such daring? But let us get on, and march along the causeway. When we arrived where another small causeway branches off [leading to Coyoacan, which is another city] where there were some buildings like towers, which are their oratories, many more chieftains and caciques approached clad in very rich mantles, the brilliant liveries of one chieftain differing from those of another, and the causeways were crowded with them. The Great Montezuma had sent these great caciques in advance to receive us, and when they came before Cortes they bade us welcome in their language, and as a sign of peace, they touched their hands against the ground, and kissed the ground with the hand.

There we halted for a good while, and Cacamatzin, the Lord of Texcoco, and the Lord of Iztapalapa and the Lord of Tacuba and the Lord of Coyoacan went on in advance to meet the Great Montezuma, who was approaching in a rich litter accompanied by other great Lords and caciques, who owned vassals. When we arrived near to Mexico, where there were some other small towers, the Great Montezuma got down from his litter, and those great Caciques supported him with their arms beneath a marvelously rich canopy of green colored feathers with much gold and silver embroidery and with pearls and chalchihuites suspended from a sort of bordering, which was wonderful to look at. The Great Montezuma was richly attired according to his usage, and he was shod with sandals, the soles were of gold and the upper part adorned with precious stones. The four chieftains who supported his arms were also richly clothed according to their usage, in garments which were apparently held ready for them on the road to enable them to accompany their prince, for they did not appear in such attire when they came to receive us. Besides these four chieftains, there were four other great caciques who supported the canopy over their heads, and many other Lords who walked before the Great Montezuma, sweeping the ground where he would tread and spreading cloths on it, so that he should not tread on the earth. Not one of these Chieftains dared even to think of looking him in the face, but kept their eyes lowered with great reverence, except those four relations, his nephews, who supported him with their arms.

When Cortes was told that the Great Montezuma was approaching, and he saw him coming, he dismounted from his horse, and when he was near Montezuma, they simultaneously paid great reverence to one another. Montezuma bade him welcome and our Cortes replied through Doña Marina wishing him very good health. And it seems to me that Cortes, through Doña Marina, offered him his right hand, and Montezuma did not wish to take it, but he did give his hand to Cortes and then Cortes brought out a necklace which he had ready at hand, made of glass stones, which I have already said are called Margaritas, which have within them many patterns of diverse colors, these were strung on a cord of gold and with musk so that it should have a sweet scent, and he placed it round the neck of the Great Montezuma and when he had so placed it he was going to embrace him, and those great Princes who accompanied Montezuma held back Cortes by the arm so that he should not embrace him, for they considered it an indignity.

Then Cortes through the mouth of Doña Marina told him that now his heart rejoiced at having seen such a great Prince, and that he took it as a great honor that he had come in person to meet him and had frequently shown him such favor.

Then Montezuma spoke other words of politeness to him, and told two of his nephews who supported his arms, the Lord of Texcoco and the Lord of Coyoacan, to go with us and show us to our quarters, and Montezuma with his other two relations, the Lord of Cuitlahuac and the Lord of Tacuba who accompanied him, returned to the city, and all those grand companies of caciques and chieftains who had come with him returned in his train. As they turned back after their Prince we stood watching them and observed how they all marched with their eyes fixed on the ground without looking at him, keeping close to the wall, following him with great reverence. Thus space was made for us to enter the streets of Mexico, without being so much crowded. But who could now count the multitude of men and women and boys who were in the streets and on the azoteas, and in canoes on the canals, who had come out to see us. It was indeed wonderful, and, now that I am writing about it, it all comes before my eyes as though it had happened but yesterday. Coming to think it over it seems to be a great mercy that our Lord Jesus Christ was pleased to give us grace and courage to dare to enter into such a city; and for the many times He has saved me from danger of death, as will be seen later on, I give Him sincere thanks, and in that He has preserved me to write about it, although I cannot do it as fully as is fitting or the subject needs. Let us make no words about it, for deeds are the best witnesses to what I say here and elsewhere.

Let us return to our entry to Mexico. They took us to lodge in some large houses, where there were apartments for all of us, for they had belonged to the father of the Great Montezuma, who was named Axayaca, and at that time Montezuma kept there the great oratories for his idols, and a secret chamber where he kept bars and jewels of gold, which was the treasure that he had inherited from his father

Axayaca, and he never disturbed it. They took us to lodge in that house, because they called us Teules, and took us for such, so that we should be with the Idols or Teules which were kept there. However, for one reason or another, it was there they took us, where there were great halls and chambers canopied with the cloth of the country for our Captain, and for every one of us beds of matting with canopies above, and no better bed is given, however great the chief may be, for they are not used. And all these palaces were coated with shining cement and swept and garlanded.

As soon as we arrived and entered into the great court, the Great Montezuma took our Captain by the hand, for he was there awaiting him, and led him to the apartment and saloon where he was to lodge, which was very richly adorned according to their usage, and he had at hand a very rich necklace made of golden crabs, a marvelous piece of work, and Montezuma himself placed it round the neck of our Captain Cortes, and greatly astonished his [own] Captains by the great honor that he was bestowing on him. When the necklace had been fastened, Cortes thanked Montezuma through our interpreters, and Montezuma replied—"Malinche, you and your brethren are in your own house, rest awhile," and then he went to his palaces, which were not far away, and we divided our lodgings by companies, and placed the artillery pointing in a convenient direction, and the order which we had to keep was clearly explained to us, and that we were to be much on the alert, both the cavalry and all of us soldiers. A sumptuous dinner was provided for us according to their use and custom, and we ate it at once. So this was our lucky and daring entry into the great city of Tenochtitlan Mexico on the eighth day of November the year of our Saviour Jesus Christ, 1519.

Montezuma, the Aztec emperor, vainly tried to rid Mexico of Cortes, first by force, then with bribes. Finally he received the invaders at Tenochtitlan. Here Diaz describes the state of uneasy cordiality that prevailed until the emperor was openly made a hostage.

He also told them that, in course of time, our Lord and king would send some men who among us lead very holy lives, much better than we do, who will explain to them all about it, for at present we merely came to give them due warning, and so he prayed him to do what he was asked and carry it into effect.

As Montezuma appeared to wish to reply, Cortes broke off his argument, and to all of us who were with him he said: "With this we have done our duty considering it is the first attempt."

Montezuma replied: "Señor Malinche, I have understood your words and arguments very well before now, from what you said to my servants at the sand dunes, this about three Gods and the Cross, and all those things that you have preached in the towns through which you have come. We have not made any answer to it because here throughout all time we have worshiped our own gods, and thought they were good, as no doubt yours are, so do not trouble to speak to us any more about them at present. Regarding the creation of the world, we have held the same belief for ages past, and for this reason we take it for certain that you are those

whom our ancestors predicted would come from the direction of the sunrise. As for your great King, I feel that I am indebted to him, and I will give him of what I possess, for as I have already said, two years ago I heard of the captains who came in ships from the direction in which you came, and they said that they were the servants of this your great King, and I wish to know if you are all one and the same."

Cortes replied: Yes, that we were all brethren and servants of our Emperor, and that those men came to examine the way and the seas and the ports so as to know them well in order that we might follow as we had done. Montezuma was referring to the expeditions of Francisco Hernandez de Cordova and of Grijalva, and he said that ever since that time he had wished to capture some of those men who had come so as to keep them in his kingdoms and cities and to do them honor, and his gods had now fulfilled his desires, for now that we were in his home, which we might call our own, we should rejoice and take our rest, for there we should be well treated. And if he had on other occasions sent to say that we should not enter his city, it was not of his free will, but because his vassals were afraid, for they said that we shot our flashes of lightning, and killed many Indians with our horses, and that we were angry Teules, and other childish stories, and now that he had seen our persons and knew we were of flesh and bone, and had sound sense, and that we were very valiant, for these reasons he held us in much higher regard than he did from their reports, and he would share his possessions with us. Then Cortes and all of us answered that we thanked him sincerely for such signal good will, and Montezuma said, laughing, for he was very merry in his princely way of speaking: "Malinche, I know very well that these people of Tlaxcala with whom you are such good friends have told you that I am a sort of God or Teule, and that everything in my houses is made of gold and silver and precious stones, I know well enough that you are wise and did not believe it but took it as a joke. Behold now, Señor Malinche, my body is of flesh and bone like yours, my houses and palaces of stone and wood and lime; that I am a great king and inherit the riches of my ancestors is true, but not all the nonsense and lies that they have told you about me, although of course you treated it as a joke, as I did your thunder and lightning."

from The Discovery and Conquest of Mexico

327

THE SEARCH
FOR KNOWLEDGE

While English and Spanish swashbucklers ranged over the world, others searched the skies and their own minds. Around 1530 Copernicus wrote a "little commentary" contrasting older views with his own. Here he summarizes the first principles of his startling theory.

1. There is no one center for all the celestial orbits or spheres.
2. The center of the earth is not the center of the world.
3. All the planetary orbits circle around the sun at the center of them all.
4. The distance between the sun and the earth compared with the altitude of the firmament is less than half a diameter of the earth compared with its distance from the sun.
5. The apparent movement in the firmament is due to the movement of the earth; accordingly the earth turns once a day on its unchanging poles, while the firmament and ultimate heaven remain unmoved.
6. Whatever movement we find in the sun is due to the earth and our orbit in which we are rolled around the sun; and thus the earth has several motions.
7. The apparent irregularities in the movements of the planets are to be ascribed to the motion of the earth. The motion of the earth alone is sufficient to explain the apparent diversities of movement in the heaven.

from Commentariolus *by Copernicus*

As daring as Copernicus may have been intellectually, he had no desire to incur the wrath of the Church and published his revolutionary findings with considerable reluctance. De revolutionibus *contained an apology to the pope in which this passage appeared.*

His Holiness will not wonder that I should give to light my slowly elaborated cogitations. Rather will he expect to hear from me how I came to imagine the movement of the earth against the received opinion of mathematicians and the common sense of mankind. But indeed nothing moved me more to investigate the motions of the spheres than the variance of opinion among the mathematicians themselves. I wearied of this incertitude among them concerning the scheme of movement of this world-machine established for us by the great Constructor, and I searched among the books of the philosophers until I found that some of them conceived the earth to move. So I also took occasion to ponder on the earth's mobility; and though the idea seemed absurd, yet since others had felt at liberty to imagine what circles they chose to explain the phenomena of the heavens, I felt myself also permitted to try whether some firmer demonstrations might not be reached by assuming the movement of the earth.

Now, on the assumption of the movements which I ascribe to the earth in the following work, I found after long observation that if the movements of the remaining planets be given to the earth, reckoning according to the revolution of each body, the courses of the stars and the phenomena of the heavens could be cleared of all confusion.

from De revolutionibus *by Copernicus*

Tycho Brahe meant to leave Denmark for Basel, where he hoped to inaugurate the "revival of Astronomy" and to meet the most "distinguished and learned men." Here he describes a change of plans and his final decision to remain in Denmark after all.

But it so happened that while I was inwardly contemplating these matters and was already making preparations for the journey, without however revealing my purpose, the noble and mighty Frederick II, king of Denmark and Norway, of illustrious memory, sent one of his young noblemen to me at Knudstrup with a royal letter bidding me to go to see him immediately wherever he might be dwelling on Sealand. When I had presented myself without delay this excellent king, who cannot be sufficiently praised, of his own accord and according to his most gracious will offered me that island in the far-famed Danish Sound that our countrymen call Hven, but which is usually called Venusia in Latin, and Scarlatina by foreigners. He asked me to erect buildings on this island, and to construct instruments for astronomical investigations as well as for chemical studies, and he graciously promised me that he would abundantly defray the expenses. After I had for some time contemplated the matter and asked some wise men for their advice, I gave up my previous plan and willingly agreed to the king's wish, particularly when I saw that on this island, which is situated all by itself between Scania and Sealand, I could be rid of the disturbances of visitors, and that I could in this way obtain, in my own fatherland to which above other countries I owe so very much, the quiet and the convenient conditions that I had been looking for elsewhere. So, in the year 1576, I began building the castle Uraniborg, suitable for the study of astronomy, and in the course of time I constructed buildings as well as astronomical instruments of various kinds, fitted for making accurate observations. The most important of these are delineated and explained in this book. Meanwhile I also energetically started observing, and for this work I made use of the assistance of several students who distinguished themselves by talents and a keen vision. I had such students in my house all the time, one class after another, and I taught them this and other sciences. Thus by the grace of God it came about that there was hardly any day or night with clear weather that we did not get a great many, and very accurate, astronomical observations of the fixed stars as well as of all the planets, and also of the comets that appeared during that time, seven of which were carefully observed in the sky from that place. In this way observations were industriously made during twenty-one years. These I first collected in some big volumes, but later on I divided them up and distributed them among single books, one for each year, and had fair copies made. The arrangement I followed was such that the fixed stars, in so far as they had been observed during the year in question, had their own place, while the planets all had theirs, first the sun and moon, and next the other five planets in order up to Mercury . . .

from Astronomiae instauratae mechanica *by Tycho Brahe*

Botany was a popular study in Elizabethan times. One of the best of the herbalists was John Gerard, whose History of Plants, *completed in 1597, combines description with history and even includes recipes. Here Gerard describes the Jerusalem artichoke.*

One may well by the English name of this plant perceive that those that vulgarly give names to plants have little either judgment or knowledge of them: for this plant hath no similitude in leaf, stalk, or root, or manner of growing with an artichoke, but only a little likeness of taste in the dressed root. Neither came it from Jerusalem or out of Asia, but out of America; whence Fabius Columna, one of the first setters of it forth, fitly names it *Aster Peruvianus tuberosus,* and *Flos solis Farnesianus,* because it so much resembles the *Flos solis,* and for that he first observed it growing in the garden of Cardinal Farnesius, who had procured roots thereof from the West Indies. Also our countryman Mr. Parkinson hath exactly delivered the history of this by the name of *Battatas de Canada,* Englishing it Potatoes of Canada. Now all these that have written and mentioned it bring it from America, but from far different places, as from Peru, Brazil, and Canada; but this is not much material, seeing it now grows so well and plentifully in so many places of England. I will therefore deliver you the history as I have received it from my oft-mentioned friend Mr. Goodyear, who . . . took it presently upon the first arrival into England.

This wonderful increasing plant high growing up from one root, one, sometimes two, three, or more round green, rough, hairy straked stalks, commonly about twelve foot high, sometimes sixteen foot or higher, as big as a child's arm, full of white spongeous pith within. The leaves grow all alongst the stalks out of order, of a light green color, rough, sharp, pointed, about eight inches broad, and ten or eleven inches long, deeply notched or indented about the edges, very like the leaves of the common *Flos solis Peruanus,* but nothing crumpled, and not so broad. The stalks divide themselves into many long branches, even from the roots to their very tops, bearing leaves smaller and smaller toward the tops, making the herb appear like a little tree, narrower and slenderer toward the top, in the fashion of a steeple or pyramid. The flowers with us grow only at the tops of the stalks and branches, like those of the said *Flos solis,* but no bigger than our common single marigold, consisting of twelve or thirteen straked, sharp-pointed bright yellow bordering leaves, growing forth of a scaly small hairy head, with a small yellow thrummy matter within. These flowers by reason of their late flowering, which is commonly two or three weeks after Michaelmas, never bring their seed to perfection; and it maketh show of abundance of small heads near the tops of the stalks and branches, forth of the bosoms of the leaves, which never open and flower with us, by reason they are destroyed with the frosts, which otherwise it seemeth would be a goodly spectacle.

These roots are dressed diverse ways; some boil them in water and after stew them with sack and butter, adding a little ginger. Others bake them in pies, putting marrow, dates, ginger, raisins of the sun, sack, etc. Others some other way as they are led by their skill in cookery. But in my judgment, which way so ever they be dressed and eaten they are a meat more fit for swine than men.

Books on natural history were enormously popular in Elizabethan England, although the reliability of their authors was questionable. William Harrison, for example, in writing on English serpents, provided his readers with a pastiche of old wives' tales, half-remembered remarks by previous "authorities," and the evidence of his own eyes. As an observer he was somewhat gullible, as can be seen from this account of the behavior of the "viper."

If I should go about to make any long discourse of the venomous beasts or worms bred in England, I should attempt more than occasion itself would offer, since we have very few worms, but no beasts at all that are thought by their natural qualities to be either venomous or hurtful. First of all therefore we have the adder . . . which some men do too rashly take to be the viper. Certes if it be so, then it is not the viper author of the death of her parents, as some histories affirm, and thereto Encelius, a late writer, in his *De re metallica* . . . where he maketh mention of a she-adder which he saw in Sala, whose womb (as he saith) was eaten out after a like fashion, her young ones lying by her in the sunshine, as if they had been earthworms. Nevertheless, as he nameth them *Viperas,* so he calleth the male *Echis* and the female *Echidna,* concluding in the end that *Echis* is the same serpent which his countrymen to this day call *Ein atter,* as I have also noted before out of a Saxon dictionary. For my part I am persuaded that the slaughter of their parents is either not true at all, or not always (although I doubt not but that nature hath right well provided to inhibit their superfluous increase by some means or other), and so much the rather am I led hereunto, for that I gather by *Nicander* that of all venomous worms the viper only bringeth out her young alive, and therefore is called in Latin *Vipera quasivivipara.* But of her own death he doth not (to my remembrance) say anything. It is testified also by others in other words and to the like sense that *Echis id est vipera sola ex serpentibus non ova sed animalia parit.* ["Alone among serpents the viper *Echis* lays no eggs but gives birth to its young."] And it may well be, for I remember that I have read in Philostratus . . . how he saw a viper licking her young. I did see an adder once myself that lay (as I thought) sleeping on a molehill, out of whose mouth came eleven young adders of twelve or thirteen inches in length apiece, which played to and fro in the grass one with another till some of them espied me. So soon therefore as they saw my face they ran again into the mouth of their dam, whom I killed, and then found each one of them shrouded in a distinct cell or pannicle in her belly, much like unto a soft white jelly, which maketh me to be of the opinion that our adder is the viper indeed.

from The Description of England *by William Harrison*

Other writers on natural history often substituted convenient historical milestones for exact dates, and imprecise doggerel for hard research. One author informs us that "muskmelons and tobacco came into England about the twentieth year of Queen Elizabeth," and that

Turkeys, Carps, Hops, Pickerels, and Beer
Came into England all in one year. . . .

from Annales of England *by John Stowe*

THE BODY POLITIC

Although a most impolitic politician, Sir Francis Bacon brilliantly expounded political philosophy to Tudor and early Stuart readers.

Shepherds of people had need know the calendars of tempests in state, which are commonly greatest when things grow to equality, as natural tempests are greatest about the *Equinoctia* ["Equinoxes"]. And as there are certain hollow blasts of wind and secret swellings of seas before a tempest, so are there in states:

> —*Ille etiam caecos instare tumultus*
> *Saepe monet, fraudesque et operta tumescere bella.*
> ["Often he [the sun] gives warning that
> dark tumults are at hand, and that treasons
> and open warfare grow large."]

Libels and licentious discourses against the state, when they are frequent and open, and in like sort, false news often running up and down to the disadvantage of the state, and hastily embraced are amongst the signs of troubles. Virgil giving the pedigree of Fame, saith *she was sister to the Giants:*

Illam Terra parens, ira irritata Deorum,
Extremam (ut perhibent) Coeo Enceladoque sororem Progenuit.
["Earth, so they say, wroth with the gods, gave birth to her, her last child, and sister to Coeus and Enceladus."]

As if fames were the relics of seditions past, but they are no less indeed the preludes of seditions to come. Howsoever he noteth it right, that seditious tumults and seditious fames differ no more but as brother and sister, masculine and feminine; especially if it come to that, that the best actions of a state, and the most plausible, and which ought to give greatest contentment, are taken in ill sense and traduced, for that shews the envy great, as Tacitus saith, *Conflata magna invidia, seu bene seu male gesta premunt* ["When great envy is excited, good deeds as well as bad are condemned"]. Neither doth it follow that because these fames are a sign of troubles, that the suppressing of them with too much severity should be a remedy of troubles. For the despising of them many times checks them best, and the going about to stop them doth but make a wonder long-lived. Also that kind of obedience which Tacitus speaketh of is to be held suspected: *Erant in officio, sed tamen qui mallent mandata imperantium interpretari quam exequi* ["They were in office, but yet they preferred to construe the commands of the rulers rather than to obey them"]; disputing, excusing, cavilling upon mandates and directions is a kind of shaking off the yoke and assay of disobedience, especially if in those disputings they which are for the direction speak fearfully and tenderly, and those that are against it audaciously.

Also, as Machiavelli noteth well, when princes, that ought to be common parents, make themselves as a party, and lean to a side, it is as a boat that is overthrown by uneven weight on the one side, as was well seen in the time of Henry III of France, for first himself entered league for the extirpation of the Protestants, and presently after the same league was turned upon himself. For when the authority of princes is made but an accessary to a cause, and that there be other bands that tie faster than the band of sovereignty, kings begin to be put almost out of possession.

Also, when discords and quarrels and factions are carried openly and audaciously, it is a sign the reverence of government is lost. For the motions of the greatest persons in a government ought to be as the motions of the planets under *primum mobile* (according to the old opinion), which is, that every of them is carried swiftly by the highest motion and softly in their own motion. And therefore, when great ones in their own particular motion move violently, and, as Tacitus expresseth it well, *liberius quam ut imperantium meminissent* ["more freely than was consistent with respect for their rulers"], it is a sign the orbs are out of frame. For reverence is that wherewith princes are girt from God, who threateneth the dissolving thereof: *Solvam cingula regum* ["I will loosen the girdles of kings"].

So when any of the four pillars of government are mainly shaken or weakened (which are religion, justice, counsel, and treasure), men had need to pray for fair weather. But let us pass from this part of predictions (concerning which, nevertheless, more light may be taken from that which followeth); and let us speak first of the materials of seditions; then of the motives of them; and thirdly of the remedies.

Concerning the materials of seditions. It is a thing well to be considered, for the surest way to prevent seditions (if the times do bear it) is to take away the matter of them. For if there be fuel prepared, it is hard to tell whence the spark shall come that shall set it on fire. The matter of seditions is of two kinds, much poverty and much discontentment. It is certain, so many overthrown estates, so many votes for troubles. Lucan noteth well the state of Rome before the civil war,

> *Hinc usura vorax, rapidumque in tempore foenus,*
> *Hinc concussa fides, et multis utile bellum.*
> ["Estates eaten up by usurious rates of interest, credit shaken, war a gain to many."]

This same *multis utile bellum* is an assured and infallible sign of a state disposed to seditions and troubles. And if this poverty and broken estate in the better sort be joined with a want and necessity in the mean people, the danger is imminent and great. For the rebellions of the belly are the worst. As for discontentments, they are in the politic body like to humours in the natural, which are apt to gather a preternatural heat and to inflame. And let no prince measure the danger of them by this, whether they be just or unjust, for that were to imagine people to be too reasonable, who do often spurn at their own good; nor yet by this, whether the griefs whereupon they rise be in fact great or small, for they are the most dangerous discontentments where the fear is greater than the feeling: *Dolendi modus, timendi non item* ["There is a limit to suffering, but not to fears"]. Besides, in great oppressions the same things that provoke the patience do withal mate the courage, but in fears it is not so. Neither let any prince or state be secure concerning discontentments, because they have been often, or have been long, and yet no peril hath ensued, for as it is true that every vapour or fume doth not turn into a storm, so it is nevertheless true that storms, though they blow over divers times, yet may fall at last; and, as the Spanish proverb noteth well, The cord break-eth at the last by the weakest pull.

The causes of motives of seditions are innovation in religion, taxes, alteration of laws and customs, breaking of privileges, general oppression, advancement of unworthy persons, strangers, dearths, disbanded soldiers, factions grown desperate, and whatsoever in offending people joineth and knitteth them in a common cause.

For the remedies, there may be some general preservatives, whereof we will speak; as for the just cure, it must answer to the particular disease, and so be left to counsel rather than rule.

The first remedy or prevention is to remove by all means possible that material cause of sedition whereof we spake, which is want and poverty in the estate. To which purpose serveth the opening and well-balancing of trade, the cherishing of manufactures, the banishing of idleness, the repressing of waste and excess by sumptuary laws, the improvement and husbanding of the soil, the regulating of prices of things vendible, the moderating of taxes and tributes and the like. Generally, it is to be foreseen that the population of a kingdom (especially if it be not mown down by wars) do not exceed the stock of the kingdom which should maintain them. Neither is the population to be reckoned only by number, for a smaller number that spend more and earn less do wear out an estate sooner than a greater number that live lower and gather more. Therefore the multiplying of nobility and other degrees of quality in an over proportion to the common people doth speedily bring a state to necessity, and so doth likewise an overgrown clergy, for they bring nothing to the stock; and in like manner, when more are bred scholars than preferments can take off.

It is likewise to be remembered that forasmuch as the increase of any estate must be upon the foreigner (for whatsoever is somewhere gotten is somewhere lost), there be but three things which one nation selleth unto another: the commodity as nature yieldeth it; the manufacture; and the vecture, or carriage. So that if these three wheels go, wealth will flow as in a spring tide. And it cometh many times to pass that *materiam superabit opus*, that the work and carriage is more worth than the material, and enricheth a state more, as is notably seen in the Low-Countrymen, who have the best mines above ground in the world.

Above all things, good policy is to be used that the treasure and monies in a state be not gathered into few hands. For otherwise a state may have a great stock and yet starve. And money is like muck, not good except it be spread. This is done chiefly by suppressing, or at the least keeping a strait hand upon the devouring trades of usury, ingrossing, great pasturages, and the like.

For removing discontentments, or at least the danger of them, there is in every state (as we know) two portions of subjects: the nobless and the commonalty. When one of these is discontent, the danger is not great, for common people are of slow motion, if they be not excited by the greater sort, and the greater sort are of small strength, except the multitude be apt and ready to move of themselves. Then is the danger, when the greater sort do but wait for the troubling of the waters amongst the meaner, that then they may declare themselves. The poets feign that the rest of the gods would have bound Jupiter, which he hearing of, by the counsel of Pallas, sent for Briareus, with his hundred hands, to come in to his aid. An emblem, no doubt, to show how safe it is for monarchs to make sure of the good will of common people.

To give moderate liberty for griefs and discontentments to evaporate (so it be without too great insolency or bravery) is a safe way. For he that turneth the humours back, and maketh the wound bleed inwards endangereth malign ulcers and pernicious imposthumations.

The part of Epimetheus mought well become Prometheus in the case of discontentments, for there is not a better provision against them. Epimetheus, when griefs and evils flew abroad, at last shut the lid, and kept hope in the bottom of the vessel. Certainly the politic and artificial nourishing and entertaining of hopes and carrying men from hopes to hopes is one of the best antidotes against the poison of discontentments. And it is a certain sign of a wise government and proceeding, when it can hold men's hearts by hopes, when it cannot by satisfaction, and when it can handle things in such manner as no evil shall appear so peremptory but that it hath some outlet of hope, which is the less hard to do, because both particular persons and factions are apt enough to flatter themselves, or at least to brave that they believe not.

Also the foresight and prevention, that there be no likely or fit head whereunto discontented persons may resort, and under whom they may join, is a known but an excellent point of caution. I understand a fit head to be one that hath greatness and reputation, that hath confidence with the discontented party, and upon whom they turn their eyes, and that is thought discontented in his own particular, which kind of persons are either to be won and reconciled to the state, and that in a fast and true manner, or to be fronted with some other of the same party, that may oppose them, and so divide the reputation. Generally the dividing and breaking of all factions and combinations that are adverse to the state, and setting them at distance, or at least distrust, amongst themselves is not one of the worst remedies. For it is a desperate case, if those that hold with the proceeding of the state be full of discord and faction, and those that are against it be entire and united.

I have noted that some witty and sharp speeches which have fallen from princes have given fire to seditions. Caesar did himself infinite hurt in that speech, *Sylla nescivit literas, non potuit dictare* ["Sulla did not know his letters, he could not dictate"], for it did utterly cut off that hope which men had entertained, that he would at one time or other give over his dictatorship. Galba undid himself by that speech, *legi a se militem, non emi* ["he levied his soldiers, he did not buy them"], for it put the soldiers out of hope of the donative. Probus likewise, by that speech, *si vixero, non opus erit amplius Romano imperio militibus* ["if I live, the Roman empire will stand in no more need of soldiers"], a speech of great despair for the soldiers. And many the like. Surely princes had need in tender matters and ticklish times to beware what they say, especially in these short speeches, which fly abroad like darts, and are thought to be shot out of their secret intentions. For as for large discourses, they are flat things, and not so much noted.

from Essays or Counsels, Civil and Moral   331

POPISH PLOTS
AND
TREASONS

From the beginning of the Reign of Queen Elizabeth Illuftrated with Emblems and explain'd in Verfe.

Firft are defcrib'd the Curfed plots they laid.
And on the fide their wretched ends dif. play'd.

Figure 1.

THe Pope aloft on Armed Shoulders Rides,
And in vain Hopes the Englifh fpoils divides;
His *Leaden Bull* 'gainft good *Eliza.* roares,
And fcatters dire Rebellion round our Shoars.
The Prieft *Bleffes* the Villians, Chears them on,
And promifes Heav'ns Crown, when her Crown's won.
But God doth blaft their Troops, their Counfels mock
And brings bold Traitors to'th' deferved *Block.*

Figure 2.

Don John, who under Spain did with proud Hand
The then unfever'd *Netherlands* Command,
Contrives for Englands Conqueft, and does Hope
To Gain it by Donation from the Pope.
Yet to Amufe our Queen does ftill pretend
Perpetual peace, and needs will feem a friend;
But Heav'n looks through thofe Juggles and in's prime,
Grief Cuts off Him and's Hopes All at a time.

Figure 3.

Spains *King,* and *Romes* Triple-Crown'd Pelate Joyn,
And with them both bold *Stukely* does Combine
Ireland to conquer, And the Pope has fent,
For that Bleft work, an *Holy Regiment;*
But in their way at *Barbary* they call,
Where at one Blow the *Moors* deftroy them All.
See here, what fuch Ambitious Traitors Gain,
The fhame of Chriftians is by *Pagans* Slain.

Figure 4.

The Priefts, with *Croffes* Enfigne-like difplaid,
Prompt bloody *Defmond* to thofe fpoiles he made
On Irifh Proteftants, and from afar
Blow Triumphs to Rebellions Holy War;
But againft Providence all Arts are vain,
The Crafty, in their Craft are over-tane;
Behold where *kill'd* the Stubborn *Traitor* lies,
Whilft to the *Woods* his *Ghoftly Father* flies;

Figure 5.

What trufty Janizaries are Monks to *Rome,*
From their dark Cells the blackeft Treafons come.
By the Popes Licenfe horrid Crimes they Act,
And Guild with piety each Treacherous Fact.
A feminary Prieft, like Comets Blaze,
Doth always Blood-fhed and Rebellion Raife;
But ftill the fatal Gibbet's ready fixt
For fuch, where Treafon's with Religion mixt.

Figure 6.

Mad *Sommervil,* by Cruel Priefts infpir'd
To do whatever mifchiefe they requir'd,
Swears that he inftantly will be the death
Of good and Gracious Queen *Elizabeth.*
Affaults her Guards, but Heav'ns protecting pow'r
Defeats his rage makes him a Prifoner:
Where to avoid a juft, though fhameful Death,
Self-ftrangling hands do Stop his loathfome breath.

Figure 7.

Whilft *Spains* Embaffador here Leiger lies,
Defigns are laid the Englifh to furprize;
Two Catalogues his Secretary had Got
The better two effect the Hellifh Plot.
One all our Havens Names, where Foes might Land,
To'ther what Papifts were to lend an hand.
For this bafe Trick he's forc'd to pack to *Spain*
Whilft Tyburn greets confederates that remain.

Figure 8.

View here a Miracle —— A Prieft Conveys,
In Spanifh Bottom o're the path-lefs Seas,
Clofe treacherous Notes, whilft a Dutch Ship comes by
And ftreight Engag'd her well-known Enemy:
The Confcious Prieft his Guilty Papers tears,
And over-board the fcatter'd fragments bears;
But the juft winds do force them back o'th' Decks,
And peice-meal all the lurking plot detects.

Figure 9.

The Jefuites vile Doctrines do Convince
Parry, 'Tis Merit for to kill his Prince,
The fatal Dagger he prepares with Art,
And means to fheath it in her Royal Heart.
Oft he Attemps, and is as oft put by,
By the Majeftick Terrors of her Eye;
At laft his Curfed Intentions he Confeft
And So his welcom'd a fit Tyburn Gueft;

Figure 10.

Here *Babington* and all his defperate Band,
Ready prepar'd for Royal Murder ftand,
His Motto feems to glory in the Deed,
Thefe my Companions are whom dangers lead,
Cowardly Traitors, fo many Combine
To Cut off one poor Ladies vital Twine;
In vain, — Heaven's her Guard, and as for you;
Behold, the Hangman gives you all your due.

Figure 11.

Nor was't with *Spain* alone, Great *Betty's* Strife;
Now *France* attempts upon her pretious Life;
The Guifes caufe th' Ambaffador to Bribe
Moody, and others of the Roman Tribe,
To Cut her off. To which they foon Confent
But watchful Heav'n does that Guilt prevent.
Stafford doth to the Councel All difclofe,
And Home with fhame perfidious *Mounfieur* goes.

Figure 12.

Spain's proud *Armado,* whom the Pope did Blefs,
Attacques our Ifle, Confident of fuccefs.
But Heav'ns juft Blaft doth Scatter all their force,
They fly and quite round *Scotland* take their Courfe;
So many taken, burnt, and Sunk i'th' Main,
Scarce one in Ten did e're get home Again;
Thus *England* like *Noahs* Ark, amidft the Waves
Indulgent providence from Danger faves.

Figure 13.

But now a private horrid Treafon veiw
Hatcht by the Pope, the Devil, and a Jew
Lopez a Doctor muft by Poifon do
What all their Plots have fail'd in hitherto
What will you give me then; the *Judas* Cries
Full *fifty thoufand Crowns,* t'other replies,
Tis done — but hold, the wretch fhall mifs his hope,
The Treafons known, and his Reward's the Rope;

Figure 14.

The Great *Tyrone* that did fo oft embrew
Ireland with Blood, and Popifh Plots Renew,
Here vanquifht Swears upon his bended Knee
To the Queens Deputy fidelity
Yet breaks that vow, and loaded with the Guilt
Of perjuries and Blood which he had fpilt.
Being forc'd at laft to fly his Native Land,
Carries in's Breaft a fting, a Scourge in's *hand*

Figure 15.

No Sooner *James* had bleft the Englifh Throne,
But Traiterous Priefts Confpire to pull him down.
Watfon the poifonous Maximes does Inftill,
And draws fome Nobles to Join in the Ill:
But Princes then appear the moft divine,
When they with unexpected Mercy Shine.
Juft as the Fatal Ax attempts the Stroke,
Pardon fteps in and does the Blow Revoke

Figure 16.

In this Curs'd Powder-plot we plainly fee
The Quinteffence of Romifh Cruelty
King Lords and Commons at one Hellifh Blaft
Had been deftroy'd, and half our Land laid waft,
See *Faux* with his dark Lanthorn ready ftands
To Light the fatal Train with defperate hands,
But Heavens All-feeing eye defeats their defire,
And faves us as a Brand fnatcht from the fire;

And now let us, with chearful Hymns of praife,
And Hearts inflam'd with love an *Altar* raife
Of Gratitude to God, who doth advance
His out-ftreatcht Arm in our Deliverance,
Tis only He, that doth protect his Sheep,
Tis he alone doth this poor Ifland keep
From Romifh *Wolves,* which would us foon devour,
If not Defended by his mighty power
Ti he that doth our *Church* with freedome Crown,
And beats the Popifh *Superftitions* down
Under her *feet,* and may they never rife,
Nor in vile *Darkuefs* Reinvolve our Eyes;
Since Heaven whofe *mercies* ever are moft tender
Hath both reftor'd *our Faith* and *Faith* the *Defender*
Let us to both a ftrict Adherence pay,
And for their *prefervation* ever pray.
Since thus *Truths* happy *Bark* hath reach'd our *fhore*
O may it *never, never* Leaves us more.

※※※ ※※※※※※※※※※※※※※※※※※※※※※※※

Sold by *John Garret* at his Shop, at the *Exchange Staires* in *Cornhill* where you may have choice of all Sorts of Large and Small Maps: Drawing Books, Coppy books, and Pictures for Gentlewomens works; and alfo very good originals of French and Dutch Prints

Englishmen of the late Tudor and early Stuart eras never tired of accounts of sedition instigated by the pope and Spanish attempts to bring about the downfall of Elizabeth. Their appetite for the grisly details of capital punishment seems to have been equally insatiable. In the popular broadside reproduced here, doggerel describing various and sundry "Popish Plots and Treasons" (and the bloody comeuppances of their villainous perpetrators) is illustrated in suitably macabre fashion.

IN PARLIAMENT ASSEMBLED

Some of the most stirring prose in all Elizabethan literature was forged in the heat of parliamentary debate, and members of the House of Lords were never more eloquent than when fulminating against the peril of a Catholic takeover. The inappropriately named Sir Walter Mildmay, a leading government spokesman, was one of the most vituperative of Parliament's many pope-baiters.

I beseech you consider what a change there would be if, in the place of the present rulers, those priests, rebels, fugitives, and papists, known to be cruel and dissolute and vain, were set at the helm of the Church and Commonwealth. And if any doubt what a miserable change this would be, let him but remember the late days of Queen Mary, when . . . the pope's authority was wholly restored, and for continuance thereof a strange nation [Spain], proud and insolent, brought into this land to be lords over us: which no doubt would have followed if God in His mercy had not delivered us and preserved as the apple of His eye this precious jewel, our most gracious queen. Look, I beseech you, a little back into that time and see what terrible fear all the subjects of this realm—yea, the most forward in popery—were overwhelmed with, both for the doubt they had to live under the yoke of strangers and for the fear they had to lose their abbey-lands.

Even more explosive was the Puritan Job Throckmorton, whose indictment of Mary Queen of Scots contained this rousing passage.

In a kingdom of the gospel where both prince and people, through the mercy of God, have long felt the sweetness of a holy and religious peace, let it never be said for shame that there was found a man that durst once stain his mouth in defence of her whom I protest unto you I know not how to describe. If I should term her the daughter of sedition, the mother of rebellion, the nurse of impiety, the handmaid of iniquity, the sister of unshamefastness; or if I should tell you that which you know already—that she is Scottish of nation, French of education, papist of profession, a Guisan of blood, a Spaniard in practice, a libertine in life: as all this were not to flatter her, so yet this were nothing near to describe her. Ye have seen her anatomy already, ye have heard her whole life and practices reasonably laid forth unto you by an honourable personage, to whose worthy speech yet this one thing may be added: that were his gifts and sufficiency redoubled . . . yet would her wickedness . . . still surmount his description . . . Such a creature whom no Christian eye can behold with patience, whose villainy hath stained the earth and infected the air. To destroy her would be "one of the fairest riddances that ever church of God had."

The anguish suffered by Elizabeth during the Marian tragedy was movingly expressed in this submission to the will of Parliament.

For me to make my moan were strange and rare, for I suppose you shall find few that, for their own particular, will cumber you with such a care. Yet such, I protest, hath been my greedy desire and hungry will that of your consultation might have fallen out some other means to work my safety, joined with your assurance, than that for which you are become so earnest suitors, as I protest I must needs use complaint—though not of you, but unto you, and of the cause; for that I do perceive, by your advices, prayers, and desires, there falleth out this accident, that only my injurer's bane must by my life's surety.

But if any there live so wicked of nature to suppose that I prolonged this time only *pro forma*, to the intent to make a show of clemency, thereby to set my praises to the wire-drawers to lengthen them the more, they do me so great a wrong as they can hardly recompense. Or if any person there be that think or imagine that the least vainglorious thought hath drawn me further herein, they do me as open injury as ever was done to any living creature—as He that is the maker of all thoughts knowest best to be true. Or if there be any that think that the Lords, appointed in commission [i.e. the Commissioners who tried Mary], durst do no other, as fearing thereby to displease or to be suspected to be of a contrary opinion to my safety, they do but heap upon me injurious conceits. For, either those put in trust by me to supply my place have not performed their duty towards me, or else they have signified unto you all that my desire was that every one should do according to his conscience, and in the course of these proceedings should enjoy both freedom of voice and liberty of opinion, and what they would not openly, they might privately to myself declare. It was of a willing mind and great desire I had, that some other means might be found out, wherein I should have taken more comfort than in any other thing under the sun.

And since now it is resolved that my surety cannot be established without a princess' head, I have just cause to complain that I, who have in my time pardoned so many rebels, winked at so many treasons, and either not produced them or altogether slipped them over with silence, should now be forced to this proceeding, against such a person. I have besides, during my reign, seen and heard many opprobrious books and pamphlets against me, my Realm and State, accusing me to be a tyrant. I thank them for their alms. I believe therein their meaning was to tell me news: and news it is to me indeed. I would it were as strange to hear of their impiety. What will they not now say, when it shall be spread that for the safety of her life a maiden queen could be content to spill the blood even of her own kinswoman? I may therefore full well complain that any man should think me given to cruelty; whereof I am so guiltless and innocent as I should slander God if I should say He gave me so vile a mind. Yea, I protest, I am so far from it that for mine own life I would not touch her. Neither hath my care been so much bent how to prolong mine, as how to preserve both: which I am right sorry is made so hard, yea so impossible.

I am not so void of judgment as not to see mine own peril; nor yet so ignorant as not to know it were in nature a foolish course to cherish a sword to cut mine own throat; nor so careless as not to weigh that my life daily is in hazard. But this I do consider, that many a man would put his life in danger for the safeguard of a king. I do not say that so will I; but I pray you think that I have thought upon it.

At the age of sixty-nine, in the forty-fourth year of her reign, Elizabeth delivered her "Golden Speech" to Parliament—a heartfelt tour de force that, reports say, left few dry eyes in the house.

I do assure you there is no prince that loves his subjects better, or whose love can countervail our love. There is no jewel, be it of never so rich a price, which I set before this jewel: I mean your love. For I do esteem it more than any treasure or riches; for that we know how to prize, but love and thanks I count unvaluable. And, though God hath raised me high, yet this I count the glory of my crown that I have reigned with your loves. This makes me that I do not so much rejoice that God hath made me to be a queen, as to be a queen over so thankful a people. Therefore, I have cause to wish nothing more than to content the subject; and that is a duty which I owe. Neither do I desire to live longer days than I may see your prosperity; and that is my only desire. And as I am that person that still yet under God hath delivered you, so I trust, by the almighty power of God, that I shall be His instrument to preserve you from every peril, dishonor, shame, tryanny, and oppression; partly by means of your intended helps [the subsidies they were granting] which we take very acceptably, because it manifesteth the largeness of your good loves and loyalties unto your sovereign.

Of myself I must say this: I never was any greedy, scraping grasper, nor a strait, fast-holding prince, nor yet a waster. My heart was never set on worldly goods, but only for my subjects' good. What you bestow on me, I will not hoard it up, but receive it to bestow on you again. Yea, mine own properties I account yours, to be expended for your good; and your eyes shall see the bestowing of all for your good. Therefore, render unto them, I beseech you, Mr. Speaker, such thanks as you imagine my heart yieldeth, but my tongue cannot express.

I know the title of a king is a glorious title; but assure yourself that the shining glory of princely authority hath not so dazzled the eyes of our understanding, but that we well know and remember that we also are to yield an account of our actions before the great Judge. To be a king and wear a crown is a thing more glorious to them that see it, than it is pleasant to them that bear it. For myself, I was never so much enticed with the glorious name of a king or royal authority of a queen, as delighted that God hath made me His instrument to maintain His truth and glory, and to defend this kingdom (as I said) from peril, dishonor, tyranny, and oppression.

There will never queen sit in my seat with more zeal to my country, care for my subjects, and that will sooner with willingness venture her life for your good and safety, than myself. For it is my desire to live nor reign no longer than my life and reign shall be for your good. And though you have had and may have many princes more mighty and wise sitting in this seat, yet you never had nor shall have any that will be more careful and loving.

Shall I ascribe anything to myself and my sexly weakness?

A 1590 *print shows Queen Elizabeth at prayer.*

I were not worthy to live then; and, of all, most unworthy of the mercies I have had from God, who hath given me a heart that yet never feared any foreign or home enemy. And I speak it to give God the praise, as a testimony before you, and not to attribute anything to myself. For I, oh Lord! what am I, whom practices and perils past should not fear? Or what can I do?

Christopher Yelverton, speaker of the Commons, summed up Parliament's—and England's—gratitude to Elizabeth late in her reign.

It is a wonder to other countries, amid the tempestuous storms they be tossed with, to behold the calm and halcyon days of England, that possesseth a princess in whom dwelleth such undaunted courage without all dismay of any womanish fear, such singular wisdom without insolency, and such sincere justice without rigor. If Plato now had lived, he should not only have seen the mind of a philosopher in the majesty of a queen—which he only wished; but the perfection of a Christian in a princely virgin—which he could not have imagined.

But into what an amazed labyrinth of endless sea do I run, if I do but sparingly prosecute either the glory of your virtues in yourself, or the greatness of your benefits to the Commonwealth? I can neither recount the one, they be so rare; nor rehearse the other, they be so many: for we be not more bound to Your Majesty for reducing again the golden world of Saturn, than for restoring again the peace and flourishing prosperity of Solomon. But I fear, with grief and sorrow of soul I fear, that, as it was said of Hannibal, "The glory and skill of war amongst them of Carthage, after so long and so secure a repose from it, began and ended in his excellency"; so I fear, I do wonderfully fear, it will hereafter be said of you, "The honour and happiness of peace amongst us of England, after so many and so great interruptions of it, began and ended in Your Majesty."

A KING BEWITCHED

Scientific advances notwithstanding, belief in witchcraft was prevalent throughout Tudor and Stuart times, and some of the most eminent men of the age addressed themselves to various aspects of the question. In England, James I wrote a lengthy, bigoted, and styleless treatise on the subject in the form of a dialogue between Philomathus and Epistemon, with the latter representing the king's own views.

PHILOMATHES: But by what way say they or think ye it possible that they [witches] can come to these unlawful conventions?

EPISTEMON: There is the thing which I esteem their senses to be deluded in, and though they lie not in confessing of it, because they think it to be true, yet not to be in substance or effect: for they say that by diverse means they may convene, either to the adoring of their master or to the putting in practice any service of his committed unto their charge. One way is natural, which is natural riding, going, or sailing at what hour their master comes and advertises them; and this way may be easily believed. Another way is somewhat more strange, and yet it is possible to be true: which is by being carried by the force of the spirit which is their conductor, either above the earth or above the sea swiftly to the place where they are to meet. Which I am persuaded to be likewise possible in respect that as Habakkuk was carried by the angel in that form to the den where Daniel lay, so, think I, the devil will be ready to imitate God as well in that as in other things. Which is much more possible for him to do, being a spirit, than to a mighty wind, being but a natural meteor, to transport from one place to another a solid body as is commonly and daily seen in practice. But in this violent form they cannot be carried but a short bound, agreeing with the space that they may retain their breath. For if it were longer, their breath could not remain unextinguished, their body being carried in such a violent and forcible manner, as be example: If one fall off a small height, his life is but in peril according to the hard or soft lighting; but if one fall from a high and stay rock, his breath will be forcibly banished from the body before he can win to the earth, as is oft seen by experience. And in this transporting they say themselves that they are invisible to any other, except among themselves, which may also be possible in my opinion. For if the devil may form what kind of impressions he pleases in the air, as I have said before, speaking of magic, why may he not far easilier thicken and obscure so the air that is next about them by contracting it straight together that the beams of any other man's eyes cannot pierce through the same to see them? But the third way of their coming to their conventions is that wherein I think them deluded: for some of them sayeth that being transformed in the likeness of a little beast or fowl, they will come and pierce through whatsoever house or church, though all ordinary passages be closed, by whatsoever open[ing] the air may enter in at. And some saith that their bodies lying still as in an ecstasy, their spirits will be ravished out of their bodies and carried to such places. And for verifying thereof will give evident tokens of which by witnesses that have seen their body lying senseless in the meantime, as by naming persons whom with they met, and giving tokens of what purpose was amongst them, whom

otherwise they could not have known. For this form of journeying they affirm to use most when they are transported from one country to another.

PHILOMATHES: Surely I long to hear your own opinion of this; for they are like old wives' trattles about the fire. The reasons that move me to think that these are mere illusions are these. First, for them that are transformed in likeness of beasts or fowls can enter through so narrow passages, although I may easily believe that the devil could by his workmanship upon the air make them appear to be in such forms either to themselves or to others. Yet how can he contract a solid body within so little room? I think it is directly contrary to itself for to be made so little and yet not diminished, to be so straightly drawn together and yet feel no pain. I think it is so contrary to the quality of a natural body, and so like to the little transubstantiate god in the papists' Mass that I can never believe it. So to have a quantity is so proper to a solid body that, as all philosophers concluded, it cannot be any more without one than a spirit can have one. For when Peter came out of the prison and the doors all locked —it was not by any contracting of his body in so little room, but by the giving place of the door, though unspied by the gaolers. And yet is there no comparison, when this is done, betwixt the power of God and of the devil. As to their form of ecstasy and spiritual transporting, it is certain the soul's going out of the body is the only definition of natural death; and who are once dead, God forbid we should think that it should lie in the power of all the devils in hell to restore them to their life again—although he can put his own spirit in a dead body, which the necromancers commonly practice as ye have heard. For that is the office properly belonging to God. And besides that, the soul once parting from the body cannot wander any longer in the world, but to [its] own resting place must it go immediately, abiding the conjunction of the body again at the latter day. And what Christ or the prophets did miraculously in this case, it cannot in no Christian man's opinion be made common with the devil.

from Daemonologie *by James* I

James' belief in the prevalence of witches becomes understandable enough in the light of this passage from News from Scotland, *published in 1591, thirteen years before he wrote* Daemonologie. *Agnes Sampson, who has confessed (or rather boasted) that she is a witch, is closely questioned by James, who was then king of Scotland.*

Agnes Sampson confessed before the King's Majesty sundry things, which were so miraculous and strange, as that His Majesty said "they were all extreme liars"; whereat she answered, "she would not wish His Majesty to suppose her words to be false, but rather to believe them, in that she would discover such matter unto him as His Majesty should not anyway doubt of." And thereupon taking His Majesty a little aside, she declared unto him the very words which passed between the King's Majesty and his queen at Upslo in Norway, the first night of the marriage, with the answer each to other; whereat the King's Majesty wondered greatly, and swore "by the living God, that he believed all the devils in hell could not have discovered the same," acknowledging her words to be most true; and therefore gave the more credit to the rest.

In this woodcut practitioners of witchcraft are shown dancing with daemons.

Witches, it was believed, could set houses aflame by an act of will.

ADVENTURES ACROSS THE SEA

Columbus' discovery, in 1492, that there was land in the way of the imagined Atlantic trade route to the Indies set off an international competition that has been duplicated only in our own time, after the Soviet Union launched the first Sputnik into space. Geographical exploration became the sixteenth-century sport of kings, who financed expeditions led by the best adventurers in their stables. There was no sharing of scientific information; charts, maps, and documents were zealously guarded state secrets. The original goal, and always the primary one, was to find a short route through the American land mass to the wealth of the Orient; but as more was learned, that quest became combined with a search for ways to exploit the wealth and potential of the New World itself. Like this detail (right) of a 1558 Portuguese map showing the Strait of Magellan, many contemporary maps bore the legend "Terra Incognita," a phrase that served only to stimulate the imagination of the intrepid men of the sixteenth century.

Until 1522, when Magellan's ship limped back to Spain, proving that it was possible to circumnavigate the earth, Portugal and Spain were the only contenders in the great race; then France hired its own explorers and was off and running. England and the Netherlands failed to enter the competition until the second half of the century; once in it, they too proved to be formidable contenders.

Terraargētea.

uus.

Terra Incognita

MERIDIES

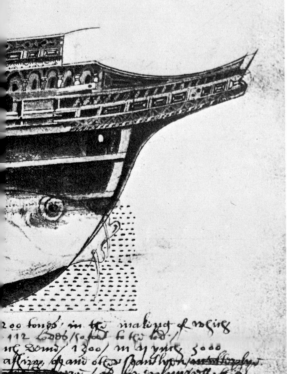

SCIENCE OF THE SEA

Experience, observation, and a magnetic compass were the tools of early fifteenth-century navigators. As the century progressed, exploration encouraged the development of new navigational instruments. Sailors learned to fix their positions, using an astrolabe or quadrant to reckon by the polar star. The tables and charts needed to utilize these instruments brought a new kind of person to the deck—one who had been trained in mathematics and astronomy. Seamen of the new breed calculated tides and invented the traverse board for measuring distances. They created a unique speedometer made of a log tied to a knotted rope (from it arose the nautical terms *log* and *knot*). Many seemingly obvious improvements were overlooked, however; not until almost 1700, for example, did someone invent a quadrant that gave seamen a reading from a shadow instead of from a painful and blinding look into the sun.

Along with such improved navigational aids as the quadrant (above), Renaissance seamen benefited from great advances that had been made in the science of naval architecture. Above left, a pair of English shipwrights are depicted at the drafting table. The result of their labors is shown at left, a faster, more maneuverable ship, superimposed on a drawing of a fish, which had inspired it.

Francisco Pizarro led a group of conquistadors into the mountains of Peru to overcome the Inca kingdom.

Jacques Cartier made three voyages to Canada and spent months with the Indians.

FERDINAN: MAGAGLIANE

Ferdinand Magellan was first to believe circumnavigation of the globe possible.

Hernando Cortes conquered Mexico after a long struggle and stayed on to oversee Spanish settlement there.

Captain John Smith explored hundreds of miles of the eastern coast of North America.

THE EXPLORERS

There is little doubt that the men who conceived and led ventures into uncharted waters in small ships manned by tatterdemalion crews had two characteristics in common: reckless courage and boundless belief in imminent personal gain. Their primary motivations for going were usually similar; but their secondary ones were varied: desire for fame and glory, patriotism, mercantile interests, religion, a hunger for adventure. Many explorers, among them Magellan, Hudson, and Drake, lost their lives, and all those who survived shipwreck, mutiny, and disease had narrow escapes at one time or another. Drake's seamen victualed on penguins at Tierra del Fuego, and in the opposite latitude Barents and his crew found themselves forced to dine on polar bear. The Huron Indians insisted that Champlain join them on a raid against the Iroquois in which he was seriously wounded. The English explorer of Persia, Anthony Jenkinson, almost died on a long camel trip across the desert with no water but "such as we drew out of old, deep wells, being brackish and salt."

Willem Barents made three voyages to the Arctic Circle to find a northeast passage that would enable the Dutch to trade with Russia. He died on the last expedition without having succeeded; arctic conditions were too severe. Bitter cold and lack of food took their toll when ice forced the expedition ashore, and the party was even attacked by polar bears (below).

MERCHANT ADVENTURERS

The Spanish and Portuguese, who courageously explored the world, established trade routes, and opened new markets, had ultimately neither the financial resources nor the organizational skills to realize all their rightful profits. The great German and northern Italian financial houses provided the necessary help for both governments and consequently reaped most of the benefits. Another share of the profits went to the English and the Dutch; as soon as the rewards of piracy and trade had become evident, they too began to take an interest in the New World and the Orient. Private investment in mercantile projects was encouraged in England, and Queen Elizabeth granted charters to companies of "merchant adventurers" to trade in various parts of the world. The Dutch government was even more concerned than the English to strengthen its trading companies, and by mid-seventeenth century England and Holland had achieved mercantile supremacy.

A Japanese screen painting shows Portuguese traders arriving in Japan. The first world-wide traders, the Portuguese, brought European manufactures to China, traded them there for silks and porcelain, and then sold those to the Japanese for silver, which they exchanged in China for gold. They traded anything: horses for hawks and tigers in India, Arabian copper for African slaves, Mexican jewelry for East Indian spices.

344

GOD BE OVR GOOD GVIDE

Arms granted by Elizabeth to the East India Company

DEVS·INDICAT

DEO DVCENTE, NIL NOCET.

England's Muscovy Company made enormous profits.

Sir Francis Drake

THE INTREPID DRAKE

Of all the overseas mariners of the sixteenth century, Francis Drake was probably the greatest adventurer. Many had his courage, but few had his compelling imagination and ability to lead. After a humiliating defeat by the Spanish in 1568, his *raison d'être* became to "singe the king of Spain's beard." Drake began his beard-singeing career in 1573 in Panama; audaciously he led his men inland, captured thirty tons of Spanish silver, and made off with it to sea before his foes could collect their wits and send their forces after him. His ship, the *Golden Hind*, led expeditions against Spanish forts and shipping almost annually thereafter until his death in 1596 off the coast of Panama, close to the site of his first great triumph.

In his 1585 campaign against the Spanish, Drake stopped at the Cape Verde Islands and sacked Santiago; his troops are shown advancing on the city from the right. He went on to hold up Santo Domingo and Cartagena for ransom.

AECK D'AVOIR CIRQVIT TOVTE LA TERRE

TERA · FVRMA

Drake's circumnavigation of the globe is charted on this Dutch map. He cleared the Strait of Magellan in sixteen days and then headed north to begin his famous raids on the Spaniards. He took 25,000 gold pesos at Valparaiso and in the next several months struck successfully time and again along the Pacific coast, completely surprising his Spanish pursuers by taking a westward route for Europe, the first Englishman to do so.

FROM THE NEW WORLD

The flora and fauna of the New World, the red-skinned inhabitants with their own thriving civilizations, the very existence of the vast, uncharted land mass could hardly satisfy the sixteenth-century European's hunger for the exotic; rather it only inflamed his imagination. To all that was new, Europeans added their own embellishments; Sir Walter Raleigh, for example, described in Guiana "a garden of pleasure . . . which had all kinds of garden herbs, flowers, and trees of gold and silver." Raleigh's precious herbs and flowers never reached Europe, but by the middle of the sixteenth century some American products had attained a permanent place in European life. Potatoes became a dietary staple. The meat of the turkey was relished, and chocolate was so popular with the conquistadors that they used cacao beans as money. Tobacco became an important crop, and smoking came to be regarded as a cure for almost any ill, as well as a pleasant social custom.

John White's paintings, such as those at right of an Indian woman, a plantain, and a pineapple, and Nicholas Monardes' engraving of tobacco at left illustrated works that were published to entice Englishmen to settle in America. The engraving at right, from a herbal, shows another plant new to Europeans: maize, or "blew turky wheat," the Indians' staple grain.

Platano. or Planten

Of Florida.

GERARD, *The herball* . . . ; NEW YORK
PUBLIC LIBARY, RARE BOOK ROOM

The Pyne frute.

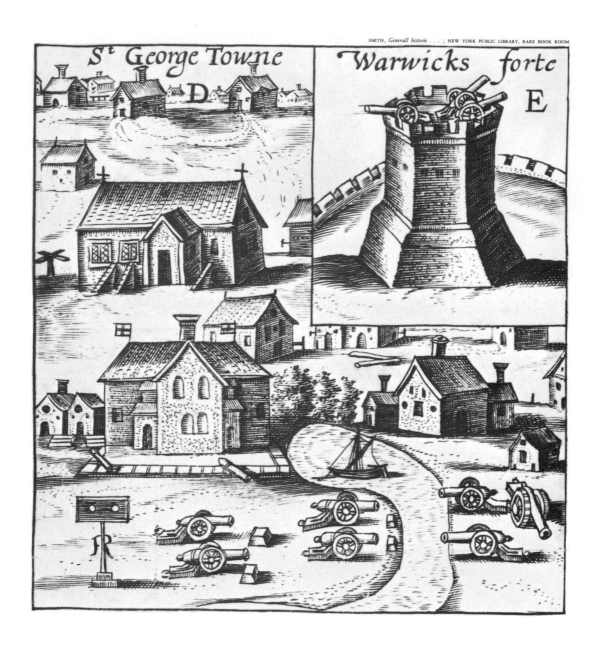

THE ENGLISH COLONISTS

The Spanish and the Portuguese had long since established colonies in the New World when the idea of settling there occurred to the English. It was first mentioned in print in 1567; but it was not until nearly two decades later that the first English colony was sent out to Newfoundland, where insurrection and inclement weather doomed the venture before the colonists had a chance to build even a hut. The scheme would not have worked anyway, for its planners judged the island's climate by fishermen's reports of summer weather; the pioneers would not have survived a winter. Sir Walter Raleigh's Virginia colony also failed, but the English pressed on, and the Elizabethan attempts provided invaluable lessons for future generations. Settlers must be farmers rather than soldiers, and a man must have his own land. Francis Bacon summed up a major problem: "It is a shameful . . . thing to take the scum . . . to be the people with whom you plant, and not only so, but it spoileth the plantation; for they will ever live like rogues . . ."

The page opposite, from A Brief and True Report of the New-found Land of Virginia *by Thomas Harriot, indicates that the unsuccessful Virginia expedition of 1585 had a happy beginning. The Bermuda colony (shown above) throve, although it was planted accidentally when a ship was wrecked on the island.*

He sea coasts of Virginia arre full of Ilāds, wehr by the entrance into the mayne lād is hard to finde. For although they bee separated with diuers and sundrie large Diuision, which seeme to yeeld conuenient entrance, yet to our great perill we proued that they wear shallowe, and full of dangerous flatts, and could neuer perce opp into the mayne lād, vntill wee made trialls in many places with or small pinness. At lengthe wee fownd an entrance vppon our mens diligent serche therof Affter that wee had passed opp, and sayled ther in for a short space we discouered a migthye riuer fallnige downe in to the sownde ouer against those Ilands, which neuerthelesse wee could not saile opp any thinge far by Reason of the shallewnes, the mouth ther of beinge annoyed with sands driuen in with the tyde therfore saylinge further, wee came vnto a Good bigg yland, the Inhabitante therof as soone as they saw vs began to make a great an horrible crye, as people which meuer befoer had seene men apparelled like vs, and camme away makinge out crys likewild beasts or men out of their wyts. But beenge gentlye called backe, wee offred thē of our wares, as glasses, kniues, babies, and other trifles, which wee thougt they deligted in. Soe they stood still, and perceuinge our Good will and courtesie came fawninge vppon vs, and bade us welcome. Then they brougt vs to their village in the iland called, Roanoac, and vnto their Weroans or Prince, which entertained vs with Reasonable curtesie, althoug they wear amased at the first sight of vs. Suche was our arriuall into the parte of the world, which we call Virginia, the stature of bodee of wich people, theyr attire, and maneer of lyuinge, their feasts, and bankketts, I will particullerlye declare vnto yow.

NICOLAO   COPERN

10

NEW HORIZONS

On March 4, 1493, Christopher Columbus sailed the battered *Niña* into Lisbon harbor and demanded that the churches be filled with blossoms and boughs in his honor. In October of the same year, a historian at the court of Ferdinand and Isabella wrote skeptically to a friend that the Italian adventurer was "back safe and sound, and declares he has found wonders." Sixty years later, any hint of incredulity had vanished, and another historian had only unqualified praise for Columbus and his achievement. The finding of a New World, he wrote, was "the greatest event since the creation of the world, apart from the incarnation and death of Him who created it." The magnitude of the exploit is difficult to comprehend; it cannot even be compared to the conquest of space, for the twentieth century is intellectually and emotionally prepared for almost any kind of discovery that may be made and expects and even desires to be astonished. The sixteenth century had no such preparation or predilection for change. Authority, blessed by generations of churchmen and supported by the giants of classical scholarship, was the intellectual rock upon which medieval society rested. Authority was a little fanciful about details, but the main outlines of its position were clear and incontrovertible. Man lived on an earth that held the place of honor at the center of the universe; it was "like the yolk in the middle of an egg," and around it the heavenly spheres revolved, making music in the firmament. Medieval cartographers accepted the word of Ptolemy and recorded the earth's circumference as just under twenty thousand miles, and they followed the leadership of the Church in assuming that the human race was confined to the northern hemisphere by an impenetrable torrid belt that encircled the earth in the region of the equator.

Within two generations of Columbus' voyage of discovery, these medieval concepts were smashed beyond recognition. The world suddenly expanded by some five thousand miles; two new continents were located; and Europeans had to accept the serious possibility that there might be an antipode whose inhabitants lived "foot to foot" with them. Even before the proportions of a new and enlarged earth had been fully realized, more unnerving discoveries were being made. Within fifty years of Columbus' voyage to America, the form of the heavens themselves was being called in doubt. The two revolutions, which overturned the traditional ideas of the earth and the universe, erupted at almost the same time, and between them they destroyed the intellectual underpinnings of the past and cast Adam and all his race out of the secure Eden of a scripturally intelligible world and an anthropomorphic universe.

Rewriting geography caught the imagination, and Europe was soon swept up in the romance of discovery. Recasting the universe, however, filled the mind with terror. Adventurers dared the unknown and went to test for themselves Raleigh's as-

This nocturnal's toothlike markers, read by touch in the dark, helped Elizabethan sailors to keep time by the stars.

surance that "there are stranger things to be seen in the world than are between London and Staines"; but it took men of even stronger mettle to risk their souls by imagining a new cosmology in which the earth and its sister planets hurtled in senseless orbit about the sun.

Medieval man was not accustomed to thinking of the earth as a geographic entity. His horizons were those of his village, his landmarks were the ancient oak and the narrow footpath, and his unknown was just over the neighboring hill. The world that lay beyond sight and sound was hidden by a heavy fog of ignorance, which was so complete that men did not even possess the vocabulary that would enable them to think in global terms. Their world was not flat, as is so often suggested, rather it lacked continents and was seen as composed of a series of separate and uninhabitable zones (the Arctic, Antarctic, and Torrid), and a single land mass, the *orbis terrarum*, of Asia, Africa, and Europe. The concept of an earth covered by seas, with occasional islands of land, was alien to the medieval mind, which visualized the oceans as lakes surrounded by land and considered Jerusalem the center of the world.

What medieval geography lacked in accuracy it made up in imagination. The garden of Eden and other regions of Christian mythology were thought of as geographic realities. The East was a land of fantasy where dwarfs and giants, griffins and unicorns, dog-headed demons and huge clubfooted men lived amidst marvelous wealth and endless commotion. The Indus, the Ganges, and the Nile were associated with the rivers of paradise, and the mysterious land of Gog and Magog was placed somewhere east of Eden. Africa and Asia were happily confused, and the Indian Ocean was often pictured as a lake bounded by India and Ethiopia. Fountains of youth and rivers of gold were always to be found in India and darkest Africa, and the Atlantic Ocean was regarded as populated with sea serpents and other grotesque monsters that fed on foolhardy mariners.

On one point learned cartographers and superstitious sailors were correct: the Atlantic Ocean was an almost insurmountable obstacle even to the most daring seafarer. Once he had lost sight of land, the medieval adventurer faced the ocean with no means of navigation, and he sailed in a frail vessel that could make no headway against a contrary wind. In the fifteenth century, just as in the twentieth, the unknown gave way not so much to boldness as to brains. As the electronic computer and advanced mathematics have been necessary prerequisites to navigation in space, so the compass, the astrolabe, the quadrant, and the compilations of Arab mathematicians and astronomers were essential to the conquest of the oceans. The first great discoverers either were able navigators themselves or had with them pilots who could combine mathematical theory with experience at sea. By 1484 seamen could venture forth into the darkness of the broad Atlantic with a fair expectation of finding their way home again, and Vasco da Gama's triumph in rounding the Cape of Good Hope in 1497 was possible only because he had the nerve and the scientific knowledge to stand two thousand miles out into the South Atlantic to pick up the favorable winds and currents that allowed him to clear the southern tip of Africa and sail on into the Indian Ocean.

In the conquest of the oceans the shipwright was as important as the astronomer. The square-rigged and clumsy medieval cog, a ship that wallowed in the high waves of the Atlantic, and unless favored with a tail wind, slipped sideways faster than it moved forward, was redesigned to incorporate features of the maneuverable lateen-rigged Arab *sambuk*. The result was the Portuguese caravel, the prototype of all sixteenth-century European sailing vessels. The caravel was a seaworthy craft that could hold its course in any but the most adverse wind, and was capable of undertaking voyages of three thousand miles without a landfall.

Even when sailors and navigators had the necessary skills and ships that were capable of taking them into the vastness of the North and South Atlantic, they required stout hearts to face the elements in vessels that were scarcely larger than today's small trawlers, to exist on a diet of salt beef, beans, biscuits, stale water, and an occasional ration of wine, and to endure months at sea with no other sleeping accommodations than the bare deck. It is little wonder that crews mutinied, pilots were disobedient, and the life expectancy of seamen was short. Even in the sixteenth century, when ships were stronger and wind and weather conditions better understood, the mortality rate was enough to discourage the most determined adventurer. Thomas Wyndham and a hundred of his crew of one hundred forty men died of fever while sailing off the coast of Guinea in 1553; the next year Sir Hugh Willoughby and most of his men perished when stranded north of the Arctic Circle; Richard Chancellor drowned in the autumn of 1556 while returning from Russia; Sir Humphrey Gilbert went down with all hands in 1583 in the North Atlantic; Thomas Cavendish never returned from his second attempt to circumnavigate the globe in 1591; John Davys was killed by Japanese pirates off the Malay coast; and Hawkins and Drake both died at sea on the same expedition.

Yet for every fatality, a dozen clamored, as one Spanish conquistador put it, "to serve God and His Majesty, to give light to those who were in darkness, and to grow rich, as all men desire to do." Whether the wide harbors of the world were explored more for gain than for adventure and Christian zeal is not easy to say. Lust for the riches of India and Cathay encouraged Columbus to believe that San Salvador lay within the Japanese archipelago, urged Vasco da Gama to risk the voyage around the tip of Africa, and fostered the persistent search for a southwestern route to the Orient and a northern passage up the St. Lawrence River or through Hudson Bay. "Spices and Christians" had been Da Gama's answer as to why he had sought to reach Calicut in 1498. A single shipload of Ceylon cinnamon, Sumatra pepper, Moluccas cloves, or East Indies nutmeg was worth countless lives and failures. Ferdinand Magellan started out in 1519 to circumnavigate the globe with five ships and two hundred thirty-four men; only eighteen of his original crew completed the voyage three years later, but in the eyes of the investors the tiny *Victoria*'s precious cargo of cloves more than compensated for the death of the ship's captain and the loss of so many crewmen.

Sixteenth-century advances in navigation did little to allay the mariner's ignorance of life in the sea itself. As these embellishments to a contemporary chart show, seagoing hulls, island-sized dragons, ship-devouring serpents, aquatic unicorns, geyser-headed hippomonstrosities, and all manner of outlandish and malefic creatures were thought to be ceaselessly thrashing about in the deep.

Europe's need to discover civilizations richer than its own in culture, luxuries, and above all in spices may have been the source of the wind that scattered "young men through the world to seek their fortunes"; but those same adventurers sailed with a double sense of superiority—confident in the knowledge that they excelled in guns, ships, and navigational techniques, and secure in the even more comforting conviction that they were bringing Christian light to those in darkness. When the Spaniards burned the priceless Maya libraries of Yucatán, they did so because they knew that the books "contained nothing in which there was not to be seen superstition and lies of the devil." The search for the legendary Christian kingdom of Prester John was as persistent as the dream of El Dorado and was almost as important in Columbus' motivation as was his desire to reach Cathay. Throughout the age of discovery, in Protestant as well as Catholic lands, avarice marched hand in hand with a sense of self-righteous superiority. Those Most Catholic Majesties of Spain, Ferdinand and Isabella, voiced the sublime egotism of all Europe when they presented Christopher Columbus with an open letter of introduction to the princes of the unknown world:

> To King ——
> We have heard that Your Highness and your subjects entertain great love for us and for Spain. We are informed, moreover, that you and your subjects very much wish to hear news from Spain. We therefore send our admiral, Christopher Columbus, who will tell you that we are in good health and perfect prosperity.

The Admiral of the Ocean Sea carried with him copies of a more sinister document: the authority to "discover and acquire islands and mainland in the ocean sea." What he encountered threw European cartographers into confusion and Spanish merchants into dismay. Painfully and dangerously, the coastline of an immense land mass began to emerge, an unknown and disturbing impediment to the important business of reaching the Indies. For a full generation after the discovery of America, Europeans continued to look eastward and southward, and the advice of the early sixteenth century was "to the south! to the south! They that seek wealth must go to the riches of the Aequinoctial; not unto the cold and frozen north." The outlines of two new continents were gradually revealed by mariners anxious to find an entrance into the Pacific, but when the western route to India, through the Strait of Magellan, was finally located on the other side of the world in freezing Antarctic latitudes, the passage proved too dangerous to be of commercial value.

However, by the time that kings and merchants came to realize that the Orient was not, as Columbus optimistically argued, only five thousand miles west of the Canary Islands, the imagination of Europe had been caught by the idea of a New World that might prove reality to be far more marvelous than even the most bizarre legends of the past.

Rivers of eternal life, fountains of youth, giant Amazons, hippogriffs, and satyrs—all the trappings of medieval fables—were transferred to the Americas; to them were added the wonders of reality—pyramids of skulls, human sacrifices, cannibalism, cities built on water, rivers so wide they appeared to be oceans, and above all, riches that seemed to confirm men's wildest dreams of the lands of Ophir and El Dorado. On Good Friday, 1519, Cortes and six hundred Spanish desperados commenced the conquest of Mexico. Within the year they had sent home to the emperor's court in Brussels unheard-of trophies of war: "a sun all of gold, a whole fathom broad, and a moon all silver of the same size," and great piles of weapons encrusted with gold and silver, "altogether valued at a hundred thousand florins." When he viewed the collection, the artist Albrecht Dürer exclaimed: "All the days of my life I have seen nothing that rejoiced my heart so much as these things, for I saw amongst them wonderful works of art, and I marveled at the subtle *ingenia* of men in foreign lands."

Twelve years later came word of an even more spectacular conquest: Francisco Pizarro, with sixty-two horsemen and one hundred six foot soldiers, had struggled over the top of the world and descended on the rich and defenseless Inca civilization of Peru. The ransom that he received from the captured Inca king, Atahualpa, became legendary—a room twenty-two feet by seventeen feet filled as high as a man could reach with articles of silver and gold, a fortune estimated at four and one-half million ducats. It was the vision of similar lands and treasures that in 1535 led Jacques Cartier ever deeper into Canada as he sought the imaginary kingdom of Saguenay, which was always just beyond the great forest somewhere up the Ottawa River. Only disappointment awaited Cartier at the end of his journey, for he never found his phantom land, and the twelve barrels of gold that he brought back to France turned out to be iron pyrites, or fool's gold. His precious stones were quartz, and sixteenth-century Parisians coined a new phrase for the counterfeit—*diamants de Canada*.

Although failure continued to dog the efforts of those who sought a golden shower in the north, the south remained an inexhaustible source of riches and reputations. The silver mines of Zacatecas, in

I. la Trinidad.

MARE del NORT.

Terra
di
PARIA.

Orenoque F.

Capuri Flu.

Raleigh's exploration of the Orinoco River in search of silver was frustrated by floods
that raised the water level "fowre or fiue foote" and drove the Indians into tree houses.

Mexico, and the Potosí lode, in Bolivia, were opened up in the 1540's and started a rush of fortune hunters anxious to share in the flood of precious metals. In the next century and a half, 18,600 tons of silver and 200 tons of gold poured into the coffers of the kings of Spain, and possibly again as much reached the pockets of private prospectors. The world remembered that Francisco Pizarro, the illiterate and illegitimate son of a Spanish officer, had won for himself a fortune and the title of marquis; it forgot that he was murdered in the process.

Until Elizabeth's reign England's role in the drama of discovery remained that of a passive but avidly interested spectator who begrudged Spain and Portugal their good fortune but lacked the energy to challenge their monopoly. English fishermen did sail out toward the Grand Banks off Newfoundland, the chimera of a northern passage to China took Richard Chancellor to Russia in 1553, and the profits of the slave trade led the cousins John Hawkins and Francis Drake first to Africa and then deep into the Spanish Caribbean during the 1560's. However, it was not until after Sir Humphrey

Gilbert presented his *Discourse of a Discovery for a New Passage to Cathay* in 1576, and Drake in the *Golden Hind* sailed into Plymouth harbor on September 26, 1580, with a forty-seven-hundred per cent profit in his hold, that England took its place as a maritime power.

Of all the adventurers who went down to the sea in ships, "putting a girdle round about the world" with their naval daring, the one most enthralled by the romance of the New World was Sir Walter Raleigh. "What shall we be," he asked, "travelers or tinkers; conquerors or novices?" In answer to his own question he set out in 1595 upon an adventure more fit for boys than for aging heroes: to find the fabled land of El Dorado, where the clothing of kings and commoners and even the kitchen pots and pans were made of gold. Stories of a city of gold had been heard almost from the moment the first white man set foot in Central and South America. Its exact whereabouts was elusive, but one persistent report located El Dorado, or what the natives called Manoa, in the upper reaches of the Orinoco River, presumably on the assumption that if the

359

A watercolor drawing by John White shows a typical Virginia Indian village of the sort found by Raleigh's ill-fated Roanoke colonists. Houses were constructed of poles and matting.

city existed at all, it could be reached only by penetrating the most pestilent and inaccessible jungles of South America.

For years Raleigh gleaned from seamen and Spanish reports every scrap of information he could find about Guiana and the Orinoco. When he finally set sail, a dozen distinguished persons had been persuaded by his silver tongue to invest in the dream or actually join the expedition. Lord Admiral Howard gave money, and the sons of Sir Richard Grenville and Sir Humphrey Gilbert both sailed with the fleet when it put out to sea with high hopes on February 6, 1595.

By chance, Sir Walter captured the one Spaniard who knew most about Guiana and who was himself obsessed with the legend of a civilization of gold located past one of the endless bends of the Orinoco. Don Antonio de Berrio, last of the Spanish conquistadors, had been searching the area for fifteen years,

and he communicated his zeal to his English captor. Encouraged by Berrio, Raleigh had one of the smallest of his ships fitted for river travel, and with one hundred men began the long ordeal of rowing up the Orinoco. For the first time he began to appreciate the hell that De Soto, Champlain, Pizarro, Cartier, and the rest of the great adventureres had endured. He was forced "to lie in the rain and weather, in the open air, in the burning sun, and upon the hard boards," and conditions became so foul that "there was never any prison in England that could be found more unsavory and loathsome."

At forty-three the gallant captain longed for the comforts of a feather bed and a decently cooked meal, but he took what comfort he could from his vision and continued on into the labyrinth of tributaries that flowed into the Orinoco. Raleigh found no golden cities, but he saw wonders that made him all the more willing to believe the fairy tales told by the Indian population. Three hundred miles inland he encountered a land rich in game and the fullness of the earth, where every pebble seemed to hold the promise of a fortune. It was "the most beautiful country that ever mine eyes beheld," he later wrote. Only the ugly crocodiles that swam in the wake of his ship, and to which one of his company fell victim, marred this demiparadise. He beheld the great falls of the Caroni, over a series of cliffs, where the rushing water sent up a mist so thick that the English "took it at the first for a smoke that had risen over some great town."

From the Indians Raleigh learned of sights even more marvelous: of kings who clothed themselves in gold dust; of giant men called Ewaipanoma, with mouths in their chests and eyes in their shoulders; and of Amazons who on the twelfth month of each year invited the lustiest warriors of neighboring tribes to stand on the borders of their territories while the damsels "cast lots for their valentines." The ladies then enjoyed their men for a month of feasting and love-making.

The rainy season came, and Sir Walter and his little band decided that they had had enough of hard boards and unsavory victuals. They returned to the ships in the estuary and sailed back to England with no gold in their pockets but with visions of paradise in their heads. When Raleigh came to write of his adventures—*The Discovery of the Large, Rich, and Beautiful Empire of Guiana, with a Relation of the Great and Golden City of Manoa*—he captured for every European who could read the thrill of distant lands, the sense of adventure, and the hope of someday discovering El Dorado.

The surge of emotion that drove Englishmen from the comforts of their chimney seats to search "the most opposite corners and quarters of the world" was touched with something more than the love of adventure and the desire for gold. The New World was "a shelter and a hiding place" where men of humble origin could carve for themselves a new and better home. At first the hope of planting a nation in the wilderness seemed unreal, part of the imaginary trappings of the unknown world. Such a vision had inspired More's *Utopia*, that philosopher's paradise where reason and wisdom reigned triumphant, and the ills, horrors, and inequalities of the sixteenth century made way for the perfect harmony of an orderly, if sterile, semicommunal state. Part spoof (the chamber pots were made of gold), part penetrating study into the social and psychological realities underlying human society, and part idealization of the medieval concept of a balanced, ordered, and integrated society, the *Utopia* had a deep impact on the Tudor mind. Throughout the century the

idea persisted that somewhere in the New World a utopia lay hidden, a haven and refuge from the troubles of the Old World.

Three men were responsible for the first efforts to transform such an aspiration into reality: the extraordinary Sir Humphrey Gilbert, who died in his futile endeavor to colonize Newfoundland, the ubiquitous Raleigh, and Richard Hakluyt, the propagandist who inspired all men with his magnificent collection of *Voyages*. From the start America was seen as a way of skimming the "milk of bitterness" from England, and Gilbert and Raleigh sought to persuade nearly one hundred English Catholics to leave their hearths for a new start in life. When many of the colonists and later Sir Humphrey were drowned, Raleigh worked on alone, urging Englishmen "to take fast root and hold" three thousand miles away from home. Of the imperial powers, only England succeeded in transplanting its people and establishing small, tough, and vital replicas of itself on the inhospitable shores and in the endless forests of an uncharted land. Spaniards went out by the thousands, but they sought gold to plunder and souls to save; Frenchmen ventured forth in far more conservative numbers to trade and trap along the St. Lawrence River; only the English sent out viable offshoots with men to toil, women to be fruitful, children to ensure the future, and laws by which to live. The achievement was a miracle of advertising: financiers were persuaded to hazard capital on a long-term investment, and the industrious workman and the thrifty housewife were enticed to the supreme folly of risking all upon the fantasy of a better life. Religious hatred, economic privation, and fear of the gallows eventually drove a multitude from their homes, but the New World could never have been successfully populated by bitterness alone. The indispensable role of Raleigh and Hakluyt was first to show how not to plant a colony and then, with Hakluyt's book, to charm Elizabethan society with the romance of colonization.

In March, 1584, Raleigh received one of those wonderfully self-assured charters issued by European sovereigns; the queen conferred upon him the authority "to discover barbarous countries, not actually possessed of any Christian prince and inhabited by Christian people, to occupy and enjoy the same for ever." Within a month two ships were sent out to reconnoiter the southeastern coast of North America for a good location for a colony. Roanoke Island had no suitable harbor, but its shores were rich with grapes and it seemed to be reasonably secure from the predatory Spanish. In August, 1585, one hundred seven colonists landed. From the start the experiment was an unmitigated failure. The

English were a scruffy lot of undisciplined ex-soldiers and incipient buccaneers in quest of easy money, and when they found little besides hard work and virgin forests they quickly lost heart. Most of their supplies had been spoiled at sea, and the landing had been made too late in the year to plant crops for the winter months. The settlers were thrown upon the generosity of the Indians, who had barely enough for themselves. When the natives refused to continue supplying food, relations deteriorated to the point of open war. Very early in the history of America the white man evolved the theory that the only good Indian was a dead Indian. Raleigh had promised his settlers that new recruits and supplies would be sent out in March, but the promise was never kept; even if reinforcements had arrived on schedule, it is doubtful whether the colonists would have stayed on. They were without heart and without women, and when Drake, who had been pirating in the Caribbean, appeared at Roanoke in June, 1586, the colonists seized the opportunity to flee back to the security of the Old World.

Raleigh was bitterly disappointed by his settlers, but astute enough to perceive the cause of their failure. The first experiment in colonization had been financed on a shoestring and manned by explorers and exploiters, not by men and women who had the strength and vision to toil in the red earth of Virginia. In a year Sir Walter had raised the necessary capital and found the volunteers for a second attempt. This time he was determined to ship out women as well as men and to ensure their labor by offering each colonist five hundred acres of land free and a voice in the affairs of the colony. One hundred fifty settlers made the two-month journey to Virginia and arrived in July, 1587, to find the original fort burned and the Indians still resentful.

Eighty-nine men, seventeen women, and eleven children, under Governor John White, elected to make their homes on the ruins of the old settlement, and all one hundred seventeen were to vanish forever. Raleigh had strained every financial nerve to supply his plantation, but even so, the colonists were critically short of the essentials of life. Within a month of their landing they sent Governor White back to England to beg for seed and iron, livestock and cloth, and a multitude of other items necessary to transform a camp into an enduring community. Before White left, there seemed to be some possibility that the settlement might take root; at least an English child had been born in the New World, his granddaughter, Virginia Dare. But by the time he returned to Roanoke, nothing remained of the colony.

John White had sailed back to England to find Raleigh close to bankruptcy and the nation arming for the forthcoming clash with Spain. The fate of the colonists soon became a tragic by-product of the momentous struggle occurring in Europe, for there were no ships, arms, or men to send to Virginia. Raleigh already had invested forty thousand pounds in the Roanoke experiment and was obliged to transfer a portion of his rights and authority to a joint stock company of London merchants, who contracted, in no great haste, to send out a relief expedition. Impatient as he was, it was not until August 18, 1591, four years to the month later, that Governor White returned to Roanoke Island to be confronted with the ominous silence of the wilderness and the impenetrable mystery of what had happened to his colony. The fort still stood, but the houses and all their inhabitants had gone. There was one clue to their fate, part of a code decided upon before White sailed for England. A Maltese cross was to be cut into the wood of the stockade in case of peril and a word was to be carved to indicate where the settlers might have fled. On one of the piles of the palisade was found the word *Croatoan*, on a tree were cut the letters *CRO*, but nowhere was there discovered a Maltese cross. The settlers had survived their first winter, for a Spanish frigate reported their existence in June, 1588, but no hint remains of what terrible events occurred thereafter. Possibly, as the carved letters might indicate, the colony had moved to Croatoan Island or had gone to live with the Croatoan Indians. The most likely explanation, however, is that the settlers were surprised and massacred by Indians.

The tragedy of Roanoke was not without its blessings. One hundred seventeen men, women, and children had vanished, but their successors learned two vital lessons that would eventually ensure the success of the Jamestown colony: first, that colonization, in contrast to plundering and gold prospecting, was immensely costly, and no private individual could carry the burden alone; and second, that there was no real hope of discovering gold and gaining a quick profit in the areas that were open to English exploration. The settlers who followed after the disappearance of the Roanoke colony, and the merchants who joined in the stock companies to supply and maintain the new settlements did so with some, if not all, of the scales removed from their eyes. The settlement of the new continent was accomplished by realists who knew the odds and were willing to accept the heartaches and the labor necessary to conquer and civilize the New World. Raleigh's labors ultimately bore fruit in 1607; and both he and Hakluyt lived to see "an English nation" in North America.

The shock of discovery, of finding the world a

different, and in some ways, a better place than the one imagined by classical and medieval authority, undoubtedly weakened the grip of the dead hand of custom. Novelty was in the air. Everywhere there were "new and rare observations," as men discovered for themselves a host of fresh wonders. Peter Martyr announced the existence of the New World in his *De orbe novo* in 1530; new theories of medicine were propounded by Paracelsus in 1526; a revolutionary book on diseases was issued in 1541 by Johannes Baptista de Cavigliolis; André Thévet published *Les singularités de la France antarctique* in 1557; William Gilbert's *New Philosophy of our Sublunary World* was written well before the author's death in 1603; and Englishmen marveled over Monardes' *Joyful News out of the New-found World* on the subject of botany. Discoveries in every area of human speculation led to questioning, and if need be, to the putting aside of ancient theories for newer ones, based on empirical evidence.

The new discoveries on earth were acclaimed even by a Church that somehow adapted the story of Adam and his expulsion from the garden of Eden to the existence of human beings in the antipodes, who could not possibly be descendants of the original biblical man. But disturbing discoveries in the heavens and the recasting of God's domain were very different matters, and when in 1543 Copernicus announced a new cosmology in *De revolutionibus orbium coelestium*, his ideas were dismissed as unsettling and silly. It was ridiculous, dangerous, and presumptuous, men believed, to argue that as massive a body as the earth, which was the center of God's universe, could rotate on its axis or hurtle in space around the sun.

The traditional view of the universe was too imposing, too deeply rooted in the most atavistic impulses of the human race to be denied. Not only did the wisest of classical philosophers vouch for the truth of the cosmos, not only was it proved by biblical evidence and by God's own voice speaking through His Church on earth but also man's every instinct and his own eyes told him that he was the central and most important point, around which the heavenly bodies marched. The dark of a winter's night provided indisputable evidence that moon and sun, planet and stars, Milky Way and the entire celestial display rose and set around the earth. To the Elizabethan observing such wonders, it seemed clear and proper that he should be standing at the core of the universe and that heaven and earth should have been created as the setting for a divine drama in which man was destined to play the leading role as God's special creation. The authority of Aristotle and the word of Scripture confirmed what

In this print, columns representing Copernicus and Tycho Brahe shore up the tottering edifice of ancient astronomy.

SPHÆRA CIVITATIS

In this graphic argument for the divine right of monarchs, Elizabeth's virtues mirror a pre-Copernican universe.

An engraving of Copernicus' system shows the sun as hub of the universe, not the earth as in the Ptolemaic system.

any simpleton could see for himself; only a tiny and suspect band of mathematicians agreed with John Donne that the "new philosophy calls all in doubt."

> The Sun is lost, and th' earth, and no
> man's wit
> Can well direct him where to look for it.

The much-acclaimed dogma that modern science is based on empirical data interpreted by reason is one of those uncritically treasured truisms that do nothing but befuddle the mind. The creed implies that old-fashioned Aristotelian science was without observation and was grounded on improbable hypotheses totally at odds with reason. Such an assumption is not only untrue, it also obscures the crucial point that many of the errors of Aristotelian science were rooted in observation and were based on too high a regard for what the eye sees and for what appears to be reasonable.

Classical cosmology was founded upon four assumptions that were derived from careful observation: the world of man had been composed of water, fire, air, and earth; the nature of all things is to remain at rest, and therefore what must be explained is movement and motion; the earth is stationary and the heavens are spherical and revolve about the earth every twenty-four hours. To this evidence of the senses, classical philosophy then added a number of suppositions about the nature of the universe: it was orderly, purposeful, and ultimately intelligible; it was finite and consisted of ether; there was a prime mover to account for celestial motion, and the physical principles that explained the actions of the firmament were not the same as those that operated on earth; and finally, the heavens were eternal and immutable, free of flux and decay.

Classical theory and observation produced a convincing picture of a universe, one that was easy to comprehend, made excellent sense, and above all else, was comfortably anthropomorphic in its assumptions. At all times man was assumed to be standing securely within an immense sphere, looking up from a central location at the inner surface of the firmament. All things were ultimately relative to a fixed point of observation—the human observer standing on a stationary earth.

Aristotelian philosophy explained the existence of change and corruption in the world by the commotion caused by the four terrestrial elements—earth, air, fire, and water—as each sought to find that location most satisfactory to its nature. Earth and water were forever attracted downward toward the center of the terrestrial globe; fire and air moved upward, aspiring to a higher and more perfect place in the heavens. Had the elements achieved their goals, the world would have died; it would have consisted of motionless and eternal layers of earth, ocean, air, and fire. But since the elements were mixed and constantly struggling to disentangle themselves, they produced change, violence, and decay on earth. Outside the world of man, a different set of physical properties operated, since the element of ether had achieved its harmonic and natural place. Like the layers of an onion the firmament extended outward in a series of rotating, crystalline, ethereal spheres, to which were attached the various points of celestial geography. First came the circle of the moon, beyond which all was contentment, ageless and enduring. Next came the spheres of the two lesser planets, then that of the sun, followed by those of the three outer planets, and then the circle of the outer firmament, where in endless incomprehensible numbers resided the fixed stars. Two more spheres remained, one classical, the other Christian: the invisible orb of the classical prime mover, which was thought to be the cause of all heavenly movement and the source of the music of the heavens; and even farther out, the empyrean, the abode of God and His heavenly hosts. There was scarcely an Elizabethan who had not been taught all or part of the Aristotelian cosmos, and long after Copernicus, Kepler, and Galileo had destroyed forever the music of the spheres, educators were still indoctrinating young gentlemen with the ancient view of a geocentric universe.

The classical world had always assumed that the heavenly spheres, so filled with harmony and virtue, could affect the destinies of men. Fortune and fate resided in the stars, and not even the Elizabethan introduction of such highly active and interfering inhabitants of the sidereal world as intelligence, potentates, dominations, cherubim, seraphim, angels, and archangels could deprive the classical cosmos of its influence in the affairs of man. If, argued Sir Walter Raleigh, God had given "virtues to springs and fountains, to cold earth, to plants and stones . . . why should we rob the beautiful stars of their working powers?" From time out of mind astronomers had been astrologers, supporting their scientific labors with the profits earned by casting horoscopes and reading the message of the stars. The sixteenth century was a busy period for those versed in the interpretation of the heavenly movements, and the year of the Armada was regarded by astrologers in every capital of Europe as an ominous date. Even the most unskilled viewer of the skies could see that Saturn, Mars, and Jupiter were in prophetic conjunction; that such a combination should occur during a year in which two solar and two lunar eclipses were scheduled to take place made the portent all the

A 1559 print shows Atlas supporting a Ptolemaic universe, though many astronomers by then supported Copernicus.

more alarming to observers.

Such was the cosmic scheme of things, and to it Elizabethans added the human conceit of believing that the celestial display had been created for their benefit. Man might live upon an earth that one sixteenth-century Frenchman described as being "so depraved and broken in all kind of vices and abominations that it seemeth to be a place that hath received all the filthiness and purgings of all other worlds and ages," but it was also evident that the heavens declared the glory of God and that the stars had been set in the skies "to adorn the world and delight the eyes of men." It was accepted by all that the sun, moon, and other stars had been ordained "for no other purpose but to serve the earth." The horse, it was said, had been "brought forth for the use of man"; the soil produced grain so that the horse might live and labor; and the skies had been instructed to water the grain. Any scientific wizard who denied such a satisfying and obvious totality of

Other views of the universe persisted despite the Copernican revolution. Here an all-nurturing World Soul, derived from Egyptian myth, serves both heaven and earth.

earth, man, God, and heavens was not just a fool but a dangerous fool, and Martin Luther voiced the common sentiment of all Europe when he said of Copernicus: "The fool will overturn the whole art of astronomy."

The Aristotelian fetters that held fast the sixteenth-century mind were so stout that even the greatest English medical scientist, William Harvey, confessed, after a lifetime of disproving classical medicine, that Aristotle "has always such weight with me that I never think of differing from him inconsiderately." Such bonds could not be broken without a total revolution within the mind of man. Answers are determined by the questions asked, and before the old physics and astronomy could be displaced, men had to pose questions that were profoundly disturbing and darkly heretical. In the face of every accepted authority, a Pandora's box of doubt and inquiry had to be opened: What if motion were natural and rest had to be explained? What if the mental picture of a universe with the earth as its center was wrong? What if mankind did not look out from the middle but stood instead on the outside and looked in? What if the cosmos was not finite but infinite, with no center at all? What if the firmaments moved only because the earth rotated? And finally the most seditious question of them all: What if every celestial body were rushing through boundless space in a fashion describable only in terms relative to other moving objects? If such propositions were true, then where was certainty, where coherence? Where was man's God-given place of honor? Such questions did not come easily even to men of great genius, and the sixteenth-century scientist, though he had his moments of inspiration, was only human, a normal mixture of erudition, quackery, enthusiasm, and blindness.

Nowhere was the ambivalence that marked the transition from medieval to modern thought so apparent as in science. Sixteenth-century scientific truth was a strange composite of the old and new, chemistry and alchemy, astronomy and astrology, mathematics and numerology, medicine and magic, observation and sorcery. A bold mind might lift a corner of the curtain of ignorance and glimpse the truth, but the man who dismissed astrology as nonsense might himself be a helpless devotee of occultism and cabala. Paracelsus announced that "the sick should be the doctor's books," but he believed in the *electrum magicum* of charms and prescribed for his patients doses of ground-up jewels on the hypothesis that the more precious the stones, the more efficacious the remedy. Sixteenth-century doctors were, by modern standards, expensive and learned charlatans who talked knowingly about choleric and melancholic influences within the body and killed their clientele with "comfortable potions" of crabs' eyes, powdered human skulls, Egyptian mummy's dust, and live spiders. Yet the greatest sixteenth-century surgeon, Ambroise Paré, for the first time made amputation an operation that the victim had a reasonable chance of surviving, and he was wise enough to say of his prowess as a doctor and a surgeon, "I treated him and God cured him." The distinguished mathematician Blaise de Vigenère argued that no one should "study the divinely beautiful proportions of numbers in order to make them serve the computation of a bank"; yet Thomas Digges, one of the most famous Englishmen versed in "cunning calculations," was an expert in ballistics and went to sea to put to a test his theories about compass variations.

Of all the scientific figures of the Elizabethan age, the most extraordinary example of intellectual brilliance combined with mental obtuseness was Doctor John Dee of Mortlake. That "arch conjuror of the whole kingdom" was the admired confidant of royalty, the adviser of mariners, the friend of the learned Dutch cartographer Gerard Mercator, the defender of Copernicus, the author of an imaginative and ambitious scheme to reorganize the English fishing industry, the queen's astrologer, and by his own confession, an unswerving believer in occultism, spirits, apocalyptic numbers, cabalistic formulas, and magic inscriptions. When a mutilated and stabbed wax effigy of Elizabeth was found in Lincoln's Inn Field, Doctor Dee assured his alarmed sovereign that the doll was the work of a silly and perverted mind. Nevertheless the sage was so deeply committed to spiritualism that he maintained a private medium by the unlikely name of Edward Kelley, to whom he paid a yearly salary of fifty pounds. The good Doctor Dee was possessed of a magic mirror, a polished stone of mystic properties, and a "gazing table," which stood on a square of red silk, with each of its legs resting on a wax seal inscribed with sacred Hebrew letters.

The liberation of the human mind from superstitions, preconceptions, and traditional habits of thinking is such a painful and disturbing process that it is surprising that Kepler, Dee, Copernicus, and William Gilbert were not burned at the stake as was the Italian philosopher Giordano Bruno. They escaped persecution primarily because they were the high priests of a mystery that very few people understood. Copernicus' view of the universe may have been as clear as "sun beams" to Thomas Digges, who pronounced in 1576 the heliocentric system to be so self-evident that "any reasonable man that hath his understanding ripened with mathematical

demonstration" must accept it; but until well into the seventeenth century *De revolutionibus* remained primarily the concern of trained scholars. Copernicus' mathematical hypotheses did not come to the attention of the public or most ecclesiastical authorities until they had been enlarged by Bruno, Kepler, and Galileo into a cosmic system of new and dangerous dimensions and un-Christian implications.

The first step of the new cosmology was built upon the weakest point of the old. Classical and medieval astronomers had long been aware that the planets did not behave with proper regard for a spherical, immutable, and harmonious universe. They traveled in a mystifying manner, usually moving in a stately and proper path from east to west across the sky, but occasionally turning about in a contrary fashion. Various theories were propounded to explain these bothersome celestial exceptions, but they all had one weakness in common: the mathematics required to explain such erratic movement was so elaborate that it contradicted the classical concept of a universe of marvelous simplicity and perfection.

Mathematicians found the planets—especially Mars—aesthetically disturbing. Copernicus resolved the difficulty by turning to the assumption that the earth rotated and the sun was the center of the universe for reasons more aesthetic than empirical. He based his new theory on aesthetics as well as on mathematics. It seemed to him that the medieval mathematics of the heavens was too complex, and that symbolically the sun, as the source of all light, should hold the place of honor at the center of the universe. Copernicus could take the first giant stride of imagining an earth spinning in space and a sun around which all else revolved, but he could not jump the next intellectual hurdle and see that if the earth rotated, the crystalline spheres of the classical cosmos were unnecessary. Copernicus had lifted the curtain and peeked under it, but he continued to stand on the medieval side and view the heavens in traditional terms.

The heliocentric theory made a deep stir within the brotherhood of astronomers. In suggesting that the earth turned, Copernicus had concluded his argument with the statement: "You will find, if you think carefully, that these things occur in this way." In the second half of the sixteenth century, two sidereal events occurred that caused scientists and laymen to think more carefully about the great astronomer's views and to reconsider their ideas of the structure of the universe. In 1572 a new star appeared in the skies, the first reported since the one that had shone over Bethlehem. For seventeen lunar months it blazed so brightly that it could be seen even in day-

Galileo Galilei

Johannes Kepler

Sir Francis Bacon

John Dee

light. Then it vanished as mysteriously as it had arrived. Astrologers, clerics, philosophers, and kings were thrown into confusion, for surely such a brilliant sign betokened some extraordinary event in the affairs of man: the death of Elizabeth, the outbreak of the plague, the approach of war.

What, in fact, the new celestial body did foretell was the demise of classical astronomy, for anyone could now perceive that the star was located in a sphere of the heavens that, by classical and medieval reckoning, should have been sublime and immutable and contain no such alien body. Five years later another exception to classical cosmology put in an appearance and presented further proof that the firmaments were themselves capable of change and corruption. In 1577 a comet raced across the sky in an area where no comet should have been.

Slowly the old concept of rigid and immutable crystalline spheres, complete with heavenly music, was set aside. When Thomas Digges saw the star of 1572, he announced that he now hoped to "discern by exact judgment whether the earth lies quiet and immovable in the center of the world." He was disappointed, for no one could give visual evidence that the earth moved and no one could think of any kind of sidereal motion except a circular one. An extraordinary mind, such as Giordano Bruno's, was capable of an imaginative leap into space and of conceiving of an infinite universe that possessed countless worlds and incarnations of Christ; but Bruno's *De l'infinito universo e mondi* was condemned almost the moment it was published in 1584, and the author was burned at the stake for the grossest kind of heresy in 1600. Until the seventeenth century, scientific evidence weighed against Copernicus. If an immensely heavy earth really did rotate at a thousand miles an hour, then an object dropped from a high cliff should land well to the west of its starting point, and a cannon ball should carry farther when shot in a westerly direction than when pointed toward the east. Moreover, if the world moved about the sun, then the fixed stars should move slightly, relative to the earth's position on either side of the sun. The stars remained constant, cannon balls refused to cooperate, and stones dropped from towers gave no indication that the earth rotates.

It was not until Johannes Kepler broke through the sixteenth century's mystical preoccupation with spherical motion, and Galileo Galilei expounded the doctrine of inertia, that the map of the heavens was rewritten and religious authority rose up in alarm. The stumbling block to Copernicus' heliocentric theory lay in the fact that the mathematics required to describe the circular movement of the planets about the sun was almost as intricate as that of the old system, which used the earth as its center. In proving an elliptical orbit for the planets, Kepler brought to the heliocentric cosmos the great advantage of mathematical elegance and simplicity. Galileo did much the same thing for medieval astrophysics. The weightiest argument in favor of Aristotle's theory of crystalline spheres had been that it accounted for heavenly motion and gave a plausible explanation of why celestial bodies remained forever in the skies. Galileo liberated the sixteenth century from the myth that an object will move only when impelled by the continuing force of a prime mover. He advanced the theory that motion, not rest, was normal and that all heavenly elements moved in orbit at a speed that was relative to their original impetus.

Although the modern concept of inertia and motion did not receive its final formulation until the time of Newton, the cosmology described by Galileo and Kepler was already depriving God of an active part in its operation. The universe was becoming a perfectly ordered but quite mechanical clock, created by a benevolent deity who was satisfied with the role of celestial mechanic and impetus-giver. In 1610, a year after Galileo first used his telescope to see for himself evidence of phenomena that already had been mathematically expounded, Sir Henry Wotton wrote to James I a letter even more skeptical than the one Spain's court historian had written on Columbus' return from the New World. He had, he said, "the strangest piece of news" to report: "The mathematical professor of Padua" had discovered four new planets rolling about the sphere of Jupiter, besides many other unknown fixed stars." Also the Italian astronomer had viewed the moon and found it not to be "spherical but endued with many prominences, and, which is of all the strangest, illuminated with the solar light by reflection from the body of the earth." The author of these wonders, concluded Sir Henry, "runneth a fortune to be either exceedingly famous or exceedingly ridiculous."

Few Elizabethans before 1600 had passed far enough over the threshold of modernity to conceive of the new and godless cosmos of endless space and mechanical motion as anything but ridiculous, but in every field of human observation the veil of myth was being drawn back. In morality, Sir Francis Bacon was writing that his century "was much beholden to Machiavelli and others that wrote what men do, and not what they ought to do." In the study of history, Sir Walter Raleigh was ready to remove God from the formula. "To say that God was pleased to have it so," he said, "were a true but an idle answer (for his secret will is the cause of all things). . . . Wherefore we may boldly look into the second causes"

and understand history in terms of human motivation. In politics, Sir Thomas More voiced in the *Utopia* the proposition that the commonwealth should be designed to help the people lead "happy lives." In charity, rich merchants gave more to benefit education than to ensure their souls' salvation. In science, men were wondering with Galileo whether God really had "designed so many vast, perfect, and noble celestial bodies . . . to no other use but to serve this passible, frail, and mortal earth?" If the theological justification for the heavens was doubtful, might not the ultimate heresy be correct after all? The universe might not have been created as a backdrop for the drama of man's salvation, but as a kingdom to be conquered and ruled by man's intelligence. The destiny of man, said Francis Bacon, was "to extend the power and dominion of the human race over the universe." Human happiness, scientific usefulness, a mechanical cosmos, all these, as Pascal complained, had turned God into a first cause who "set the world in motion by a twist of his finger and thumb," and who thereafter left the universe to man's tender mercies and ruthless exploitation.

Steadily the face of Gloriana's England changed. It was not so much that the features became, with each passing year, more Jacobean than Elizabethan; the metamorphosis was more profound and enduring than that. Imperceptibly the scientific mind, the secular frame of reference, and the mechanical concept of the universe appeared, like an ugly step-daughter, unwanted but always present. The medieval profile receded; the image of modern man with his self-confidence and his mania for definitions and categories began to emerge. Men of imagination breathed the intoxicating scent of change and announced with Jean Fernel that "our age is doing today things of which antiquity did not dream," but most Europeans were unaware of where questioning and doubt were leading. Elizabeth would have been as shocked as the cardinals of the Roman Church by Bruno's pantheistic and infinite universe. Her age may have been edging out of the feudal past, but the queen herself remained what she had always been—no modern, but the greatest Elizabethan of them all. Gloriana had always detested newfangledness; she liked her society and her heavens to be orderly, anthropomorphic, and solidly divine. Although the world was passing the old lady by, she was not yet dead; and such was her magic that history seemed almost to have slowed down to wait for Elizabeth to leave the stage. Yet before she turned England and Europe over to James of Scotland and Henry of Navarre, to Galileo and Montaigne, and to the harbingers of intellectual inquiry and political revolution, she had a few medals left to display.

SCIENCE AND SUPERSTITION

Of all the changes that took place during the sixteenth century, the most profound and lasting was accomplished by the Copernican revolution. Probably no single work ever published has so shaken and altered human thought as Copernicus' *De revolutionibus*, with its radical proposition that the earth revolved around the sun. In the years after 1543, when Copernicus' book was published, other scientists continued the Polish astronomer's work. The Englishman Thomas Digges enlarged the known universe by hypothesizing a realm of fixed stars, which "extendeth itself infinitely up in altitude"; the Dane Tycho Brahe calmly informed an astonished world that "there are not really any orbs in the heaven"—thereby discarding the long-cherished notion of a system of concentric crystalline spheres upon which the planets rode; another Englishman, William Gilbert, laid the foundations for the study of magnetism and electricity and wrote *De magnete*, the first great work in modern experimental science; and the German Johannes Kepler (an illustration from his *Mysterium cosmographicum*, showing the orbits of the planets, appears at right) used mathematical calculation to prove that the planets moved in elliptical, not circular, orbits. By 1597 Galileo had turned his attention to astronomy, and thirteen years later, with the aid of a telescope focused on Jupiter's satellites, provided final discreditation of the Ptolemaic concept of the universe.

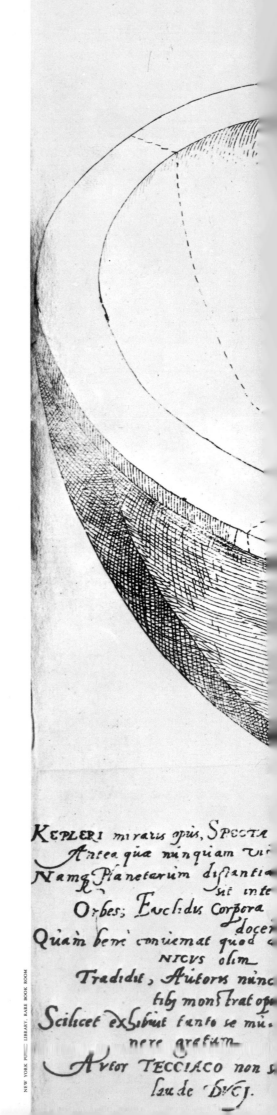

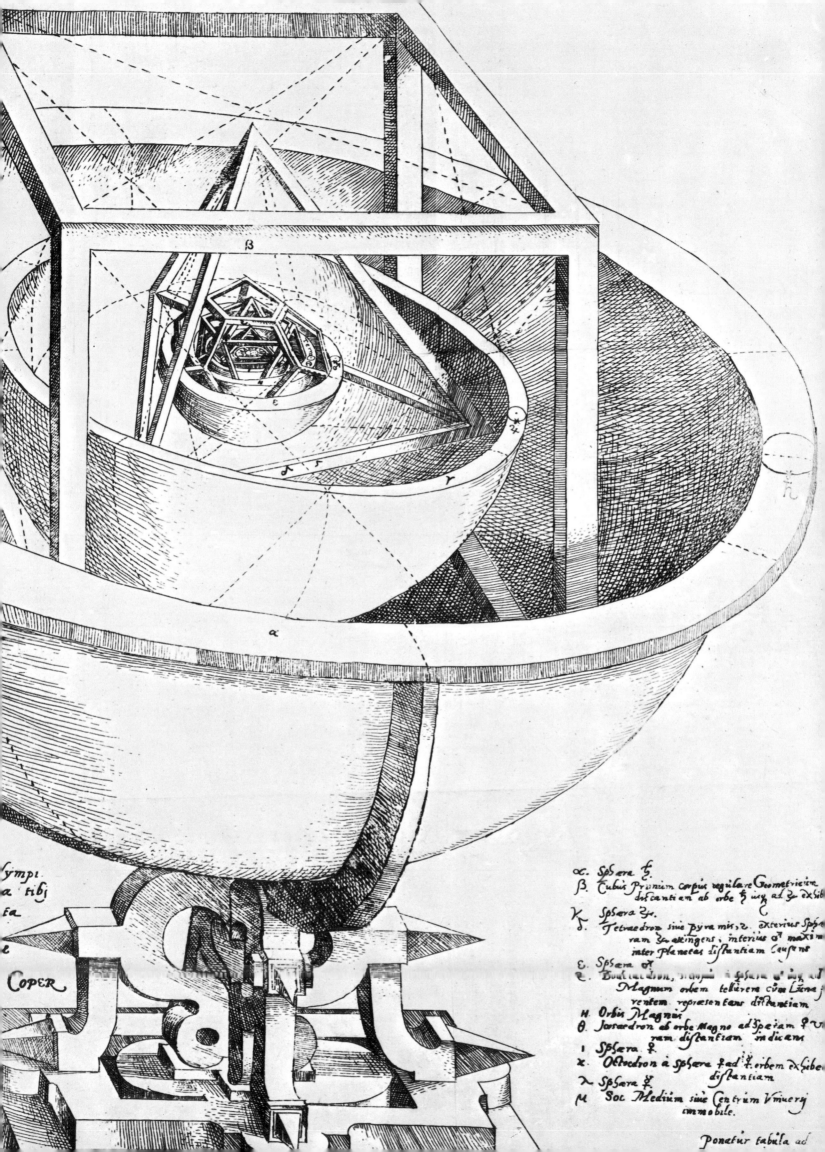

THE WORLDS OF TYCHO BRAHE

After Copernicus, the self-taught astronomer Tycho Brahe was probably the most widely respected of the great sixteenth-century scientists. Brahe, who was born in 1546, was a part-time astrologer early in his career and dabbled in alchemy for a time too; but he gradually became preoccupied with pure celestial observation. An account of his studies of the new star that appeared in Cassiopeia in 1572 so impressed the king of Denmark that Brahe was granted the feudal lordship of the island of Hveen. There he built a magnificently eccentric castle, Uraniborg, set up laboratories and observatories in it, installed the gigantic instruments without which accurate calculation was impossible before the invention of the telescope, and attracted and trained a small army of talented younger men. Throughout his distinguished career Brahe sought to find an alternative to the Copernican system that would accord with Christian dogma.

In the late sixteenth century the appearance of new celestial phenomena, the increasing sophistication of stargazing equipment, and the Copernican controversy, fanned by literary hacks, combined to make astronomy an immensely popular pastime for gentlemen, as the print above indicates. Opposite, the astronomer Tycho Brahe is shown taking measurements of the stars with the giant mural quadrant that he had installed in his famous castle observatory in Denmark.

DEUTSCHES MUSEUM, MUNICH

This illustration from an early seventeenth-century medical treatise depicts the Garden of Alchemy, with trees symbolizing various metals. The man perched on a twin-bodied lion probably represents the spirit of alchemy.

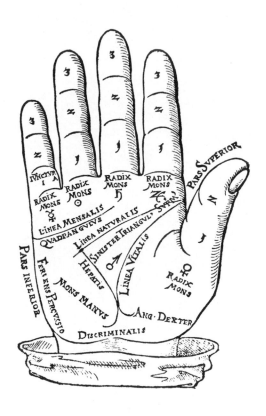

THE PSEUDO SCIENCES

Despite the scientific advances of the sixteenth century, superstition persisted—even, in some cases, among the scientists themselves. The renowned Swiss physician Paracelsus drew little distinction between alchemy and medicine, and astrology and astronomy often were confused. Demonic possession, sorcery, and magical talismans were taken with the utmost seriousness. Scholarly volumes on natural history soberly described mythical creatures, and closely reasoned treatises were written on the means of locomotion used by witches. In many cases valuable contributions to chemistry and medicine were the chance results of the continuing search for a formula for transmuting base metals into gold.

AGRIPPA, *De occulta philosophia libri III*, 1533

GESNER, *Historia animalium*

Divination by magic affected decisions by kings and commoners, and bodily movements were thought by some to correspond to a universal rhythm. A palmistry chart (upper left) and a print (left) assigning occult numbers to portions of the body are typical of the times. The bishop fish (above) was believed to exist.

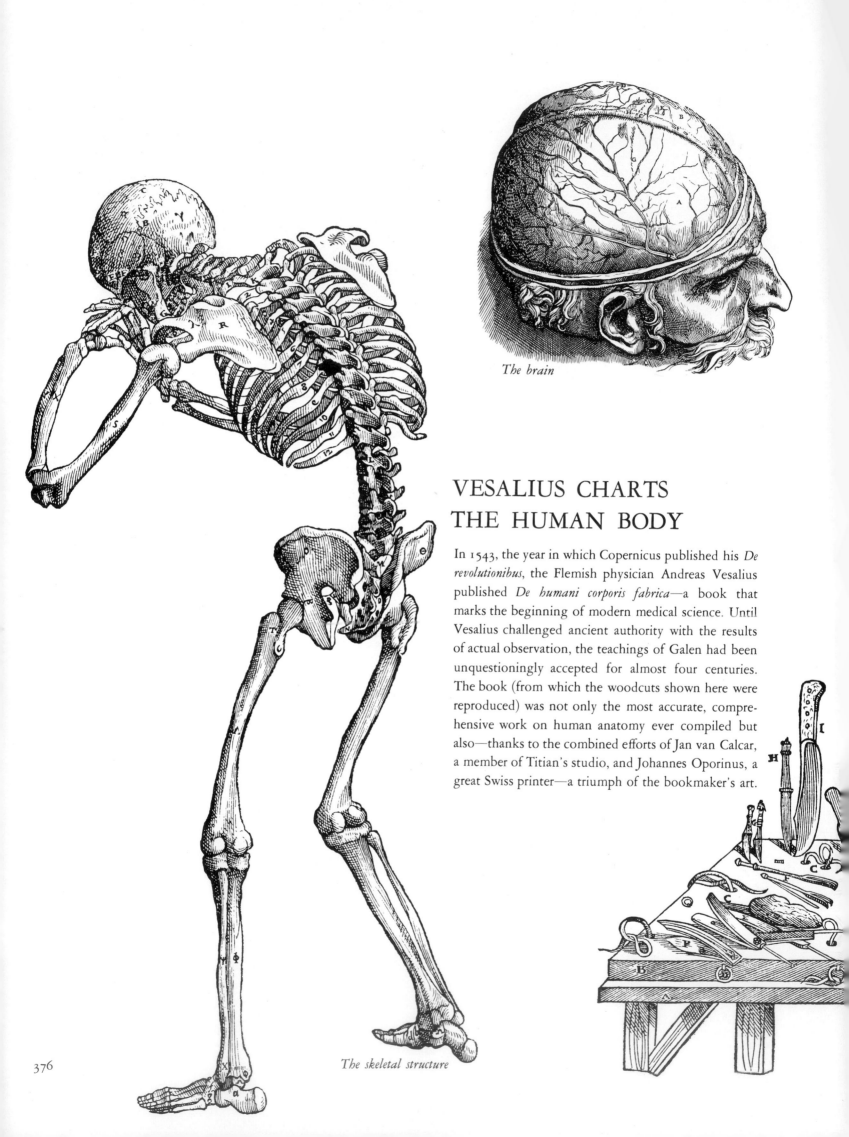

The brain

VESALIUS CHARTS
THE HUMAN BODY

In 1543, the year in which Copernicus published his *De revolutionibus*, the Flemish physician Andreas Vesalius published *De humani corporis fabrica*—a book that marks the beginning of modern medical science. Until Vesalius challenged ancient authority with the results of actual observation, the teachings of Galen had been unquestioningly accepted for almost four centuries. The book (from which the woodcuts shown here were reproduced) was not only the most accurate, comprehensive work on human anatomy ever compiled but also—thanks to the combined efforts of Jan van Calcar, a member of Titian's studio, and Johannes Oporinus, a great Swiss printer—a triumph of the bookmaker's art.

The skeletal structure

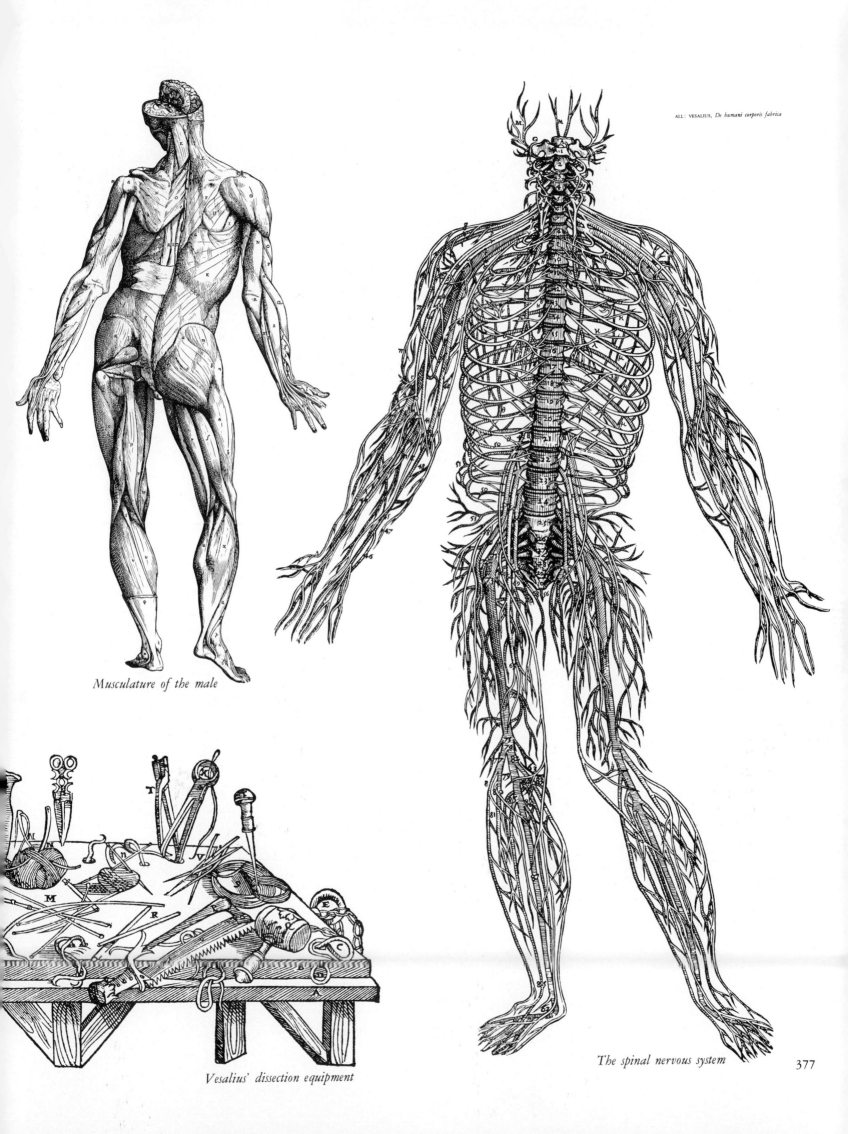

Musculature of the male

ALL: VESALIUS, *De humani corporis fabrica*

Vesalius' dissection equipment

The spinal nervous system

11

END OF AN ERA

Elizabeth was growing old, and not even the removal of the mirrors from her rooms could change the truth: she and all her generation were mortals "whom time had surprised." There is a story, "credibly reported," that not long before her death the queen had a "great apprehension of her own age" when she saw her face, "then lean and full of wrinkles, truly represented to her in a glass." Gloriana was suddenly overcome with the awful knowledge of how often she had been "abused by flatterers" who had "informed her the contrary." As age crept silently into court, management and artifice, rouge pot and wig became all the more essential to her reign. Pageantry and adoration, pomp and stateliness stood alone, devoid of the lighthearted gaiety and exuberance with which the young princess had mounted the throne. There were still moments when the queen could conjure up the spirit of those earlier days. At the age of sixty-six she danced the pavan to the sound of a pipe and tabor, but she did so in the privacy of her closet, "none being with her but my Lady Warwick." Her tongue remained as sharp as ever, her laughter as cutting, and her anger as majestic. When in front of the entire court the Polish ambassador criticized her policy toward Spain and threatened war, she stormed at him in impromptu Latin, so vital and colorful that all England delighted in the ambassador's discomfort and their queen's brilliance.

After four decades the charm still worked, and her people continued to talk of "her mind of gold, her body of brass"; but with each passing year Elizabeth depended more and more on artful staging to achieve her effect. As the queen's face became wrinkled and her body grew stiff, ceremony waxed all the more lavish. Her table, reported a foreign traveler in 1598, was set out with carefully arranged solemnity. "A gentleman entered the room bearing a rod, and along with him another who had a tablecloth, which, after they had both kneeled three times with the utmost veneration, he spread upon the table, and after kneeling again, they both retired. Then came two others, one with the rod again, the other with a saltcellar, a plate, and bread; when they had kneeled as the others had done and placed what was brought upon the table, they too retired with the same ceremonies performed by the first. At last came an unmarried lady (we were told she was a countess) and along with her a married one, bearing a tasting knife; the former was dressed in white silk, who, when she had prostrated herself three times in the most graceful manner, approached the table and rubbed the plates with bread and salt, with as much awe as if the queen had been present: when they had waited there a little while, the yeomen of the guard entered, bareheaded, clothed in scarlet, with a golden rose upon their backs, bringing in at each turn a course of twenty-four dishes, served in plate, most of it gilt; these dishes were received by a gentleman in the same order they were brought, and placed upon the table, while the lady-taster gave to each of the guards a mouthful to eat, of the particular dish he had brought, for fear of any poison."

During the tasting and laying out of the meal, "twelve trumpets and two kettledrums made the hall ring for half an hour together. At the end of this ceremonial a number of unmarried ladies appeared, who, with particular solemnity, lifted the

As time and death look on, an elderly Elizabeth receives a heavenly diadem.

Essex as lord deputy of Her Majesty's forces in Ireland

meat off the table and conveyed it into the queen's inner and most private chamber, where, after she had chosen for herself, the rest goes to the ladies of the court. The queen dines and sups alone, with very few attendants; and it is very seldom that anybody, foreigner or native, is admitted at that time."

Elizabeth supped alone with her memories while her people made do with ceremony. Old Burghley was content that it should be so, for he had been arranging the pomp and circumstance for as many years as Gloriana herself had reigned. The queen knew her servant's worth and her own indebtedness. In his final sickness she came to his bedside to feed him with her own princely hand, and the old man was so moved that he told his son that in heaven he hoped to continue to be "a servitor for her and God's Church." There were, however, younger men who were not so willing to serve God by bowing low before a bejeweled and bewigged virgin queen, whose harried worshipers never knew from one day to the next whether she fancied herself as a coquette or a schoolmistress. The time for change was approaching, and Lord Burghley's death on August 4, 1598, at the age of seventy-eight, was the signal for a new generation to begin a struggle for English political power.

Two men bid for the old Lord Treasurer's powers and titles and looked ahead to a day when Elizabeth must step down and her cousin from Scotland sit in majesty upon the English throne. One was Burghley's second son, Robert Cecil; the other was the earl of Essex. Even the most wanton of the gods might have hesitated to arrange so uneven an encounter. In 1598 Essex was thirty-two, Cecil thirty-five; one had been trained as a peacock of the court and was obsessed with the vanity of his species, the other had been carefully and lovingly educated by his father in the art of government. Robert Cecil had been a member of Parliament at twenty-one, had been sent on a diplomatic mission at twenty-five, admitted to the Privy Council at twenty-eight, and at thirty-three made principal secretary, a post he had already been administering without title for more than five years. In a world that jibed cruelly at his hunchback and his spindly legs, Cecil made his way partly by his father's influence but more by his own industry. Almost alone of the second generation, he could match his sovereign's attention to detail. There were few secrets that the Cecils, father and son, did not possess; there was little stirring at court or elsewhere in the land to which they were not privy; but both Cecils were content to operate in the shadows, to exalt the cult of royalty, and to possess the substance of power behind the glitter of a goddess-queen. Burghley, her "Spirit," and Robert Cecil, her "Pygmy," had been indispensable to Gloriana's reign, and she knew it.

In contrast, Essex was loved, pampered, and treasured, but he was always expendable, and this Elizabeth also knew. Not all the vitality of his youth nor the virtuosity of his Renaissance heritage could altogether obscure an ugly egotism, made doubly sinister by the presence of deep-rooted baronial pride. Essex claimed power as his due, as his forefathers had done, because he had been born to the ermine; he was an earl and one of the natural leaders of society. But joined to anachronistic feudal pretension was a more dangerous quality: he demanded a place beside his queen because he was Essex, a hero, and a man. Etiquette required that he dance attendance upon a goddess and mouth the formula that transformed a capricious and crusty old woman into a semideity. No one knew better than the irresistible earl how to speak to perfection words that in his secret heart he denied: "When Your Majesty thinks that heaven is too good for me, I will not fall like a star, but be consumed like a vapor by the same sun that drew me up to such a height."

Elizabeth was too much a realist to judge her courtiers by their honeyed phrases, but she believed in artifice and she knew her authority to be of God. She could swallow her anger as a woman and forgive her handsome Essex his melancholic brooding and petulant outbursts, but when he publicly questioned her divinity as a queen in 1598, and announced that he could see upon the throne of majesty only an aging and cankered female whose mind was "as crooked as her carcass," then he passed beyond the pale and committed a crime not just against her sex but against "God's immediate minister on earth." "Those who touch the scepters of princes," she warned, "deserve no pity."

As long as Burghley lived, the conflict between Essex and Cecil was contained. Essex glittered at court and sought to satisfy his thirst for honor and popularity by feats of heroism at Cadiz and in the Azores; Cecil remained discreetly behind the scenes, "with his hands full of papers and his mind full of matter." Very early a pattern began to emerge, one that augured ill for the unstable earl and drove him to ever-greater acts of frenzy and hysteria. Essex could touch Gloriana's heart but never her mind. He could block Cecil's advance so long as he remained close to the queen, but the moment he left for adventures upon the high seas, Elizabeth quietly gave political office to his rival. While Essex strutted before the walls of Rouen, Cecil was placed on the Privy Council; when in 1596 Essex was off in search of military laurels at Cadiz, Cecil was made principal secretary. By 1598 it was painfully clear that the earl of Essex was gaining all the honors and Sir Robert Cecil was winning all the offices. It was bad enough that the queen should have rewarded hard-working Cecil, but it was even worse when she honored Charles Howard, Essex's old military rival, by creating him earl of Nottingham. The new title plus his office of Lord Admiral gave Howard precedence over Essex. Enraged and mortified that his queen could possibly recognize military service in someone other than himself, Essex sulked, feigned sickness, and refused to appear at court until Elizabeth had rectified such an insult to his honor. On December 18, 1597, she gave in and created him Earl Marshal, the highest military post in her gift.

Essex was extremely pleased; his honor had been satisfied and his rank sustained. Elizabeth had acceded to his demand, and that was only proper since she was a woman and he was a man. But as always, Essex had no sense of proportion and no idea when to stop. He insisted that all men should be either with him or against him. He never realized that parties did not belong to him but to the queen, and he wrote one of Elizabeth's foremost soldiers, Lord Thomas Grey, to demand that he present his colors and declare himself to be a friend or an enemy. When Grey refused to commit himself, Essex bluntly reminded him that he would do well to remember that the Earl Marshal controlled all military promotions. In answer Lord Grey posed an issue that Elizabeth could not long ignore. The queen, he said, could not permit men of the sword to owe their advancement to the whim of a party leader and court favorite. If she did, she would endanger her throne, and her faithful nobility would "languish under the despised yoke of one of their own rank." The truth of Grey's observation became apparent in 1598 when the queen and Essex clashed over the appointment of a lord deputy for Ireland.

Trouble had been brewing in Ireland for more than a decade, and strong military action was required in that graveyard of English reputations, but no one wanted the post of lord deputy or the chance to rescue English honor. Elizabeth favored Essex's uncle, Sir William Knollys. The earl urged the appointment of his old enemy, Sir George Carew. The queen grew weary of Essex's pleading and angrily told him to have done with it. In a fury of contempt, he turned his back on his sovereign and received a box on the ear for his discourtesy and the order to "get him gone and be hanged." At that moment Essex lost what little self-control he possessed, and his hand reached for his sword. Nottingham stepped between prince and subject, and Essex in a blind rage stormed out of the Presence chamber. Wiser and more dispassionate heads reminded him that "there is no contesting between sovereignty and obedience," but Essex would have

William Cecil, Lord Burghley, Elizabeth's closest confidant, is shown here with his hunchbacked son, Robert, who successfully outmaneuvered Essex in the struggle for high office during the declining years of Elizabeth's reign.

none of it. "I owe Her Majesty," he said, "the duty of an earl and of Lord Marshal of England. . . . What! Cannot princes err? Cannot subjects receive wrong? Is an earthly power or authority infinite? Pardon me, pardon me, my good lord; I can never subscribe to these principles." The mirror of majesty had been smashed. The principle that would one day pull monarchs by the dozens from their thrones, and for which in later centuries men the world over would gladly die, unexpectedly appeared in the unpleasant mouth of a fatuous sixteenth-century egotist.

Matters between the queen and her difficult earl were patched up when he fell ill in September, 1598, but reconciliation failed to bring a respite in the jungle warfare of court politics. With Burghley dead, trouble immediately broke out over the inheritance of the old man's most coveted and lucrative office, Master of the Wards. Essex felt that he must have it, both for honor's sake and to save himself from bankruptcy. As early as 1589, scarcely two years after his arrival at court, he was at least twenty-two thousand pounds in debt. On the earl of Leicester's death he had been granted the income from the customs of imported sweet wines and had been able to borrow heavily on the strength of this, but his household was steadily growing in size and expense, and his political influence depended on his ability to place his friends at court and in his own

house. Control of the Court of Wards provided immense patronage and wealth, and the moment Burghley died, a would-be guardian to a rich orphan wrote Essex: "I pray that we may hear that you are Master of the Wards, for then I shall hope that you will bestow a male or female upon me." The queen's solution was, as usual, to take no irrevocable step; she delayed and presented the prized office to no one, telling the earl she would be her own master.

Deprived of one of the richest plums of political life, Essex did the expected: he wrote the queen a hot, almost threatening letter, demanding that she "think again" of his suit, and when she continued to refuse him, he announced that he deemed it "the fairer choice to command armies than honors." He forced Elizabeth and the Council to select him as lord deputy of Ireland, where Hugh O'Neill, earl of Tyrone, was successfully harrying the English out of the land.

For most Elizabethans Ireland was a damp, disease-ridden bog of barbarism into which the English poured men and money without profit. In 1596 the queen had sent three thousand five hundred soldiers to fight; within a year two thousand five hundred were "either dead, run away, or converted into Irish." For much of her reign the Irish clans disliked one another so ferociously that they had little time to hate the English and less occasion to unite against them, but in 1593 Ireland found in Tyrone something approaching a national leader. Tyrone's rebellion was serious, but to make matters worse, behind him stood the Spanish, always waiting, always hoping that Ireland would become Elizabeth's Dutch ulcer.

Into this land of rebellious clans, where witches and unseasonable weather abounded, marched the earl of Essex with the strongest force Elizabeth had ever sent into Ireland—sixteen thousand foot soldiers and thirteen hundred horsemen at a cost of one thousand pounds a day. Everything depended on success. As one observer cautiously put it: "If the lord deputy performs in the field what he hath promised in the Council, all will be well; but though the queen hath granted forgiveness for his late demeanor in her presence, we know not what to think hereof." If Elizabeth was providing her Essex with enough rope to hang himself, she must have been well satisfied with the results. In early April, 1599, he set out with carefully drawn plans to attack Tyrone in his Ulster fastness. Moreover, he had stringent orders from the queen not to promote the earl of Southampton, his worthless crony, to the post of second-in-command as Master of Horse, and to use his authority to create knights only with discretion. Instead of searching out Tyrone, Essex

The brightest moment in Essex's futile Irish campaign came with his capture of the ancient castle of Cahir in 1599.

went off on a series of wild goose chases into Leinster and Munster, which cost thousands of men to no purpose except the capture of a decrepit Irish castle "from a rabble of rogues." Instead of destroying Tyrone, he negotiated peace with him, and to make matters still worse he made Southampton Master of Horse and lavishly bestowed knighthood on thirty-eight henchmen with little to recommend them except their loyalty to Essex.

As might be expected, Elizabeth was furious, but she was also frightened by conduct that smelled of treason. In letter after letter, the sting of her invective lashed at her deputy. Why had nothing been accomplished after so many loud boasts and so great a financial effort? "If sickness of the army be the reason, why was not the action undertaken when the army was in better state? If winter's approach, why were the summer months of July and August lost? If the spring were too soon, and the summer that followed otherwise spent, if the harvest that succeeded were so neglected as nothing hath been done, then surely we must conclude that none of the four quarters of the year will be in season for you . . ." The miserable Essex sat in his tent and complained that nothing came from England except discomforts and "soul's wounds." He had cause to feel bitter; ridiculous failure confronted him in Ireland, and behind his back the queen had given the mastership of the Court of Wards to Robert Cecil.

At what point treason actually entered Essex's mind is difficult to say. Possibly the notion had been lying dormant ever since he dared deny the divinity of kings. Still more probably he spoke treason when he and Tyrone secretly discussed terms of peace. At any event, he decided to throw caution to the wind and return to England at the head of three thousand men. Even in rebellion, however, Essex was too egotistical to be successful.

Instead of arriving at court with an army to give weight to his treason, he chose to travel with only a select company to guard him from arrest, and he depended on his fatal charm to confound his enemies and renew the queen's love. He sought only to exercise his male prerogative to rule over womankind and to demand his historic due as the barons of Runnymede had required of King John, but, as he sadly confessed, he spoke either "a language that was not understood or to a goddess not at leisure to hear prayers." When on the morning of September 28, 1599, he strode unannounced and covered with filth into the queen's chamber at Nonsuch Palace, he encountered a goddess who was in no mood to hear prayers spoken by a subject teetering on the brink of treason. For once Elizabeth was caught totally unprepared, with the adornments of her

Essex had always been a favorite of the public. This woodcut, depicting his execution, comes from one of the many popular ballads of lament published after his death.

divinity and the trappings of her vanity put aside. Had Essex found a queen attired in regal splendor, and not a wrinkled old woman without her wig or makeup, the meeting might have been more dramatic. As it was, the disobedient earl thought he had again won the day, for the queen was strangely quiet and deceptively gracious. Not until she had donned the accoutrements of royalty, put on the face of a queen, and talked at length with Robert Cecil did the storm descend, and was Essex called upon to explain his insubordination.

As the days passed, Gloriana's anger increased, and she recalled Lord Grey's warning. "By God's son!" she stormed, "I am no queen; that man is above me. Who gave him command to come here so soon? I did send him on other business." Essex was imprisoned two days after his return, but the Council hesitated to bring him to public trial. He was the darling of the London rabble and the leader of a dangerous band of impecunious soldiers, disappointed office seekers, disgruntled noblemen, and lawless and landless knights of his own creation—in fact, of all the outcasts of Tudor society whom the queen had been unable to charm by her artistry or satisfy by her patronage. The walls of Tudor popularity were being assaulted for the first time since the uprising of the northern earls in 1569, and cautious councilors urged Elizabeth to curb her fury and cancel the trial. Against her better judgment she allowed Essex to escape the consequences of his idiocy, but it was clear that she had neither forgotten nor forgiven, and she turned a deaf ear to "shaming, languishing, despairing Essex" and his pleas to be allowed to return to court. Gloriana had learned that "affection is false," and in September, 1600, she forced into the open the treason that she knew still lay within an unrepentant heart. She refused to renew the earl's lease of the customs on sweet wines, and Essex's entire financial structure collapsed, forcing him to gamble all on an act of political madness.

Nemesis had long withheld her hand, but from November on, she moved swiftly to prove the truth that "character is man's fate." By the time Essex had turned to open treason, the deterioration in his character had passed beyond the point of hysteria; it was bordering on an insanity that led him to confuse the fantasies of his own sick brain with reality. "He shifteth from sorrow and repentance to rage and rebellion so suddenly," reported Sir John Harington, "as well proveth him devoid of good reason or of right mind." Essex's house was turned into an arsenal and the headquarters for rebellion, and early on February 8, he and Southampton, with a company of two hundred henchmen, rode into the city to raise the apprentices with the cry: "For the queen! A plot is laid for my life!" A few of the citizenry cheered, but no one stirred, and when a royal herald proclaimed Essex to be a traitor, his own following began to melt away. The throngs watched but made no move to help their darling Essex, the victor of Cadiz, and by evening the farce had been played out. Essex's Sunday parade was over, his senseless rebellion dead, and retribution swift and decisive.

On February 7, Essex and his colleague Southampton were brought from the Tower to appear before a jury of their peers. For a time the earl's dark pride and obsession with honor sustained him. At his trial he was magnificently scornful, and like Mary of Scotland, his dramatic instinct was superb. When Raleigh was sworn in as a witness against him, Essex wanted to know: "What booteth it to swear the fox?" To the court he proudly disdained to speak: "To save my life, for that I see were vain: I owe God a death." Essex persistently denied he had been disloyal or "ever wished to be of higher degree than a subject," but the evidence against him was overwhelming. It was manifest to the court, as Cecil remarked, that the earl had "a wolf's head in a sheep's garment," and Tudor society agreed with Francis Bacon when he said of Essex's behavior: "Will any man be so simple as to take this to be less than treason?" When the terrible sentence was read—"to be laid on a hurdle and so drawn to the place of execution, and there to be hanged, cut down alive, your members to be cut off and cast into the fire, your bowels burnt before you, your head smitten off, and your body quartered and divided"—Essex answered that he thought it only fitting that his "poor quarters, which have done Her Majesty true service in diverse parts of the world, should now at the last be sacrificed and disposed

of at Her Majesty's pleasure." Again, however, Essex was posing; he knew full well that his mistress would never expose him, to such an indignity. The hangman would be cheated and he would die as became his rank, by the axe.

Elizabeth had won the battle, and in the end she won the war, for Essex's defiance did not long withstand the teaching of a lifetime: "He that nameth rebellion, nameth . . . the whole puddle and sink of all sins against God and man." Conceit had brought him to such a pass, and every Christian knew that unrepentant pride must inevitably lead to eternal damnation in the fires of hell. Before the day of execution, Essex made confession of his faults, and when he faced his executioner on February 25, 1601, he did so "in humility and obedience," and prostrated himself before his "deserved punishment." A "nature not to be ruled" had finally been tamed.

With Essex's passing, something disappeared from England and from Elizabeth's life. The ramparts of Tudor popularity held firm; the queen had triumphed, but the Essex tragedy had clearly shown that the cult of a virgin queen could not forever satisfy all manner of men and that Elizabeth's system of government was not immune to attack. The queen never really got over Essex's treason or his disloyal words about her mind and heart being "as crooked as her carcass." Sir John Harington reported in October, 1601, that "the many evil plots and designs have overcome all Her Highness' sweet temper. She walks much in her privy chamber, and stamps with her feet at ill news, and thrusts her rusty sword at times into the arras in great rage." Still later he described her as "reduced to a skeleton, altered in her features" and even "her taste for dress gone." It was pathetically clear that Gloriana felt "creeping time" at her gate.

More and more the queen remembered what used to be and grieved for it. Old, sightless Blanche Parry, who had rocked the princess in her cradle, died in 1590. Leicester, her "Robin," had already gone, and soon stiff, hard-working Walsingham and Chancellor Christopher Hatton, her "Mutton," would face their turn. Knox and Calvin, Drake, Hawkins, and Essex, Catherine de Médicis and Henry III of France, William of Orange and Suleiman the Magnificent, Ivan the Terrible of Russia and Mary Stuart of Scotland—Elizabeth outlived them all. Even the oldest of her enemies, Philip of Spain, died in 1598, in the forty-second year of his reign. When the bells of the Escorial tolled their message of grief, they rang out an era that both Elizabeth and Philip had known and respected: a century of divine-right monarchs and paternalistic governments, when men still paid respect to the fiction of religious unity and dressed their thoughts and motives in proper Christian platitudes.

Internationally the old and well-understood configurations were passing. Spain remained a great power, but by the time of Philip's death, Spanish belief in miracles was sadly shaken, and the old crusading zeal was so dim that most Spaniards were ready to make peace with the heretic Jezebel in England and to accept Dutch independence. Pride, not religious conviction, kept the war alive, and within a decade of the king's death, it was clear that Spain could no longer afford to maintain its honor. Peace with England in 1604 and with the Dutch in 1609 were the inevitable consequences of economic and spiritual exhaustion. Spain's misfortunes were, as Philip had sadly explained, partly the work of God who had granted him many kingdoms without "a son fit to govern them," but the blame rested as much with Philip as with his worthless heirs. His empire was withering away from within. The silver and gold of the New World stayed just long enough to inflate the economy and destroy Spanish industry before passing into the pockets of heretical Dutch merchants, who supplied Philip's fleets with the hemp and tar of the Baltic and the salt herring that his Hieronymite monks ate on fast days. Philip had inherited a kingdom richly diverse in culture and tradition, and like Elizabeth, he sought the unity of his realm, but the final irony of his reign was that he succeeded too well and finally imposed an intellectual and spiritual straitjacket on his subjects. In 1598 Spain still looked impressive, but intellectual and economic sclerosis was already well advanced. Wealth and confidence were moving northward to the Netherlands, and the weight of military power was slowly shifting to France.

The tides that flowed into the estuaries of the Dutch coast carried on their crest the riches of the entire globe, and merchant princes in their counting houses stood knee-deep in gold. At Amsterdam the acquisitive spirit was permitted full rein; the economic freedom to buy and sell without regard to religious belief, state policy, social welfare, or the soul's salvation gave the city a position unequaled in Europe. The Dutch provinces could send out ten thousand ships and more men-of-war than England and Scotland combined, and at least half those sails made their port on the Amstel River. Antwerp died, but Amsterdam flourished; the southern provinces bled, but the northern cities prospered; and baffled observers noted the strange riddle of the beleaguered Dutch towns and ports: "It is known to all the world that whereas it is generally the nature of war to ruin land and people, these countries on the con-

Henry IV of France is shown here abjuring Protestantism, supposedly after remarking: "Paris is well worth a Mass."

trary have been noticeably improved thereby."

In 1600 it seemed to many Elizabethans that the junior partner in the war against Spain had gained the most profit from the decline of Spanish sea power and had taken to heart Raleigh's advice that "whosoever commands the sea, commands the trade; whosoever commands the trade of the world, commands the riches of the world, and consequently the world itself." While famine, inflation, and commercial recession plagued Elizabeth's England, and dreary guerrilla warfare in Ireland absorbed its revenues, Dutch merchant princes waxed fat on the profits of both war and peace. The Netherlands stood on the threshold of fifty years of economic and cultural pre-eminence, a golden age in which Amsterdam would be rechristened the "crowned queen of Europe."

In France the shape of the future was evident to those who could discern the realities of international power. By 1600 a new Bourbon dynasty under Henry IV was recasting and revitalizing the land. When the last Valois, Henry III, was stabbed at St. Cloud on the morning of August 1, 1589, the first reaction had been shock that God could have permitted such a deed and could have turned the kingdom over to a heretic. But that reaction was quickly followed by an angry determination that Henry of Navarre should never live to make good his claim. Followers of the dead monarch vowed that they "would die a thousand deaths" before accepting Henry IV as king.

At thirty-five the new king of France dubbed himself "a king without a country, a soldier without money, a husband without a wife." Like Elizabeth Tudor, Henry was a master of the well-turned phrase, but his situation was not quite as desperate as he mockingly portrayed it. As a king, time and history were his indispensable allies. The exhaustion of over thirty years of intermittent war eventually silenced even the most vocal bigot and salved the most tender conscience, and despite papal excommunication and Satan's blessings, his claim to the throne remained inviolate. No one had a better right to the Valois crown than Henry of Navarre. Nor was he a soldier totally without resources. The Catholic League might have the consecrated banners of the pope to sustain its candidate for king and the gold of Spain to pay its armies, but Henry had Valois and Capetian blood in his veins and English silver in his pockets. Only the final witticism was true: he was indeed a husband without a wife. His marriage to Margaret Valois, in 1572, had proved to be the preliminary to the blood bath of St. Bartholomew's Day, and their connubial life continued to be as tumultuous as its start, vacillating wildly between bouts of sensuous reconciliation, mutual promiscuity, and bitter recriminations.

Henry IV is as much a legend as Elizabeth—viewed by posterity as the savior of his realm, an apostle of sanity, reason, and tolerance, the architect of French greatness, a benevolent and patriotic king who sought the welfare of the peasantry and the prosperity of the commercial classes, and above all, a royal lover from whose lusty caresses no woman was safe. As with Elizabeth, the myth becomes the historical figure; Henry hardly exaggerated when, toward the close of his life, he wrote: "France is deeply indebted to me, for I worked hard for it!" Certainly he labored long to outwit Philip of Spain, foil the fanatical designs of the Catholic League, and secure his throne. The great strength of the League was that it represented all good Catholics who were horrified at the thought of a Protestant monarch; its great weakness was its dependence upon Spanish money and troops and its bafflement over who would be the legitimate sovereign if Henry were barred from lawful inheritance. As long as Cardinal Bourbon, Henry's Catholic uncle, lived, the cardinal could legitimately be recognized as Charles X, but when he died in May, 1590, the League was torn apart by contending candidates. Fat Charles, duke of Mayenne, brother of the murdered Henry of Guise and leader of the League, aspired to the throne. Philip of Spain, however, planned to bestow the crown upon Isabella Clara Eugenia, his daughter by Elizabeth Valois, and

Mayenne never dared push his own claims too hard since he was dependent on Spanish arms and money in the struggle against Henry of Navarre.

For four years France endured a war in which there seemed to be no possible solution. Isabella Eugenia was unacceptable because she was Spanish, Mayenne had little support because he was a Guise, and Henry of Navarre was detested because he was a Protestant. At first it appeared as if God, after all, might be on the side of legitimacy when Henry IV's starving, ill-paid, and desperate little army routed Mayenne's superior force at the battle of Ivry in 1590, but without the capture of Paris, no victory was complete, and the city withstood a siege of four hellish months and remained stubbornly and violently Catholic. The aristocratic and commercial classes of the city might have capitulated, but the rabble, who suffered most, were strongest in their determination to resist a heretic king even unto death. Monks and priests, thirteen hundred strong, donned breastplates and helmets and marched the streets as a sign that the spiritual sword of Christ was not without its fighting edge. As the months slipped by, dogs, cats, even rats began to disappear from the cellars and alleys of Paris, sacrifices to the city's determination to remain alive and to add a little variety to a diet of oatmeal and water. Grim stories were reported as hundreds starved and died. Flour for bread, it was said, was mixed with human bones, and other cases of cannibalism were suspected; the revolutionary Council of Sixteen announced that it was preferable in God's eyes to eat children than to recognize an apostate monarch.

Just when it seemed as if the city must surrender, the duke of Parma came to its rescue and marched his invincible Spanish legions out of Brussels to relieve the siege of Paris. Fanatical Catholics gave thanks with a solemn *Te Deum*, but artisans and peasants, moderates and skeptics, and the party of the politique wondered whether such a miraculous eleventh-hour reprieve was worth the price of three more years of bloodshed and confusion. Henry of Navarre, for all his flamboyant courage, was no military match for Parma, and Paris remained adamantly determined never to accept a Protestant sovereign. The Catholic League was paralyzed by quarreling within its own ranks when Mayenne and the left-wing Council of Sixteen clashed over the leadership of the League and the control of Paris. Philip II annoyed his Catholic supporters by sending as his representative the duke of Feria, undoubtedly the most tactless diplomat of the sixteenth century, and antagonized all Frenchmen by putting historians to work to prove that France's cherished Salic law, limiting succession to the male line, was invalid.

The signing of peace with Spain the year after Elizabeth's death is shown in a painting attributed to Marcus Gheeraerts. One English signatory was Robert Cecil (right foreground).

If France were to be spared further agony, and if Henry of Navarre was ever to possess a kingdom commensurate with his exalted title, it was evident that he must renounce his Protestant faith and turn Catholic. Such a solution had been voiced as early as 1589, but it took the king four years to realize he had no other choice. On July 25, 1593, dressed in white and escorted by the highest dignitaries of the realm, Henry made formal recantation at the abbey church of St. Denis. A minority remained unconvinced and regarded his conversion as "supping with the devil," but most Catholics jumped at the chance to end more than thirty years of chronic warfare and return to their pigs and crops, their warehouses and ledgers, and to the serious business of civilized existence. Paris voluntarily opened its gates on the morning of March 22, 1594, and when Henry rode through the streets, the crowds, which a year earlier would have torn him from limb to limb, greeted the king joyously.

Like his royal cousin in England, Henry preferred mercy to revenge and realized that diplomacy was a surer weapon than war. He won the regional governors and the noble magnates of France with fat gifts and lucrative titles, and, when his Council complained about the price, he explained that "the things they are delivering up to us would cost us ten times as much if we had to take them by force." Even for the duke of Mayenne he demanded no punishment. The duke was made governor of the Ile de France, and his many debts were assumed by the crown. Henry was content to walk his obese and rheumatic old adversary, for whom every step was a torment, at a brisk pace through the gardens of the royal chateau of Montceaux during the heat of the day, and the king happily whispered to a friend: "If I lead this fat lump a long enough dance I shall have my revenge."

Catholics could be won to peace by honors and silver. Protestants, however, proved to be more difficult, and Henry was forced to give up a portion of his sovereignty and to recognize the legal existence of a Calvinist state within a Catholic kingdom. By the Edict of Nantes, in 1598, Huguenots were allowed to practice their faith in all towns except Paris and the episcopal cities. They were made eligible for all government offices; a special law court was established to handle cases involving their faith and their persons; and for a period of eight years they were given control of two hundred towns where they were permitted to maintain armed garrisons, supported in part by the king. The practice of religious toleration in a century that absolutely denied the principle was established by a monarch who had deemed Paris to be worth a Mass. When conservative lawyers tried to block the promulgation of the edict by arguing that it violated the historic laws of France and the Holy Church, Henry assured them that they stood in far greater danger of being declared heretics for not obeying him than for sanctioning an act that might be displeasing to God.

As Henry himself said, he worked hard for France, checking the resurgence of feudal anarchy, cooling the heat of religious ardor, profiting from the discrediting of old ideas and institutions, which seemed capable only of producing further war and disunity, and rebuilding a land that was potentially the richest and most powerful in Europe. By 1600 the essential condition that had made Spanish hegemony possible and had been the major consideration of Elizabethan foreign policy had disappeared: France was no longer a weak and divided realm to be sacrificed at the bidding of another state. It was once again the senior kingdom of the Continent; and before the century was out, England would again view France, not Spain, as the enemy.

At home, too, life was passing the old queen by. For a few brief decades Renaissance egotism, religious zeal, the acquisitive spirit, the thirst for adventure, and even lingering medieval chivalric posing and love of display had been harnessed and put to work by the Tudor state. The result had been a perfectly balanced yet wonderfully buoyant and sensitive society. Elizabethans wrote with the boisterous grace of a Shakespeare; they were glad to be alive, yet profoundly aware of their own mortality and just a little afraid of the life to come. Even the Puritans, although they continued to warn of God's punishment upon the wicked, enjoyed the world in which they lived; if they hadn't, they would not have been so anxious to improve it. But as the years passed, the static and ordered society grew rigid and unwieldy, and Renaissance confidence and vitality slipped into self-satisfaction or rebelliousness. By 1600 landed country gentlemen, Puritan zealots, and city merchants were growing restive under a divinely sanctioned and paternalistic regime.

After Elizabeth died and the irritating element of the Stuart personality was added to a dangerously unstable political, religious, and economic situation, elderly Elizabethans looked back with nostalgia to a golden age and remembered far more than had in fact existed. "During her life, what peace in her country! What plenty in her land! What triumphs in her court! What learning in her schools! What trades in her cities! What wealth in her kingdom! What wisdom in her counsel, and what grace in her gov-

ernment!" Actually the final decade of Good Queen Bess' reign saw neither plenty in her land nor grace in her government. Between 1594 and 1597 the harvests failed every year and the poor starved. In the popular mind hoarders and usurers, those medieval caterpillars of the commonwealth, were to blame, and Elizabeth's government was severely criticized for doing little about them. As the price of food soared, the buying power of wages dropped to an all-time low, and Oxfordshire peasants took up arms against the queen's sheriffs and justices.

A paternalistic government was not completely devoid of ideas on how to handle the economic crisis, and the most revolutionary of all Elizabethan poor laws was enacted in 1601—a law that for the first time recognized that poverty was a social not a spiritual or individual ill. Humane as Elizabeth's economic views were, her policy remained essentially medieval and anachronistic in an age that was casting off its feudal and religious approach to economics. The Tudor state believed in curtailing cutthroat competition, fixing wages and prices, and licensing all production under grants of monopoly to achieve a stable and contented society and a fair living for all. Unfortunately, medieval guild economics applied to the entire kingdom did little to curb the recession, and they antagonized the most vocal and wealthy elements of the society. If peasants and apprentices censured the crown for failing to keep wages and prices in reasonable accord, and for its inability to appease a wrathful god who had brought unseasonable rains for three summers in a row, landlords and merchants were irritated by a paternalistic state that strangled free enterprise, failed to recognize the dynamism of an expanding commercial and industrial economy, and raised the cost of living by issuing monopolies to favored courtiers in order to finance their lavish and uneconomic ways.

Tudor England was changing. A few great peers might continue to maintain households of two to three hundred retainers, but iron smelters employed as many as four thousand workers. During Elizabeth's reign coal production increased by seven hundred per cent, and iron production was up fivefold. By 1600 it was noted that a London merchant might be worth one hundred thousand pounds, as much as the greatest peer in the realm. Slowly but surely Englishmen began to perceive that the search for the black coal of Yorkshire was more rewarding than the quest for silver, and that the mining of iron might be more profitable than digging for gold.

The wealth, prosperity, and domestic peace with which Elizabeth had blessed her people produced within the landowning and commercial groups a new sense of their own social and political importance. In 1500 Erasmus had described the prince's threat as an eagle's scream before which all men and interests gave way; by 1600 a new note was heard, the idea of service to the state as a public and landed obligation and not as a duty to the sovereign. Elizabeth's loyal Commons were evolving a new and revolutionary conceit, viewing themselves as legislators, not as humble petitioners, and demanding a share in the government of the realm. Members of the lower house, though they hesitated as yet to answer the question, had heard and recorded Essex's fateful outburst: "What! Cannot princes err?"

To merchants anxious to search out new avenues of trade, to country gentlemen groaning under a decade of wartime taxation, to entrepreneurs with clever schemes to improve production and reap a quick profit, and to a realm that was suffering from the long trade depression of the 1590's, government monopolies regulating and licensing almost every item of life from buttons to tobacco seemed to be an immoral and unwarranted interference in the rights and economic activities of the individual. It was over the abuse of such monopolies that the most serious and concerted attack on the structure and theory of Tudor government broke in 1601 with a fury that alarmed Elizabeth almost as much as had the Essex rebellion. Three vital issues were at stake: the royal prerogative that stood above earthly criticism, the right of the crown to interfere in the actions of subjects in order to ensure the welfare of all, and finally the role of Commons as humble adviser to the crown, not as arrogant initiator of policy. During the controversy over monopolies, Commons listened in hostile silence to the efforts of privy councilors to explain the royal prerogative and the crown's right to license and control trade and production. When one of the Council suggested that in theory all men's estates belonged to the sovereign, he was shouted down by landowners who had long since forgotten their feudal obligations and viewed their lordships and manors as private property. Worse yet, when at the close of the first session the queen passed through the Parliament chamber, the traditional cry, "God bless Your Majesty," was weak and halfhearted. Gloriana was thoroughly alarmed, for the mortar of her entire governmental edifice—the indispensable personal popularity that she treasured above her constitutional prerogative—was turning to dust.

Elizabeth had fought long and hard to conserve her subjects' resources and to win victory in the war against Spain with the least loss of English blood and the least expenditure of English money, but the war had been long, the cost heavy, and her kingdom belabored by famine and war weariness. She had sacrificed to the war effort almost her entire inheri-

Elizabeth's tomb, with the arms of her realm and a mourner representing sorrowing England, is shown in this 1625 print.

tance from her father's confiscation of the monastic lands, and as her capital dwindled her income declined, and her dependence upon parliamentary subsidies mounted. Gentry and merchants, who more and more often paid the royal piper, sought to call the governmental tune. As yet they demanded only the redress of evils and the reform of monopolies, but in so doing they implicitly championed the doctrine of economic liberalism, and by seizing the initiative and forcing their views on the crown, they raised economic and constitutional problems that were insoluble within the structure of the Tudor state.

Elizabeth's sense of political survival was matchless. She realized that should Commons present its demands in statute form, a dangerous precedent might be established for a further assumption of the legislative initiative by Parliament. Consequently, she promised immediate and complete redress of

This contemporary watercolor of Elizabeth's funeral procession through the streets of London shows the coffin surmounted by the queen's effigy and flanked by "gentlemen pensioners."

wrongs and the revamping of the entire system of monopolies. By surrendering and admitting the existence of abuse, she saved her royal prerogative from being made the subject of a constitutional debate. As always Gloriana was willing to stoop to save what she held most high—her reputation and the unity of her kingdom. In her Golden Speech to Parliament in November, 1601, she told her loyal Commons: "I was never so much enticed with the glorious name of a king or royal authority of a queen, as delighted that God hath made me His instrument to maintain His truth and glory and to defend His kingdom from peril, dishonor, tyranny, and oppression." With unerring political sense Elizabeth knew when to present her divinity dressed in the guise of utilitarianism.

At the conclusion of her address, Gloriana bid each of the gentlemen present approach and kiss her hand. It was the final farewell; sixteen months later the queen was dead. She died, as she had ruled, when her "own great judgment advised"; Elizabeth elected death when she realized that she had no further reason to live. Throughout the winter of 1602 she had been suffering from bouts of melancholia and had aged visibly. She seemed to have little concern for her health, almost inviting pneumonia by wearing summer clothes. For days on end she sat looking into a past that no one at court could share. She must have known that Cecil, Raleigh, and the rest were more mindful of what they were soon to get than of what they were shortly to lose; and the queen

allowed Cecil to rehearse her Scottish heir and to arrange the details of the succession behind her back. She saw but said nothing, except to sigh that "her authority among the people was sensibly decayed."

In early March a "heavy dullness" seized her, whereby she could neither sleep nor eat, and she sat waiting to leave an England to which she had nothing more to give and in which she no longer took interest. Years before, she had said that she had no desire to live if her life and reign were no longer of profit to her subjects. In March, 1603, Elizabeth knew that moment had arrived, and the time for a new master had come. She died with quiet dignity and perfect timing, slipping rapidly from disinterest into speechlessness, coma, and death. On March 24, 1603, she turned her head to the wall and her eyes to God.

The magnitude of Elizabeth Tudor's success is baffling; the historian may record it, but he can scarcely explain it. With failure, the dark necessity of circumstances and personality stand out, and the chain of events leading to despair, death, and perdition can be traced back to the first false step. But success is too mercurial, too volatile, to be disciplined by causality. It seems to possess no roots, no history; it merely exists, blooms, and dies. What, after all, is success? Is it really what it appears to be, or is it a trick of historical hindsight? Elizabeth was successful in doing what? In bequeathing to her Stuart heir problems of state beyond his, or possibly any king's, ability to solve? In holding time at bay and allowing a later generation to pay the price? In

avoiding, through feminine guile, her subjects' mounting pressure to have done with benevolent paternalism and "degree, priority, and place?" Elizabeth was a success, but might not another sovereign have been more successful? What wonders might have taken place had she acted with the resolution of Henry VIII? What might she have achieved? The answer, very likely, is nothing; her reign might have ended in catastrophic failure. And there's the rub. Gloriana rarely did the things mankind most admires, yet she is judged pre-eminently successful. She contrived to elevate inconsistency to a virtue, turn vacillation into wisdom, and translate half measures into policy.

The secret of Elizabeth's art was that she was blessed with ambitions commensurate to her abilities. She demanded no windows into men's souls, she neither coveted her neighbor's lands nor sought to carve out an empire. She was content to preserve the unity of her kingdom and to earn the devotion of her subjects. In the months before she died, the queen had occasion to speak of her life's achievement, and she told her loving and loyal people that "though you have had, and may have, many mightier and wiser princes sitting in this seat, yet you never had, not shall have, any that will love you better." Alone among her royal contemporaries she possessed the skill and the means to achieve her end. Philip of Spain consumed himself and martyred his kingdom in demanding that all men subscribe to the absolute truth. No matter how estimable his vision, it was

doomed to failure, for not all the gold of the mythical El Dorado, let alone the resources of the Spanish empire, could have transformed such a dream into reality. Catherine de Médicis' purpose was simple and domestic—palaces and scepters for herself and all her brood—but historic circumstance and the shallowness of her own mind made a mockery of even such modest ambitions. The same was true of Mary of Scotland and of Essex; their hot desires took no account of reality. Only Elizabeth succeeded. She was no modern woman, but at least she was an adult and a realist free of obsessions. "She only is a king. She only knows how to rule!" was Henry of Navarre's tribute.

Gloriana achieved her life's ambition: "To do some act that would make her fame spread abroad in her lifetime, and, after, occasion memorial for ever." In this she was supremely successful, for the century that produced Shakespeare, Donne, Drake, and Bacon bears her name—the age of Elizabeth.

> Even such is time which takes in trust
> Our youth, our joys, our all we have,
> And pays us but with age and dust;
> Who in the dark and silent grave,
> When we have wondered all our ways,
> Shuts up the story of our days.
> But from this earth, this grave, this dust
> The Lord shall raise me up, I trust.

The words are Raleigh's, but the conceit belongs to Elizabeth and to the golden heroes of her age.

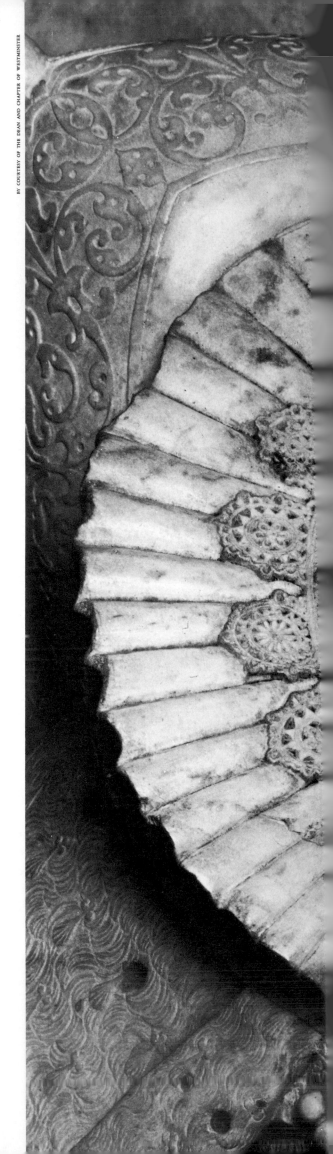

A CHANGING NATION

During the long reign of Elizabeth (whose tomb effigy by Maximilian Colte appears at right), the queen's personal magnetism, strength of character, and plain good luck carried England through times of change and crisis and set the precedent for "muddling through" as the English way of political life. Under Elizabeth's successor, James I—a far more systematic monarch, but a narrower human being and one utterly devoid of the charisma that sustained Elizabeth—the divine authority of the throne was first seriously challenged, religious discord reappeared, and the nation's navy went to pot, and the Renaissance exuberance that gave the Elizabethan era its tone and panache was gradually replaced by the leaden sobriety of an emergent puritanism. Elizabeth and her court had paid lip service to religion but left God to look after His affairs while they looked after their own. By 1605, however, two years after the death of the queen, the visiting Dutch jurist Grotius could sum up the climate of James' England with the words: "Theology rules here." With his accession James had automatically brought about the unification of Britain by bringing his two kingdoms, Scotland and England, under one crown. Yet throughout the newly united kingdom his reign was marked by political disunity as James and his Puritan-dominated Parliament entered into a struggle for supremacy that eventually was to culminate in civil war.

Jacob der 6. Königk
inn Schottlandt.

ENGLAND UNDER JAMES

Thanks largely to the efforts of Robert Cecil, James I succeeded to Elizabeth's throne without incident or dispute. Indeed, Englishmen, who for many years had dreaded the chaos that the death of a childless queen might bring, greeted their new monarch with enthusiasm as he made his way from Edinburgh to London. James soon proved, however, to have no comprehension of conditions in England and no understanding of Parliament. Where Elizabeth had exercised royal prerogatives with the warm approval of her subjects, James tried to impose his will autocratically and met with cold contempt. His uncompromising stand toward Puritan and Catholic alike won him the enmity of both, and his attempts to raise money without Parliament's consent led to a series of bitter court battles.

James (opposite) considered himself a theologian; he commissioned the Bible translation that bears his name, and often wrote on religion. In the painting above, the king (in balcony) hears a sermon at St. Paul's Cathedral. Above left, the arms of a unified Britain

395

Procerum   Cācellarius   Thesaurarius   primogenitꝰ

R. Scotie

Cancellario sedes vel

Prolocutor

Milites Provinciarum & Burgenses (quos vocant) utrinꝗ, qui Cameram Parlamenti inferiorem constituunt. Prolocutorem conducentes.

PARLIAMENT VICTORIOUS

Like his father before him, Charles I, James' son by Anne of Denmark, was popular when he first came to the throne but soon alienated his subjects. Charles' first mistake was marrying a Catholic, Henrietta Maria, sister of Louis XIII. Unsuccessful foreign expeditions under Charles' favorite, the duke of Buckingham, in no way enhanced the king's popularity. When the king proposed to send aid to his sister, Elizabeth of Bohemia, in the Thirty Years War a recalcitrant Parliament defied him. Parliament's differences with Charles finally erupted into a revolution. The king's armies were defeated by troops raised by Parliament; his favorite, Buckingham, was impeached, and Parliament passed—over his objections—the Petition of Right (a guarantee of civil liberties). Charles' unhappy reign finally came to an end when he was tried by a committee specifically convened for the purpose, found guilty of treason for waging war against Parliament, and beheaded.

Even under Elizabeth (who is shown in Parliament opposite), Parliament had grown increasingly restive in its passive, humble petitioner's role. During the reign of James I Commons grew more and more assertive of its rights, and three years after the overthrow of Charles, could proudly proclaim its "freedom by God's blessing" on the medal shown above. Charles' trial before a committee in the House of Commons is depicted in the contemporary print at left.

397

The hapless Charles I was the first Western monarch ever to be tried, condemned, and executed by his own people. This painting, supposedly by an eyewitness to the grisly event, depicts the execution at Whitehall Palace. In reality, the headsman (who is shown on the scaffold and in the vignette at upper right) wore a mask and false beard, and many mounted troops had been ordered to interpose themselves between the scaffold and the crowd.

OVERLEAF: *As the disruptive reign of the Stuarts wore on, many Englishmen looked back with increasing nostalgia to a more settled era when Elizabeth occupied the throne and kept her national house in order. In this engraving the Tudor queen is surrounded by figures of Astronomy (left), Geography (right), and Fortitude and Prudence (on the plinths of the pillars). Peace and Justice embrace in the medallion above her head.*

Clemens et Regni moderatrix iuſta Britāni
Hac formâ inſigni conſpicienda nitet.

Triſtia dum gentes circùm omnes bella fatigant,
Cæriæ errores toto graſsantur in orbe.
An·Dni pace beas longa, Vera et pietate Britannos: 1579
Iuſticia moderans miti ſapienter habenas.
Chara domi, celebrisæ foris, longæuaæ regnū
Hic teneas, regno tandem fruitura perenni.

ACKNOWLEDGMENTS

Bibliotheque Publique et Universitaire,
  Geneva
  Miss Idelette Chouet
Bibliotheque Royale de Belgique, Brussels
  Martin Wittek
British Museum
  John McKenzie
  Edward Croft-Murray
R. B. Fleming and Co., Ltd., London
Folger Shakespeare Library, Washington,
  D.C.
  Dr. Louis B. Wright, Director
  Mrs. Gordon Fowler
  Miss Jean Miller
  Horace Groves
Mrs. Miriam Koren
Dr. M. E. Kronenberg
Kunsthistorisches Museum, Vienna
  Dr. Erwin M. Auer, Curator
Lord Chamberlain's Office, London
  D. V. C. Buchanan
Marlborough Gallery, London
  James Kirkman
Nationalmuseum, Copenhagen
  Miss Fritze Lindhall
Nationalmuseum, Stockholm
  Dr. Pontus Grate
National Portrait Gallery, London
  Dr. Roy C. Strong
New York Public Library
  Lewis M. Stark
  Mrs. Maud D. Cole
Patrimoine des Musées Royaux des
  Beaux-Arts, Brussels
Royal Library, Windsor Castle
  Miss J. Holt
  Miss A. H. Scott-Elliott
The Shakespeare Birthplace Trust, Strat-
  ford-on-the-Avon
  Dr. Levi Fox
Staatliche Museen, Gemäldegalerie, Berlin
Miss Annette Wells

NOTE ON ANTHOLOGIES: *Elizabethan spelling was devoid of standardization and based on a highly individualized and altogether capricious approach to phonetics. Seventy-three contemporary spellings of Raleigh's name have been recorded, for example, including several variants used by Sir Walter himself. Moreover, the typesetter's craft was far from perfect in the sixteenth century—a circumstance that added considerably to the vagaries of published Elizabethan prose and verse. For the convenience of today's reader, the spelling of material anthologized in this book has been standardized and modernized wherever it was possible to do so without distorting the sound or meaning of the original. Punctuation too, which was equally haphazard during the period, has been revised somewhat in accordance with modern usage. In most cases the titles of English works, from which quotations are taken, appear in the original versions in order to retain some of the flavor of the language of the times.*

Grateful acknowledgment is made for permission to quote from the following works:

pp. 326–27 *The Discovery and Conquest of Mexico* by Bernal Diaz del Castille, trans. by A.P. Maudslay. Copyright 1956 by Farrar, Straus & Cudahy. p. 328 *Tycho Brahe's Description of His Instruments and Scientific Work,* trans. and ed. by Hans Raeder, Elis Strömgren, and Bengt Strömgren. Copyright 1946 by Munksgaard, Copenhagen.

pp. 133–35 *Advice to a Son,* ed. by Louis B. Wright. Cornell University Press, Ithaca. Copyright 1962 by the Folger Shakespeare Library.

pp. 135, 136–37 *Middle Class Culture in*

Elizabethan England, ed. by Louis B. Wright. Copyright 1958 by Cornell University Press.
pp. 248–49, 255–56 *Elizabethan Lyrics*, ed. by Norman Ault. Capricorn Books Edition, 1960.

Map on pages 7–8 and genealogy on pages 8–9 by Francis & Shaw.

NOTES ON ILLUSTRATIONS: *Many of the pictures in this book are reproduced from unique original manuscripts and rare contemporary printed material. The following list of sources is designed to supplement the credits accompanying the illustrations for those cases where more detailed information may be helpful. Page numbers appear in boldface type.*

12 Ms. 9 242, fol. 184 **13** Ms. Fr. 83, fol. 205 **14** King Rene's Book, Ms. Fr. 2692 **24–25** Amann, *An Allegory of Trade* **27** Ms. 1672 **32** Chants Royaux du Puy de Rouen, Ms. Fr. 1537, fol. 29 v **33** Machiavelli, *The Art of War*, trans. by Peter Whithorne, 1560 **37** Bovillus, *Liber de intellectu*, 1509 **38** Ms. 5116, fol. 71 **39** Ms. Add 28330 No. 33 **42–43** Vallard, *Atlas of Portolan Charts*, c. 1547, sheet II **52** The Great Bible, 1539 **56** Calais-Cotton Ms. Aug. I, ii, 70 **60–61** Westminster Tournament Roll **61** *both* Ms. Roy. 2A XVI Plut. IIIc fol. 636 **68** Anthony's Roll, 1546, pp. 6, 7 **68–69** Cotton Ms. Aug. A iii **72 73** Foxe, *Acts and Monuments*, 1563 **76** *bot.* Mss. Roy. 18a xlviii **82** Ref. Additional Ms. 28330, Corte Beschryvinghe van Engheland, Schotland, Irland—Halberdier **83** Drayton, *Poly-Olbion*, 1612 **84** Ms. Add. 34,605 No. 563, 24 verso **85** *both* T. F., *A Book of Divers Devices*, 1585–1622 **87** Braun,

Civitates orbis terrarum, 1577 **88** Duchy of Lancaster; Accounts various **92** Mss. Harley Charter 83 H 14 **96** *cen.* Harley Ms. 3885 # 19r **96** *top* Turberville, *Book of Falconrie*, 1575 **96, 96–97, 97** Turberville, *Noble Arte of Venerie and Hunting*, 1575 **98** Teshe, *A Book Containing Divers Sorts of Hands*, 1589, Sloane Ms. 1832, fol. 7 **112** Schopero, *De omnibus illiberalibus sine mechanicis artibus* **124** *Theatrum crudelitatum haereticorum nostri temporis*, 1587 **128** Roxburghe Ballads, vol. I, no. 95 **145** Hill, *The Gardner's Labyrinth*, 1577 **152, 153** T. F., *A Book of Divers Devices*, 1585–1622 **154–55** Cotton Augustus I.I. 74 **156, 159** Roxburghe Ballads, Vol. I **183** Shahanshahname (The Book of the King of Kings), Turkish Ms. **196** Munster, *Cosmography* **198** Codex Mendoza, Aztec Tribute Roll **199** Codex Mendoza, Tribute Rolls, (Loubat Copy) **200** Colophon of a Hebrew Bible written in Toledo in 1492 and completed in Constantinople in 1497 **212–13** *top* Bruyn, *Omnium pene Europae, Asiae, Aphricae atque Americae gentium habitus* **218** *top, all* Codex Florentine **218** *bot.* Histoire Mexicaine depuis 1221 *jusqu'à* 1594, 17th century Ms., from collection of E. Eugen Goupil No. 44 p. 55 **220** De Bry, *Voyages* East Indies Series, part VIII, first German edition, Frankfort/Main, 1606 **225** *De Nederlandsche Provinciewapens Naar Heraldische Gegevens*, c. 1500 **236** Cornelius Danckwerts, engraver, *A Thankful Remembrance of God's Mercy* **257** Month of May T. F., *A Book of Divers Devices*, 1585 1622 **262** Roxburghe Ballads **262** *bot. rt.* Kemp, *Kemps nine daies wonder, performed in a daunce from London to Norwich*, 1600 **268** *bot.* Ms. Funeral procession of Lady Lumley, early 17th century **272** *bot. The Groundeworke of Connycatching* **272** *top rt.* Bateman, *Chrystal Glass of Christian Refor-*

mation, 1569 **272–73** Holinshed, *Chronicles . . .*, 1577 **273** *bot. lft.* Dekker, *The Belman of London*, 1608 **273** *bot. rt.* Ballad: *The famous Ratketcher, with his travels into France, and of his returne to London* **273** *top* The life apprehension, arraignement, and execution of Charles Courtney, 1612 **300–301** Holinshed, *Chronicles . . .*, 1577 **295** *top rt.* Antwerp View of London **309** De Bry, *America*, part VIII **310** Harriot, *A Briefe and True Report . . .*, 1588 **314–15** Braun, *Civitatis orbis* **316** Zarate, *The Strange and Delectable History . . .* **318–19** Waghenaer, *Marriner's Mirrour*, 1588 **338** Map by Diego Homen **340** Baker, *Fragments of Shipwrightry* **342** Smith, *Generall historie . . .* **342–43** Barents expedition, account by De Veer, Amsterdam, 1598 edition **345** Stow, *Survay of London*, 1633 **346–47** Vellum sheet Eg. Ms. 1579 **350** Monardes, *Joyfull Newes Out of the Newe-founde Worlde*, 1577 **352** Smith, *Generall historie . . .* **353** Harriot, *A Briefe and True Report . . .*, 1588 **357** *Carta Marina* by Olans Magnus, Venice, 1539 **359** Hulsius, *Die Funffte Kurtze Wunderbare . . .*, Part 5, Edition III, 1603 **363** Kepler, *Harmonice mundi*, Libri V, Lincii, 1619 **364** *top* Case, *Sphaera civitatis* **364** *bot.* engraved by Andreas Cellarius, 1660 **365** Cuningham, *The Cosmographical Glasse* **366** Fludd, *Utriusque cosmi majoris scilicet . . .* **370–71** Kepler, *Mysterium cosmographicum . . .* **374** Mylius, *Opus medico chymicum . . .*, 1618 **375** *bot. lft.* Agrippa, *De occulta philasophia, Libri III*, 1533 **381** Stafford, *Pacata hibernia* **383** Shirburn Ballads **389** Purchas, *Purchas his Pilgrimes*, 1625 **395** *lft.* Blaeus, *Grooten Atlas . . .* **396** Glover, *Nobilitae politica* **397** *lft.* Nalson, *Journal of the High Court of Justice* **397** *rt.* Reverse of 2nd great seal of the Commonwealth, 1651, Thomas Simon, medalist **400** C.I. 481, 1579

INDEX

INDEX